House of the Angels

Also by Timothy Wilson
ALL ONE BODY

Carol: 'That's the way the ball is bouncing.'

House of the Angels

LOVE NOTES FROM THE ASYLUM

by TIMOTHY WILSON

A Richard Seaver Book

THE VIKING PRESS   NEW YORK

Acknowledgment is made to the follow-
ing for permission to quote material:
BASIC BOOKS, INC.: From "The Skull Bal-
lad" by Andrei Voznesensky, translated
by Stanley Kunitz in *Antiworlds and the
Fifth Ace*, edited by Patricia Blake and
Max Hayward, © 1966, 1967 Basic Books,
Inc., Publishers.

NORMA MILLAY ELLIS: From *Collected Poems*,
Harper & Row. Copyright 1931, 1958 by
Edna St. Vincent Millay and Norma Mil-
lay Ellis.

SE

To Kibria, with love
from us all

Contents

Illustrations

Part One: *Introduction*

Love is so small who cares for love
in times like these men build
and set a world on fire—you kiss
me State in blood in blood
                     Voznesensky, The Skull Ballad

1. *The Return*
31 March 1971

Bill Berger got out of the car just outside the village and walked across the road. It was a few hours after midnight. In front of him was a high stone wall, in the middle of which was an iron gate. It was firmly locked. The wall was too high to climb and the gate had sharp spikes on the top. He walked up and down to see if the wall was lower at any point. It was the first time he had been back to the village in eight months.

Earlier that day he had sat at his trial in Salerno which had lasted seven hours. He had said very little, watching the farcical game that was being played in the name of justice. But now he was free, after eight months in an insane asylum and then a prison, he found himself locked out of the graveyard where they had buried Carol, his wife.

All around was silence, semi-darkness. There were no cars on the road—it was early spring, not yet the beginning of the tourist season. Like the surrounding vineyards, the cemetery was tiered because it had been built on the side of a steep mountain. Below was the Mediterranean. From where he stood he could see the tiers of graves rising up the mountain and the neatly planted trees. The formality of it seemed to mock the nightmare of separation he felt tearing his heart. He pocketed the torch, gripped the iron bars and scrambled up, gashing his trousers as he balanced on the spikes. He jumped on to a ledge on the other side.

He had no means of identifying the grave. He walked up the steps to the first tier and shone the torch along the terrace of graves. The graveyard had four tiers. Most of the graves on the first tier were slabs of white marble, some gruesomely ornate in a baroque Italian style. He shone the torch around in a despairing gesture. At the second tier he wondered whether or not to give up. He had been told there was a number on a simple wooden cross, but he didn't know the number. The graves on the second tier were set into the wall. At the end of the terrace was a tall palm tree.

He climbed up to the third tier and walked more slowly along a narrow concrete pathway between the rows of graves. All of them were simple—mounds of earth with crosses stabbed onto them. Any one of them could have been Carol's. Intending to go on up to the fourth tier, he walked back past the last grave on the third tier, the one nearest the steps.

Instinctively he shone the torch on a small marble plate with a number on it. He sat on a stone wall by the side of the grave, looking at the number on the marble—221. Rain began to fall. He felt no energy, just emptiness—not what he had expected when he had lain awake at night in prison longing for this moment which would mean his freedom and a sign from Carol.

It didn't matter any more. He closed his eyes and felt how absurd is the human need that death be tragic. Nothing mattered any more. Her deep black eyes, her wicked grin. . . .

'Where are you, baby, where are you?'

He shivered and walked down towards the gate, forgetting to pick up the torch he had thrown down by the side of the grave. He was buried above ground. The world would never be the same without her big beautiful eyes to filter it for him. He would have to pretend to be alive.

Getting back over the gate was more difficult; then he walked down the hill to the main road. A deadly calm had come over him giving him the feeling of ghost-like transparency. He saw the glow of cigarette ends inside the car. He got in, hugging his arms round him. No one said anything. A woman turned down the window, threw her cigarette out and they drove through a dark tunnel under the mountain into another part of the village. The car stopped near some shuttered shops. Bill opened the door, turned as if to say something, then got out. The woman turned round.

Before Bill could close the door, she said 'I'll phone. . . .'

Bill waved. The car drove slowly off, faces pressed to the window pane. Bill turned and walked wearily across the road towards the three hundred twisting steps that led up to the house.

He had a peculiar walk. His legs moved with a springing lope while his head was kept still and his shoulders slightly hunched.

The clock on the church tower in the village chimed as he climbed the first narrow steps. In the silence between the chimes it was as if nothing had happened—the sound connecting two different worlds: that of before and after death. He stopped—half thankful, half resentful. It was now 4 a.m. and still no light in the sky. The houses with their large wooden doors opening on to the steps and nibbled stonework were all silent. Not even a dog barked.

At the top of the first flight of steps was a long pathway, sloping upwards at a slight angle. Above the pathway, flanked by a high stone wall on the mountain side and a shorter wall overlooking a vineyard on the sea side, a dim light creaked and swayed in the wind. Near the end he could see nothing—a tangle of darkness that seemed an oblivion into which he could fall, for ever unconscious. He wasn't carrying anything since he had left all he had in prison with a cell-mate. He felt confused, dizzy and suddenly old. He raised his eyes.

He must have been standing there a long time because the clock struck another quarter as he groped along the path. Rounding a corner he saw a long flight of steps above him, slightly steeper, with cactus trees on either side. Somewhere above him was the house, the crumbling paradise where tomorrow the slow sunsets, oranges ripening, tomorrow the emptiness. . . . He wanted to hold back the dawn and stay for ever in the darkness. Why had Carol made him return to endure her absence?

The last flight of steps became steeper and he kept looking up to the house as though it might not be there. No lights were on, no one was there except the ghosts. The garden door with the inverted silver cross Carol had painted on seemed unreal. For a crucial moment he stood there.

Then he pushed open the door and went into the garden. He waited to see if his dog would come. The tinkle of bells on the back of the door was the first shock of familiarity. He left it open. The house was threateningly dark, yet he went in.

It was like walking into his own skull.

2. *Most Intimate Strangers*

William Berger, 43-year-old American actor held in Italy for eight months awaiting trial on a drugs charge, was finally acquitted at the end of March 1971; but the scandal surrounding the case was to go rumbling on, with Italian politicians citing it as a glaring example of the need for judicial reform.

The case began in August 1970 when Bill Berger's villa south of Naples was raided at 2 a.m. by forty policemen during a nation-wide drug witch-hunt. He, his wife and seven others staying in the house were committed to asylums for the criminally insane—one for the men, another for the women—charged with being in possession and under the influence of drugs. In October Bill's wife—the American actress, painter and member of the Living Theatre, Carol Lobravico, aged 38—died in mysterious circumstances after an emergency operation. At the time, the press were informed that the cause of death was deterioration due to intensive drug taking; later the causes of death were given as cardiac collapse and pneumonia.

A few days after her death, the seven others arrested at Bill's house were released and expelled from Italy. Bill was then kept in prison while evidence for his trial was being gathered—it turned out to be less than half a gram of stale marijuana found in a tobacco box at his house on the night of the police raid. At his trial in Salerno on 30 March 1971 he was acquitted of all the charges brought against him—possessing and using drugs and permitting others to take them in his home—on the grounds of lack of sufficient evidence.

In the immediate weeks after his acquittal and return to the house, Bill was interviewed by the press and television from Italy and America. He described the appalling circumstances under which his wife had died and made an indictment against the indifference and hypocrisy of the Italian authorities involved in the case, as well as the American consulate, whose total ineffectiveness he saw as one of the most important contributing factors to Carol's death. During the numerous interviews that he gave, Bill talked about his wife's death quietly and without bitterness. What actually happened and who was responsible seemed to concern him less than a determination to go on relating to her. During the five months after she died, while still in prison, he went on writing daily letters to her. 'But I can't spend the rest of my life writing dead letters to keep feeling alive,' he said. 'Before she died we were . . . most intimate strangers. . . .' Extracts from Carol's prison letters and from a diary which Bill kept after she died were quoted in the press—all of which vividly conveyed the human tragedy within the bare facts of a story, with the result that it had caught the imagination of Italy and solicited international comment.

Having presented the facts accessible to him to the Italian press, Bill arranged with his lawyers to make an appeal for an inquiry into the way the case was conducted and into the causes of his wife's death, none of which was even referred to in his own trial. But Bill was pessimistic about proving negligence by the authorities, because the facts of the case were not available. In fact, shortly after her death an inquiry was started into its circumstances; but Judge Verasani, who had control of the case, refused to grant an autopsy on the grounds that her death was entirely 'normal'.

In April 1971 Bill travelled to the States at the invitation of Congresswoman Bella Abzug to discuss what action could be taken, through censure of the American consulate, to find out the true causes of Carol's death. At a press conference in Washington on 13 May 1971 Bella Abzug committed herself to seek a congressional investigation of the conduct of the State Department in the case of the Bergers, saying: 'I have made a number of inquiries to the State Department, but its replies do not fully square with the actions—or lack of actions—of consular officials in Italy. This is a tragic case with possible serious implications for thousands of Americans visiting and living abroad. There are now more than 1,000 U.S. citizens being held in foreign countries, including approximately 700 detained on narcotics charges. It is important that through a thorough and impartial investigation, we find out specifically what happened in the Berger case; whether there is any

possibility that U.S. officials provide less assistance to those
arrested on narcotics charges than to those accused of other
offences and, finally, whether the case reflects a general pattern
of conduct by State Department representatives which could
adversely affect the safety and well being of American citizens in
foreign nations.'

Answering questions from the press Bill said, 'Carol's incredible mental, spiritual and physical suffering during those
seventy-seven days are a thing of the past and cannot be annulled.
My own suffering and grief are a matter I should much prefer to
keep private. . . .' Then he went on: 'In Italy the press as well as
various judicial and political groups have seized on this case as an
example of an outrageous miscarriage of justice. Orlandi, the
capo-gruppo of the P.S.D.I. [Social Democrats] has initiated an
inquest in parliament and has publicly stated that he feels there
has been a violation of article 27 of the constitution which states
that persons convicted of crimes may not be subjected to in-
humane treatment. There have been similar statements by
members of parliament of all parties except the extreme fascist
right. At the same time the State Department in answer to congressional inquiry states that: "The consulate general, which has
followed Mr. Berger's case closely, reports that it is satisfied that
Mr. Berger has received all the rights and privileges accorded to
an Italian citizen accused of the same crime." If that phrase is
interpreted as including all miscarriages of justice that may occur
in a given country it leaves American citizens abroad without any
protection by the representatives of their government.'

That first night back in the house, before meeting journalists
and travelling to America, he must have felt lost and over-
whelmed by her absence in the place where she had been most
present. He had sat in a chair in front of the window in the long
upstairs room. A strong wind blew out the candles he had lit.
Doors rattled and banged all night.

He would journey to America, he would go on working in
films, but he would live in the house.

Nothing he did could ever bring Carol back. He could only try
to reach a sense of at-oneness with her, exorcising the pain and
separation from within himself. In the beginning he tried to do

this by moving outward, publicising the facts of his and Carol's story as an example of the atrocities committed by society on the individual under the guise of 'justice', 'democracy' etc. His way of externalising his grief and sense of loss was ruthlessly to attack the 'system' in order to seek an admission of responsibility from the authorities involved—and he used all the conventional means available to the private citizen—the media, parliamentary and congressional inquiries. Yet his determination to seek justice or at least admission of responsibility was a hopeless struggle of an individual against society.

The journey he began in prison after she died when he started writing a diary in the form of a letter to her, and which he continued to make after returning to the house alone, was in fact an intensely inner journey, painful and very lonely, yet in a remarkable way healing and transcendent. His story has a far more personal and enduring quality than could possibly be revealed in the public row it excited but which quickly blew over. It is a story of a rare and remarkable relationship, the story of a difficult, often dangerous journey of two people towards each other and a unity that transcended death.

Apart from brief journeys away from the house, mostly to work in films to pay his lawyers and support the people who came to stay at the house, for the next year and a half after his release from prison he continued to live there surrounded by all the reminders of Carol: photographs, her paintings, clothes, rooms she had made for herself, the huge wooden bed she had insisted on bringing from New York to Rome, then to Praiano. For six months in prison Bill had had one photograph of her and a cross he had taken from her body after she died. Her death had awoken in him a passion for her, a passion she had always longed for and could not live without but which he had denied her in her lifetime. Now the only way he could express that passion was in a mental and spiritual search for her within himself, searching moments of their life together for the lost chord, the missing harmony. Perhaps it was the house itself which contained the key, since it was only when they decided to leave their apartment in Rome and find somewhere more peaceful and creative to live a different kind of life that they began to overcome the emotional crises which had dogged their lives together.

Asked why he left Italy shortly after his trial to go to the States Bill replied: 'Mainly I reacted from impulse. I wanted to see what was happening to the revolution. I wanted to see the people involved in the demonstrations to get me out of prison. I went to see my mother in Innsbruck. Carol told me to go . . .'

Born in 1928 in Innsbruck to Austrian parents, Bill spent his first twelve years in a Germany that was gradually coming under the dominance of the Nazi party. Both his parents were doctors—his father, William Berger, was a brilliant skier and an outstanding medical student who graduated with the highest honours. He became the director of the University Medical Clinic in Graz; then in September 1939, while the family were on holiday in Northern Italy, war broke out. Abandoning all their possessions, money and status—because of Nazi persecution of their Jewish colleagues—the family journeyed across Europe, from Geneva to Lisbon, in a battered refugee bus during the autumn and winter of 1939 to queue for a boat to the United States.

Bill went to high school in New York, after which he attended Columbia University, where he studied engineering. At the same time he was pursuing an athletic career. At twenty he qualified for the finals in the selection for the Olympic team, running the 1500 metres; but in a run-off for the final selection he did badly, clocking in a time far below his previous best. After graduating from Columbia he was drafted into the army at the time of the Korean war, then was transferred to the Air Force, where he did very well for some time; but after three years in the Armed Forces, during which the initial romanticism of a military career waned, he was demobbed, got married to his first wife and worked for a short time in I.B.M. Then during the ten years 1954–64 he became deeply involved in the New York theatre scene. He studied acting with Curt Conway and various other teachers, and started teaching acting at his own theatre studio. The most successful play he acted in was Albee's *Who's Afraid of Virginia Woolf*, which ran for two years in New York.

Bill had two daughters from his first wife, but the marriage started to break up. He and his family moved to California in an attempt to start a new life there, Bill working as an actor in Hollywood films, but the marriage proved irredeemable, so he returned to New York to continue in the theatre on his own—leaving his wife and two small children in California.

It was during this period that he met Carol Lobravico—'Crazy Carol'—from the artistic jet set of New York's beautiful people. Carol, whose grandparents had emigrated from Italy, had run away from home when she was seventeen to go to art school in Paris. After that she had lived between New York and Paris and Rome, and for a while on Ibiza, earning a living from portrait painting and fashion drawing. She had never married, nor had she ever lived with anyone for more than two weeks—all of which indicates her own restlessness with herself, her continuous need to create an illusion of her own fascination. Devastatingly sensitive and giving the impression of living precariously from moment to moment, Carol could at times be very insensitive. When she spoke to people she talked straight from herself, never polite conversation, debunking romance and conventions with an alluring mixture of compassion and cruelty. Bill and Carol met off and on for two years at parties, and although Bill felt an attraction for her, she invariably ignored or rebuffed him.

The point at which Bill entered Carol's life in October 1962 marked a turning point for both of them. They both found a love they had been looking for yet hardly dared believe existed—when fantasy and reality suddenly became one in a self-expression that is complete and total, when their inner and outward lives harmonised in a love-making that inevitably became harder and harder to sustain but without which all else seemed worthless. At times both of them, especially Carol, found it hard to believe that it had happened. In a letter to Bill written in 1967 Carol wrote about a friend who had committed suicide, saying 'Anyway I guess she wanted to go to her next life fast—sort of the way I felt before I met you.' In fact, soon after they began living together, Carol did try to commit suicide, by taking an overdose of sleeping pills. Bill returned and rushed her to Bellevue hospital just in time. For his part, Bill had exhausted all the possibilities he had tried and found very little creative satisfaction in his life—it was all adapting to the immediate situation. But this adaptive quality was one of his main strengths and something which Carol must have been attracted to, though probably unconsciously.

For the first two years they lived in New York—in Carol's apartment—beginning an exploration of love that was intense, sometimes frightening, sometimes hilarious, and which contained what at first might have appeared contradictions to a relationship —promiscuity, bi-sexuality, wild raving parties and long-distance journeys. But they were unconventional people, made more so by the use of drugs. At the time Bill was running an actor's workshop which Carol attended and she painted the sets of plays he acted in. This was the height of the L.S.D. revolution in America. Both Bill and Carol started taking L.S.D. during this time, and it pushed them further away from conventional living—into discovering more about themselves and the kind of life that could accommodate the true 'eccentricities' of their personalities.

Bill recognised the dangers of a relationship that was so total and tried to pin them down in a letter to Carol:

> These wounds we inflict go deeper with each fight, with each year. They test love. It's a dangerous game because it must necessarily get more and more dangerous. The scars of love get re-opened with each fight and with each test they get deeper. They must eventually cut through the veins, the arteries, the tissues, the bone, the marrow . . . unless we can learn, unless we can mature. I need your love but I know I must be able to do without it or I can't have it.

Carol's reaction to their separations, however brief, was much more physical:

> I'm sitting here longing for you so much that I'm crying tears. As for feeling horneeeee, I'm climbing the walls and I hate everyone and everything that's not you. You and I are the only people in the world. I am making love to myself and wearing your dirty shirt and thinking of you.

Then in 1965 came the decision to leave America and settle in Rome—Bill had already had parts in Italian-American films in Rome, the first being *Von Ryan's Express*, because he had been growing disillusioned by the New York theatre scene. Before they left they were married in a Sunset Strip wedding parlour in Los Angeles, Bill having been advised by his lawyer that it was the best way of gaining custody of his children from his previous wife. Carol didn't like the idea of marriage, but she agreed. However, immediately after the ceremony she tore up the wedding certificate and locked herself in her room, crying all night.

In the two years they were living together they had been taking flying lessons, and both of them acquired flying licences. Carol's idea was to buy an old plane and fly themselves to Italy. Bill's more rational, compromising voice prevailed and they took a Pan Am flight instead.

Carol hated being considered an American and always told an elaborate story of how it was her parents, instead of her grand-parents, who had emigrated from Italy. From the time they started living together in 1962 Carol never once returned home or ever saw her parents, as though refusing to admit that she had them. Bill never really considered himself an American either. They were like two people in search of a country or an identity, each return-ing to where their journey had in a sense begun. Bill, an eleven-year-old boy when the Second World War broke out, had been in the Hitler Youth and had attended strict Catholic schools. When the family emigrated to the United States, Bill had left behind a rigidly disciplined and authoritarian upbringing that was to shadow him for a long time, causing him to over-romanticise the freedom he had found in America, then in disillusionment to turn abruptly against it—influenced by the brilliantly satirical book *Dangerous Thoughts*, written by Michael Quinn during the McCarthy era and banned in the States. In 1948, a disillusioned idealist, he had planned while on holiday to Paris to immigrate to Israel because of the excitement of building a new state. Instead he had returned to the States and found an outlet in pursuing his career. When he left America with Carol in 1965, he had a powerful ally and an opportunity of being successful as an actor. But the journey to Italy was to bring new disasters and lead to a fundamental change in his outlook.

At first they lived in a house outside Rome and Bill went to and fro all over Europe, pursuing his career, mainly in films. A certain distance built up between them during 1965, largely be-cause Bill was away a lot but also because Carol had an affair with a well-known British actor—perhaps out of revenge against Bill for making her marry him. In a letter to a friend of hers in Paris where Bill was staying, Carol wrote to say that they were separated, then added:

> I'm working very hard since I want to make a lot of money and be independent. I'm not in the most fabulous humour and I'm trying to deaden my mind by indulging in sex as much as possible. It helps a little, especially when one has the makings of a nymphomaniac, except now I'll probably get pregnant or something. I really miss Billie, but I'll live because I've discovered that I don't have the guts to kill myself.

Bill appeared to be cultivating the distance, revealing the ambiguity of his commitment and philosophising away the very real barrier that existed between them. From Paris he wrote:

> My love for you is very deep and very strong, and so is my need for you. My pride is also very large and I find it degrading when I am forced to prove my love on challenge. I love you to the point of cherishing your happiness more than your physical presence. I certainly detest the idea of your sacrificing your happiness for me.

However that particular crisis passed and Bill returned to Rome to live with Carol. In the next year he started working in the theatre again, organising and running an actor's workshop in Rome. Carol joined in and continued the acting work she had started with Bill in New York. Early in 1966 they put on a series of plays for English-speaking audiences in the crypt of an American church in Rome. These plays won widespread critical acclaim and Carol's talent as an actress was recognised as being exceptional.

Later in 1966 Carol returned to New York to close up her apartment there and began doubting the relationship, writing a number of letters to Bill that reveal her inner conflict between the need for freedom and the need for someone, an either-or that is the murdering ambiguity of love. It was a conflict that they both faced and which was to separate them two years later. However, in her first letter she wrote from New York, Carol was able to be light-hearted, only hinting at the tension:

> My darling. The scene was too much last night. I made E take Roscoe to dinner at Orsini's and after made him call you.

A young lady appeared about 2 a.m.—very attractive—and I knew why she was there. E's way of providing all possible forms of titillation for me as he is dying to have me in the biblical sense. How did I put them all on—it was beautiful. I watched a James Mason movie while she sucked my cunt for about an hour and then went home. E made her see me to my door in a cab. It was too much. I love love love love you. You are so beautiful. What are you doing to whom, my darling? Anyway I still haven't fallen madly in love with anyone so I will probably be back around your neck no doubt. I was very uncertain while I was on the plane with all that time to think. Are you sure that all these domestic things aren't getting to be too much for you. Not me. Please write me a long love letter.

The second was more explicit:

What I am trying to say to you is that I don't love you. I am afraid of you and feel that you want to love me very badly sometimes but that hatred is there and I think it's time to stop playing games and be honest. I prefer quick death and I only say that because I'm delicate, very fragile and whether you like it or not I'm not going to pretend otherwise, I'm not going to pretend not to care and I'm not going to pretend to be cool. I didn't expect you to be the archangel Gabriel, so actually I'm not complaining—just running out.

Carol returned from New York at the end of 1966, and they found a new apartment in Rome which Carol furnished with bizarre and beautiful objects she had collected from different corners of the world. Bill made a circular tent room with drapes and cushions, and their apartment became a crash pad for actors, hippies and friends. There were candles all over, most of them burnt all the way down since nobody bothered or wanted to put them out—there were beads and Japanese paper flowers, some huge, hanging from the ceiling. There were L.S.D. trips, group love-making scenes and the tent-room where everything happened in the womb-warm atmosphere of a magic circle . . . trekking slowly towards paradise—Bill getting nearer to God, the kama sutra saint, while Carol fought the devil-angels. Life was about the other side, the beyond death, the paradise they glimpsed but couldn't quite get to. On this side they lived spontaneously and crazily—painting the street walls outside their apartment with signs from the Tarot pack; suddenly deciding after supper in a *trattoria* to drive out of Rome to Florence in a friend's white Bentley, but Bill having to get up early next morning to shoot a film and having to fight Carol in the back of the car, then getting out on the autostrada to Florence at dawn and having to hitchhike back to Rome in time for the film.

In 1967, when Bill went to Israel to make a film, Carol flew to London to consult some doctors to see whether or not she could get pregnant. She desperately wanted a child but, in spite of never using any contraceptive devices, had never been pregnant. At this time Carol was playing her last cards in an effort to retrieve or revitalise the relationship, throwing everything in to try and make their life work. Besides trying to get a child, she worked hard to try to help Bill with his acting career, seeing agents and producers in London and trying to get him parts.

From London she wrote: 'I have just read that you and Carroll Baker have run off together—*bonne chance*.' Then just before flying to Tel Aviv to meet Bill she wrote him a letter from Rome:

I am in our own bed finally which by the way looks very big and empty. I have been holding court here in bed, draped in arab veils. Today I am going to the dentist. My two front teeth fell out—it looks fabulous. This will delay my arrival in Tel Aviv I think. Darling please don't worry about me. I am fine and this thing with the baby is going to take time. I had a minor operation in London. I might get pregnant now. Your letters are so beautiful, I can't tell you what they do for me. Don't send the semen to me, for godssake. Just have it tested. I am leading a life of contemplation, thinking very seriously about my problems, which are suddenly becoming so clear to me it's incredible. I've kept my promise and haven't touched acid—only with and only 'planned trips' as they say. Do you remember that fabulous beautiful trip when you read the poems to me? That's what I mean. I love you more than anything else in the world and what I do means nothing unless it gives you pleasure. Your loving wife, Carolyn (I've changed my name again).

Then in February 1968 the lives of Bill and Carol changed radically. Carol had a talent for being devastatingly dramatic and she put it to powerful use. They had a row and Bill walked out of the apartment, as he had done many times before, but this time he couldn't get back to Carol. They seemed to have come to the end of their marriage—each struggling for independence yet also wanting to be able to be dependent. Carol decided to abandon the marriage and join the Living Theatre, a company founded by Julian Beck and his wife Judith Melina and dedicated to revolutionising the theatre. Both Bill and Carol had had some slight acquaintance with the Living Theatre in New York before the company left America in 1964 to tour Europe; and Carol had spent a short time with them in the winter of 1967–8 when she went to Cefalu in Sicily with Rufus Collins, black ex-Jesuit member of the company, to watch the rehearsals for their newly written play *Paradise Now*. Carol had asked Julian Beck a number of times if she could join the company, but joining wasn't a formal affair that depended on his assent. It was more a question of an individual's commitment to the company's anarchic life style and the general consent of the whole company.

When Bill had first met Carol she was only interested in painting and creating a survivable private life for herself. Bill was much more of the crusader, searching with Teutonic intensity for some outlet or further fuel for his radical intellectual views. But Carol lived radically, working far more with raw emotion than thought. In the early years of their relationship she didn't really care much about the outside world; but the effect of their living together, Carol's development and confidence as an actress and her sense of becoming more and more of a weight round Bill's neck, pushed her towards some kind of action to escape from the hot-house, somewhat egocentric atmosphere Bill created and also to express herself more freely. Bill was always theorising, changing his own and other people's attitudes but unable to put his beliefs into action. He waited for things to happen rather than making them happen, which could be excruciatingly frustrating for others.

Carol's decision to join the Living Theatre in 1968 was a step towards an independence she had tried but couldn't sustain in 1966. It was an escape from the tangled involvement of the marriage by an intense form of exterior activity. Bill, on the other hand, retreated deeper and deeper inside himself, becoming more detatched from involvement with Carol and exterior activity. Already disillusioned with the film business, he went on working to gain freedom and money enough to make his own experimental films.

In February 1968 when Carol decided to leave Bill, she didn't go immediately to the Living Theatre, but first went on a cruise on Aristotle Onassis' yacht S/Y *Christiana*, sailing from the Mediterranean to the Bahamas with her friends Paul and Talida Getty as well as Onassis and Maria Callas. It was an extraordinary decision, considering the fact that she wanted to join the Living Theatre. She couldn't have chosen two more contradictory extremes. It was as if she couldn't join the Living Theatre, which preached poverty and anarchy, without first being able to be a part of the world she was going to attack. Her gift for being uncompromisingly contradictory is summed up in a sentence she wrote in a letter, arguing in favour of living without money: 'It's not that I've never had the opportunity to have diamonds.'

Carol joined the Living Theatre in Avignon, where they went after taking an active part in the Paris street revolution in May, to put on the first performance of *Paradise Now*, and she became one of the outstanding female performers in the company. *Paradise Now* created a great impact in the theatre, though its effect was not totally theatrical. It aimed at breaking down all the established theatrical conventions and succeeded in creating pandemonium wherever it was performed, more often from the police than the audience. Even before it was put on the stage at Avignon, there were hysterical outbursts in the press, and during the Festival lynch mobs roamed around the street grabbing kids with long hair and beating them up, the police calmly watching. The building where the Living Theatre members were staying was repeatedly stoned and finally they had to be escorted out of the city.

The kind of effect which the play created inside the theatre is brought out in a tape which Carol made with Bill about an experience in Geneva.

CAROL: No, I went to talk to him because I thought he wanted
to——
BILL: To whom?

CAROL: This man in the audience in Geneva. When I said my line . . . somebody screamed, somebody yelled and I turned round and said . . . and I saw this man waving his arm and I thought he wanted to come down. I thought he was answering me, he was volunteering but he wouldn't come down, so I went up to where he was sitting and I got up there and instead of . . . I mean his first words to me were . . . I said something about do you want to come and be in the cell? And he said '*Non, je suis contre vous*'—'I am against you'—which flipped me out anyway. Those were his first words and he said, 'I am against everything you are saying and I'm against everything you're doing and I think you're disgusting, I think these women . . . girls running around in slips, little panties is completely unnecessary, it's exhibitionism, I think . . .' He said, 'What little I understand I disagree with completely and the rest I just don't understand at all.' And he went on like this for about ten minutes and I was completely horrified. I didn't know what to say. I was shocked, he really was . . . he was putting me down and then after all of this he said 'and this is the fourth night I've been here'—which blew my mind and I said 'That's fabulous'. He said, 'Yes, I've been coming here four nights and I still don't understand what you're talking about, it doesn't make any sense'. And I said, 'That's fabulous that somebody like you . . . doesn't understand something . . . don't you see that in itself it's groovy, you know, it's crazy . . . you've come here four times to try to understand something that you don't understand.' He must have a more or less open mind . . . and then he started asking me to explain it to him.

BILL: What? To explain the play?

CAROL: But I did very little talking. I just let him talk and talk and talk, and he said things like . . . I mean the typical answer of the typical bourgeois respectable Swiss man who probably, I'm sure he does, work in a bank because all of those people either work directly in banks or they work for the banks and they all get . . . I mean it really is the money machine in Switzerland, that's it and they're all involved very closely with it, they're involved with it . . . and he said . . . O and when he said 'How can you possibly expect to change the world, it's too difficult . . . it's impossible, it's not . . . you can't live without money' and I said 'Maybe you can't live without money, but what we're trying to do is making people see there is a possibility of living without money. That's what is destroying man and what is sick is the fact that people all think they can't live without money and it's very difficult for people to change their ideas. But the first thing they have to do is change their ideas before they'll ever be able to change the world or change reality because his mind . . .' The information has been fed into his mind, it's been fed into his mind for hundreds of years that this is the way he exists, this is the way to live. It's a capitalist structure and sure he has an easy life because he has money but he doesn't have an easy life. My life is much easier than his, and this is something he couldn't understand.

BILL: That your life was easier.

CAROL: That our life is easier because he said 'Your life is so difficult, your life is so difficult' and I said 'But *your* life is difficult because you are chained to a machine, you're chained to a plastic world . . . you're chained to a reality that someone tells you that's your reality and this is the way it's got to be.' And his wife was upset because one of the babies was sleeping on the floor in a blanket in the dressing room with all that noise and all that screaming and all that yelling. And I said 'Yes but that child is very peacefully sleeping in the midst of all this chaos. That child's needs . . . that child doesn't have to be in a little bed, shut up in a little room someplace *at home* while its mother is at the theatre all night, maybe having nightmares, maybe waking up in the middle of the night and screaming for its mother and its mother isn't there and there's nobody there.' I said it's very happy. . . .

BILL: He knows where his mother is.

CAROL: He knows where his mother is. No but it's true. I said you go . . . the way you have to live you have to leave your children at home if you have to work or if you want to work. You're not allowed to see your children all day if you want to see them. And that really got him. I said, 'That child is perfectly happy.' I said, 'Tell me why it shouldn't be sleeping there?' and she couldn't. She said 'You're right'. Well, I mean that's the thing . . . it's communicating with people like that which is *really* difficult.

BILL: That was her.

CAROL: That was his wife. No, I'm saying it's difficult communicating with people, but it's not really so difficult because if you can . . . I mean I wonder now if that man will ever think again. I'm sure he will, about his life . . . and about the fact that he is so rigidly confined to an idea of his life the way it should be or the way it *has* to be. If he can see himself . . . this is what I was trying to do when I was talking to him, I was trying to let him hear himself and when he can hear himself saying 'I *have* to do this' and then I can say 'I *don't* have to do that' and he said 'How do you live? It must be so difficult' and I said 'Well, how do you live? It's difficult, isn't it, it's difficult to live? But it's more rewarding if you can live the way you want to live.'

His root of life may be in that bank vault but it's only because of the sick reality that he's living in, and it's only because he's been told that it's only because he doesn't realise that he's living his life through one minute percentage of his capacity. He doesn't realise what he's capable of. Mankind doesn't realise what it's capable of any more . . .

When Carol left him in February to go on Onassis' yacht and then to join the Living Theatre, Bill realised that there was little hope of winning her back. But later, while Carol was in Avignon, Bill came from Germany where he had been acting in a film and decided to make his own film of the Living Theatre, as a way of staying in touch with Carol and also because for a long time he had wanted to make a film of his own. For six weeks he went everywhere with them—filming, talking, sharing their life. It had a profound effect on him in that they were living out and extending into action many of the ideas that he and Carol had been working on, but he never let himself be drawn fully into their activities, partly because of the tension between him and Carol, partly because of his own intellectual resistance to commitment and the extremism of their ideas and lifestyle.

However, for the next year and a half, while the Living Theatre toured Europe and America, Bill stayed in close contact with Carol, trying all the time to work out their relationship and to win her back. In a letter to her he wrote:

> I shall have to search the four corners of the earth and try to buy you back from whatever slave trader possesses you or seduce you away from the Voodoo priest who has bewitched you.

And when he finally did win her back, it was only after a white magic witch, a girl in Rome called Maya, saw a drawing Carol had sent Bill from Morocco. Maya thought Carol was shouting for help as though possessed or bewitched, so she came to Bill's apartment in Rome, felt the strong presence of black magic there; then together with Bill and some friends conducted a ritualistic exorcism of the black magic to bring Carol back.

Although in the first five years of their relationship they had been together a lot, to a certain extent the relationship thrived on separation, each needing to provoke reasons for it to prevent the other from coming too close. This was more true of Bill than of Carol. There seemed to be a barrier in him that neither he nor Carol could break through, and he thrived much better on freedom than Carol, stabilising himself and finding a powerful inner strength, free of dependence on anyone. Carol, on the other hand, desperately needed the intimacy and love of a close relationship in order to survive. If Bill was unable to provide it because he felt his independence threatened, Carol always found what she referred to as her 'golden boys' who gave her the attention she needed.

In the Living Theatre she had found something she had been searching for a long time—a supportive group and an opportunity for radical expression. But her escape into the exterior world also had an almost pathological desperation about it—she started taking drugs indiscriminately, swallowing whatever was put into her hand or mouth (in contrast to Bill's use of drugs which was always directed towards self-discovery and penetrating to deeper levels of consciousness); and she threw herself into the activity of the Living Theatre with incredible zeal, taking things further than anyone else dared to go—she was the first member to take off all her clothes on the stage, starting the whole cult of nudity in the theatre. It happened in the Brooklyn Academy in New York when Carol started dancing naked in some kind of ecstatic trance while club-wielding police broke up the performance all around her.

But the Living Theatre's American tour in late 1968 was so strenuously demanding that it burnt many of the performers out. They were constantly harrassed by the police—there were at least fifty police at every performance—and everyone was very paranoid, although in fact they were only busted once, at Yale, when actors and members of the audience went out of the theatre into the streets. People began to get sick from not eating and taking too many drugs. There wasn't a performance when everyone in the company didn't take L.S.D. Performing night after night on L.S.D., although it gave the actors power to face five thousand people in opposition, without apparently draining their energy, in the long term was bound to burn out the body.

When she joined the Living Theatre, Carol was aware that her body might give out. In July 1968, writing to Bill from Avignon, she said of *Paradise Now*: 'This play is so physically demanding that I really have to work hard to get strong before I can make it. My body is really weak and everyone else is of course in incredible shape.' During the American tour she went down with a cold, then complained of stomach pains. While she had been performing in America, Bill had been in Paris editing the film of the Living Theatre he had made during July and August. But it all seemed excruciatingly masochistic—to be working on a film of his wife's lovers at a time when he knew she really needed him.

One weekend he couldn't bear the pain and absurdity of it any longer, so he drove out to Orly airport to take the next plane to New York, though he didn't know where Carol was. There wasn't a plane that night, so he drove into Paris and had supper with some friends. He talked about the situation between him and Carol. A girl there said she had a friend who was a medium— Yaguel—who had an unusual gift for seeing the future. They ended up driving to Yaguel's house late at night and she told Bill that the healing of his relationship with Carol would take much longer than he anticipated. She also told him other things which in fact were to happen in the next three months. That meeting was the beginning of a friendship that was to become important to both Bill and Carol later.

However, next day Bill flew to New York and started looking for Carol. He found her with the Living Theatre at Stony Brook, a small university town on the north coast of Long Island. Carol looked very sick—she had lost about twenty pounds—and Bill wanted her to come back with him to Europe. There was a dramatic moment when they sat together talking in a car Bill had hired, while the yellow Living Theatre bus waited to go. Carol said she would return with Bill. She got out of the car and went to the bus to get her things and to say goodbye to the Living Theatre. She boarded the bus and a few moments later it drove off, Carol still inside. Bill was left sitting alone in his car in an empty parking lot.

He drove back to New York and took the next plane back to Paris. He had only been in America for a few days, and it seemed the end for both of them. He went on working at editing the Living Theatre film, then on 6 November—the date predicted by Yaguel—Carol phoned to say she wanted to come to Paris to see Bill. For two weeks he heard nothing, then she suddenly arrived. She looked even more sick, and so Bill took her to see a doctor in Paris, Dr. Fribourg, who said that tests had to be made and they would have to wait a week for the results. Since 1967 Carol had been having pains in her stomach and had been in hospital in Israel and in Rome, but nothing serious had been found wrong.

In Paris Bill and Carol talked together but were guarded with each other, Carol still not sure of what she wanted. Then one night—about ten days after she had arrived—they were driving down the Boulevard Saint-Germain when they saw an old friend they hadn't seen for four years and had dinner together. He said he was going to London the next day and Carol said she wanted to go with him. Next morning she left—before the results of the doctor's tests had arrived. Again Bill was left alone, though he refused to let himself believe he had lost Carol.

Then Dr. Fribourg telephoned him and said that it was serious —the tests had shown that she had cancer of the uterus. All Bill knew was that she had gone to London. He tried to get her there on the phone but found she had left for America. Finally he found her with the Living Theatre—by telephone—and told her the news and that she should go to his brother-in-law, Dr. Rudolf Colmers, and his sister, who was also a doctor. Carol went to their house in Connecticut. Bill went from Paris to Rome, back to their apartment and stayed there. His apparent detachment at such a crucial time seems strange, but it was the beginning of a turning point in their relationship, which was to hold together for the next year and a half.

All that happened, including Carol's leaving for London with an old friend and her illness, had been forecast by Yaguel in September—also that Carol would come back. Perhaps the accuracy of the predictions up to that point gave him confidence that they would get through this crisis.

Bill's brother-in-law got Carol admitted to Stamford Hospital, where she was examined under anaesthesia and had a biopsy taken. The cancer proved to be highly malignant. Then she was transferred to the Cancer Memorial Hospital in New York, probably the world's most outstanding cancer hospital, and operated on by Dr. Brockunier, top gynaecologist at the hospital. The operation took place on 6 January and lasted seven hours.

At the end of January 1969 Carol flew from the States and arrived at Rome airport, carrying only her guitar. The operation had been successful and she had recovered remarkably quickly. The doctor had been able to remove all the diseased tissue and the probability of further problems was judged to be no greater than twenty per cent. Just before the operation Carol had been asked if she wanted any special pain-killer. She replied that she wanted L.S.D. The doctors said they couldn't give her that, but she managed to get some from friends who visited her and she took it every day before and after the operation. She also went through the operation on L.S.D. It was a very 'clean' operation—she lost only one and a half pints of blood instead of the normal seven or eight. Then she was out of bed a week later, telephoning Bill and arranging to leave America. Two weeks after the operation she was on the aeroplane, fully recovered from an operation that normally needs a long convalescence. A doctor at the hospital told her that it was the most remarkable recovery he had ever known. Carol told him she had been taking L.S.D. every day.

Just before she had arrived back, Bill had received a letter from his brother-in-law telling him of Carol's condition. Carol had obviously not been a 'conventional' patient, and this had caused some problems:

> As you well know, we had quite a problem with Carol whom we took into our home when she called me in desperation from Boston. Unfortunately Carol as well as her friends with their non-conformist way of life caused problems at Stamford Hospital. Other patients were disturbed and complaints were received from many sources so that during her short hospital stay she occupied three different rooms. Obviously she received adequate medication for pain and no unreasonable restrictions were placed upon her. Certain minimal rules and regulations—*re* number of visitors and strict enforcement of visiting hours, particularly during a flu epidemic—have to be enforced for protection of the patients. Bill, I hope you realise that Carol's problem is not one of eccentricity alone but she is suffering from a serious mental illness for which she had been hospitalised on a previous occasion. This illness is presently quiescent but may recur at any time.

Carol had changed a great deal as a result of the hospital experience. She felt that she had died, was already dead, and talked a lot to Bill about the experience and how it was possible to cut out from one's immediate environment and leave one's body—possibly the L.S.D. she had taken made her aware of what is called 'astral projection'. She had returned to her body reluctantly, though she was happy to be back in Rome and together with Bill again.

One of the reasons why the operation had been so traumatic for Carol and gave her such a strong sense of death was that it meant she could never have a child. In the years before going off with the Living Theatre, she had constantly been trying to get pregnant —seeing doctors and specialists in London and Geneva, cutting out clippings from the newspapers about new clinics and advances being made—but it never happened. In the time immediately prior to her departure with the Living Theatre, she and Bill had begun to accept the idea of adoption and had wanted to adopt a Vietnamese baby. They went to the South Vietnamese embassy in Rome and filled in forms, but found that they would have to go to South Vietnam to make the adoption. Although Carol had begun to face up to the impossibility of getting pregnant then, her leaving with the Living Theatre had a lot to do with her disappointment and inability to face it fully. It was one of her deepest needs or instincts—to have a child by Bill and create a large family around them—and to face up to the impossibility of this was one of the hardest and saddest things for her. She thought that if she couldn't give Bill a child, she was failing him as a woman and that he would ultimately leave and find someone else.

What Bill never told her and she never knew was that when they operated on her to remove the cancer, they found that she was pregnant—there was a living foetus in her womb which they had to cut out to make the operation.

While she had been in hospital Bill had become involved with a mysterious new religious sect called The Process. They gave the appearance of being a cross between Catholic priests and the S.S., and wore black uniforms with an emblem of two crosses. They were a split-off group from the Scientologists and, although they never communicated their beliefs directly and no one was quite sure who they were, the predominant theme of discussions was the interconnectedness of good and evil, creation and destruction, rather than their being polarities or opposites. They kept coming to Bill's apartment, which was open to everyone, staying for several hours—just talking or sitting silently. They lent him Satanistic books and tried to get him committed; but Bill was content to watch them, fascinated by some intuitive or psychic power they seemed to possess. He had stopped smoking while Carol was ill in hospital as an act of prayer towards her, but never told anyone this. Father Malakai, the most striking-looking member of The Process, who hardly ever talked, indicated one day that he knew all this. Also, he and Bill once played a series of chess games that to Bill seemed like mystical chess, as though he were being hypnotised. Bill is a very good chess player, but Malakai would always win, deliberately sacrificing an important piece early on in the game then catching Bill completely off guard later. The Process intrigued Carol because she was always fascinated by something strange and was becoming more interested in magic. Then one day they suddenly left Rome and never appeared again.

A friend of Bill and Carol—Joe Wheeler, an American actor working in Fellini's *Satyricon*—described an evening at the apartment not long after Carol had returned from her operation:

It was the time when The Process were in Rome—everyone was into one kind of magic or another—but they gave the impression of being involved in Black Magic and sacrifices and all kinds of rituals. They haunted people, wanting to know where everyone lived and inviting people to weekends in the country. I was talking to Carol in a downstairs room—we were both sitting on the bed and Carol was on a death trip, saying that she felt she had died in the hospital. We started making love on the bed when the words ran out—Carol couldn't fuck but we took our clothes off and stroked each other. Suddenly we both sat upright because a black silhouette with a longish kind of oval head and a hookish nose but a face without any definition appeared in a corner of the room. He was short, about five feet tall. Carol turned to me and said 'Did you see that?' I nodded, then the figure appeared again, for a very short time—just enough to see him. Carol got up and said 'I'm getting out of here.'

Less than two months after leaving hospital, Carol rejoined the Living Theatre. After a tour of Northern France and London, in the summer they went to Morocco in an attempt to write a new play, staying in the remote village of Esauria. From the time of her return to the Living Theatre earlier that year, things had become much more difficult for the company, and this had its effect on Carol's already weakened body. From London she had written to Bill about the difficulties, indicating that she really needed him and wanted to be with him:

The tour was really crazy, driving back and forth from one end of France to the other, all in the north of course—cold and raining mostly and disgusting people who threw eggs at us and rotten tomatoes. London is a drag—everyone is exhausted and in pieces. The London critics are trying to destroy us. One paper even tried to defame us, if that were necessary, by writing an article saying that we are all drug addicts and homosexuals and that Julian Beck makes it with men and his wife says it's all right and all the chicks are lesbians. Everyone is flipping out from exhaustion.

A mystic saw us together riding on an elephant with a buddha over us—a very euphoric vision. My feelings for you are so complicated that sometimes I find tears coming out of my eyes, just pouring out and I know it's because I miss you. It's very difficult to make love by mail and I have a strong desire to hold you in my arms.

On the way to Morocco Carol saw Bill briefly in Spain where he was acting in a spaghetti Western, *Sabata*, with Lee Van Cleef. In Morocco the Living Theatre began to lose that cohesive momentum that had made them such a powerful force in the theatre, and they were unable to create any new work.

In a long letter to Carol while she was in Morocco Bill wrote:

I cannot force you out of your rut, I cannot even seduce you and I certainly cannot offer you something 'better' than the Living Theatre, because as long as you are a Living Theatre zombie, nothing can be.

Bill was becoming more and more impatient with Carol's attachment to the Living Theatre, and felt he had to present the situation as he saw it clearly and forcibly to Carol because he sensed a dangerous resignation and despair in her. In the past he had always reached out to her and taken care of her when she had been at the point of suicide, but now it seemed she was unable to respond. In the same letter he went on to write:

The Living Theatre is terribly strong and they have managed to make you accept that fact, and that is probably a part of the hold it has on you. I'm not saying the Living Theatre is bad for you but that hold which you accept with less and less struggling every day is what is destroying your soul. It is not their fault. You did the same with me for such a long time till you got to the point of desperation and split. There you were lucky there was a Living Theatre to split to, and now I feel you're looking for an even stronger drug, a greater high, and that obviously can't be because no matter how much you talk of changes it will always seem a going back to a prior addiction. If you didn't feel this, you wouldn't still be talking to me in terms of ivory towers. I never put you in an ivory tower, the Living Theatre doesn't put you in an ivory tower—you do it yourself. The fact that you've got to have something 'better' to split to seems to prove that. I know you realise this and you accept it as part of your nature that you cannot change—but there you are wrong. You can change your hang-ups, you can change your destiny.

Bill's strength and his sense of urgency obviously communicated themselves to Carol because on the boat from Morocco to Naples, the *Cristoforo Colombo*, she dropped one of her bombshells when she drew up a manifesto 'The King Must Die', attacking the Becks, Julian and Judith. On the boat in the midst of all the discussions, the Becks had proposed that they should cut down the numbers and that several members should leave. In her manifesto Carol suggested that the Becks should leave, expressing a common feeling that the Becks were dominating the theatre company, taking the lead parts and controlling discussions.

Bill met the boat in Naples, hoping that Carol would get off, but she was so involved in the break-up of the Living Theatre that she wanted to go on to Sicily, so Bill boarded the boat and went to Sicily with her. But he hardly saw Carol there because of the intense discussions that were continuing—sometimes all through the night. After three weeks of hanging around and getting no nearer to sorting out their own problems, Bill told Carol he was leaving—the next morning. When he got into the car to drive it to the boat at Palermo, Carol was sitting in it with her bags packed.

The decision to leave the Living Theatre had finally been made. The problem facing them was where to go now? The lease on the Rome apartment had run out—Bill's twelve-year-old daughter Debbie was with them—and neither of them wanted to go back to the old life, of living in the city, hustling for work and unable to be alone together because of all their friends dropping in and staying for weeks. Also, when in September 1969 she got into the car with Bill in Sicily and said goodbye to the Living Theatre, Carol was still ill, not having allowed herself enough time to fully recover from the cancer operation earlier in the year, and she had further exhausted her body by continuing to take numerous 'hard' drugs in an indiscriminate way. On the drive from Sicily,

she was nervous and physically run down, though she was happy
to be with Bill again and happy that he was there to look after her.
In the past one of the most serious problems that had created
difficulties between them was their totally different attitude
towards money. Carol had never taken any notice of money at all,
doing what she wanted regardless of the cost, and although she
was a very good painter, she refused to sell her canvases but
instead gave them away to friends—usually rich friends. Bill, on
the other hand, was always 'responsible' and careful with money,
making sure that he always had enough to pay for his and Carol's
needs, although Carol's spontaneous living threatened to exhaust
even his bank balance. Bill invariably tended to solve their
emotional problems by plunging himself into his acting career,
which gave him independence as well as financial security, all of
which possibly had deep roots in his early life—breaking away
from home and his undoubtedly powerful parents. Although it is
a well-known cliché that acting is the profession of rebels—from
authoritarian parents or educational upbringing—it nevertheless
seems true in his case.

Before joining the Living Theatre Carol had tried to work on
this problem with Bill, suggesting that he take time out to solve
it:

> Artists have to be selfish—that is the only way they can exist.
> I feel if you really want to work, really work, you are just
> going to have to make up your mind to be a bum and an
> independent one. I am not interested in leaving you and if
> you leave me I'll kill you and that will make matters much
> worse because then who do I tell my troubles to?

However, Bill became more and more isolated from Carol,
seemingly distant and cold, acting an intimacy he wanted but
couldn't really express and waiting for Carol to break through the
barrier they both knew existed. Whenever Carol tried to escape
from the relationship, it was largely out of frustration at being so
financially dependent on Bill and also because Bill obviously used
the money he could earn to dominate or imprison Carol. Joining
the Living Theatre had given Carol the financial security and
freedom she had needed, and it was no coincidence that when the
Living Theatre started to have serious financial problems she

returned to Bill. The difference in their attitudes to money, together with the emotional and sexual implications, is brought out clearly in the tape already quoted which they made just before the Living Theatre's American tour in 1968:

BILL: You're just as much part of the money machine as anybody else.

CAROL: I understand we're part of it, but our only answer to that is that we're living in a society where you can't exist without money.

BILL: Yes, but how does that make you any different from anybody else?

CAROL: However, we manage to exist on a lot less money than most people.

BILL: Doesn't the Living Theatre live on 1,500 lire a day when they don't have much money and 3,000 lire when they have more and 4,000 lire a day if they have more money? You live on what you have.

CAROL: No, it's a question of principle.

BILL: When you have twice as much money you live on twice as much money like everybody else.

CAROL: Bill, it is a question of principle. I'm sorry, it is a question of principle. The Living Theatre could be rich . . . see, that's where you're wrong. The Living Theatre does not live on 1,500 lire a day because we're incapable of making money.

BILL: That's not true, otherwise if you were going on principle you would live on 1,500 lire a day no matter how much money you had.

CAROL: Don't you listen to Julian's performances? Don't you listen to Julian's speeches? Don't you listen to the discussions about money? Don't you understand that we work in theatres where people sell tickets only so that we have only the basic minimum amount of money that we need to eat . . . ?

BILL: The Living Theatre gives performances and charges money for performances.

CAROL: I mean Jenny explains it so much more clearly than I do. My mind is still so completely . . . unclear about it.

BILL: How does she explain it?

CAROL: Oh it's what she said . . . in the world that we're talking about, you don't have to go and make these movies to get money to do something that you like to do.

BILL: Oh yeah. But that world doesn't exist.

CAROL: No, it doesn't exist now. That's the world we're trying to make.

BILL: The Living Theatre does exactly the same thing that I'm doing. They charge for tickets although they don't want to charge for tickets because they have to have the money to travel, to eat. Even if you live on little money, you still have to have it.

CAROL: Unfortunately it's true. But Julian Beck has been wearing the same pair of pants and the same shirt for I think like six years. But Richard Burton hasn't.

BILL: But the members in the Living Theatre spend a lot of money on clothes.

CAROL: No they don't.

BILL: Relatively speaking.

CAROL: They do not.

BILL: That jacket that Sandy has.

CAROL: They do not. Which jacket?

BILL: That beautiful jacket with the brocades and all.

CAROL: Somebody gave it to him. I mean the Living Theatre is a marvellous . . . I think the Living Theatre is a marvellous example of how you can live on little money. People give us things all the time.

During the long separation when Carol had her operation and then when she rejoined the Living Theatre, both of them had begun to isolate the money problem in order to stop it from coming between them in such a predictably disastrous way. In a letter to Carol during that period of separation, after Carol had made a number of collect calls from America to Rome, Bill wrote to her:

I have a feeling that the bull in the china shop technique may in the long run be easier to take than the Mount Olympus self-righteous stance. When I analyse myself I find some basic weaknesses that fuck up my thinking and they are all intertwined: sex, money and a kind of self-righteousness that stems from an ability to see things too clearly from all sides or perhaps only seeming to do so, and last but not least a driving desire to be the good guy, at least in my own eyes.

By the time they were together again in the car driving from Sicily, both of them had changed a great deal and they were more able to accept and enjoy one another instead of endlessly fighting to preserve their identities. Such an acceptance stemmed largely from the fact that Bill had been able to stand back from the relationship and acquire an inner strength and peace that was beginning to communicate itself to Carol, also because both of them had been able to concentrate on the difficulties and solve some of the tensions that divided them. But it was dangerously precarious, and Carol had a destructive tendency that stemmed from a deep insecurity about herself. It was something she recognised but couldn't always control. In a letter to Carol in 1967 Bill was confident that they would be able to live together and get through the difficulties, saying: 'I know now that it will happen, provided we don't kill each other before.' The trouble was that in spite of the fact that Bill's letters contained deep insights into their relationship, they remained merely insights that got discarded on the way. In the light of what was to happen exactly a year later, they have a terrifyingly prophetic quality.

Bill drove Carol to Positano on the mountainous Amalfi coast just south of Naples, where he had rented a small house, in a maze of alleyways in the older, poorer part of the town, where some remnants of the artistic clique that had made Positano famous in the 1930s still survived. The rest of Positano, nearer the sea, had by now become a fashionable tourist resort. After a few days there, the three of them (Debbie, Bill's twelve-year-old daughter, had come from California to Italy for the summer holidays) living in one large room, Bill and Carol decided to look for a larger house somewhere near Positano. A friend of Bill's, the owner of a restaurant in Positano, said he knew of a house in Praiano, and one morning both he and Bill went to look at it—Carol meanwhile having gone off on her own to look at a small castle on some rocks by the sea near Positano.

Praiano is a small village, five miles from Positano, along a precariously narrow mountain road, with a few shops and hotels on the road, but otherwise unspoilt by the influx of summer tourists. Most of the village consists of old houses with several acres of cultivated land above and below the road, the houses being interconnected by a series of narrow twisting alleyways and steps. The people mainly live by fishing and farming. The house Bill was going to see could only be reached by climbing over three hundred steps that led up from the main road. In spite of the arduous climb, as soon as he walked into the doorway of the house he decided it was the place they had been looking for. Normally indecisive by nature, it was one of the only immediate and clear decisions he had ever made in his life.

The three-storey house is very large, with fourteen rooms, a garden and a series of caves underneath the main part of the house. In fact, the house—the oldest in Praiano—was built as a stronghold capable of a prolonged resistance. The earliest building records date back to 1750, but it is probable that the house is considerably older than that, at least some parts of it. The purpose for the defensive construction could either have been to ward off Saracen raiders who had control of the Mediterranean before the sea battle of Lepanto in 1571, and then briefly during the Thirty Years War, or because at one time it was a pirate stronghold, as local rumour has it— the house is supposedly haunted by a white-haired pirate.

Apart from the size and number of rooms, the most striking feature of the house is its unique view. Built half way up a mountain, it overlooks the village of Praiano with its mosaic domed Romanesque church and large square, and beyond is the huge expanse of blue Mediterranean, with several small rocky islands half way to the horizon. In the distance below the high range of mountains that continue right along the Amalfi coast is Positano, then the mountains curl round to form a long peninsula that extends as far as Capri, which is visible on the horizon. Behind the house is a steep mountain terraced with vineyards and fields, and on a higher level than the house is a large fifteenth-century cloistered Dominican monastery crumbling into disrepair.

The mountainous region above the road, where the house is situated, is a strange and remote part of Italy that has a timeless quality about it—the life on the mountains is substantially the same as it was in medieval times, being very little touched by the modern industrial world or even by Catholicism. The local people entertain each other on long winter evenings by playing medieval-type instruments or by spinning tales of ghosts and spirits in the mountains—the monks in the monastery above the house were supposedly driven out by ghosts—and religious festivals in the mountain villages manage to interweave the Christian drama with local myths of much more terrifying and sinister happenings. Praiano was a Greek settlement, then in Roman and early medieval times was more densely populated than it is today—because of the fertility of the land and because people moved to the remoter mountain areas to escape the plagues that ravaged the plains of central Italy.

After looking round the house Bill drove quickly back to find Carol to tell her about it. Sitting in a café in Positano, Carol was adamant about buying an old castle, until Bill eventually per-suaded her at least to look at the Praiano house. In the past Carol had often had mad impractical schemes of living in a palace or a castle and had often tried to persuade Bill to buy one. But as soon as she saw the house she fell in love with it, renamed it The House of the Angels, and shouted out lines from *Macbeth* from the balcony while Bill signed a three-year lease with Signor Zingone who owned the house.

When they moved in everyone said they were crazy because Praiano was so remote—but that was what they were looking for. Bill wanted to find a place to think, somewhere where they could live quietly away from all the storms that had been blowing them about in the last two years. Carol was still very nervous, distracted and uncertain what she wanted; but Bill was convinced that it was important to pursue an inner search, to gain strength, choosing the right moment to move off into some new activity, learning to wait from inside oneself. During Carol's illness in December 1968 he had written a poem for her which described what he wanted a house to be and which ended with these lines:

> *Thoughts rest your wings.*
> *Here is a hollow nest of silence*
> *A nest of stillness*
> *In which to hatch your dreams.*

They moved all their things from Rome and started to transform the house into the magic atmosphere that Carol always created wherever she lived. They opened up caves below the house and made new rooms; Bill started building a swimming pool in one of the caves and a tepee on the roof.

Although the house symbolised a new coming together, an acceptance of each other, the peace and stillness they had wanted was hard to find. Carol went into manic depressions and wanted to distract herself with some kind of frenetic activity—as she had done in the Living Theatre. Some invisible, intangible disharmony that had existed throughout their lives together, remained smouldering ominously beneath the surface—Bill who could murder to get what he wanted and Carol whose suicidal tendency could cause her to provoke those she loved into killing her to escape from what she found too painful to face. Also the fact that Bill's daughter Debbie was living with them caused explosive conflicts, Carol being jealous of Debbie and feeling she had a stronger hold over Bill than she herself did—which in a way was true, as a letter from Bill to Carol in Morocco had indicated:

> Debbie is really an extraordinary being and has the ability to become one or stay one, to put it better. She has more wisdom and psychic forces going in her body than you and I and the whole Living Theatre together. She's like where we're all trying to get and she doesn't yet have the hang-ups that make her want to hide it in some corner like the rest of us do. She's at that point without having as yet had to pay the price in cynicism to the devil. It's beyond any incestuous love affair feelings I have for her and beyond the automatic narcissism one feels for one's offspring, and I am learning and growing from her. She is Demain.

Carol had never treated Bill's daughters as children, and from the time they first met in California she had seen them as a threat, though it was a conflict she tried to overcome as she said in an early letter:

> I promise you I won't be the wicked stepmother. And Billie, I do love big familes. I know that you think I'm unstable

but *in fondo* not when it comes to your children, you and your happiness. I could never hurt someone you love and you must know that.

In a sense the house was a perfect place for them, since it was large enough for them to lose and find each other again—it created the distance and privacy they needed for themselves—Bill building things and Carol holding court in a cave or on the mountainside, talking or making music. It seemed as though Carol was gradually beginning to control her jealousy of Bill, who occasionally stayed with different girls in Rome or slept with someone else in the house, as she herself did. One time in the house when Bill became upset because Carol was angry and jealous, she said, 'What's the matter, can't I be jealous—let me be jealous.' It seemed she had begun to accept it and go beyond it. The same was true of drugs. The experience of living a more settled calmer life had enabled her to see that she could do without them. This was one of the most important, yet sadly ironical aspects of their new life together. The biggest problem for her was that she sometimes felt trapped in Bill's life, trapped in the house and wanted to escape again into a sort of suicidal activity or go back to the Living Theatre people. But she was beginning to work towards creating what she wanted for herself, talking about starting a street theatre in Positano or working with Bill on the films he was planning to make himself.

Sometimes there was a rare harmony between them that radiated out to everyone who came to the house—it wasn't long before more and more people, especially other members of the Living Theatre, came to stay with them.

What Carol found by living in the house and the journey she made towards Bill in the last year of her life is hinted at in a series of diaries she kept—containing drawings, poems, songs, letters. One of the dairies was titled *House of the Devil*:

You are leaving tomorrow. You planned it all. You have me where you want me and now you will go off to your Living Theatre, feeling good knowing I am where you want me. Alone in your palace, in your cage. Well, a cage is a cage,

I'm not choosy. A candle in a roll of toilet paper. I only wish this one had a large stash of opium.

It can only be. It can. Me. Positano—a new life. A big house on the mountain. The potato room. The little house. My cave. Petra arrives. Is it possible I've been here so long. I cannot leave. Where have all the beautiful people gone? Where are they? It is finally night and I can breathe. Today was a bad day. My body full of tensions. Restless people all rushing. Restless spirits around here today. And last night wandering through the rooms. My orphans wearing the clothes that I once wore. No need to paint. No more paintings flow from my fingers, no more oneness and joy of creation. Making messy water colours and criticising them, judging. They get worse. Mud pie again. No oneness with the universe, but tonight it feels better. A little more easy. Now the tape recorder blows. Now I play my guitar and everything is cool. Then everything is in pieces again. Why hang on?

The tortured twisted mind. The fear, the paranoia and guilt. I must be punished. The hate and violence. Every nerve in this body is raw and in shreds. Two days of screaming, one day of desperate crying. I watch myself speaking words and hallucinating things that can only make me loathe and despise myself and no effort of will can stop it. I feel as though I'm suffocating. This is not me, I am watching from within. Without is the person speaking, doing things. It's not me because I have no control over these things. Am I going to go through this whole life tortured like this or am I ever going to be delivered? Where is the release? It's not true that you can flip out and it's over. It never ends. Winter is coming. If I were a bear. Or a tree. Maybe I can become a tree.

I'm expecting no more than anything and everything. I will come to the crossing and fingers rise out of the wall and we held hands for valuable years. Could you tell that mine was empty? We must go to the rooms again where you do not ask for love. We do not have to ask. Loved and envied. Shake the

sand from your shoes she said, a wrecked and rotten shell
with needs, or walk forever crawling. Dirty deeds dirty deeds.
Not a sound I utter. Sleep forever, hold your head, rest your
brain. A shudder passes through my eyes. One looks out, the
other looks in. Turns back. She walks ahead. We arrive at the
outside. Left us here again. It's a long time and music sounds
the sickening uniformity of conformity and coffee cups with
cigarettes and pinpoints the glancing lies lies where I lies.
Makes you nervous. How did you know I needed O to cross
the great water and stand away. Nothing more, nothing less
than anything. Good fortune, I see far into the future for
you.

So happy to see you again my friends! We all know we're
in the same world. It's as strong for you as for me. We feel
the same thing. I long to have you close for a while again, to
see you every day, to spend some days in close communion. I
cry, *ich schriee, ich schriee,* our love I sing. Demanding lovers,
O you are so hard with me, each to make me choose against
the other. The one that says—this is the last time—it is the
one I have conquered and who no longer hides me from you
or you from me.

You are looking for a place to fold the wings. I am looking
for the silver key. How to soften the hearts of others. How to
stop the pain in my own. How to find the gods again. What
to say to you from the void. I am on the abyss, this mountain,
helpless before the abyss—wishing I could fly, not even able
to run. I want to help you. Give to . . . a place to float down
to. My hands are tied. You must move. Move. I feel like
Steppenwolf. Shunned by humanity I found the magic theatre
and lost it again. This place where I am is very painful. I have
no power, I am completely alone. Lost. Here on the mountain. No drug can take me through. I can't even bother. I am
erecting a monument here to death. There is much here
for those who make the trip. Hepatitis. That too. Over-
whelmed by the scent of death around here they say. O god
where is love? Where are we? Imagination takes power.
Carol.

Billie's song

> *It's come to me slowly*
> *turning around*
> *always uncertain but always there*
> *always fought in so many ways*
> *but it just stays and stays*
> *no one beside me*
> *tears in my brain*
> *heart like a stone*
> *always I know that I'm alone*
> *without you*
> *without you*
> *and I know the answer I'll find*
> *the one that'll bring me peace of mind*
> *is with you*
> *yes with you*

My darling you are not entirely right. I have faith in you and I love you more than money, gold filthy lucre and will love you for as long as I live. It's you who keep me from despair after I have been through all the shits, and that's what really matters to me. But I cannot have you lose all respect for me because I am incapable of earning enough pennies to keep myself in cigarettes. I am not and cannot stand the shadow this casts over our lives. This is part of my frustration and anger. I love you I love you I love you. Carol.

Just before Christmas Bill got a part in a film in Egypt. He, Carol and Debbie, who was still with them, all planned to go to Egypt together, but there was a chaotic week of fights and tensions to break through that indicate the difficulties of living together. Jimmy Tirof from the Living Theatre was staying at the house during this time.

Bill went to Rome to get a visa for Carol but forgot her passport so had to come back. Then he, Jimmy Tirof and Carol went to Naples because Carol had to have photographs taken for the visa and Jimmy Tirof said he would take the passports to Rome by train. Carol was in a truculent mood—half wanting to go to Egypt, half not. She went in to have her photographs taken and came out with photos of her making funny faces. Bill said they wouldn't do and more would have to be taken. Carol said, 'What's the matter, they're photos of me aren't they?' Eventually she had some more taken; then they put Jimmy Tirof on a train for Rome, telling him to take the passports to Bill's agent, Perrone. During the drive out of Naples Bill and Carol got into a traffic jam; then Bill hit Carol because she was taunting him. She got out of the car in the middle of the traffic and walked away. Bill spent three hours trying to find her, then drove back to Praiano without her. When he got home he found Carol, who had hitch-hiked back, having a fight with Debbie, banging her own head on the stone floor and screaming like a madwoman 'I don't want your child!'

The next day Jimmy Tirof returned from Rome . . . with the passports. He had become so paranoid because of the number of police at Rome station that he had darted into a phone booth, phoned Perrone to say he had the passports but couldn't possibly leave the station. Perrone sent his chauffeur to pick them up, by which time there was no sign of Jimmy Tirof in the station bar where a meeting had been arranged. Bill drove to Rome again . . .

They spent Christmas in the house and went to Egypt—Debbie and Carol getting parts in the film—then, when they all returned to the house in early spring, Petra Vogt, Carol's closest friend from the Living Theatre, came to live with them. Shortly after, Carin, Bill's elder daughter, arrived from America for the 1970 Easter holidays. Carol and Petra decided to go to Paris—to leave Bill and the girls alone in the house but largely because the tension between Carol and Debbie had not subsided. Before they left for Paris Carol wrote Bill a letter about the situation:

Things are actually much worse than you realise. You couldn't possibly know all the evil things I do are not conscious. I cannot possibly stop myself. I watch from afar like another person, incapable of stopping it, and with horror and disgust I watch myself turn into an ugly cruel vicious madwoman. I need help desperately and I have to find it soon. You can't give it to me because you don't have time and you are too emotionally involved. It is very difficult for us to see ourselves, and just as difficult for you as anyone else. We also are each other's mirrors. I know that I am the one in this whole situation that is the most fucked up, and I feel very helpless. Of course I understand that all the things that used to be important to you are no longer important. Your love for me is only secondary to having someone who will take care of your child and who she'll love. What drives me away is that you will probably find that person. There are thousands of them, each one who would give anything to be where I am before I can get it together. All you know is I've failed, and you have already given me up. That's why there's never any room in the bus. I can see you sitting there, reading this letter and judging everything I am saying—which is why I had to write it. I must try to communicate something to you which is breaking my heart and tearing my soul. I cannot say it to you without our getting emotional and screaming at each other since we both know that we are right and will not stop judging the other. We both know that people are what they are and feel what they feel and there is no judgment of right and wrong, don't we? We know this about each other, so I think we can say the same for ourselves. Every day I wake up and hear the birds and look around me and know that this is paradise. But there is still a snake in the garden.

By the time she got to Paris Carol had cooled out and wanted to be back in Praiano, hating to be in the city again. In Paris she saw Yaguel, Bill's medium friend, as well as several members of the Living Theatre—notably Henry and Nona Howard who were to come to Praiano later—and they told her that Rufus Collins, who had left the Living Theatre in Morocco just before Carol finally left, had decided to go to India to start a centre for dance, meditation and yoga. Then she went on to London with Petra and wrote another letter to Bill in Praiano.

I keep thinking about the mountain and how far it has taken me. It's been so emotional seeing everyone but beautiful. Everyone is very together. Yaguel also says that she doesn't see me in Praiano for three months. I was horrified and am going to see what I can do to change destiny. My magic is becoming stronger and I feel very confident. I do want to talk to Rufus. Odile and Gunther have told me the plan and it sounds the most interesting plan to me—just living, studying and growing. I can't help thinking how beautiful it would be for Debbie, instead of sending her to a European school, if we all went to school in India for a while. Rufus is there now working with the masters who will be working with everyone. But first and foremost I am going to straighten out my physical scene. I miss you both very much. Henry had asked me to work with the group in Paris but I told him I couldn't say anything right now because my personal situation is uppermost in my mind and being separated from you—and the kind of life, living condition-environment we are in.

Bill drove Debbie and Carin to Paris to put them on a plane for America, met Carol and Petra there and they all drove back to Praiano together. As it grew hotter and the summer began to make people think of leaving the city and heading south, friends started coming from different parts of the world and the house became a kind of crash pad summer commune, a larger family— Bill wanting it to be open to everyone but Carol remaining watchful of who came into the house, wanting to preserve a privacy she needed. And she could be severely protective of that privacy. Once Bill brought a friend from Rome who one day started arguing with Raffaela, a woman from Praiano who worked in the house. Carol stalked into the kitchen, took hold of the man by the ear, marched him to the front door and stood there until he left. In fact, Carol was beginning to grow bored with having so many people around all the time—it was merely an extension of the Living Theatre scene, but without the opportunity to perform. She wanted herself and Bill to be alone, with time to grow closer together again and recapture moments when this had happened in the past.

By May things had become tense again. Bill was due to work in another film in Spain and Carol wanted to go with him, but he didn't want her to go. They all went to Rome together, Carol even thinking of going to Spain independently, then Bill flew to Spain alone and wrote in a diary:

Bad scene with Carol—can't figure it out any more—know I have to get away. It's the same scene in Praiano or in Rome when I want to be on my own—I have to actively avoid her and I'm aware of it and she's aware of it and it increases the tension. This morning she said I'd never see her again—she may well do it I know. I don't think I want that, but at this point I have to take the chance, I have to get away—have to make my own scene, have to think, have to find out who and what I am in relation to the world. I'm not Mr. Carol Lobravico any more. I'm completely hung-up, up-tight, strung out sexually and emotionally. To what extent after all the rationalising is done am I trying to punish her? The whole thing has been evolving in such a headlong rush with so much emotional impact right from the *Cristoforo Colombo* meeting and so much has happened that there was never calm and time and distance to adjust to it.

After Bill left for Spain Carol hitch-hiked back to Praiano in utter despair. Petra and the others staying in the house, all of whom had gone to Rome with Bill and Carol, drove down worried that Carol would kill herself. They found she had locked herself in the house. David Naylor—26-year-old Cockney, ex-croupier who was now making a living from leather bags and staying in a nearby house in Praiano rented by an English actress, Marilyn Woolhead—had to climb in to get to her. She was sobbing and hysterical in bed, at the point of suicide. David, who had been in love with Carol for a long time but from a distance, talked to her and calmed her down.

In June she wrote a short letter to Bill, without any of the tensions that had been there before.

Cherie.
Everything here is blossoming and beautiful. Richie Havens had two kittens. Yaguel is coming next week. We have six hampsters, two pigs and eleven rabbits. I miss you. I went diving for sea urchins with Katrine. It's the first time since years that I could get myself to go deep underwater with only a mask and no air. I love you.

When Yaguel came to the house they all had a seance and Yaguel told Carol that she had seen that Bill was in danger. Yaguel's premonition was later to haunt Carol when she was put into an insane asylum and separated from Bill. In fact, Yaguel told Bill later that she had seen everything that was going to happen in the next three months, but she didn't tell Carol because she was never certain that she was a hundred per cent right. Then suddenly Carol became very sick and the local doctor diagnosed it as hepatitis and prescribed injections twice a day. At the beginning of July Bill returned from Spain early, the film there having to be cut short for lack of money.

The next three weeks in Praiano were a strange time—people coming and going a lot. Carol sleeping with David, and Bill with different girls who came to the house. On the surface it seemed a satisfactory arrangement, since by then their relationship apparently depended very little on sex, more on an undercurrent of commitment and acceptance of one another. However, the balance between a more accepting, tolerant marriage and all the old tensions, frustrations and jealousy was still very precarious— Carol all the time needing reassurances and love from Bill. And the stronger her demands, the more Bill kept a distance between them, an area for his own freedom—all of which seemed to Carol like a slow death driving her in turn to more extreme and desperate measures. In a way Carol was using David to provoke Bill to respond to her, and when he didn't she became hysterical.

During this time after he returned from Spain, Bill was spending nights in a small house in the garden with Karin Christensen, a young Danish girl who looked very like Carol and who had come from Rome to Praiano for a few weeks. Carol became so jealous that she used to walk sleeplessly around the house all night, crying and talking of death. One night she became so upset that she crept into the little house where Karin and Bill were sleeping, poured gasoline all over the bed and on the walls and tried to set fire to the room; but Bill woke up, calmed her down and shortly afterwards Karin left the house.

But Carol wasn't only having problems with Bill. Ever since she returned from Rome after Bill flew to Spain, she had begun to fight with Petra who had been as close to her as anyone else apart from Bill—largely because Petra liked living in a chaotic communal atmosphere whereas Carol wanted to make a more creative, family kind of community at Praiano. In the three weeks after Bill returned from Spain, the feud between Carol and Petra grew stronger—which left Carol more and more isolated except for her relationship with David, to whom she began to cling with increasing passion and tenderness.

On good days in the house life could be beyond thought, beyond intention, just being. The rest was the normal labyrinth of ego needs, illusions—a labyrinth into which the pursuers were about to enter and from which no one, except perhaps Carol, would escape. What neither of them knew, though they had their suspicions, was that for the past eighteen months or more they had been closely watched by the Italian police, who suspected that Bill was the organiser of a drugs ring and who were merely waiting for the right moment to swoop down.

The night before the police arrived David and Carol came back to the house after spending the day on a yacht owned by a rich woman from Positano, swimming and taking opium. They found several people had taken L.S.D. and the whole house was raving. Carol and Petra had a battle over Norman Davis, a black American dancer who had just left after having a bad time on L.S.D. David, who had brought the L.S.D. from London, took the strongest trip of his life and crashed right out.

During this time Carol had hardly been sleeping at all, just a few hours every night. Since she had been going out with David every day, either to Positano or to the beach at Praiano, climbing the steps was arduous and David invariably had to carry her up. Also, apart from hepatitis, Carol had been kicked in the face by a mule on the steps and was wearing a black patch over one eye. Meanwhile during the last days Bill was working on the roof of the house, finishing the tepee he had been building there and hardly seeing Carol at all.

On 4 August Carol and David went down to a little cove away from the main beach of Praiano, took off their clothes and swam there most of the day, then came back at about 7 o'clock in the evening. Bill and Carol were going to go out fishing for *calamari* that night but Raffaela was sick and Carol wanted to stay and help her, so they didn't go out. Later Carol went upstairs and drew a picture of Petra. Then she came down, sat with Bill and Florence, a young French girl, in the fireside room and strummed her guitar.

There was a certain nervousness and tension in the house that night. But outside all was quiet.

3. *Messages from Limbo*

1. 1962–1964, NEW YORK

Bill to Carol   Miss Lobravico. Don't read this if you are about to ball anyone because it will make you love me so much, you'll really enjoy it. Read it after—it will make you sick.

My beautiful darling cunty sometimes perverse sad-eyed shy-smiled impish Carol. My God! I must still be rather stoned. I've been sitting on the crapper for twenty minutes and never realised the seat was up until I flushed and the bowl tide came roaring up my arse. I hope you feel all right. I'm a little worried you'll be depressed today. Are you? If you are or were, I will be sad tonight. Not because I will care how you felt this morning but because right at this moment I love you. so very much and want you to have everything. Of course I suppose that if you really want to be sad, you must have that too. I wish I could have taken that boy and made him make you beautifully. You were so marvellous—like a little girl who wants her teddy. Whether it seems that way to you in restrospect doesn't matter. You were radiant. Not saying of course that when I want to (try to) ball someone it is unpleasant, but you are basically so much more selective and discriminating (and not a pig like me) that it is a sin for it not to happen, unforgivable of God. I wonder what's making me write this letter? But I don't give a shit. I won't psychoanalyse myself out of a feeling of absolute bursting with the joy of loving Carol Lobravico. Whenever I tell you this you seem scared and sad which of course you must if you feel it, though I understand not why. It's just that you're always so goddamn intuitive I find myself wondering if I'm really happy or only think I am. But now writing in a hot sweaty tub I can indulge in my own feeling. I love you I love you I love you I love you. As concerns the fucking you missed last night due to the incompetence of our new social director, the management assures you that we have reminded ourselves of our

staunch motto: If you want it fucked up right do it yourself. Why
are people. . . . What I mean is—there is probably nothing in this
world that people are more fucked up about than sex. I love my
neuroses because they're fine. And yours because they're mine—
tits I mean not neuroses. . . . My god, not only am I unable to
finish that sentence I can't finish this goddamn letter.
P.S. I got a hard on writing it and jerked off but I still love you
just as much but I think I had better tear up this letter—you might
be sane when you read it. All of which foregoing is in explanation
of why this letter has been destroyed and does not exist except as
a figment of your lovely imagination. You're sick. . . .

Carol's Diary

26 DECEMBER 1963   I am nervous, almost hysterical. I have no
hope, no consolation, no desire to go on. I have no strength to do
the simplest thing. God help me. Help, help.

24 JANUARY 1964   The silence in this place is drowning out
every single bit of noise! Today we've had the worst scene we've
ever had. No violence but icy coldness, which is much worse. We
both manage to stay cool and polite. But that is what is so frightening. What's more frightening is that I'm not flipping and not even
particularly unhappy—just 'un po soffocata'. This makes me worry
and even doubt the existence of this extreme masochistic tendency
which I'm supposed to have. Norma just called. She makes me
laugh—especially when she laughs. My mind seems to be wandering around a lot. I feel like Fillip Wylie on L.S.D., or Max on
opium. But since these lovely 'aphrodisiacs' are not at my disposal–it
must be me. Nothing else to blame it on. Billie tells me today that
he goes to 'the coast' on Saturday—he asked me if I would 'like to
go'—I know that if he gets on that plane and I am not on it I shall
probably suicide after one hour. I think he was born to be a star,
even though he denies it. I want for him everything.

SUNDAY   I have nothing to do. Yesterday I insulted Tom. So
I supposed my ears were burning all night. Billie is ignoring me
all day and left to go running. I don't think he loves me so much
any more. I wish I were at work. I am still 'soffocata'. Fausta is
sitting next to my head staring at me again.

FRIDAY   I am giving Miss Bloom and Dajda back to Dorothy. She and Billie had a date the other night but she didn't show up so he made it with Ruth. We made love once this week and now I have the curse. Awful cramps. My breasts are throbbing, my leg is swollen—I wish I were dead. How long are people expected to support bodies which are always falling to pieces? And now Billie isn't speaking again. He just called—he sounds like he hates me. At least he doesn't apologise now—when will people understand that apologies have absolutely no meaning. When people say what they say, and especially when upset, it comes from the truth—and 'I'm sorry' is a crutch without which they couldn't say these things. I am convinced now that he feels I am using him—I suppose he is justified—the last one is still bleeding him. I thank god every day that I have never got pregnant or anything. That would be a mess. I have got to get some money. I wish I could leave but I don't have the courage. It would be like suicide. It would be hell—how could I live alone without Billie? I cannot conceive of it. I am so miserable—but so is he. When I told him I have no guts, he thought I meant because I have no money. That is a laugh! No one has ever given me anything. I had to sweat out a pair of stockings—everything—always so. I *wish* I could *understand* people! Maybe it excites him to think that way about me. It's like sleeping with a whore. I wish I could get some work. Please let me do those portraits. God! If only I had the strength to destroy this body that is becoming such a bore. If he left me I could. I just don't have the will power to leave. I will stay and watch this resentment grow. Christ, it's not my fault what happened. I can't make up for ten years. I am almost sure that now he could live with her to have his children and it would not be intolerable. Perhaps he is afraid that she won't do it. I am not a wife or a mother or a child. I guess I am just a whore.

SATURDAY   I've had enough of hate . . . she is becoming different. I have just taken sleeping drugs. . . .

TUESDAY 6 FEBRUARY   The worst nightmare of my life is over. I can only remember waking in a hospital with Billie. It was all unclear but I was in an ambulance that was taking me to Bellevue where I spent the most tortured nightmarish twelve hours of my life. Surely this must be hell. I cannot describe the horrors, the filth, the insanity. I have never been so full of despair, much more I am sure than when I took those pills. I thought everyone had abandoned and betrayed me, even Billie. This was really despair. But Billie finally came and fought for hours to take me out. He was frantic but so determined that I knew he would have taken me out by force if he had to. Then to another hospital, a proper plush nuthouse for lady-like loonies. By this time I didn't care any more. All I could think of was to try not to become hysterical and why they were doing this to me. All I could think of was Billie—I can't remember anything else. I don't want to remember any more than I do. Only from the moment when Billie finally came and said he would take me home, and I knew he still loves me. I can only remember that feeling of peace when we sat in that room alone and he held me in his arms for hours. I love him so. I cannot live without him or bear to be separated from him. I am afraid all the time. I know this is wrong. I want to hide and see no one but him, but he protects me and loves me and I feel safe only when he is here. What it is I am afraid of I don't know but it is there, I must admit it to myself now. But I can't find help in a place like Gracie Square. I am not insane and not violent. I do not have to be locked up like an animal in a cage. I am so happy to be home. When I saw the suffering in Billie's eyes that I had caused, it was like a terrible physical pain. I will never hurt him again. I would give my life for him.

6 APRIL   I placed an ad in the *New York Times* today—I hope to get rid of this fucking apt and never see it again. I saw a fantastic dress for Ivy but I am not going to give it to her. O what a fool—insane fool she is to have attacked me—all those hysterical accusations—I cannot tolerate this sickness. I remember the happiest time of my life once in Spain—completely alone for months, with no one to talk to except servants and myself. Everything must end. Where is it—this place? Love, hate—making love.

2. 1966, PARIS

Bill to Carol

> *Friend, Roman and cunty girl, lend me your ears.*
> *I come to bury Edward, not to praise him.*

The fucking that men do lives after them,
Their faults are oft interred with their cocks,
So let it be with Edward. The noble Linda
Said Edward was capricious—if this be so,
It were a grievous fault and grievously
Has Edward answered it. Here under leave
Of Willis and the rest come I to speak
In Edward's funeral. He was my friend
And just; but you have said he was delicious,
And sure you are an honorable chick.
He hath brought all his oboes home to Rome
Whose sounds the general eardrums filled.
Did this in Edward seem malicious?
Yet Linda says he's vicious, and sure Linda's
An honorable chick. But yesterday
The cock of Edward stood against you hard—
Now goes he there and none so hot to do
Him reverence. You all did love him once,
Not without cause. What cause withholds you now
To mourn for him? O judgement, you have fled
These brutish feasts and we've all lost our reason.
Bare with me, my hardon's in your cunt—there
Where was Edward's. I must pause until it come. . . .
You all did know this pussy. I remember
Well the first time that I tried it on—
'Twas an October's evening in your pad,
That day I called on you. See what a rent
Was made where Edward's envious cock did stab.
Mark how your dried up come did follow it,
As gushing down your leg to be resolved
If darling Edward knocked you up or no—
For Edward, as you know, is not an angel.
Judge, O ye Gods, if really you did love him.
O what a fuck was there my cunty men.
There you and I and all of us went down,
Whilst cruddy reason flourished over us.

3. 1968, ROME

Bill's Diary of a Crisis, February

THURSDAY   8 am call, drove to location, rain, drove back. Got the bomb film at Kodak—it's out of focus but filming projection works amazingly well. I go to see Patrizia. She says it's OK to shoot there tomorrow night. I keep trying to rent a camera with no luck. Phone Claudio. He sounds very down. Dominique has left. He says he'll come tomorrow to shoot the film. Went home to get some things. Carol makes me lunch. She's so beautiful. I want to explain, but how can I when I can't explain to myself? She wants to talk too, I sense it but neither of us can find the words. I feel extremely close and miles apart. I sense her slightest vibration but I can't touch her—'most intimate strangers'. Her love hangs heavy in the air, it caresses me, it is ecstatically painful like an extremely slow orgasm. I think she feels me the same way. I hope it reassures her somewhat, but of course it's no answer. It's all so stupid, so awkward . . .

I leave. Carol can't restrain herself. As I get in the taxi she is screaming something from the balcony and a shower of papers rains down on the startled taxi driver who is just closing the door. I tell him to drive off. Hotel de la Ville. Johanna and Mickey Knox, Fred Segal, Renzo at the bar. They go to dinner. I wait for Bergonzelli. He has me sign some papers and tells me his troubles. I can't quite get with them. I join the Knoxes and others at the Taverna Flavia. We go to the Bunk House. I have to split. Carol has been to the hotel and has left me a pair of sunglasses she bought for me with a note of 'You were right, I am unstable'— something like that. I call her. Her voice when she speaks caresses my ear. But we hardly speak . . . just long silences and nothing is said except 'No, it's not your fault, it's my problem. . . . No, it's mine, I don't know. . . .' After the Bunk House I had to see someone. I go by Donyala's pad. She's gone off to London and Georg is there with the Living Theatre crowd. They have just left Carol at Equippe 84 Club. Says she looks marvellous. I stay half an hour then split.

FRIDAY   All day at Manzano. I ride my horse, play poker but don't work. I seem to have two separate lives. While I'm on location I manage to shut out all personal problems. I don't even do it consciously—they simply don't exist. I buy 16 mm film for tonight's shooting. Call Patrizia . . . it's OK. I call Claudio . . . OK. I go to Patrizia's. Claudio has called—he's too upset about Dominique, he doesn't want to see anyone. *Niente da fare.* I decide to shoot it on 8 mm. Patrizia goes to dinner. I set to work. Fiddling around getting things set up but can't find the light plug. I stop and get hung up on proof sheets of Gerry Malanga's *Rome Diary.*

Patrizia has come back. It is 3 o'clock. She goes to bed. I would like to join her but I get the feeling she doesn't want to and I make no move. I sometimes feel I'm the only one left in this world who wants to ball. Everyone else seems to have their 'prior conditions'. Or maybe Carol is right—it is all part of the game and I don't know how to play it or refuse to, which is equally stupid.

On the Spanish steps bathed in artificial light there stands a poetic solitary figure. Actually there are two. Julian Beck and that sweet really cool boy from the Living Theatre whose name like almost all their names disappears into a sea of familiar individual but nameless or name-confused faces that make up the Living Theatre in my mind. The three of us stand on the steps hardly moving except for an occasional smoke, talking little, saying less and yet communicating something intangible that bounces back from the atmosphere that is Rome at 3 o'clock in the morning. I go on to the Cowboy for a hamburger . . . very depressing scene. I split and stop off at the Little Bar. There sits Dominique and we exchange a kind of nuclear reaction, emanating from our groins. We both want to make it. For a while it looks like we can recapture the beautiful spontaneity that was Almeria one night, but the problem of where to go at 4 o'clock in the morning brings the spontaneity to a halt and from there on in it is just a mental dry fuck. I walk her home to her pensione and say goodnight. Shades of Gerry Malanga!

SATURDAY   9 am call. All day at Manzano. One fight sequence and a lot of dull poker. In the end I play so badly I lose 70,000 lire in about ten minutes for no other reason than I want to create some action. My adrenalin isn't charged. I feel nothing. I really don't care. It seems idiotic to worry about losing a few lire in a

Carol to Bill, 1963

Carol before meeting
Bill

Bill and Carol, 1964

place where I shut out all the rest of my existence. I have a feeling that when I am at Manzano I am suspended in space, completely irrelevant of the life outside. It even extends to the fact that at Manzano money is meaningless since there is no need for it while there. I get back to the hotel at 11 pm tired but hopped up on nothing. Carol has called twice. I call her back but she's out. Birgitte says she'll be back soon. I go to the opening of the new club the Knoxes have invited me to.

SUNDAY   I have just gone through eight or ten different motions. Looked for cigarettes, then went down to the bar to get matches, returned, worked on figuring out how to open the wooden screen that covers the window-sill outside my room which they call a terrace, sat down again at my typewriter.

Have I left home or am I just kidding myself to play a game? Perhaps it would be better if I didn't try to analyse it and just let things happen. Cast adrift on the ocean and see where it leads me. I can't. There's a meter inside me that wants to look for answers even though the answers will do no good, in fact may do harm. If I see Carol and have it all figured out in my head and it all makes absolute sense, I will try to convince her of it, then she'll either say 'yes, that's true' (fat chance) and I'll get bugged wondering if she's only saying it to be nice or if she really believes it, or else she'll disagree and we'll have a fight about that.

Last night I was supposed to see Dominique. I'd been off and on hopped up all day. She said she'd gone to bed and was very tired. I was somewhat bugged but surprisingly little disappointed. I tried calling Carol but she wasn't there so I went to the opening of the new club Mickey and Johanna had invited me to and I planned to call her from there . . . after I'd scouted the action. The scene was total drag. Fred Segal described it as 'Nescafé Society in the lounge of a second class ocean liner'. I am becoming convinced that I am really making it—all kinds of people kept coming up to me and were nice to me though I was nothing but a dull bombed out shit. Bob Palmer asked if I'd get into a photograph with him. I see always more clearly why 'making it' turns so many people into rude evil bitches. Then I sat myself in a corner with three cunts coming on very strong with me—while I was trying to decide which one, like a kid with a nickel to spend in a candy store. I became very dragged with that scene and left them all sitting there with each other. I couldn't decide whether to leave and call Carol from outside or stay. . . .

Couldn't decide . . . till that little blonde—the one we met with Eddie Chapman who later did the discs at the Madison and who had been sort of avoiding me till she found out that I'd 'left Carol' —started coming on and that was the final straw that made me split. No taxis, no telephone.

I am now determined to call Carol, to see her, to seduce her like a first date. The idea was exciting. I went through the whole bit. I call . . . no answer. I go past the building looking for lights, and though the keys are in my pocket they cannot be used. I look for a cab and there aren't any. I take the car instead. Back at the hotel I call Carol and the line is busy. I tell the operator to keep trying. She does . . . it's always busy and I pass out.

I think I'm playing a game with myself and she is the ball or the trophy, depending on how you look at it. Having come to that conclusion it is stupid to say 'I'm sorry if I've hurt you', although I desperately want to say it . . . because it's all part of the game. Saying 'I'm sorry' is part of it too, and if one plays a game one must get caught up in it. It breaks my heart to see Carol with that sad, hurt, understanding and not-understanding-at-all look. Day before yesterday when I came to get my clothes and she made me lunch, I wanted so desperately to touch her and to hold her and to say it was all my fault and to beg her forgiveness and to ball her, and yet I couldn't do it . . . and I couldn't do or say anything else. That's why I left so abruptly.

Whether there is something within me that I must find out for myself—if I can and what it means to function on my own—or whether the whole thing is a masochistic sadistic game revolving about Carol. . . . I must do it. I must get it out of my system. I realise it's a most dangerous game, a kind of Russian roulette. I may lose her by the time I arrive at the point where I know that the answer is that I can't live without her. It's a cross between a compulsion and an intuition. No matter how dangerous it is to pursue, I feel it would be more destructive not to go with it.

Had lunch with Fred Segal. There is a marvellous kind of communication between us—perhaps we are so very different and still in some way alike. He's the first person that's turned me on in a long time. Marlon did it too but that was in an 'unsaid' way. He turned me on but we didn't communicate. I think I just presented him with a puzzle that he sensed but couldn't figure out. I think communication with Marlon is in terms of vibrations that he sends out and sucks in.

At six I start shooting. The work is very tedious and I go on kind of mechanically, really hating every minute of it. By 2 o'clock I wrap it up. I have finished one roll of 8 mm film. Carol's phone is still busy and when I get to the street I get a panicky feeling. I go over to the house and she is in bed. For an instant it seems time stopped five days ago, but then it is ever-present. It weighs us down. We finally manage to talk a little after some verbal sparring. I try to tell her about my feelings last night, about the game I wanted to act out, but she doesn't buy it. I want desperately to make it happen. I suddenly want her more than I have ever wanted her for as far back as I can clearly remember. She seems marvellously contained but sad and confused. I start making love to her . . . she wants to but holds back. Strange that she should suddenly be on the side of reason and sensibility, and I lost in wilful intuition. She says she is leaving for Sicily with the Living Theatre. It seems like escapism into a fire because she has no enthusiasm for it. I feel a little pang of jealousy, thinking of her in that ambience and a need to protect her . . . but I know I am in no position to give advice. What I don't know is why that should stop me from giving it. Am I getting wiser or more cautious? I go from home to the hotel.

4. 1968–1969, NEW YORK—ROME

*Carol to Bill**   And Carol takes you with her. You know that she's half crazy, but that's why you want to be there. And we'll go mad together. Or I go alone. Here in this house I became aware of millions of miles between what we have each come from. My insane violent father, my crazy mother who wears feathers and strange clothes. Their fucked-up lives, chaos all around. And this, your family. I don't want to involve them in this, but you know

---

* Carol's first letter was written from Bill's brother-in-law's house just before she went into hospital for her cancer operation.

best and I suppose you felt that it's the normal thing to do—and you're right. I'm going to see Rudi's doctor tomorrow. I hope I have the strength to get out of here before they start to dissect me, cutting me up, taking out all the pieces. You are watching another woman lie down and surrender to the surgeon's knife. I'm terrified. I want to walk and keep walking until I drop someplace and never have to rise up again. How do I get such a thing as cancer anyway? What is it that I'm paying for? I think that I just about can't go on. You're fed up too and you know it. Only you always live up to your responsibilities. You are too good just to leave me to my fate. But I'm over. This operation might stop it, stunt, cure, arrest it—whatever—but then again it may not. There's a 50-50 chance. Meanwhile all my precious tubes and womb and eggs and pods and things—gone, all gone—poof! Maybe I could grow a cock. I'm bisexual of course, but you aren't—so that might create a problem as to our relationship. I wish you were here. I'm so afraid and desperate. If only you could hold me in your arms and make me feel it's OK. But you are very far away. When I call you, you can only think of money. How can you expect me not to worry about the bread when you come on like that? I mean, who's going to pay for this scene? Santa Claus? God Bless him. And how am I going to get out of this miserable fucking country —on Santa Claus' sleigh I suppose. I think your relationship to money is even more weird than mine. Don't laugh, I'm serious. Which is sexier—a parasite or a vulture? And how do you feel about adopting somebody's baby? I prefer it to having my own actually.

Bill to Carol

CHRISTMAS EVE   I am very happy that you made it to Stamford over all the obstacles of distance and psychological. I was convinced all along that it would be the best possible solution—at least you will have the optimum good will without which the best technological capability remains a sterile thing of medical acrobatics—it is also the most difficult thing to be sure of. As for yourself, I have the feeling that you have taken a first step to get off the 'running away rollercoaster' you have been on for so long and are truly giving yourself to the flow rather than searching for foreign rivers with stronger currents. As for your coming to Rome for a rest when you are better, do come by all means if you truly want to. I think that all the problems that have made that decision so difficult have disappeared. I know now there is no 'going back' for either of us, and once that knowledge moved out of my brain into the rest of my body and organs, I could feel the great weight of accumulated hang-ups lifted from me. Hang-ups of wanting you to conform to my illusions of you which did not allow me to conceive of loving you in any other way, I am now able to love you in whichever way the future will evolve. I hope this will also let your problem disappear or at least resolve it. We are both free now to begin whatever is possible. If you decide you want to come here, it will be fine; if not, it will be equally fine—which is more than just 'cool'. Whatever happens, I still love you, but I am no longer possessively hung-up with desires that originate in my own fantasy and have nothing necessarily to do with yours. You can write or not write, come or not come as you wish—without guilt, without obligation, without need to run away. In that sense the whole awful mess may seem like a painful but necessary operation that will leave us both free to breathe, to live and to love. I shall be with you and holding your hand in my thoughts.

Carol to Bill   Well, I went under ether this morning for an examination—god knows what they did. Blood is pouring out in buckets. When I came to I was in another room in the old part of the hospital. This is the third time I've been moved. It's very depressing down here—no television, no radio, no music, no guitar.

I am in a much better state. It's Sunday morning. I just found out that I am on the floor with all the naughty people and negroes. That's all right, I feel more at home. Rudi still won't let me have my guitar. The nurse told me that they had three boys with guitars last week and they sat around at night and played and sang and everybody loved it. I'm not blaming Rudi. He just can't help being that way. Rosemary and Oma have been here twice. Opa wants to come and spend some time with me, but they won't let him. I love him very much and wish I could take him to live with us. They are still treating him like an invalid and are very impatient with him because his mind gets a little befuddled. Why can't people understand that it doesn't matter, that he should just get a lot of love and the only important thing is to make his life as sweet as possible. But he never gets angry or upset. He's like a wise old child. When I first got here I asked Rudi to give me some pain-killers—I have a lot of pain all the time now—he refused. Opa sneaked me two Codeine pills when they weren't looking. I wonder what makes people think of life as some kind of punishment instead of just grooving. I mean, all life is just a period between deaths. We are in the lowest state of reincarnation—I suppose that's why people who are able to make the death trip in a highly prepared condition are granted rebirth as something superior than what we are now. But most people remain trapped in the third state of death—on the Sidpa bardo where complete illumination takes place and then becomes faint and is replaced by visions of horror. They become trapped in a womb and are reborn into this same static humanity or whatever you want to call it. I think this has happened to me at least—probably my last birth. But this time is going to be different. With all my love.

P.S. You're not going to believe this, but when I woke up this morning I realised I was in the psychiatric ward. Also Rudi hasn't told anyone in this place that we are related. Do you think he is ashamed of me? Anyway, it's much more pleasant down here—especially because they scare so easily. When I spoke to you last night I really was still out of my head from the sodium pentathol. You keep forgetting everything and you're still not really back yet. It's like you're dreaming but you're asleep.

Bill to Carol

CHRISTMAS DAY   It came to me as I hung up the phone after I called you in Ithaca. I realised, and I was somehow aware while I was doing it but couldn't stop it, that I had reverted to all the old times. I had intended to let you know that I had resolved my problem with you, had accepted the necessity of living alone and leaving you free and had even begun to groove with it. Instead, as I thought of our conversation, I realised I had been whining, had tried to make you feel guilty and 'responsible' for my sad condition, tried to influence you to say you would come back by appealing to some stupid sense of 'duty', to love, past, etc.—all the things I knew perfectly well would influence you to do all the opposite, would frighten you into running away even further.

This puzzled me because this time it was no longer even an expression dictated by my actual state of mind. My actual state of mind when I called you was that I wanted to help you somehow at a difficult moment, to convince you not to run away from the doctors, the operation; and that whatever mind games we were playing with ourselves and with each other should not be carried over into the sphere of health and body, that the problems of the head and soul—while possibly more important, more intricate and more sensitive—did not demand the same urgency of time as the problems of illness in body at this time. I wanted to tell you that our personal problems and games no longer had any great urgency of time and required no immediate decisions.

After your awful visit to Paris that ended in such a sublime moment at Orly, only to be followed by your inexplicable silence for no apparent reason at all, I realised that we had become involved in a hopelessly stupid sado-masochistic game. I knew you were aware of my love and my need, that you were aware of the pain I experienced through your rejections, but that though you still loved me, you could not do otherwise. I knew that the worst thing we could do was to repeat that Paris experience and yet on the phone I had sounded as if I wanted you to pack your bags and come right back, which was really the furthest thing from my conscious mind.

Then it came to me—that the part of the game I was playing and why it was continuing was that I was continuously putting myself in a pleading position where I knew you would have to reject me, that I was just as responsible for it as you were. When I realised that, I suddenly felt free—free of rancour, free of a sense of betrayal, free of the hang-up that I had to 'get you back', had to hold you, possess you, consumate you.

I think we are both still in love with each other. The trouble between us has been due to the fact that we have been in love with illusions. It has been your illusion that you want to 'come back', because your wanting to come back represents your love for me. That is why you continually speak of doing it yet choose to go with anything that will keep you from doing it, because doing it would bring you face to face with the reality of me, would alter your illusion of me and that is what frightened you so much—why your visit to Paris as you saw it or your coming back as I saw it was such a total disaster—why you couldn't be with me, talk to me or make love to me. (Your cunt problems were only the rationalisation of that because one can make love without cunt in so many ways, even without sex, but you're incapable of any.) And why you had to run away again. There was no insurmountable urgency to get back to the Living Theatre or you would have gone to them directly—there was an urgency to get away from me, getting away from the intolerable necessity of having to run away from me while sleeping in the same bed which had sooner or later to destroy your illusion and make you face some reality you were unable to face.

All this explains why you sincerely felt your decision to return was true and yet let a slight nudge from Jimmy Tirof put you on the yellow bus, why you decided and changed your mind when Pierre Clementi dangled a possible movie in front of you, why you went to Pittsburgh after wiring me you were coming to Paris, why you severed all contact when you left me at Orly, etc. etc. It explains why you had such enormous difficulty in making the simple decision to stay or go. Part of your illusion of me is that we have something indestructible although nothing in this world is totally indestructible. As long as you hang onto that illusion you will continue to try to destroy it while asserting your belief in its beauty simply to protect that illusion from being shattered. I patiently tried to understand you and reassure you, but the more you had to try to destroy it (to test its indestructibility), the more the process tormented you.

My illusion of you has been that you would certainly respond to my needs if you knew how desperate they were. The truth is that you could not, precisely because you knew how desperate they were. My illusion has been that I could not face living without you and that logic, reason, patience and love would solve all. I was in love with my illusion of you and as long as that love was true, I could not love anyone else, could not allow myself to know the real you, could not possibly love the real you. My illusion of you was that you could not possibly live without me, that you needed me to save you, to protect you, to love you. I have now cut loose from all those illusions and I think it will allow me to get to know you, to give you the freedom you crave and to find what transmutation our love can take, in terms of the possibility, the reality and the needs that exist—and not as dictated by our illusions. I am certain now that I shall continue to love you and that I am freer to discover you than I was. This in itself has given me peace from the terror that our love was irrevocably heading towards a disaster so that it would have to transmute itself into a hate-apathy relationship. I am confident now that this will not happen. I always knew that neither of us wanted it to happen, but it was beginning to look as if it would happen in spite of us—perhaps in a more polite, more sensitive and intricate form, but happen nevertheless. It was the fear of that which supplied much of my desperation which in turn was setting me up for your eventual rejection—and so the fear itself was bringing on the thing it feared.

I think that if you can rid yourself of the illusion that you want to come back but cannot decide because of the perversity of your head, because of your need of identity with the Living Theatre, because of all the thousand things that you think have been fucking you up—then you will see that there is no longer any decision to make, to torment yourself with. You cannot come back. You can only go forward to wherever you want to go, that it is possible to go. If we can both realise that, we can be free to find love wherever it lies without hang-ups, without jealousy, without torment—and maybe it will be a love more beautiful than the one our illusions have been promising—if not we will at least be free to find it elsewhere.

I do love you, but I no longer need you in that desperate possessive sense that destroys what it seeks.

Carol to Bill

CHRISTMAS DAY   Well, somebody finally gave me a writing portfolio and a pink nylon nightgown. It was Rosemary I guess—she came with Oma. We chatted for five minutes, then they went home to baste the goose. It was very pleasant. Also got a box of marron glacés. I had mince pie with ice cream—two orders. My Christmas meal. Something I always wanted to do. I ordered a third but I didn't get it.

Later. I feel very rich—Kathy and Pierre just left. They drove all the way from Woodstock, and they threw them out after 45 minutes. They came with gifts—beautiful groovy cakes and goodies.

26 DECEMBER   Today started off with no breakfast. Two enemas, a barium enema which is torture—no food for lunch because the kitchen fucked up. I decided to accept and nap all day. Was awakened by Kathy, Pierre and Petra who drove up again today from New York. They are so groovy to come up every day like that. And they take my mind off things. They were going to split for Paris but are going to stay until I get out of the hospital. But that turned into a bad scene. All of a sudden the nurse came in and said they'd have to leave because only my mother or father could visit me. I flipped and said Kathy was my sister. The nurse evidently split and two minutes later two policemen walked into the room, laid hands on Pierre and said they had to get out immediately. Petra tried to reason with them, then they got nasty and said some far out things about how he heard that one of them was in bed with me. Before he let this out he said he'd heard something so disgusting he didn't want to repeat it. This was from the nurse of course. Some more nasty cracks and insinuations, including a few 'dirty beatniks', 'people like you' and 'this is a respectable hospital', etc. I was really embarrassed and mortified. They drove all the way up here from New York and are coming every day and what's worse, I can't get Rudi to do anything to help me. Doesn't he understand that I love these people and they love me, that they know what hell I'm in and are trying to make this trip less of a horror as hard as they can. Besides I was moved out of my room yesterday because the woman in that room complained about my 'smell'. Rudi went along with that one too, saying I must have been smoking something strange or some reason. I really don't think he even believes me—that all I did was walk into the room and lie down on the bed.

Anyway, now I'm in a room with another lady who's unconscious all the time—coma—it's pretty depressing but at least she doesn't complain. So I can't have visitors, can't make any phone calls unless I make them collect, can't do anything. I have never been so lonely in my life. I am virtually a prisoner because they won't let me leave. There are police guarding the exits. It also seems that I signed some paper when I came in, saying they could operate whenever they see fit. I thought I was signing myself into the hospital. I give up. People just don't care any more about anybody—there is no humanity any more, just a bunch of machines, rules and regulations. I surrender. I just hope they all get cancer. I miss you so much—I haven't let Rudi talk me into staying here.

Tomorrow they are going to examine me under ether and probably operate Saturday. There's nothing I can do about it. I wrote poems for you for hours last night. Now I know I am mad and unable to exist in this world with these people. They keep talking about prolonging my life. I want to laugh. I've failed at everything, most of all with you. I know I'll never love anyone else, not really. And I have enough love to make up for a lot of other people. But no one wants it—they're afraid. O Billy, what's left? I'm over. I want children and a beautiful life and I have nothing but this thing growing inside.

Well, try to forget.

It is very nice to hear your voice. The human mind is incapable of forgetting anything. What you mean is you'd like to shove me into that crazy niche where we put things that we are incapable of facing or accepting, dealing with, afraid of, etc.

I have so many dreams lately—whatever I want will come true. I know the value of positive energy. Some of us pushed this huge greyhound bus, equivalent of 2 blocks, after a Paradise show and it was like moving a chess piece. I can wait for you to get high but I am afraid way down deep that you will never get high enough; that you will never make the film; that you don't know how to get what you want, without using force, that you are in the void; that you are full of frustrations; that you are trying to punish me; that when I hurt or have pain you can't stand it. I know for certain that you are going to nag me about the fact that I haven't written to you for two weeks because that's what your mother does to you. I know that I am mad, and that you cannot understand me; that you will probably go insane trying to figure me out instead of enjoying me; that you think too little of me—partly because you think too little of yourself.

I'm going through a new phase—how to fight for myself, how to make judgements, how to appreciate myself. I've moved again to a higher Bardo plane (read *The Tibetan Book of the Dead*).

Please—before you do anything rash—don't burn my clothes

and paintings. I am going to need them when I get back. Kathy has informed me that she will be staying with you in Rome or something like that. I will write to Attilia and tell her what to do with my clothes.

I have really learned an awful lot in the past three months about you, about me, about the Living Theatre, about comfort and prosperity, about love, giving and taking, my own importance and unimportance. I am digging myself and really I like me much more than I ever thought I could, flabby stomach, sagging titties and all. I found out for the first time in my life that physical perfection is not important and also the kind of people I dig. More people are like me than I imagined. I do love you and I am very sad. Well, maybe you can figure Kathy out. I should think so.

Bill to Carol   Listen Baby. I don't know how much time I've got but I'm inside a trip inside your house inside your things. I don't care what old fuck-face says with his logic shit—I dig you, I mean I really dig you much more than him. I mean, he's all right when you need traveller's cheques cashed and so on because he passes for square. Trouble is he's been passing for a square so long, maybe he is. If he is—Oh God, I can't leave him but you should—though I'd miss you. You should see this back room—total shambles. Fabulous. The outside of the tent is up and there are endless numbers of fabrics and Donyala regalia hanging from the scaffold. I know you dig the idea that I'm off on a trip right in the middle of all this serious shit we're involved in—you of course in particular. Old fuck-face will try and tell you somebody slipped him something but you know better than that. I'm not much good at thinking and words and so I don't know if I'm saying it right (said the coy Indian maiden before being violated by 568 mad Hungarian Buggars) but if you were here I'd show you. I mean, shit baby, you groove me so much—I really don't know what I'll do if you decide to leave Billie—maybe I'll leave him too but I'd much rather not—we've been together so long.

Carol to Bill   I am getting out of here tomorrow—Tuesday—and I am so happy I could scream from the rooftops. I would have told you to come and get me but I didn't know that Kathy was gone. Anyway I feel fabulous and the doctor seems confident that I'll be all right. I should be in Rome next week. I am dying to get home, but I have some bad news—I can't fuck for three months. Also I have to be checked every two months for three years, every three months the fourth and every four months the fifth year. During this time I have to come back here every six months. I don't want to worry you. I just want to prepare your head and mine. Do you really want to live with this thing? I don't but I have to. The six months deal goes for the rest of my life. I love you. I can't wait to see you. Will wire where I am.

The doctor told me that the effects of the past year are bound to have fucked me up psychologically. He was going to write to you about this, but not till I told him to—I haven't yet.

I keep wishing you were here. I almost got on the plane for Rome last night but was so weak after eight hours out of the hospital that all I could do was take a sleeping pill and relax enough to float off into rest. I was also getting very up-tight. The first big move out of the womb. I can't wait to find out who I am. But it's a little frightening. I keep wishing you were here but not just for two days. I could say fuck the doctor and split, but my practical side says no, don't split without a stamp on my birth certificate. And I don't want anything to go wrong this time. I want to take very good care of my body and not feel any more pain. I want to come alive, feeling every second of it as a pleasurable one.

Well, I am bound to be twisted after all the sexual inactivity. But it's very far out.

Did you ever get my birthday card—this is the Aquarian age and things are all right for you this year. You certainly sound as though you've been going through some weird changes. I love you very much. . . .

5. 1969, MOROCCO—ROME

Carol to Bill   To Love Machine. The hermit is in the head. Why can't we be together? There must be a place. I am coming close to finding it. Living in a smaller universe that mirrors a larger one. Makes it all easier to see and for my simple mind to understand. I want our paths to stop crossing and come together. There really is nothing more than that, nothing so important or meaningful. Only what I am and what I am doing. Juna said you were coming here—I've been waiting. Now I hear you're in Venice. I thought all this time you were in New York. The Living Theatre is planning to stay here [Esauria in Morocco] another month I think. All around me I see that you are not here. What a drag. I do not want the rest of this life to be without you in it. Dig. How is that for admission or starters. Not bad. I do not want to become a Living Theatre zombie or a cripple, that's for sure. Your message is getting through to me out here. And I am very far out here and I hope you understand that. Falling through the stars. No word from you though. I need a letter from you soon.

I am coming as fast as I can but it's a long way—especially when I think about how you will probably throw me out, maybe either for shooting or freaking out or because I don't want you to make it with anyone else. O let's not talk about it. St. Ronnie Laing says that when people become cold and hungry and dirty they become frightened. Well, we are cold, hungry and dirty. We have trances and get weird and draw labyrinths. Anybody who doesn't want to make this trip can leave. Well, I'm here so I'm making it. Saint Bleklop says the way to understand how to understand how to communicate to people so that they can live together without hurting-destroying-breaking each other is to do all these things to each other. Only aching labyrinths. There are only thirty something of us so it shouldn't take long. Maybe someone will come after all on a big fiery steed and looking-glass pictures and nice big feet. Did you ever notice? It will be perfect for a while if you put a magic spell on me to change my life. It had better be a good one. It must be a better one because I must keep on learning. The wandering sickness that only can be cured if you are going to help me. I want some sanctuary. I would rather it be with you than without you. We are trying to leave Morocco but we have no money. Three days so far no money for food or drugs. We are trying to find a boat to get us out of here. It's very far to Italy. I hope the money comes soon but this state of emergency is making things get very far out. I wish I had wings—or you did. Soon, soon friends, soon. I love you. You're the mountain.

Bill to Carol   My dear Virgo. I don't understand our phone conversations, I don't know what motivates them and drives them to wherever they go. I do know that I feel a desperate need in you, especially in the last letter—the one with the nightmare map. I moved everything I could to get to you in Morocco. Unfortunately this time I found myself in a Diner's Club Cardless trap of no money. I concentrated all my powers and knew I would make it and I did, but I was too late—tragedy. The tragedy is that you call me like you call the doctor—only when you are at last resort desperate. It's like you used to call the doctor at three o'clock Sunday morning when you could no longer stand the pain for another second. But no one can help either me or you except ourselves—by using our own powers which are enormous when we have faith in them and are nothing when we have not.

I had an incredible experience of that when I was in New York. I had a terrible confrontation with my mother and I may have killed her. I don't say that lightly and it wasn't anything reasoned out—it just happened. When I saw Debbie I was determined to take her away with me. My mother took a ten-hour bus ride from Vermont and got Tom to invite her to stay with us (Tom went to Porto Rico). Debbie was sick in bed and we could not go out of the house. It wasn't terrible on the surface but underneath I felt a foreboding and then it happened. I sat across the table from my mother and it came to me in a flash. I looked her hard in the eye and said 'You came here to take Debbie away from me but I will not let you do it. I will do anything to stop you or anyone else.' I said it like that—quiet and cool—but the amount of psychic strength that I felt going out of me frightened me and my mother backed down. She denied that's why she came and early the next morning she left and that was it. But now in her letters, which are full of a deep shocking anguish that I sense but cannot alleviate, she admits it. She writes to me of wanting to die and for once I know she is not exaggerating. It is a terrible terrible thing, but I know I had no choice. But I also know that the powers I called up could not be denied, changed psychic hang-ups, emotional, evolutionary bonds, destiny. I only tell you this experience to let you know that I know what I'm saying. It is possible to change anything and obliterate all obstacles when the will and the need are concentrated enough, and the motive pure.

I still love and care desperately for you. If I no longer cared, it would be simple not to say all this, to let you go on and on and have a ball with you on 'vacations'. But as long as I do care I must write this and I cannot join you all on the *Cristoforo Colombo* and have a ball in the Mediterranean.

I will always love you and cherish you and be grateful to you for all you have given me, but I think now finally that it is too late.

4. The Sound of Someone Coming   5 August 1970

Before anyone knew what was happening police were everywhere —shadowy figures pouring into the candle-lit house. Over thirty police had surrounded it, then a group of them ran in through the open door, along the garden path, up some more steps to the front door of the house itself—also open. The police were out of breath and nervous. The leaders ran into the front room shouting 'No one move'.

Carol was strumming her guitar, singing quietly. It was a peaceful Southern Italian evening—stars, sea, drowsy talk or sleep—then at 2 a.m. there came the sound of people running like invaders or Saracen raiders. She continued to strum louder and louder.

Eleven people, including a child, were in the house at the time, some living there and some just there for the night. The first person to see the police that night was Robert Peitscher—a boyish 29-year-old American drop-out from a Madison Avenue advertising firm and an aspiring actor. He had only been in the house for two days, having just come from staying with the Italian millionaire Agnelli, and was sitting on the upstairs terrace overlooking the steps up to the house. Suddenly he saw a stream of people running up the steps, flashing torches. He ran inside to tell David Naylor.

David said 'Fuck, it's a bust.'

Robert looked startled. 'What's happening?' he kept muttering.

Before either of them had time to warn the others, the police were already in the house and they heard Carol's voice shouting from a downstairs window 'It's a bust'.

Bill, Carol and Florence had been sitting by the fireplace where there were several mattresses on the floor. They were the first people the police saw and tried to seize when they ran into the house. But Carol had broken free and ran to the kitchen window to warn the others.

Ted Edwards—a black American actor who had recently

finished working in Fellini's *Satyricon*—was on the roof with Petra Vogt. Ted was wearing a long magician's cloak with mirrors and myriads of colours in it, Petra a suggestively clinging white gown. They were dancing and laughing when the police ran up the wooden steps to the roof and seized them roughly, dragging them downstairs.

In another room—a long upstairs room overlooking the sea— the police woke up Nona Howard who was sleeping there with her young son. She pushed them away and refused to get up, arguing with them and trying to prevent them from disturbing her son who was still asleep. Michael Dunkley, a 19-year old English boy, was sleeping in a cave when he heard a barrage of shouting Italian voices. He tried to yank his trousers on when the police burst into the tiny cave with torches and excited shouts. They thought they had caught him trying to hide something. Florean Gehlhaar, was asleep in another room.

Later the police were to claim that they had found all the people in the house 'naked, lying on the floor of a circular room which obviously had been made as an opium den'. This 'circular room' was called 'the mediatation room' and had foam rubber cushions formed in a circle and Day-glo lighting with posters on the walls. Also, the success of their operation was described as depending on 'total surprise' and on the fact that 'everyone was so intoxicated with drugs and confused that they couldn't resist arrest'. In fact, it was the police who appeared more nervous and confused than the occupants. They brusquely seized everyone and herded them into the kitchen, then began searching frenziedly all over the house and grounds for a large cache of drugs they suspected were hidden somewhere. After a short time their torches ran out and they had to resort to candles. Meanwhile everyone sat calmly in the kitchen, discussing what they should do—the mood changing from anxiety to hilarity, from passivity to boredom.

The police raid on the Bergers' house was part of the largest drugs operation ever carried out in Italy. Over two hundred police were involved—*carabinieri* and police from the *squadra-mobile* from Salerno, agents from the *guardia di finanza* in Salerno in co-operation with members of the South Criminapol from Naples. They converged on the area of Positano–Praiano on the night of 4–5 August to take repressive action against foreigners who were suspected of using and trafficking in drugs. The operation had been planned for the end of July. An application for a search warrant had been made to the *procuratore della repubblica*, Dr. Antonio Marchesiello, on 25 July—and there were eight names on the search warrant, including William Berger and Ted Edwards. But the main thrust of the operation was directed against The House of the Angels or Villa Zingone where the Bergers lived. Other secret police reports exist, some of which were compiled a year before the raid, on William Berger who was being carefully watched because he was considered to be one of the chief drug traffickers among foreigners living in Italy. Also, a more recent report of the house stated that it was one of the main drug-trafficking centres of Southern Italy. All the time the Bergers had been living there, the police had been watching the house, planting spies and waiting for the right moment to strike.

The general political climate in Italy began to change dramatically in 1969. Three governments fell that year and there was the 'hot autumn' during which there were widespread strikes when workers, ignoring the lethargic inactivity and compromising attitude of the unions, took matters into their own hands. As a result, ironically enough, the unions gained a considerable increase in power and for the first time it seemed possible that the Left in Italy might organise themselves more effectively and perhaps swing the balance of power. The authorities anxious to direct attention from a potential crisis situation, reacted promptly to redress any swing to the Left that might be threatening. It was a situation analogous to Greece before the colonels' coup.

Late in December 1969 there were several bombings in Milan banks killing sixteen people. An anarchist New Left group were arrested and charged with the bombings, though later it was proved that the bombings had been made by a right-wing group with the aid of the Greek embassy in Rome—in order to discredit the New Left and make them into scapegoats, also to show the people that the government was strong and capable of dealing with the unions. Then in 1970 the right-wing backlash that was necessary to keep the government strong started to seize on the drugs issue. In the preceding years the government had moved spasmodically to check the Mafia drugs traffic from Turkey–Sicily–America but more as a publicity stunt than with any real attempt to stamp out the big dealers. Typical of the kind of measures taken was the famous trial of June 1968 against the Mafia for exporting drugs to America. The investigating judge in the case, Binieri, who was co-operating with the F.B.I., went to America to pursue his inquiries. On his return the trial was held and everyone who was involved was absolved. Binieri then left the magistrature, was appointed secretary-general of the Sicilian mines and is now one of the richest men in Sicily.

But in 1970 it wasn't the Mafia who were the targets of the anti-drug campaign. They were too powerful. It was the carriers and users on whom the police concentrated—people who would create adequate political publicity for the anti-drugs campaign and also foreigners living in Italy—hippies, anarchists. Obviously the drugs issue was of little importance compared to the political capital gained from showing up the pernicious and corruptive influence of the 'long hairs', as they are called in Italy, besides removing any foreigners who were in fact having a political influence on Italians. The first sign of the anti-drug campaign was the arrest in April 1970 of Lutazzi and then Walter Chiari, both cases causing a splash of publicity. The second sign was the raid on William Berger—*Sartana* in Italian Westerns—in August 1970.

The Bergers knew at least a year before the raid that the police were investigating them. Although at this time members of the Living Theatre had not been busted for drugs, all their contacts and activities were obviously closely watched because 'fringe' people were continually being picked off and arrested on drugs charges. But in May 1969 an acquaintance of the Bergers who operated as a drugs dealer was arrested in Italy on his way back from Pakistan and was questioned at great length about the Bergers and the people who came in and out of their Rome apartment. Then during the three months immediately prior to the raid, the Bergers were aware that the police were watching the house— snooping around the house in civvies, coming to check their *permesso di soggiorno* up three hundred steps, then on another occasion coming to investigate a rumour that Bill had murdered Carol and walled her up in one of the caves below the house, and also examining the garbage for signs of drugs.

Besides these warnings, there was a persistent rumour in Positano, of which the Bergers were aware, that a large anti-drugs operation was being mounted and was timed some time towards the end of July—a rumour that made everyone in Positano, where drugs were fairly widespread, take precautions so that on the night of 5 August when the police searched restaurants and the houses of foreigners no drugs were found anywhere in the town. Not only were these warnings evidence enough of a bust, but exactly five days before 5 August Gaetano (the garbage collector of Praiano and husband of Raffaela who worked in the house cooking and cleaning) came to Bill and told him that he had heard in the village that there was going to be a police raid in five days time—a prediction that proved to be accurate. When Gaetano told this to Carol and Bill, Carol had become very upset and distraught, but Bill had calmed her down and promised to take care of it.

But on the night of 5 August all the doors were wide open and several people in the house that night were on L.S.D. trips, though not the Bergers themselves; and from statements made by several people involved there were small quantities of drugs in the house that night, though Bill has consistently denied that he was aware of it. In fact, Bill had specifically asked everyone not to bring any drugs into the house during this time, but people had ignored his request—in spite of the fact that Carol was very sick and obviously could not cope with the rigours of imprisonment, especially in an Italian jail.

If the doors had been locked when the police arrived, it would have taken them a long time to break in. The house is surrounded by a high wall in which there are two doors—one at the back and the main door from the outer steps into the garden; then there are a short flight of steps from the garden leading up to a heavy double-door to the main part of the house. Supposing the police had got into the grounds of the house, it would have been impossible to enter the house itself—even if they had carried a battering ram up the three hundred steps, an unlikely prospect, the narrow porch gave no opportunity of wielding it. But none of the doors was locked and the police action was total surprise.

Carol said 'O God, what do they want? Have they got a warrant, Billie?'

Bill asked an officer if he had a paper giving the police right of entry. The officer produced a document signed by the *procuratore della repubblica*.

At one point Nona was brought in carrying Ben, her son, in her arms. He was just waking up and asked 'Who are all these men with guns?' Nona put him down on a counter next to the fridge and looked for something to give him to eat.

Ben said 'You see, I told you they were coming and now you're all on the train.'

While everyone was sitting in the kitchen discussing what should be done, the police had cleared the table of coffee cups and the débris of supper and kept bringing in whatever they considered to be likely evidence of drugs. Although they were supposedly a trained anti-drug squad, none of them seemed to have the least idea what a drug looked like. At one point when an officer was asking for everyone's passport and asking questions about another house owned by foreigners in Praiano, there was a great flurry of activity outside the door and a number of police ran in holding a lump of something wrapped in silver paper, shouting jubilantly 'hashish! hashish!'. The officer unwrapped it, smelt it, dabbed at it with his finger, then said flatly 'Chocolate', which caused an outburst of laughter from everyone in the kitchen. Also humped on to the kitchen table for examination were a chlorine testing kit for the swimming pool, twenty packets of incense sticks, and a quantity of flour wrapped in a plastic bag to keep the ants away.

Later the police found about forty plastic (use-them-once kind) hypodermic needles in a drawer, thinking that at last they had found definite proof of drugs. Carol immediately protested, saying that they were hers and had been prescribed by the local doctor. Although Bill repeatedly explained that Carol was sick and that the police could check on the prescription by asking the local doctor who lived only five minutes away, they persisted in regarding the syringes as definite proof of drug-taking in the house and never consulted the local doctor.

After their initial hostility and aggression the police had calmed down somewhat—largely because everyone in the house was calm and unexcited. At one point they asked Bill meekly if they could use the telephone—apparently to call Lt. Col. Capone who was in charge of the whole operation, to say that they had found some evidence of drugs. Then the police who were keeping guard in the kitchen kept asking Bill questions about his most well-known Westerns, treating him with a kind of reverential curiosity at the same time as trying to prove that he was a dangerous criminal.

The discussion that took place round the kitchen table as to what they could do in the situation revolved around whether or not they should stick together as a group. Carol wanted everyone to stay together, partly because she was frightened that Bill would take the blame and partly because she knew from the experience of the Living Theatre that they stood a better chance if they acted as a group. Bill argued against this, saying that it wasn't the same kind of situation the Living Theatre had been in and that people could be more useful out of prison than in. But no one knew what the police would find in the house or what would happen. There was a general feeling of optimism, in spite of everyone being exhausted, and they thought they would all be back in the house in the morning laughing about it.

What kind of experiences were had by those who had taken L.S.D. is hard to imagine. The only thing everyone could do in such a situation was to form a circle of energy within the group and cut out the outside reality, which is what they tried to do.

After the discussion Carol became very quiet and in the next few hours hardly spoke at all. Meanwhile the police had discovered a cupboard upstairs full of private films which Bill had made, also reels of a film he had made on the Living Theatre. Suspecting that they were pornographic films, the police demanded to see them. Bill set up the projector in the long room where Nona had been sleeping and most of the police abandoned their search when they heard there was going to be a film show of pornographic movies and crowded into the room. One of the officers pointed at random to a reel and asked Bill to show it. It turned out to be a reel of the Arab–Israeli Six Days War. The police soon became disinterested and wandered away to continue their search of the house. The two police who remained in the room pointed at another reel—of Bill's two daughters playing when they were very young. They lost interest and tried to get Bill to talk about working in films. Meanwhile the projector had started to go wrong and film was squirling out all over the floor, so the police helped Bill rewind it before giving up the idea of pornographic films.

That incident captures the whole absurdity of that night in precise detail—the police fantasy of the kind of life lived by a well-known movie actor with money and freedom enough to do everything they would have liked to do, in other words to make or watch pornographic films. In fact there were several films of Carol—one of her running naked by the sea—which the police mentality would probably have considered to be pornographic, but they never saw it. However, the police did seize a still photograph from the recent film Bill had made in Egypt—of him carrying his younger daughter Debbie who was naked—hoping to use it against him later.

While Bill was upstairs everyone in the kitchen had begun to chant OM, at first softly then louder and louder. The police rushed in, furious, but everyone went on chanting. Then at four in the morning David and Michael were led out of the house, taken down the steps and driven to Positano police station—a distance of about five miles. In the next two hours everyone was driven to Positano in groups of two, Carol being one of the last out of the house. The police had found an enormous wooden box into which they stuffed all the articles they had seized in the house as evidence.

As Carol walked out of the house and down the steps, it was light but the sun hadn't yet come from behind the mountains. In front of her she could see the long promontory of mountains that ended in Capri, the sea, and the rocks and the two islands of the sirens and beyond them the wide horizon. Then she looked back at the house—it was the last time she was to see it.

In fact nine people had been taken out of the house. The police had not arrested Nona Howard and her son—they didn't even take her name because, they said later, 'She was with her son who was sleeping'. Yet it was in the room where they had found her that they discovered the only evidence of drugs in the house that night—a half gram of stale marijuana in a small tobacco box.

When Raffaela, who lived just below the Bergers' house, came to the house at 7.30 that morning there were police everywhere keeping guard. She walked straight past them slamming the front door behind her.

A policeman came up to her and demanded angrily 'Who are you?'

Raffaela answered 'Who are you?'

The policeman shouted 'Who are you?'

She pushed past him and found the whole house in a shambles, drawers and cupboards turned out all over the floor. Nona and Ben were sleeping in the beds they had been in before the police invasion, but there were also five police in the room, some sleeping, some pacing around.

By the time everyone arrived at Positano police station it was seven in the morning and they were tired, subdued. But there for the first time they found out the vast scale of the operation, because a large number of the foreigners living or staying in Positano were there as well as some Italians. Most of the people there were known to the Berger group and some were close friends—in particular a group from the house below them in Praiano that the English girl Marilyn Woolhead had rented for the summer and in which some of the people arrested in the Bergers' house actually lived. Everyone stood or sat on the terrace of the police station, on the right of which a table had been placed for an impromptu tribunal of about twenty police and officials. Meanwhile two officially appointed doctors were examining the evidence which the police were bringing in.

It was the beginning of a hot summer's day and the sea was shimmering with the heat.

Carol said 'Did you see Fabrizio's face?'

Fabrizio Elefante, who lived in Positano, had been a frequent visitor to the house and had become friendly with the Bergers. In the police station he warily avoided them and seemed very agitated. Later Bill, who knew there had been a spy in the house, deduced from various incidents that Fabrizio Elefante was the only person who could have betrayed them.

By nine o'clock everyone else except the Berger group had been released.

In spite of the huge expense and organisation that had gone into mounting such a large operation, no drugs whatsoever had been found in Positano. The police had broken into the Positano Art Workshop which encourages foreigners to come to Positano and where an exhibition was being held. They even broke open the statues in an effort to find something, but without success. They swooped on the discothèque The Quicksilver, where a large number of foreigners and Italians congregate at night, and set up a table in the restaurant upstairs so that they could question everyone there. But as soon as they arrived they said 'Foreigners to the right, Italians to the left' and then told all the Italians to leave. The foreigners who remained were called upstairs one by one from the dancing floor where they waited to be questioned and searched— which included stripping all their clothes off. Drugs that were there that night were passed down the line and hidden in odd places to be retrieved later, so again the police found nothing. Individual houses were searched, including the house of an eighty-four-year-old American woman, Edna Lewis, who had lived in Positano for at least ten years.

Meanwhile in the police station the evidence found in the Bergers' house was being analysed. At the first interrogation that took place there Bill was shown a bottle of methedrine pills which he identified by saying they could be his, incense sticks which he identified as incense sticks and several other items such as ordinary cosmetics, spices. . . . They were then told that the reason why they were being held was because 'the evidence seized had to be sent away for analysis'. Bill was then shown a small silver box and asked if it contained marijuana. He opened the box. He said he thought it could be marijuana but repeated that he didn't know where the box came from. He was told that it didn't matter since it had been found in his house.

All the time they had been at Positano police station Carol had said nothing, just resting with her back against a wall. But when Bill was being questioned about the tobacco box she moved forward as though to admit that the box was hers. Bill and David restrained her from saying anything.

Then the man at the head of the table for the first time identified himself as a judge and asked Bill if he was prepared to submit to a judicial interrogation. Bill agreed. At that point he wasn't aware that the purpose of the interrogation was to gather more police evidence and that it would be used against him later, though a uniformed policeman sitting at the table reminded him forcibly each time he wanted a different answer that 'it was a very serious offence to lie to the judge'.

The judge asked him if he knew Saint? He said—yes, he had heard that he had been arrested in Rome. Another person named

Jim? Bill said he knew a Jim slightly but he wasn't sure which Jim the judge meant. The others were also interrogated but they refused to make a statement after they realised the implications of the questions.

The significance of the interrogation was that out of four members of the Living Theatre who were in Italy, four were now in custody; and the police were obviously trying to implicate the four in drug-trafficking activities.

At 9.30 Bill was driven back to the house so that a more extensive search could be made. This time some of the police refused to climb the three hundred steps and shoved off to a bar. The second search of the house lasted an hour and a half and produced nothing new.

The others were left at Positano police station sitting on the terrace in the sun. They were given nothing to eat and weren't allowed to sleep. By then Carol was completely exhausted and weak. She lay on the concrete floor, her head in David's lap. At one point he got up and asked if Carol could lie down, explaining that she was sick and needed rest—he had seen that there were six unoccupied beds at the police station, but the police said it was out of the question. Then they kept coming up to him, asking why Carol was sick and sneering that it was because of the 'drugs'.

David said 'She's got hepatitis.'

The police laughed and said 'Come on, tell us what's really the matter with her—she's a junkie, isn't she?'

Carol kept silent the whole time.

At one o'clock most of the group were driven from Positano to Amalfi, but before they left Positano police station they were all manacled together with long rusty medieval-type chains. As they came up the stairs out of the police station, they were met by crowds of onlookers as well as photographers. Then they were pushed into waiting cars which couldn't get through the crowd. Marilyn Woolhead, who had waited outside after being released, ran up and shouted to the cars as they moved off 'Don't worry, I'll get my lawyer from Rome. . . .' It was a poignant moment because two days later she was arrested and put in with the others. Then at four o'clock in the afternoon the last two from the Berger group were taken out of Positano police station, filmed by television cameras which had turned up and driven to Amalfi to join the others.

At Amalfi jail the atmosphere was completely different. The police who had been involved in the anti-drug operation had all disappeared, presumably to sleep, and the group was left in the hands of the local Amalfi police, the jailer and his family. As soon as they arrived, the jailer introduced his family to them, gave them food and wine and two large rooms where they could sleep. The informal atmosphere there contributed to a feeling of optimism among the group. No one thought anything very serious would happen—there had only been hints that everything had been pre-planned and their fate already decided, but no one was alert enough at the time to piece together the fragments.

At 6.30 p.m. a doctor and a judge arrived. The group were woken up and the doctor proceeded to carry out a medical examination of everyone there. The doctor, Dr. Luigi Testa, could speak no English and all the questions were asked though an interpreter—a waiter from a nearby restaurant. The examination consisted of a scanty routine check-up—peering into people's eyes, testing their reflexes, taking blood pressure. The doctor also looked for possible needle-scars. Bill hadn't had an injection for at least six months, but the doctor thought he detected 'possible needle scars' on a thirty-two-year-old vaccination scar.

The result of Dr. Testa's scanty examination was that he signed papers stating that everyone in the group was 'under the influence of drugs'—this was seventeen hours after the police raid, during which time everyone had eaten one light meal and drunk some wine but had not slept, except for an hour or so in Amalfi jail, for the last thirty hours.

Dr. Testa's report on Carol, similar to the others, read as follows: 'I examined Mrs. Carol Lobravico Berger, born in 1932, and found her in a bad general condition, not well adjusted in space and time. Pupils overreact to light. Reflexes of arms very quick, legs very slow. Disturbance of equilibrium. A state of confusion. Blood pressure 110/70. Pulse 95. Diagnosis: state of the brain confused from suspected use of opium alkaloids. We strongly advise that she be transferred to a psychiatric ward because she is dangerous to herself and to others.'

The examinations made by Dr. Testa and their consequences

were legally very dubious. Dr. Testa was not the officially appointed medical examiner—the two doctors Dr. Romano and Dr. Losalzo at Positano were the official doctors but they had not examined the Berger group. Dr. Testa was obviously brought in by the police to sign statements that confirmed police suspicions rather than the facts.

At this point Bill could have refused to undergo the examination without a lawyer being present, as he could have done with the interrogation at Positano. If a lawyer had been present at this moment, which turned out to be critical, the whole case would probably have been very different. As it was, no one at the time knew what was happening and Bill's main concern was to communicate the fact that Carol was very ill and needed special medical attention—the police had seized her medicines as 'evidence'—and he repeatedly explained the seriousness of the situation. At no point had anyone been told they were under arrest or why—they all thought it was a matter of clearing up a misunderstanding; nor was Bill ever told that his absence from the house would be of any duration so that he could take the precaution of closing it or instructing anyone in how to do so.

At 11 o'clock that night—still 5 August—after the group had been given another meal by the jailer's wife, numerous police appeared carrying the same type of antiquated manacles used in Positano. Everyone was chained together in pairs—the young policeman who fastened chains to the Bergers kept apologising for putting them on. Then they were all led out of the jail to the street where there was another crowd and flash bulbs sparking off. Four cars stood in line, ignitions on. Bill and Carol got into the same car, not knowing where they were going.

The newspaper stories describing the police raid which appeared that afternoon and the next day were written from police reports made on the afternoon of 5 August—no one arrested was allowed to talk to the press—and they were the first official statements made on the case. Besides cashing in on the publicity value of busting a famous actor, reference was made to 'the brilliant police operation on the Amalfi coast'; and 'the luxurious Berger Villa', as it was described, was made to sound like a disease in an otherwise innocently happy tourist area 'noted for its tranquility and serenity'. A number of controversial and, in the light of what subsequently happened, contradictory facts emerged—the police stated they had found 'a considerable quantity of narcotic substances in the house', that 'everyone was under the influence of drugs' (this was before any medical examination had been made), and everyone would shortly be 'imprisoned in Salerno jails'.

The caravan of cars set off, driving through the streets of Amalfi and heading for Salerno. Carol was sitting beside Bill in one of the cars. They both felt surprisingly calm.

Carol said 'It's crazy but I have the feeling I'm free and they are in prison.' She pointed to the people in the street with their frightened yet curious glances.

For a long time they were silent, both feeling an extraordinary sense of togetherness as though they had suddenly found what they had been looking for for so long, something which had started to come in Praiano and which they were to get closer to in the next months . . . an intertwining of their destinies, a sense that the long and difficult journey they had made together had a meaning beyond words or immediate events.

As they got nearer to Salerno Carol asked Bill about trances. Bill told her all he knew about it, to help her cope with the prison experience and to enable her to cut out of an oppressive sense of the immediate environment.

Just before they reached Salerno the cars turned towards the autostrada to Naples and stopped by the entrance to the autostrada. Bill was ordered to get out of the car. He kissed Carol and got into another car. The women were all put together, the men in two cars and Bill in another. Separated from all the others, Bill was driven into Naples. He thought he was being taken to an ordinary prison. He was hustled in through a small side door of a large building. The manacles were taken off.

'Does he need a strait jacket?' the guard on night duty asked the policemen who had brought Bill in.

One of the policemen crushed his cigarette out slowly and laughed. Only then did the impact of where he was suddenly strike Bill—a mental asylum.

He was led up some stairs and put in a small cell, bare except for a cot. The iron door clanged shut. He lay down on the cot, went into a trance then fell asleep. He woke up with a start, not knowing where he was. He had been woken by the rumbling of a coffee can trolley doing its morning rounds. Bill had a coffee and wished he had brought some cigarettes. Soon after people started milling around his cell, peering in through the grill and shouting 'Hey, you there, movie star . . .' Rumour that the new inmate was the movie actor they had seen on television the night before had got around fast and people were curious to see the 'bad man' of many Italian Westerns.

Later Bill was told by someone that the week before his arrival the Sunday film show in the asylum had been *Sartana*, one of his most famous Westerns. 'Nice publicity for my arrival,' he commented dryly in a letter to Carol.

Then he found out that he had to write a request to see the director of the asylum. When he saw the director later in the day he was told he wasn't allowed to make any phone calls. However the director was sympathetic and friendly. For the first time Bill was told that Dr. Testa had signed a paper stating that he and his guests were all under the influence of drugs and needed psychiatric treatment. The director then examined Bill and said that he could see that he was neither drugged nor dangerous.

The director said 'It's all crazy', waving his hands in the air to indicate non-involvement and helplessness.

He offered to pass on Bill's request that the United States consul in Naples visit him immediately.

Later that same day Bill was moved to another cell with more privacy. But outside in a long corirdor was a row of 'insane' patients strapped down to their beds, pounding and screaming.

After the convoy of cars had stopped at the autostrada into Naples and everyone divided up, the rest of the men were driven to the outskirts of Naples where they stopped outside a grey rectangular building in rural surroundings. A policeman got out of the car, rang the front door bell. After everyone was let inside it seemed as though they had come to an enormous hotel—they were in a spacious lobby with potted plants and a twisting marble staircase—then the guards removed the handcuffs and they were all taken to a room to be weighed and signed in. A door was opened to reveal a long dismal corridor with cells on either side. As they walked down the corridor they passed an open door.

Inside a room were beds to which people were tied, groaning and struggling.

Meanwhile the girls were taken to a suburb of Naples—Pozzuoli. The car pulled up outside an old renaissance building—above which was a large green sign: Women's Mental Asylum for the Criminally Insane. The doors opened and they were pushed inside. The girls, walking three abreast down a marble-floored corridor dressed in semi-transparent brightly coloured gowns, were met by three black-robed nuns. The girls' faces registered disbelief, horror, then they broke down into fits of laughter. The nuns, exuding pious disapproval, immediately led the three girls—who must have appeared like satanic creatures read about in refectory and sent to tempt saints—to the bathhouse and ordered them to undress and wash, all of which was mimed since the girls pretended not to be able to speak Italian. A crazy old woman came in and picked up their pile of clothes, smelling and caressing the materials. Then she started rubbing the girls' backs with a large sponge, crooning and talking to herself. Later they found out that she was the notorious woman who during the war had boiled children alive and made them into soap. Cleansed, the girls were given white night-shirts with brown stripes that hid their femininity, then locked in a cell together—narrow iron cots, tiny barred window, a crucifix and a picture of a burning sacred heart. They sat on their beds, looked at each other for a long time, then laughed themselves to sleep.

Exactly twenty-four hours after the police had burst into the House of the Angels—where the doors were never locked—gates had opened and closed, doors had been locked, there were bars on the window and everyone had been separated. Between the two places where Bill and Carol had been imprisoned were at least six locked doors, judges, the police, doctors, the *procuratore della repubblica*, lawyers, consuls—the whole system of organised society—that had suddenly come between them in those twenty-four hours. Neither of them knew what was going to happen. It was *ferragosto*, when everything closes down in Italy. There was the problem of communicating with each other—letters that had to be censored and which were delayed at crucial moments. No one co-operated, treating them as criminals or drug addicts—even the United States consulate. But through all the difficulties

A page from Carol's diary

A birthday card for Bill

Carol, 1969–1970

and impossibility of direct communication there was an extraordinary feeling of togetherness between Bill and Carol that is partly expressed in their letters, partly in the last moments they were to spend together.

5. Notes from an Insane Asylum

Carol to Bill. 6 August   My darling Bill. I'm fine, how are you?
I love you very much. I hope to see you again very soon. Don't
worry about us, we're all fine. I love you, I love you. I love you
very much. Many many kisses. Much much love. Many greetings.
Many kisslets. Much love. Carol. Please write me darling.
P.S. Is it possible to send me some money?

Bill to Carol. 6 August   Dear Carolissima. . . . There's a cat
here who keeps screaming over and over: 'This is a madhouse,
one must have patience. . . .' I'm studying to be a nigger. This
world is a little speck in the solar system. They now think that there
are something like three hundred new solar systems formed in the
universe every hour. It is therefore most unlikely that this world
of ours is not *not* duplicated somewhere in the universe of which
by definition however there can only be one. After all if you take an
infinite number of suns and an infinite number of typewriters, one
of them is bound to look like a monkey. That's a serious depressing thought for you in case all the humour and joy is getting you
down once in a while. Going down is a groove when you're in
love. I think it's a worthwhile experience as long as you don't get
hooked on it. If everyone spent a little time in prison and nobody
spent a lot, they would soon disappear. It sure helps to cut away a
lot of pretension and bullshit. I miss you—and Petra and the
beautiful people. I was wrong, I do love you.
P.S. Just got your letter. Am sending ten thousand. Love B.

Carol's Diary
6 AUGUST   First day in prison. In the prison madhouse,
Pozzuoli. Heavy scene. Of course no one tells us that we are to
be locked up. Or for how long, or why. A madhouse full of
women all raving, screaming—no way of telling if they came here
this way or are this way from being here. Where is Billie? Nothing

to do. No possibility to contact anyone outside. I know this country. I know they can just let us sit here and rot. No one has any rights. Transfer me from the raving ward to the sterile hospital ward for physically ill. A health cure gratis from the state. Go to bed at six o'clock. Put myself into three or four trances to get through the night. Rosalia—what incredible pain in that face: 'My child where is she? They keep telling me that she's dead, but I know it's not true. They say she died from gas and that it was me, but it's not true. Five years tied to this bed for something I didn't do.'

7 AUGUST   Last night was a horror. I couldn't sleep—endlessly waking up and tossing and nightmares. I know if I stay here I am going to flip. It's not possible to keep cool here. This clean sterile hospital room, locked in all day. At least in Section I one can laugh. I would much rather be back there with those madwomen than here with all the sterile cleanliness and sane straight *bonnes femmes* and nuns preaching to me morning to night. My God, what a horror and sticking needles in me all day. This morning I had a visitor. To tell the feeling, it was ecstasy until I saw two men in grey suits, white shirts and ties with American embassy written all over them. So embarrassing because they can't do a fucking thing for me except make a phone call and who do you call when you have to scream for help. Maybe they have a direct line to God, I said. They kept their eyes averted throughout. Oh god, *quelle angoisse!* Better some friend with a bonbon and a smile. But at least they brought me news of Billie. He's in prison in Naples. Oh god, I hope he's doing better than I. I'm sure he is.

Antonella—the ray of sunshine of Section 4, running up and down the halls sneaking in and out of the rooms with thermoses of coffee and cigarettes. I have to get some money, we can have anything we want. The ten thousand will be gone very fast. If they separate us it will really be rough but I can't keep it together much longer. And I can't take much of these shots, they are killing me. Today they also took our blood to be analysed. What a surprise when they don't find any drugs. The American says we got an awful lot of publicity in the papers and television. Hah! Too bad we're not allowed to have any newspapers. I know what they mean—a few days in jail really straightens out your head. My god, that air, that palace we live in, the sea, that peace. . . . I can't even breathe here. It must be 100 degrees in this room. O Lord, I am going to be punished, and Florence also, punished because we can't sleep. I'm terrified, terrified.

8 AUGUST   Fourth day. For the first time I fell into a peaceful sleep for about an hour and forgot completely where I was. Woke up feeling the slow and agonising recognition. Morning lecture from the good sister on decency and original sin because we take off our clothes in front of her. No one slept all night of course. Today we shall have to stay in the room. The director is not here yet and may not come as he did not come yesterday. Today is Saturday, he's probably at the beach. I really goofed with the consul—he was in such a hurry and I know they won't let me call him again, even though he says they will. I must find some way to keep my mind free from all the vibrations around me, to have no walls in my mind . . . to stop thinking of 'outside' because it doesn't exist. This is a play and I will play it until the end and will take my bows and move on to the next change. Flowers in the room, a statue of the Blessed Virgin, flowers in a terracotta vase . . . not plastic, real flowers in water, not plastic flowers. Johnny Cash singing on the radio . . . *If I Was a Carpenter*. The time has come to sing a travelling song. I really don't see how they can keep Billie in jail. The newspapers say evidence of drugs, which means my medicines which they have analysed by now and have found to be only that. Walter Chiari was caught using narcotics which makes his case a little more reasonable, not really, but anyway legal. But we haven't been charged with anything yet. We're waiting to be all interrogated by a judge I think.

9 AUGUST   Eeek.

10 AUGUST   Help! What am I doing here?

Bill's Notes. 10–11 August   At the beginning I was outraged by my innocence, outraged by the 'injustice' that *I* should be subjected to the indignity, the cruelty that is this place. I was obsessed by the fact that I was 'not guilty'—not guilty because I cannot conceive of smoking hashish as a crime, not guilty because at the moment I was arrested I did not have any hashish, because

months before I had flushed what was in the house down the
toilet drain like a 'good boy', because I was not stoned, etc.
Now I have felt the small kindness of being given generously
cigarettes, pieces of fruit and above all understanding and human
comfort—by some genuinely kind people here, people who have
been here for twelve, fifteen, twenty-five years and yet who are
still able to respond to my stupidities as if they had meaning, had
importance. Here inside there is compassion, there is no judgment. I truly sense that I can learn here and if fate really has prison
in store for me it can be a positive experience—the ultimate sense
of letting go of pride, of anxiety, of responsibility; the ultimate
sense of 'going with the flow'. So far this is only a thought in my
head, it is not organic. My soul, my entire being strives to be rid of
this horrible nightmare. But what is . . . it? It is a small death
experience that may help prepare for and embrace the big one.
It's all part of life, part of being free. You can't be free and at the
same time rigidly stiffen against the flow of things.

The sweetest cat here, the one who takes care of the poor
buggers they have tied to their beds in the ward outside my cell,
the one who brings me coffee and kindness and gentleness—he
has been here for twenty-five years and he can cheerfully explain
that he only has seven more to go. When I asked him why he was
here, he sheepishly pantomimed a pistol and bang bang! What
bearing does the guilt or innocence of a young man of twenty-five
years ago have on this kind, gentle man?

If I have found one truth here, it is that I cannot look into the
eyes of a man who is enduring his sacrificial burial to the totem
god of justice and then be upset for long at the 'injustice' of being
here for one day, for one week, for three years. When one chooses
to live amongst the savages, one takes chances of being eaten by
the cannibals. All this does not mean there is not a tremendous
surge of outrage swelling my soul, because I too am a savage and
I have tasted of the cannibal's meals. If I can aspire to something
higher, I will be able to convert that negative energy into something more cosmic, into love instead of the excrement of hate.
That is the supreme test.

They've swept back into Praiano and blocked it off for another
nine hours. Probably the same 'army' with their squad cars, their
guns and their flashing lights. Result: they busted Marilyn,

Widget, Desna, Steve and Allain. Three little girls sitting quietly in their home and who knows, maybe smoking a joint! And the black avengers start their way home again to Salerno—one hour's drive down the Amalfi coast. Can you imagine the cost in bureaucratic effort it must take to organise such an invasion! What does it do to the local tourist business? No matter, if the end is worthwhile, *sans doute*! What is the purpose of the end? Is it to teach Billie Berger a lesson? Is it to make Widget Murphy be a 'good girl'? Why don't the taxpayers protest? Because there must be some higher purpose behind it all . . . and obviously there is.

'*La droga e un grande pericolo!*' How do you know? I read it in the papers. What is '*la droga*'? It's an '*assurdo paradiso artificiale*'. Yeah man, sure, but like what is it? Are there different kinds? Why out of all the three hundred cops with their flashing lights is there not one who knows what it looks like? Or do they? Then why do they seize the incense sticks, the flour, the medicines, the chocolate, the spices and the chlorine test kit for the swimming pool, etc.? Step right up folks, see the magnificent Marvello. . . . Nothing up his sleeve, nothing in his hat. . . . poof!

Carol to Bill

16 AUGUST   Dearest William, of course you love me. Don't you know by now that I always have the best of everything. Marilyn, Widget and Desna are here. Quite a jolly group. It was getting a little heavy in the beginning, but now it's much better. They are treating us like the queens we are and my only worry is you. If I know you are free, I could be free of most of my anxiety and be more capable of dealing with the vibes. Do you have books and things to read? How are they treating you? I am trying hard to keep my cool. I realise now that my basic training in the school helps and taught me a lot of games. I miss you very much. I hope they send you this letter—if not, I'm writing another in Italian just in case. But please don't worry about me. I'm not afraid of anything. I'm taking vitamin shots for my liver and they give us special food, even some vegetables and fruit. I can tell you I know we're getting special treatment. I think of you all the time.

20 AUGUST   Dearest Billie. I received your letter. It really made me feel much better. I must confess, I don't have your strength

and your extraordinary ability to accept things in a way that's really fabulous. But you are fabulous darling, a very special man. Now I too feel able to accept everything. Before I was thinking too much about everything I've 'lost' because we were truly in paradise. Those last three months were probably the most beautiful of my life. The only thing I miss now is my guitar. But that too will pass. I also had a letter from Raffaela. I wrote Raffaela and Gaetano because Marilyn told me Raffaela was very afraid, especially for you of course, and was crying all day. I told her everything would be over soon and all right and not to be afraid. I also have a great need to be near you, to touch you, but I feel your presence here with me *very* strongly every minute night and day. I too will try not to think. Here there are some very nice people. But they're always saying the same thing, like your friend —'*pazienza*'. We're trying to put on lots of shows here in the clinic. Yesterday we presented *Tableaux Vivantes*. Marilyn, Florence and Petra. It was a lot of fun. There's an organ here. I'm going to ask for permission to play it. I hope so. They haven't refused anything yet. I love, I kiss you, I think of you always. Caroline.

30 AUGUST* My darling. Please don't lose hope. I know you're very much alone. At least we're all together, but we all have the same problem—lawyers that disappear after one visit, letters that don't arrive. Your letter made me a little depressed. Maybe you like to stay in prison. *I don't*. I can't stay like an idiot waiting for a miracle. I want so much to talk to you. I'm beginning to be afraid that you're in danger. I asked the director if he could ask for permission that I could visit you. Otherwise how is it possible so many months without seeing each other. We're in the hands of the law. *Pazienza* I have little.

I love you with all my being. If I cry I cry for you. I can support anything if only I could be sure you are free in the world. I also don't understand why I find myself in the madhouse, I really don't. It's very difficult, but more difficult for you I think. I've

* During this time Bill wrote four letters to Carol in which she was meant to read only the first letter of every line to get the message. One letter in which Bill said everything a 'good' prisoner was supposed to say, decoded said 'Dearest cunt I love you'. Carol didn't understand the code and became worried that Bill was unable to cope.

lost all my sense of humour without you. I need to be near you. I can't understand why you don't get my letters. I write every Sunday. I wrote last Sunday, the 23rd. Maybe some letters they didn't let pass. I'm sorry. I beg you to think carefully about the lawyer problem. Oh God, how I miss you. It's not possible, all of this. It's terrible to think you're all alone. But maybe you're all right. Chicks are not my scene, you know . . . eeek. They weighed me. I weigh 44 kilos (98 lbs!). I've lost four kilos. I'm always getting vitamin shots. *Che tristezza*. I want to fly, I want to dance, I want to sing, I want to laugh with you, I want to feel the joy of living again. *Quelle tristesse!* Locked up with two hundred mad-women. I love you, I love you, I love you. Your Carol.

Carol's Diary. 2 September One month in the *manicomio giudiziario* [prison lunatic asylum] and I am not gone all the way up the walls yet. Called the director's office. Seems I've been accused of trying to strangle a *guardiano*. Not bloody likely I told him. Marilyn was called down too, attacking a nun or something. Only trying to get her cigarettes. My lawyer came today again. He's growing a beard. He still looks like an Italian spiv. Told me we're being held illegally. I'm here baby. Billie sent his book on self-hypnosis. I guess after my last letter he must think I really need it. I keep having this vision of all the inmates over there trancing out in the 'playground', Billie going 1000-1, 1000-2, 1000-3. And they probably think he's really nuts. I mean they think everybody's nuts in these places. HO HUM. We had salad for dinner, no vinegar again. Lawyer says he'll get me out of here and jail quickly. I hope! Or maybe even a private clinic. I keep losing weight. Gets everybody up-tight. I want to see Billie, I miss him. Raved all night, no sleep again. Still saving my vitamins.

Bill to Carol. 3 September Carissima. They've sent me to the *infermeria* where I'm not alone any more and I've met a nice cat who is an engineer, teacher and a socialist and with whom one can talk quite well. But there is no one here who plays chess. I have to play with myself and always lose. The engineer's name is Blasi and when I didn't have a lira for two weeks he bought me cigarettes and everything. I've found some really nice people here. Still it's difficult to find things to laugh at, which is so very important.

Here no one speaks my language and laughing by oneself is first of all very egocentric and second highly dangerous in these places! I have such need to laugh at the things only we can understand—it's such an essential form of human communication. I too have great need to see you but I don't think they'll let us. Rest assured that I am free in the world, at least half of me—my world is inside me and inside you.

La lutte continue. We have to do our thing and play our part. I don't think it is all quite so absurd, quite so useless as it seems now. At least we've passed the first month and even if it should not be the last it is one less. If I were shooting a film I would be away longer; when you were with the Living Theatre we were separated much longer; and when we were separated by our own madness we were separated much longer and in a way much more terrible than now. In a way I feel much closer to you and also much freer than in that period.

If you really believe that I might like it in prison you've really flipped your lid. It also means you've truly lost your sense of humour and must recover it at all costs and adapt it to the situation which is so very absurd that it's impossible you can't find food for laughter if you search. One way you'll succeed without a doubt is to buy a kilo of bananas. Eat as many as you like, then place the peels about the floor and take turns slipping on your arses while saying '*Etre libre, c'est etre libre de planer*'. Then—ask Petra to recite German poetry. The sound of German to all those fortunate enough not to understand it produces laughter the world over, even amongst the Japanese who have great difficulty laughing because as we all know they are constantly smiling. I've been told, for example, that during the war they had continuous transmissions of the latest speeches of Adolf Hitler for all the *Kamikaze* pilots on their missions. Then—Richard Nixon. Then there are so many words that are sure fire laughs: kangaroo, impotence, mass media, hippy etc.

I have to stop now because even though it's good to laugh you must not overdo a good thing otherwise you won't eat—and you've got to eat. It's absurd for you to lose 4 kilos, you were too skinny already. You must think of your public image and the '*la moda*' and all the *paparazzi* and the mad crowd that will greet you when you're out of prison! Please thank Florence for her dear letter and tell her not to be too diplomatic with her thoughts or she'll ruin my dreams. Love, kisses, courage, love Billie.

Carol's Diary. 3 September   Today was really exciting. Got some money. Director told me he can send me to Billie's prison to get my head examined and maybe get to see him. I'm so excited, I can't believe it. Tonight Florence and I had a complete orgy of laughing imagining him hypnotising everyone in the prison. It's the first time I've really laughed in a month. O god, I hope it happens. But I think I will. Marilyn, Desna, Widget, Petra and Florence went over to the looney bin to have a bath. I still can't make it over there. Gives me the horrors, all those people tied up and the last time I stepped in shit. Supposed to be lucky. I have to say that Widget is the coolest person I have ever met in my life. She has never once got mad at anybody. I mean, we could still be in Praiano. I wish I could be like that but it sure helps being around her. She never brings anybody down. Maybe I'll get out for my birthday. I wrote a really weird, sarcastic letter to the American consulate today. But it was brilliantly disguised in flowery compliments. My passport expired yesterday! O dear, dear, talk about troubles. Potatoes again. I made stewed fruit. Everybody was still fasting. I ate the whole plateful. I really feel sick.

Bill's Notes. 5 September   Dream. Just got out. We are in an apartment. Friends drop by. I've never seen them before. I think they're friends of Carol's. She thinks they're people I know. It's cool—they're groovy people. I start getting nervous because of all the noise and ask them to keep the noise down. They all understand, but the noise keeps getting more and more. I keep turning off the music. They are very understanding though they look at me as if I'm nuts. Everytime I turn the music off in one room, there is another tape recorder going in another room. People want to dance and I stop them from dancing, from singing, from laughing, from talking! By now almost all of them are stoned out of their brains. I finally flip out and tell them they have to leave.

Everyone is so nice and understanding and everything calms down. Now they all have babies with them, all kinds of gear to pack and they have come here to live. They wake up their kids and tell them they have to leave. The kids ask 'Why? We just got here. It's the middle of the night.' The mothers all say 'It's all right, it's cool, the man just doesn't dig music—he's got a right, it's his scene.' Some people are very stoned. Somebody says 'How can you kick people out into the street in this condition? The cops will pick them up in two minutes.' But they all leave. I go to sleep.

There is music in the next room. I go there and find there are more people. I say 'OK, but keep the noise down, please. I just got out of jail . . . the police.' I'm very paranoid. They all say 'Oh sure sure man'—and the whole thing starts all over again.

One of the chicks is very sexy. I touch her and she's very hot. She says 'Oh sure, I fuck everybody.' We go into a room and she takes off her clothes. She's still very exciting but has become grotesque—one huge tit and the other very tiny, fat legs. I can't stand fat legs with bulging skin—but I'm still very excited, excited and at the same time disgusted. She's very sweet, but before we do anything someone calls her and she has to go outside. She doesn't return. I'm just as glad. Then later when I'm telling people to leave, I find her in a bed. After a while I realise there's someone else in the bed, way over on the other side. It's obvious they're not making love—in fact, she still has all her clothes on. I can't ask her to leave. She realises that I was disgusted by her appearance and she just cooled it so as not to embarrass me. There was no other place for her to sleep so she just flopped in that bed, keeping way over to the edge so as not to disturb the other person who is sleeping.

If I ask her to leave now, she'll think I'm kicking her out because I didn't get to fuck her or because I'm jealous—as though I only let people stay until or if I get something out of them. The others now tell her I'm making everybody get out. She just looks at me and says 'OK, I understand'. But it's still cool with her.

Carol to Bill. 6 September   My dearest dearest beautifulest adorable love. Your letter made us all laugh. It arrived during dinner. And then, did you feel something last night? You were here (the table flew around).* Also Yaguel. More successful than

* Carol was refering to a seance they held in their cell. See pp. 126–127.

I've ever seen. We've had a complete change of humour since yesterday (Yaguel says all is well—it was incredibly powerful—I will tell you about it when I see you). I feel so happy. What joy.

Marilyn, Widget and Desna's judge came Friday. Then there was also the doctor who looked at all the arms in Positano for 'needle holes', you remember? His name is Testa. He said we were all normal. I don't think they'll make any more blood tests because they've already seen here that we're all normal, no trace of 'those things'. Evidence no? Maybe they'll begin to understand their absurdity. It hurts me to think that you wrote your mother. I hope it won't do her too much harm. You are god for her and prison is something that not even as a word enters her world. I know that the love she has for you will be stronger than all other thoughts. It's only that she's very weak now. I too want to write mine, but I don't know how.

I can't understand why you are all alone. We're always thinking about that. We at least can laugh together, put on our shows, amuse each other, keep up one another's morale; but we talk all day about you and there's not one of us who doesn't love you. . . . You mean to tell me that all this time you've been right in the middle of all the madmen? How is that possible? Have you spoken to your director? I also want you to talk to them about the letter business. I write every week, sometimes twice. It's not possible you only got three letters from me—*all written in Italian*. What a bore only one piece of paper to write on. I have so much to tell you. I started a diary. I dreamed of Debbie, all of us together—I, you and she. Today I'll write Jacotte and Yaguel. It's terrible this three letters a week.

I eat a lot. We have a kitchen. It's not true I don't eat. Today we're making *consommé*, liver with onions and *zucchini*, then stewed fruit, cheese. This morning oatmeal, eggs, tea with (*voilà* another sheet of paper thanks to Widget) milk and honey. Don't despair, I think it's very possible they'll let me come and see you. You didn't tell me if you have books. I'm having some sent from Elsa Morante and Jacotte. I found her address.

M., D. and W. have a consul who's really adorable. His name is Baker. He comes every week, brings books, coffee-maker, coffee biscuits, toilet paper, so many things. Then he was also here when the judge came. I've met him—really special. But darling, that consul americano—I've asked him twice to come. Nothing. Really! They're here to help people and they do nothing! Why don't you write Senator Javits or something. It's really too much. Then there's the fact that my passport expired 2 September. What diplomacy. Why didn't you have money? Did you send it all to me? The salad works great even when there's no apple pie. Florence already found it out a few days ago. Some evenings we put on little shows for our friends here. The last one was *Rosa la Rosa*, a period piece style *Tom Jones*. Rosanna who weighs 130 kilos in prison is awaiting her love on horseback (Florence); there's the drunken jailer who comes to say that at midnight . . . etc., etc. and it goes on like that. We laughed for five hours.

Widget really is cool. She made a little garden on the window sill in a cardboard box. She's planted seeds of lemon and nuts and watermelons. What joy! Little green plants are sprouting. A miracle! It's really true. *Allora* a game. Take a bucket of water, put it in the sun near the window (if there is one), stir it a little and look—a light show on the ceiling. I too think myself very close to you because every year that passes I love you more. C x x x.

Bill to Carol. 8 September   *Mia Cara.* If I write you light banalities you mustn't think I don't understand your situation. Needless to say we're all in the same stew, the same boredom, the same desperation and so on, with all the negative thoughts and emotions. There's no need to communicate them. It also does not mean I've abandoned myself to nihilism. I do everything possible that comes to my mind, even though to date it's been almost useless and without positive results. I've done much thinking in these days and it seems to me that the foremost thing is always—fear— even though it is usually disguised by other considerations, other arguments, other emotions. We must win out over fear, eliminate it from our soul, from our life and attempt to reduce it in the society. It's easy to speak of these things in theoretical discussion; it is most difficult to apply in our own life in diffuse situations like the one in which we now find ourselves. It is easier to say: I'm not afraid. It is also easier to combat the fear when we are confronted with actual physical violence than to combat our fear when it is most subtle. But it is precisely that type of courage we personally must learn. I don't want to oversimplify in generality but I believe if you analyse profoundly your negative emotions—be they hate or exasperation, disapproval or frustration or whatever— they all stem from a certain fear. Perhaps it is precisely to realise this that destiny has put us into this situation. It's the same for me as it is for you. But if we cannot face our fear, we can never be free. We shall always have to lock the gates of our soul. I ask myself what is this fear? We have already overcome so many fears: the fear of being put down, the fear of not having money, I don't know, these fears I believe I have overcome now seem so stupid, so infantile I'm ashamed to even enumerate them. All in all this place here is not so frightening. It's ugly, it's a bore, there is exasperation etc., but. . . . I'm afraid for your health, yes, but even there I can only hope and have faith in your ability to take care of yourself. There is the fear of losing my sense of freedom, of losing universal love, the hope in humanity, the fear of learning cynicism, compromise, the fear of learning to fear. But all these are things one cannot lose so easily if they have value. I try to enumerate the possible fears because I believe once they are known they no longer exist. As long as we concentrate ourselves on hate, on exasperation, on all the negative emotions caused by fear, we will never be able to conquer them and overcome them.

Basta with this discorso. I just wanted to say: We've got to stay cool. These are all things the black people have suffered so much more severely and for centuries—it has given them a spiritual life, a spiritual essence that I envy. Try to write, but if you can't don't worry about it—I understand. Many kisses, tante amore. Billie.

Carol's Diary. 10 September   4 a.m. So many things have happened I don't know where to start. First of all I had two beautiful letters from Billie that made me all hysterical for hours. I love him so much. I really feel very close to him. Sunday was rather uneventful. Anyway I was really in excellent spirits, then Monday came the disaster. Petra and Marilyn pulled one of their disgusting scenes, screaming like harpies much worse than any of the guardianos. It was really disgusting. As soon as I saw it coming I immediately split from the kitchen and put myself in my bed. It seems Petra had a knife—they scared the shit out of everybody (after all this is a looney bin), somebody called the director, they were taken downstairs where I understand Marilyn punched a nun and scratched all the skin off the arm of a guard. Petra more or less the same. They've been in strait-jackets ever since. We have all to be punished. I am in a room with dear Widget. We are locked in all day and night and cannot leave the room. Florence and Desna are next door. Yesterday I had a letter from the lawyer asking me to telegraph an answer, it is important. Wouldn't let me send a telegram. We are all now in great danger of being accused of insanity and being dangerous to society and they can if they want ask to keep us here for observation for one year. I am ready to give up. It just seems too impossible. If you don't do anything they make something up. I am so weak I faint practically every time I stand up. I weigh about 98 pounds and all my hair is falling out, also my teeth. . . . I have a fever every night, of course no one seems to know why. It's really all too disgusting. In two days my birthday . . . thirty-seven years old and I look about eighty . . . this sometimes I think is the biggest bringdown of all. I look like a skeleton and my tits are two shrivelled up prunes . . . *charming*!

Bill to Carol. 11 September   Man suffered from cold. Out of his fear of suffering came the idea to build a house—a city. He suffered from the attacks of other beasts and from that fear came the idea of arming himself with a weapon. He suffered from the attacks of other men with their weapons, and thus he developed all his instruments of peace—like society, civilisation and his instruments of war. Fear has helped us develop our world as we know it today. The idea that love too can be a force for development is relatively new—a mere couple of thousand years. That's why it's so difficult to change. The battle of reason over emotion over instinct is also quite recent. We must not despair that neither love nor reason have overcome fear and instinct. The marvel is that these yet persist in whatever poor and impotent form we find them. Fear has proved itself for a million years as a beneficial instrument for mankind, it has thus become an integral part of our society. The child is taught what it must learn through fear of punishment, through fear of disapproval. We work for fear of losing our job, for fear of society's disapproval, etc., we make war and also peace for fear that the 'others' may do us harm.

Undoubtedly the men of power in each country use this fear to keep them in power. But they too have their fears; fear of losing power, fear of losing esteem and so on.

It's all very complicated but also quite simple. Hate, violence, brutality of man against man are products of fear. Jealousy is caused by the fear of not being loved; it is not the product of love. Until yesterday it seemed that this system based on fear could function, at least with more benefits than bad effects. Only today can we see clearly that the tools developed in this way lead to a total destruction that seems inevitable. The beautiful cities are suffocating the spirit and even the physical life of man. Technology seems incapable of turning backwards and continues to produce even more efficient means for the suicide of mankind with the bombs, the anti-missile missile, and all the other things that are leading to a gradual destruction of our environment, of nature. The world of technology can analyse with increasing precision and predict the cataclysm that awaits us, but it cannot arrest itself from its very production activity which is causing that cataclysm. The radar becomes ever more perfect—the man directing the missiles has not changed. I have a vision of myself watching a television interview by RAI-TV either in Washington or in Moscow with the man who is about to press the button to launch the missile that will obliterate the Italian peninsula. He is explaining how he has the most lovely memories of Italy and its people. If we truly want to avoid that *ultima transmissione* we must eliminate fear and the use of fear. We must begin at the bottom and work to the top. As long as fear is an essential and useful tool for governing human relations, even if a messiah of superior wisdom and super power were to arrive he could do little more than arrange a truce. That is why Christ arrived in such a humble form. The elimination of fear must begin inside each one of us.

The opposite of fear is not courage but love. Courage is simply a way of controlling the negative results of fear, is simply a way of directing our actions to positive ends. Curiosity can examine the causes and develop the means to eliminate or neutralise them. Love will render man-made fear impotent and useless. Hate is not the opposite of love—it is something else entirely. Hate is the product of fear when there is no love. Artificial ignorance is a means created by man for instilling fear. Natural ignorance instead

House of the Angels and Carol's portrait of Bill

Self-portraits and
other moods

Carol's drawings of the
house made on the morning
before the police raid, and
(below) of the Angels

is a protective shield that lets us incubate our love and our curiosity. It is a shell with many many layers which separate us from the brilliant energy of God until such time as we have gained enough force, enough strength of love to absorb that total energy in all its glory. Our way is to break these shells one after the other. Fear can give us the force to develop means of making life inside the shell more comfortable, but it will never help us to break the shell. Prisons, wars, 'justice' and artificial ignorance are all symbols of fear created by fearful men. Love does not even admit concepts like 'justice', duty, punishment and sacrifice. As I love you, as I love my children, it is absurd to say I make sacrifices for you or I'm fulfilling my duty or it is not just you should get the bigger piece of the cake or that I want to punish you because you hurt me. It's obvious that those concepts come to mind only when we no longer love. To the extent that I love you, everything I can give you, everything I can do for you, everything that pleases you is a joy for me and the same for every one of us, the same for all humanity. It is the simple message of Christ. This is precisely why he did not write a book on theology but lived a humble life like all of us; he ate with us, shared with us, touched us and kissed us because it is with these simple actions that we can find our way towards spiritual love.

Carol to Bill
13 SEPTEMBER   Darling, we must admit that we are being cut off. I sent you last week two telegrams plus a registered letter express—all pertaining to the lawyer problem. Have sent letters to Baldings, Hitchcock, Van Wolf, Bertran Castelli, etc. to send us a few million. I don't have that 'tic' of not asking for 'favours'. That's the only thing I don't understand about you—you do everything for everybody—if someone asks you a favour, you do it—you are the most generous man in the world—there doesn't exist a friend whom you haven't helped—*allora*?

Yesterday, I must tell you, I had one of the most beautiful birthdays of my life. Everybody brought me presents. The sisters ordered me a beautiful cake and we celebrated all day long. Raffaela also sent me a *galabea*, yours from Egypt, only you were missing but not really. They all hope you are well. I hope you're not upset about the lawyer, but something very strong pushed me and I had to do it. I adore you as always. I now feel that this whole story will end very well for us and all the others. I swear to you, *all* the signs show it. I feel very happy. Try to sense me. You are not alone there, I'm with you every minute. I send you all my strength. We are always thinking of you. If you want Jacotte's address, I'll send it to you. Widget gave me a little garden and I've put it on the window sill. It's truly a miracle. We planted two lemon seeds and now they've already grown into two little trees of 3 cms. Every day there is something else beautiful. How sweet you are to write every day. You can't imagine how happy it makes me. Every day I love you more. Every day I feel your incredible strength. Every day it makes me laugh just thinking of some little thing of the past, of your beauty. I see you building your tree house, your swimming pool. I think of how you've brought joy to so many people without even thinking about it. I've never thought this but now I understand how there are people who pass their whole life together. Florence and Marilyn said how they've never seen a couple with such a perfect relationship. Nothing can destroy it, I've learned too much from you. I close with much love, also from the others. Your Lobravico.

P.S. Why don't you ask Peronne to send me a beautiful picture of you?

17 SEPTEMBER   Dear. What joy that you got my letter. I too write with much difficulty in Italian. In my last letter I told you all about the feast they made for me Saturday. I was overfilled with joy. I also got a letter from you. But don't worry, I get a letter from you almost every day. Every day I feel happier. Also on my birthday the director gave me my guitar that Raffaela had sent. I love you very much. Gaetano carried the motorcycle all the way up to the house. He told me was sorry he couldn't carry the car up! Like I said I feel happier every day, there are always beautiful things happening. We'll be out of here and together very soon, I know that. I'm completely sure. Why don't you write Yaguel? I think you can write her in French, I wrote last Sunday. The consul told me that the Rome consulate will ask about the passport . . . same old story. Good news in the horoscope—it says Friday is a favourable day. I love you with all my heart. Don't worry about me, I'm fine. I stay in bed and read lots of books. No

bother, they're all *super* nice with me. Almost *clinica Mater Dei*, but it doesn't cost half a million. Many kisses, I adore you. Carol x x x

19 SEPTEMBER   Dearest Love . . . Other good news. The director said yesterday that in a few days we'll leave here. He's only waiting for a telephone call that the *carabinieri* are coming with the car. We'll go to Salerno and maybe *liberta provisorio*. I think we'll go to Salerno to finish everything. How beautiful it would be if this letter would fly immediately to you like a bird. How good I feel now; I've felt like this since I saw Pirrongelli. I love you much. Did you hear that Tim Leary has escaped! You should get this letter right away because the *perizia* is finished and the director said there was no more censorship. I've had a beautiful letter from Jacotte and also from Fabienne. I'm enclosing a photo of Nino guess who. Are you sure you're not really him? It's incredible how you have the same face, only that you're more beautiful.
P.S. Last time I saw Eduardo di Giovanni I gave him a wristband for you—I made it with needlepoint. It took me a week to make it. It's the Phoenix above the pyramid where we were in Egypt. Don't tell me you didn't get it!
P.S. I'm closing because maybe I write my letters too long.

25 SEPTEMBER   Dearest mine. Don't worry about your letters, I get one almost every day. They're the most beautiful things I ever read. You're right, *in fondo* you are a writer. I know the whole story about Nona. I asked them to leave from the first days. Also Raffaela was very upset. She refused. She's never written me a line since we left. It's all been a terrible story. I didn't tell you because I didn't want to give you any more headaches. Really I don't understand people any more. I'm sorry my letters are so boring, but that letter about love and fear in the world is something that's made me understand you. I've also understood why our love, our life has to continue. Such a relationship between two people is so special you almost never find it, at least rarely in these years. I'm making this letter very short, that way maybe it will pass more quickly. I just have to tell you that the little hints are '*in giro*' that we'll soon be free! I love you with all my being. Your Caroline cherie.

27 SEPTEMBER   My *caro*. Do you like this drawing? I made it for you. I'm all right. I sleep a lot, make beautiful dreams about you. This drawing is the sunset we see every evening from our *palazzo sul mare*. Why don't you buy yourself things to eat? I also think of you, I also think of love, I also wonder what use is fear that I have never known. I think now I am here and I am very calm. I love you. I love you because you still think about love. Your Carol.

Bill to Carol. 29 September*   Every night I wake up two or three times. It isn't insomnia, but for an hour at a time I'm completely awake to write, to read or to contemplate. I think my subconscious (without the aid of self-hypnosis) discovered that this is the time I can be truly alone with myself without any effort. It's mostly for contemplation because usually there's no light except for the soft light that seeps in through the peepholes from the corridor. What usually passes through my head are memories of the past. I recall happenings and also emotions that take me back into another past way of thinking. It's a little like getting to know an old friend but always someone outside myself.

I've never been stupid (at least not more stupid than I am now) but it seems to me now that my visions, my horizons have always been limited. My intellect was always busy finding explanations, accommodations within these limits, and I must say it's always worked well that way, but always in an adaptive sense, not in a creative sense. It's saved me from serious frustration but at the same time it also blocked the force necessary for a true evolution of my spirit. Every now and then this process of liberation happened because of some outside 'accident' that now seems to me to have been inspired by my subconscious. The great changes like the emigration, the army, my marriage, my children, the theatre, always made slight adjustments in my way of thinking. Perhaps they opened new emotions, new instincts, which in their turn conspired to influence the subconscious to 'prepare' the 'little accidents'. These 'accidents', these seemingly outside forces in

---

* Bill was writing daily letters to Carol, filling them with bits of news, songs, poems, satirical fables, Italian translations of English 'hip' words and phrases. He had found a dictionary and was teaching his cell-mates English. Trying to keep in touch with Carol at all costs, he started thinking back over his own life and wrote an autobiographical letter.

their turn always inspired actions and decisions which little by little freed my rational brain.

I've always been successful at everything I've ever applied myself to, always successful up to a certain point. At this point always when the ultimate success, the ultimate goal seemed inevitable, something always happened—some bad luck, some 'accident'. When I was an athlete I was totally absorbed with all my energies, all my heart. I was twenty years old when I easily qualified for the finals in the selection for the Olympic team. Then in the actual race, the most important race, I couldn't do anything, absolutely nothing. It was like a nightmare where you have to run and can't move your legs. Still there were always the Olympic Games of 1952, 1956 and 1960 and I had no doubt about that. It seemed a sure thing. Then the next year I developed a strange pain (never explained by the doctors I went to) that forced me to stop my 'athletic career'.

I went into the army against my will, but then I soon found myself very well there. I was the 'bright young man' of the colonels at Wright Field, the protégé, and I decided on a military career. Now in the Air Force if you want to get to the ultimate top you have to be a pilot—so I went to pilot training. I found out that flying a plane comes easy to me and even then I didn't have the slightest fear or doubt. Then a strange thing happened—all of a sudden I couldn't concentrate on the simplest manoeuvres, I became a bundle of nerves and they kicked me out of flying school. At the time it was a big blow and I couldn't explain it to myself, but after that I never again thought of 'making it' as a general. Then there was my first marriage. I made a fabulous adjustment to the good bourgeois life, the *pater familias*. All of a sudden Marj went completely 'crazy' and neither I nor anybody else could understand why. Today I'm quite sure that in some way I was responsible, I caused it to happen. End of the good bourgeois life with divorce and total flight.

The more I get towards the present, the more these radical changes in my life include some conscious contributing awareness. For example, when you left me for the Living Theatre. There I had found the *grande amore*, a love no longer tied to outside life circumstances, a love that seemed indestructible. I still believe that today, although different from the 'old form'. That form of love seemed the ultimate ideal but compared to today it was limited. Before this there was the 'bright'—no longer quite so young—actor of Broadway. Then came the Uta Hagen incident that changed that contemplation. I've rethought all the old arguments, the former ways of thinking. Today I've arrived at an explanation. I've always had a rather healthy respect for my reasoning mind and intellect, probably too much so because it always served me well. Still it served me always to adapt myself to existing conditions, always within the limits of 'duty', of 'responsibility', the limitation of being reasonable, of being a good boy. It was always an effort of repair, of justification, of adaptation—never a creative force to let me soar beyond 'things as they are'. The success I was looking for was never of my own choosing, was never for something I profoundly felt. It was always simply the race I happened to find myself running in, and the measures and means of the success were always those prescribed by others and accepted by me without question. I never used my mind to search deeply to see if the desire was really part of my soul, if the goal was truly in harmony with my spirit or just any kind of goal for the sake of having a goal. Today I can see clearly that the goals themselves and my success towards these goals were blocking me, that in order to free the scope of my mind I had to change paths. My subconscious always came to my aid, in spite of myself. In some ways it always made the path I was on impossible and forced me to find another. This way, at each 'change of path' I had to rethink a little. I was able to free myself a little of preconceptions. It was a long, long, slow slow process. I always had that impulse to jump on that tramp steamer going into the unknown; I always resisted it. In 1947 I wanted to go to Israel to be there to be part of that adventure—a new nation, a new society. In 1948 I found myself in Paris. My subconscious was working very well. I overslept the morning the boat left. But then my rational mind and resourcefulness took over and still got me on board at the last minute, not to miss the beginning of the new semester at Columbia. What a fabulous opportunity to be in Paris in 1948 without money, twenty years old . . . forced to drift on one's own, to learn, to discover.

So many roads, so many steamers that I never tried because I was too sensible, because my mother might not understand, because I didn't want to miss the next track season, etc. So many roads that Roscoe opened to me—the Red Rooster scene—the village scene, the Peggy Hitchcock scene—that I never really allowed myself to pursue in full because I was too blocked off; roads that might have opened to me so much sooner what my soul had always been searching. Instead I used my energy, my curiosity to adapt myself better to where I happened to find myself, to adapt myself to competition, to bourgeois values of success—all things that have no inner meaning for me, all things outside my nature. That damned adaptability that comes so easy for me, *even here*, that we should use in order to fly, to soar out into space, I always misused to make the chains more comfortable, to make the chains tighter. More than anything else I think I was always afraid that those who happen to be near me would not be proud of me— forgetting that the only thing of value is to be proud of oneself. How beautiful to find myself in this humiliating condition—a criminal in prison. Not one of those people can now be proud of me. I only regret that I'm not here for some abominable crime, that I am innocent instead of guilty. I must content myself that for 'them' my very presence here is enough to suggest *ipso facto* something far worse. I no longer regard it as inevitable misfortune but embrace it as a penitence that cleanses the sins of omission, which gives it all a sublime meaning. I'm proud of myself. Love, love, love, Billie.

Carol's Diary*

> *I surrender I surrender*
> *All to thee I freely give*
> *May the love of full salvation*
> *Glory glory to my king*
> *I surrender I surrender*
> *I surrender I*
> *All to thee my blessed saviour*
> *I surrender I*

* In the two account books in which Carol had written her *manicomio* diary, alongside lists of how she had spent her money, were these three songs which have no dates but must have been set down towards the end since they were in the second exercise book.

One bright morning when my life is ended
I will fly away home
I will fly away home to glory
Fly fly fly away home to glory
One bright morning
When my life is ended I will fly
Fly away home
Fly fly fly
Home to glory

I've been here too long
For reasons I don't know
But I'll get gone
On my own
So I'll be walking by the river
Till I'm home
Yes I'll be walking by the river
Till I'm home
I've surely served my time
Ain't no use in crying
I'll be gone shining on my own.

6. The Angel of Death

On the first day inside the *manicomio* Bill had tried to make contact with the American consulate. A vice-consul, calling himself the consul—Donald Lautz, together with his interpreter—came the next day—7 August. But the visit was frustratingly formal. The vice-consul merely handed Bill a pamphlet prepared by the consulate on the complications of the drug laws in Italy, then insisted that the consulate could not assume financial responsibility in 'cases of this sort'. Bill told the vice-consul that the police had seized Carol's medicines and that she was in urgent need of medical attention. Immediately the vice-consul went to visit Carol at the Pozzuoli *manicomio* where the same formal procedure took place.

A further visit by the American vice-consul, when he handed Bill a list of over two hundred lawyers, showed that the consulate were clearly not prepared to co-operate in even the functions they were empowered to perform beyond the mere formality of 'doing their duty'. By 13 August Bill had found a lawyer, Eduardo di Giovanni, through his agent in Rome and he telegrammed Carol to advise her to nominate Di Giovanni which she did. The next day Bill received a visit from this lawyer who said he had already visited Carol on his way there, and she was well. But Carol was becoming desperate and made several appeals for help. On 10 August she wrote a letter to a consular official in Naples, De Luzenberger, whom she had met in Positano and who told her to contact him if she was ever in any trouble. Vice-consul Lautz replied to her letter over two weeks later: 'I regret to inform you that Mr. De Luzenberger performs an activity separate to consular work.' She also telegrammed Di Giovanni, requesting an immediate visit. By 30 August he hadn't appeared so she wanted to nominate another lawyer, Giovanni Leone.

On 2 September, Di Giovanni came from Rome and Bill asked him to see Carol—by then he had not heard from her for nineteen days though she had written twice a week. On 4 September he wrote to Carol: 'When I saw the lawyer I couldn't think of anything else but the necessity that he should get to see you and bring you money.' Bill also told her not to be too disheartened by loss of faith in the lawyer: 'We always have to bear in mind that time doesn't pass the same as here, especially in Italy and in August, that lack of faith in the lawyer is a prisoner's disease.' Meanwhile he was working on ideas which he later wrote about in letters to Carol to help her keep calm in the midst of so much madness and which he was to develop so forcefully after she died. He had said: 'I've finally found my "message". For this cause, for the need to substitute fear with love as the driving force—I have no doubt. It's the first time I've truly, profoundly believed in something.'

As long as we are addicted to the rationalisation that prisons are necessary, we sustain our ability to rationalise My Lai, even Auschwitz and Hiroshima and preventive war. It is the ability to rationalise avoidable man-made horror that is kept alive in the prison system, like a cancer in the body. It is our denial of love, the switching off of our humanity that allows the rationalisation of violence.

Justice is a false dream. It exists nowhere in nature. It is not the bad worm who is eaten by the bird, it is not the bad baby who dies of famine in Biafra. Justice is an artificial concept the human mind has developed to protect itself from the obligations of love. To believe that something as finite as the human mind could truly conceive of real justice and, having conceived of it in its pure state, to be able to implement it . . . is absurd. Since it does not exist in the universe, it is even debatable whether justice is desirable. It is an opiate far more dangerous than the one I am accused of having enjoyed. It is an ego-satisfying idea that allows the 'fortunate' of this earth to maintain precariously their hoarded goods. It lets people commit acts of horror against their instinct of love and in return substitutes the lost love with self-righteousness. I want no part of it.

After Bill had told Carol of the trance experience during the taxi-ride to Naples on 5 August and then had sent her a book on self-hypnosis, Carol had 'the hilarious vision' she mentions in her diary of him trancing out all the inmates. She herself seems to have used the trance as Bill suggested 'to cut out of the immediate surroundings', but her letters and diary show how hard it was for her not to react to the pitiful conditions of the *manicomio* and the insanity all around her with panic and fear, though there were occasional moments in the midst of it all when she found peace and strength to combat the physical illness that was gaining control over her. One day when everyone was in the courtyard for the morning walk, Carol and Petra caused an uproar by suddenly whirling into an ecstatic dance with the madwomen. The importance of the trance experience which both Bill and Carol used, especially Bill after Carol's death, was that it recreated the positive drug reactions—energy, relaxation, expanded awareness of physical surroundings and intellectual perception, conscious dream fantasy; but for Carol the *manicomio* experience plunged her right back into the atmosphere of the hospitals she had been in when she was undergoing her cancer operation eighteen months earlier. The tragedy was that she was only just beginning fully to recover when she was put back into a situation that was worse—that of being treated as criminally insane and of being surrounded by so much suffering.

In a letter to a friend in America Carol had described the *manicomio* she was in as a 'snake pit'. What exactly it was like is only obliquely described in Carol's *manicomio* diary. A more vivid description was given by Petra Vogt in a tape, covering the first few days, which she made shortly after being released.

During the first two or three days we weren't allowed to go into the courtyard—they were afraid of the reactions of the other women to us because we were very strange. I think they were very unsure the first few days about our being there. They expected that after two days we would break down because they were sure we were junkies. All the women seemed to be extremely frightened of the nuns, and I saw how the nuns started all sorts of little tortures. For example, a lot of women had to work in the laundry or in the kitchen and most of these women were sick with pains and all sorts of serious diseases; but if they refused to work, the nuns told then they wouldn't get medicines anymore. Also every nun, every warden, every prisoner is a spy. There's no possibility of trusting anyone because everyone's situation is permanently desperate, and if you ever get into a scene where you're wrong you get more time—maybe two years more.

There's this hate. You feel it very strongly. It came out in the first few days when we went to the courtyard and there were all these rumours about why we were there and who we were. They kept asking us, 'How long are you going to be here?' We said, 'Very few days'. It was the first time they had seen anybody who came in for a few days, so they came up to us one by one and started talking, at first very very carefully. Then suddenly a lot of them came and said, 'If you get out tell them how it is in here'. Not only this but some of them said specifically, 'Tell them that I'm here and should be out'. They saw we were young and I think they felt we weren't really evil. They said, 'You must tell them because nobody ever comes in this courtyard or ever sees the rooms and no one knows. Tell them how it is'. It was very difficult to be in the courtyard because we were surrounded by fifty women. It was very hard to take because I remember looking in all those faces, seeing this terrifying hope.

There was this one woman in the courtyard who came to me and talked very low and secretively. She said she was a journalist who had put herself into this situation to write to three newspapers outside. I looked at her and was fascinated by the idea. I said, 'Who knows about it? Does the director know?' She said, 'Yes he knows and I can give you this address and I know people who can get you out of here'. She gave me a paper on top of the table and another underneath. I immediately told Carol and Florence and Carol said, 'Are you sure she doesn't think she's doing all this?' Slowly we realised there was no way to find out. We started watching the women who looked most normal and slowly you could feel that madness which isn't hard to see.

One afternoon one of the prisoners came in and whispered, 'Take this piece of paper'. Carol took it and said, 'They busted Widget and Desna'. It was the first really horrifying moment because we knew that this meant time, we knew it would mean possibly two cases. We were wondering why

Marilyn wasn't busted and we were hoping she had split; then this woman told us, 'If you go to the window you might see them because they have to give up their clothes'. We were standing at the window, waiting and waiting and suddenly they came and Marilyn was with them. We shouted down, 'You too baby'. They were laughing and it was very nice because we had almost stopped laughing at that point. They came in and we called down, 'Keep laughing, keep laughing— you'll see how it is'.

From the beginning we all had doubts, but we knew we couldn't afford to get depressed and we kept up this enormous energy and we laughed a lot, thinking we would get out tomorrow, if not today. Carol was the first one who thought about time. If you have money you can order food, cigarettes too. A girl came the second day and said, 'D'you want anything?' We said, 'Oh yes, cigarettes'! then, 'When does it come? Today? In the afternoon?' She said, 'Next Saturday'. I said, 'Oh no, I'm not going to be here . . . ever'. Carol said, 'Are you sure?' She said, 'Yes'. I was completely horrified. I thought when we start ordering things here and think we can wait until next Saturday. . . . I just really didn't want to know about it at all. Carol said, 'It really doesn't matter. If we get out before, groovy. If not, we have it.'

The day when the lawyers first came was frightening because each of them had a different opinion of how the case looked. Florence's lawyer said that it looked very serious and could go on for a really long time. When my lawyer came I couldn't believe it because he told me the story he had heard from the judge and the doctor, and I suddenly got the impression of how the story was being told outside.

He said, 'You lived in this house for three months. Don't you think it's strange?'

I said, 'What's strange about it?'

'Where is Mrs. Berger?' he asked.

'She's upstairs with me', I said.

He didn't even know that Carol was in prison because she was using her second name—Lobravico.

He said, 'Ah, but was Mr. Berger paying for you to stay

there? Don't you think it's strange you people living there and not working?'

I said, 'No, I live with my money and I'm a friend of both of them and I don't think it's strange to live in a friend's house that long a time'.

He went carefully through all his points then he said, 'Is it true there are pornographic pictures and paintings everywhere?'

I said, 'I wouldn't call them pornographic because there are paintings with naked people. Through all the centuries (they'd call the Sistine Chapel pornographic!) people are naked in paintings. . . .'

The point he made at the end was that if they couldn't get us on drugs, they'd try at least to get Billy on pornography or on paying all these people to do orgies. Suddenly I got this completely other picture of the whole story, which was that they really wanted at least one of us for something because they couldn't allow themselves to have a failure.

We just knew there was a long time to pass, so we started thinking how to pass the time.

In her letters Carol kept reassuring Bill about her health, though her diary tells a different story. But Bill had not received these letters and grew more and more concerned. On 7 September he wrote: 'Since I only get half your letters, it's a little like getting a message with every other word missing. Most important, you have to watch your health and not give way to depression and desperation.' Because he had no direct contact with Carol, either through the American consulate or his lawyer, the only practical solution he could think of was to try to find another lawyer on the spot in Salerno where the case was being decided, to act as a go-between.

At a point of desperation because of having no contact with Bill, Carol resorted to less practical but more direct means. On the night of 5 September she and the other girls held a seance in their cell. Having taken sleeping pills and drunk bottles of beer, the girls draped a sheet over the night light and sat round a table they had moved to the centre of the cell. They all made themselves up with flour, eyes outlined in black from burnt matchsticks, and covered themselves in sheets. One of them even made a silver moon from cigarette foil and stuck it in her hair. A passing warder looked in and asked them what was going on. They said they were going to play cards. First they contacted Yaguel, then Bill. Carol sat hunched over, breathing with difficulty, tears streaming down her face. Suddenly the table started to pound around the cell. A warder appeared with two plainclothes policemen who shouted and banged on the door. The warder had the key in her hand but was so terrified she didn't dare to enter the room. Shortly afterwards the seance ended.

On 8 September Bill telegrammed Carol saying he wanted to nominate a lawyer from Salerno, Avvocato Grisi, but would wait for her reaction. Next day he sent her a letter for her birthday on 12 September which she didn't receive until two weeks later:

> It seems a bit stupid to wish you a happy birthday, at least the best possible. The bars on your window are the same as the bars on mine. I don't think I could bear your imprisonment if I could not at least share the same fate. Here at least we can see the bars, but the bars are everywhere—the frontiers, the laws, the customs, death, conformism, etc., even if they are less evident, less ugly. They are all bars of our very fear; they are all of them indicators, images of the fear inside the soul of humanity, inside our very own soul. If we do not succeed in breaking these bars inside us, it will avail little to break the bars of the window. On the other hand, if we succeed in breaking those inside us, the others no longer exist. Let's wait to celebrate your birthday till we're out of this nightmare.

On 10 September Bill, having heard nothing from Carol, nominated Grisi as his second lawyer and telegrammed Carol telling her to make the same nomination so that Grisi could visit her. Carol couldn't understand that Bill hadn't received her letters nor what he was doing, and wrote angrily: 'Your letters are full of desperation and you haven't chosen with your sense of discretion.' At this point crossed communication—due to the delay of their letters and lack of co-operation from the American consulate—became so impossible that Bill tried once more in desperation to establish contact through the American consulate. When he had received no answer to a pre-paid telegram to Carol, he had assumed that she was either so grievously ill or in restrained isolation that she could not reply.

As the situation stood, he had nominated one lawyer—Grisi—on 10 September and she had nominated another—Pirrongelli—and neither of them could nominate a third. In answer to his urgent request, the secretary of the *manicomio* agreed to ask the consulate to send a representative to visit Bill. In fact, the registered letter in which Carol explained to Bill what she was doing, written on 13 September, never reached him. The letter she wrote on the same day, elaborating the explanation, reached Bill when she was already in Cardarelli hospital and dying. It was postmarked Pozzuoli 3 October. Vice-consul Lautz arrived on 15 September in response to the phone call by the secretary. Bill's account of the meeting reads as follows:

> I presented Mr. Lautz with my letter declaration* and asked him to investigate possible discriminatory and extra-legal actions and delay regarding our detention. I asked him to inquire if my letter to Senator Javits had been forwarded by the censor and to arrange for at least weekly visits to Carol because of the state of her health. He responded with the usual superfluous explanations about *ferragosto* [that almost everything in Italy shuts down during the August holidays], lack of responsibility and very general explanations of Italian law and responsibilities of Italian legal counsel. In response to my request for regular visits to Carol, he claimed press of other duties.
>
> General impression: Mr. Lautz is not interested to do more than absolutely necessary and is not very sympathetic towards us. He also left me two books to read. I asked him why Carol's two previous request for visits had been ignored. He replied that according to her letters, her wishes could not be complied with, i.e. liberation or transfer to a regular prison; further, that her desire to change attorneys was a matter she had to attend to herself.

* This 'letter declaration' restated the facts about Bill's legal position which he had written in the letter to Senator Javits three days earlier. This letter is quoted in Diary Notes 3 on pp. 278–279.

The vice-consul refused to make the visits which Bill asked for, so Bill decided to write a 'peace' letter to Lautz, trying to reach him on some level since he was the only one who could see Carol apart from the lawyer Di Giovanni whom Carol wanted to drop and who kept disappearing to Rome. But even the reasonableness of Bill's 'peace' letter failed to win any response from Lautz whose attitude throughout remained as unco-operative as it could have been.

On 16 September a notification was sent from the director of the Pozzuoli *manicomio* to the investigating judge, stating that Carol was suffering from continuous high fever and should be immediately transferred to a better medical facility. Numerous applications were made to the investigating judge to have Carol transferred from the asylum to a clinic for better medical treatment, the last being made by Pirrongelli in a telegram on 3 October. This was the only way Carol's life could have been saved at this stage. According to Di Giovanni (who never made a written request) and Pirrongelli, the investigating judge's attitude was to dismiss Carol's sickness as a 'fake' to get her release. The similarity between the investigating judge's attitude and that of the American consul calls into question the impartiality of the consulate in this case. The indication on 16 September from the director of Carol's *manicomio* about the decline in her health, contrasts strangely with a letter from vice-consul Lautz to Bill after his visit to Carol on the same day (16 September):

I visited your wife at the hospital in Pozzuoli yesterday. She seemed to be in much better spirits, but quite naturally she wishes to gain her freedom. As the hospital authorities are aware that she had an operation eighteen months ago for suspected cancer, they are arranging for her to undergo an X-ray examination and other tests that there is no recurrence of this affliction.

Apart from the misleading optimism of this letter, Lautz referred diplomatically, as he persisted in doing throughout, to the insane asylum as a 'hospital' and also stated that Carol's operation was for 'suspected cancer' when in fact the operation had involved cutting out a particularly malignant growth of cancer from the uterus. But since no attempt had been made to find out

Carol's medical history, any tests or medical examination was relatively worthless—especially since the doctors in a Neapolitan insane asylum were hardly competent to deal with a situation as serious as this.

When the vice-consul saw Carol that day (16 September) he told her not to change lawyers because an analysis of the evidence seized was due to be made on Friday.

Once the Bergers and their 'guests' had been put in *manicomios*, the case was in the hands of the investigating judge, Verasani, in Salerno. Its outcome depended on two factors. The first was psychiatric and medical reports on all those arrested to determine whether or not they were under the influence of drugs when arrested; the second on an examination of the evidence seized at the Bergers' house, to be made by court-appointed experts to determine whether in their professional opinion any drug or narcotic was present. The first had already been questioned by Dr. Rosapepe, director of S. Eframo *manicomio*, when he discredited Dr. Testa's examination in Amalfi by stating that in his opinion Bill was not under the influence of drugs and needed no psychiatric treatment. The second issue was more complicated. Practically speaking, the analysis took only two hours, but legally the experts had up to forty days to make their examination and it is common practice that they take as long as they are allowed because they get paid during that time.

The date set for the analysis came and went—18 September. It was not until a few days later that Bill learnt it had been postponed until 25 September. In fact, the analysis wasn't made until 19 October, five days after Carol's death.

On 19 September Carol wrote to Bill about 300,000 lire he had given to Di Giovanni to give to her, saying she hadn't received it. She never did because neither of them saw Di Giovanni again—he never came back. Carol also wrote optimistically about her new lawyer, Pirrongelli:

He is a hundred times more informed about our case than Di Giovanni. He knows the judge well and he gave us good news and much courage that everything will be over very soon. He said we lost a lot of time with Di Giovanni and we should have been out a long time ago. When you speak with him you'll understand everything. This is an *avvocato*—competent, brilliant, efficient, one who's in control. He told me not to think anymore about anything, that he will speak with Eduardo, that I should only think about beautiful things and he will do the rest, and that's what I intend to do.

Then she added mysteriously 'He says not to think about *that* either. I can't say who, but he's the lawyer of someone who sent him to help us.' By this time Carol was clutching at straws and projected into Pirrongelli what she actually needed, though as it turned out he did nothing to help her. The mysterious person to whom Carol referred was an Arab prince whose mistress Marilyn Woolhead had at one time been and by whom she was still supported financially. He had instructed Pirrongelli, his own lawyer, to involve himself in the case on Marilyn Woolhead's behalf and to keep his name out of the newspapers.

On 23 September Bill telegrammed Carol, saying he had finally received a letter about Pirrongelli from her and he had decided to nominate him as his own lawyer. The next day he sent 5,000 lire, all he had, to Carol. On the same day Carol, who now had a continuous high fever and was in great pain, sent a telegram to the American consulate pleading for an immediate visit. She received a letter, signed 'Cordially yours, Donald Lautz (American consul)', in reply:

I regret not to be able to satisfy your request in as much as all consular officials are most busy organising the visit of President Nixon to NATO which is due to take place in the following week. However, if you wish you may write to this Consulate General and this office will be glad to answer your questions and problems concerning your detention at Pozzuoli.

By then Carol was only able to communicate to Bill about the immediate problems in a desperate attempt to get something done. On 25 September she telegrammed him, saying she had eliminated Di Giovanni whom she hadn't seen since 3 September. Then on 1 October Carol sent a short letter to Bill mainly about the problems of paying Pirrongelli. It was the last letter she wrote, and at the end she added a P.S.:

I love you. When we get out I want a white Bentley and a black yacht with sails fairly large and two little babies.

On 2 October Carol became so ill that she was rushed in an ambulance to Pioggioreale prison hospital. Two hours later she was moved to Cardarelli, a large public hospital in Naples, where she was immediately operated on—without prior consultation of her previous medical history or permission from her husband.

Later the State Department in Washington, defending the Naples consulate and the Italian authorities after congressional inquiries, were to claim that Carol's lawyer—Pirrongelli—had given permission for medical treatment. Pirrongelli's answer to this attempt to cover up the chaotic circumstances surrounding Carol's illness reads: 'The American consulate never contacted me about Carol. It was I who complained to the authorities through a series of telegrams. I never gave permission to anyone and was only informed incidentally and mysteriously that Carol had been taken to a Naples hospital.'

The medical records, supplied by the authorities, of Carol's treatment at Pozzuoli manicomio indicate that although Carol became seriously ill in early September, no diagnosis of the illness was ever made. However, the doctors there continued to give her various medicines—hoping in a haphazard way that she would respond to the limited amount of medical treatment they could provide. In other words, she was kept in the manicomio, where there were inadequate medical facilities, for a month after becoming ill; then after failing to respond to any of the medication there and after suffering a serious relapse, she was transferred to a prison hospital. There, where the medical facilities were obviously more advanced, the seriousness of her condition was realised and she was transferred, after a delay of two hours, to Cardarelli hospital where the illness was immediately diagnosed, though by then it was too late to prevent further and fatal deterioration.

The crucial period obviously was the month spent in the primitive conditions of a manicomio where, if the illness had been diagnosed in time, her life might have been saved. Certain facts gathered from the others in the manicomio with Carol indicate the lack of any proper medical attention there. As her diary shows, her health started seriously to decline on 10 September and it became steadily worse after her birthday on 12 September. She couldn't sleep and wasn't receiving the right kind of food for hepatitis, except through the intervention of the British consul. On one occasion, according to Petra Vogt, Carol was tied down to a bed because she complained of sickness. Petra took the injections that Carol was supposed to be receiving for a liver complaint and found they were depressants used to calm the insane patients.

Petra, who until the last moment had kept distant from Carol, even believing her illness to be faked, was with her the day she was rushed to the hospital. Half Carol's hair had fallen out and she was being fed intravenously. Petra sat with her in her cell, comforting her and talking quietly. Then the ambulance men came to take Carol away. She looked very wasted.

As she was being taken out of the door she smiled at Petra and said 'I'm dreaming of a white Bentley—there'll be a white Bentley outside the house.'

Petra followed her down the corridor, then they had to say goodbye.

They embraced and Carol whispered 'That's the way the ball is bouncing.'

According to Pirrongelli who visited Carol in Cardarelli hospital the day after her operation, when she arrived no one knew who she was or what she was suffering from—also Carol seemed to him to be very ill and was still unconscious from the anaesthetic. The operation, officially described by the American consulate after Carol's death, was stated to be a 'laparectomy (exploratory surgery) for diffused peritonitis due to a perforated intestine which may have been caused by abdominal typhus'. The consulate's report went on to state: 'There were no complications after the operation and the attending physician prognosed a normal convalescence . . .', although the medical records make no reference to the peritonitis being cleared up and indicate that Carol was in a critical condition. Pirrongelli also stated—he was the only one to see Carol during this time—that it was his impression that she was treated badly in the hospital because she had come from an asylum for the criminally insane and there was a shortage of beds in the hospital.

When Pirrongelli visited Bill on 3 October he wrote a note saying that Carol and the others were expected to be released the following week and that he would probably have to wait another two weeks. Also Pirrongelli had arranged for Bill to visit Carol in Cardarelli hospital the next day. Although there had been rumours before, this was the first intimation Bill had received that something definite was happening in the case. At that time he was too preoccupied with Carol's health to pay much attention to the news, except to regard it as yet another optimistic forecast from his new lawyer. He wasn't to know what had been going on behind the scenes, and Carol who had been more involved in it all— because of contact with the English consul, Anthony Baker, and the lawyer Pirrongelli—couldn't communicate anything in her censored letters except ambiguous instructions.

Between 2 and 14 October a number of puzzling factors about the case began to become clearer. The other men in Aversa asylum, who had been treated very well by the authorities, had been questioned on a number of occasions but no one had 'talked'. They were obviously separated from Bill in the hope that some of them would betray him. Also, Raffaela, who was in the most vulnerable position since she was Italian, was visited five times by the police in the weeks after the bust in an attempt to pressurise her into talking, but she refused to give anything away. Then on 9 October, five days before Carol died, Robert Peitscher was suddenly released from Aversa asylum, driven by an American consulate car to Rome airport and flown out of the country. He was the first to get out.

From what the lawyers told everyone and from other sources, it appears that in the middle of September it had been established that the people involved in both cases, including Carol, were due to be released 'early in October', although Bill would probably have to remain inside a little longer—information that reached him via Pirrongelli on 3 October. The investigating judge in Marilyn Woolhead's case was sympathetic, lenient and willing to interpret the law liberally; but the investigating judge in the Bergers' case, Judge Verasani, was fascist, with a reputation for slowness and severity. So the date predicted for everyone's release—10 October—was chosen because it was when Verasani was due to go on holiday and when another judge could assume temporary responsibility and sign the release papers, as in fact happened.

The organisation and guidance for everyone's release came from the English consul, Anthony Baker, who from the beginning of September worked full-time on the case (although at one point he was transferred to Turin but refused to leave until the case had been resolved), making daily visits to the various *manicomios*, bringing special food for Carol, getting the lawyers together to work out a common strategy. But nothing could have been achieved unless considerable sums of money were paid to various key officials, notably the experts appointed to examine the evidence.

On 4 October, two days after Carol's operation, Bill was driven to the hospital to visit her. He was told he was only allowed to stay five minutes. Outside the room they took off Bill's handcuffs. A crowd of people—doctors, priests, police—were standing around the bed. At first Carol didn't recognise Bill—she was barely conscious. There weren't any chairs so he had to kneel on the floor beside her. He tried to talk to her, telling her what Pirrongelli had said—that she was going to be out in a day or so, that he was sure it would happen. Bill wasn't allowed to touch Carol because the doctors said she had typhus. They tried to talk to each other through the noise in the room, though Carol still couldn't believe that it was Bill. Then after five minutes Bill was told he had to leave—regulations, patient tired, etc. He dragged it out for a few more minutes. As he was led out of the door by more policemen, the doctor said that Carol would have to go to an isolation clinic because of the typhus.

This was the first time Bill had seen Carol in two months. She was in a terrible condition as though she had just come from Auschwitz—her whole face had collapsed, her arms were covered with severe bruises and she looked seventy years old. At the time it didn't occur to him that he wouldn't be allowed back to see her again.

Bill was driven back to S. Eframo *manicomio*, uncertain how long Carol would survive. Everyone kept telling him that she was all right, though intuitively he knew that she was dying. He sent her a letter, then an express letter, then a telegram; but she didn't reply. For three days he heard nothing, then on 8 October he wrote a letter to Carol that reached her at the same time as he did —seven hours before she died and when she was already in a coma.

It's been thirty hours that I have not smoked, thirty hours when I have thought the whole time about you. Every time I want to light a cigarette I think that if I don't smoke Carol will be better and so it is a joy not to smoke. I'm only afraid that after a few days I'll lose the desire to smoke. Today the consul stopped by. He told me he tried to see you but they wouldn't let him in because of the contagious disease. He told me you've been transferred to the Incurabile hospital—what a name for a hospital. The secretary telephoned today and they told him you're still in a critical condition. I feel it in my heart but I also feel your incredible strength and I'm trying to send you mine. It's so much more difficult than the last time when we were separated only by the Atlantic ocean which after all is not such a formidable obstacle. Today there's a much more imposing barrier between us—the abyss of the lack of human compassion which is confined by the rules. . . . To fly we need things that are strong, but also light and delicate—like you, my love.

At a meeting with Lautz on 8 October, Bill expressed concern that Carol should be transferred to another hospital so soon after the operation. He also asked if permission could be given for him to stay with Carol longer than the prescribed five minutes. Lautz told him that nothing could be done. In fact, Carol was moved from the Cardarelli to the Incurabile hospital on 7 October. Later Bill was told that when she was brought in she was naked except for a thin sheet. In view of the fact that the doctors said, after she died, that she had pneumonia, one can only suppose that throughout those critical days she was treated with the same kind of carelessness reserved for criminal patients.

On 10 October Bill sent roses to Carol, and a doctor from S. Eframo *manicomio* who visited Carol in the Incurabile hospital returned to say she was well. Two days later a doctor came to examine Bill, apparently to find out if he was sane and under the influence of drugs. In the course of the examination the doctor asked Bill why he smoked so much. Bill asked if he was aware that his wife was between life and death. The doctor replied 'Oh yes, yes, of course.'

On 14 October Bill was driven to the Incurabile hospital for another five-minute visit. A policeman still stood guard outside the door to Carol's ward. The doctor couldn't understand how she remained alive for so long. He kept saying 'Her heart is incredibly strong.' Bill wrote about the last hours with Carol in a diary:

14 October. At 1 o'clock they take me to Carol. She's not conscious, little hope, horrible. I must go back after five minutes. I have to ask them three times not to try to slap her awake. I plead with the priest to do something to let me stay in the name of God. I turn to the doctor and ask him to confirm that the only slightest hope is if I might give her the will to live. He nods. He's told me that she's been in a coma for 36 hours and marvels that her heart is so incredibly strong. Says she was practically dead on arrival. Seems she also caught pneumonia. The general opinion is that only the American consul might get special permission for me to stay. The priest goes to phone but returns saying the consul could not be reached.

They take me back to the *manicomio* (mental asylum). I plead with the secretary to do something. He talks about maybe tomorrow. I say tomorrow is too late. The *carabinieri* agree. The secretary gets on the phone—after many calls he gets extra permission for me to stay with Carol. I return at 4 o'clock. She has no blanket, it is freezing cold. They say they cannot close the window because she needs oxygen.

The nurse finally brings a blanket and I get them to change the sheets which are soaked. The other patients tell me they had brought her in naked—one of them had lent her the little cotton jacket she is wearing. My roses stand on the bureau. A fellow patient tells me how Carol laughed and cried when she got them, how she was in ecstasy. It was the day before she went into a coma. 11 o'clock . . . it is all over.

He had stayed kneeling by her bed for seven hours, holding her, stroking her hair, reading letters he had written to her but which she hadn't been able to open.

It was the end of their journey together in squalor, appalling suffering and anonymity.

What happened to Bill in those last seven hours is indirectly communicated through his diary. In that time Carol lay dying in front of his eyes and he was powerless to bring her back or go with her. He could only ask why, why, why . . . until the question became an answer. He knew that something in him had let her go or allowed it to happen and that he was partly to blame—the open door, the careless freedom of the house, the determination to remain 'cool' instead of fighting . . . The suffering of that knowledge, which in those last hours and later became exaggerated to the point of suicide, cannot be imagined. Another emotion, apart from the self-inflicted judgment, predominated in those hours—a sense that Carol was the victim not of any one individual error of judgment or incompetence or deliberate evil but of the system operating in society in which most people are trapped in some form or other, in the dehumanising system to which the poor and non-conforming are sacrified in the name of so-called 'higher' goal—expediency, justice, productivity, etc. The endless cycle of atrocities or 'accidents' some of which are reported or protested against but most of which remain nameless, ordinary events which are all too easily taken for granted, suppressed or forgotten. Ever since the doors of the *manicomios* had closed on them, Bill and Carol had been forced to struggle against 'the system' which had suddenly and sinisterly trapped them during those twenty-four hours after the police raid. It was a futile struggle—the 'system' granted Bill the right to be with Carol when she was already dying, but not for her life to have been saved.

A few minutes after Carol died a doctor came into the room. He said brusquely 'She's dead', then pointed at Bill and said aggressively 'Who the hell's this?'

Bill said he was Carol's husband. The doctor nodded and told him to wait outside.

Bill picked up a pile of loose papers from beside Carol's bed, gave her a last kiss, walked past the guards at the door and sat on a bench in the corridor. The papers he had gathered up consisted of his letters to her, a brief diary she had kept of her long nights in the asylum and an exercise book with nothing written in it except a title *The Final Judgment on Us of Ourselves* in Carol's hand-writing. Five minutes after she died, he started writing in the otherwise empty notebook:

> You did not give any sign of recognising me. Perhaps you did but couldn't. I held your hand and sat by your bed till now. I tried to get you to keep fighting . . . to keep living. But I understand you no longer wanted to, and at 11 o'clock I had to let you go. My love, I know you are better now— you are free. But I am not. I cannot conceive of it ever again without you. I am not grieving because you have left me. I grieve that it had to be so horrible for you, so pointless. I grieve that a last moment of conscious recognition of togetherness was denied us. I love you, my love, you are so beautiful. Even in the ugly hands of death that is here. Death of spirit or is it lack of birth? It is over.
>
> Forgive them father for they know not what they do.
>
> This book is our last togetherness, our last love-making.

It was the beginning of a diary in which he made daily entries for the next six months. In all he filled nineteen notebooks—the first which he picked up by Carol's bedside, covering the first seven days after her death and the last ending the night before his trial in Salerno.

Part Two: *The Final Judgment on Us of Ourselves*
(William Berger's prison diary)

You will travel unrestricted in my heart in the
vast universe of my dreams.
The Diary

7. 15–21 *October*

15 October   Today is the first day you couldn't share with me, my love. Today is the first day our love must exist in my breast alone. It is the ultimate unification—the coming together totally in one cell. It is a painful union, just as birth is a painful separation. There is a promise of temporal joy as my capacity to love has been doubled for the remainder of my time. You have made the ultimate trip through the portal of death. It is the first experience you could not share with me until my time comes. When my time comes I shall think of you and we will find the completion of our union.

I speak to you with silly finite words; to you who are already in the infinite they may have no meaning. I speak to you that has remained within me.

They asked me just now to write a note of thanks to the investigating judge for letting me stay the last seven hours with you instead of the usual five minutes when you were dying. You never knew about it because you were no longer conscious. The director and the secretary did their utmost, calling all over from Rome to Salerno, finally reaching the investigating judge at his home—all of which I appreciate all the more because actually they are on the 'other side'; but I had to tell them that I could not do it until I felt it. I could not commit, at least today, an act of hypocrisy. I could not help the investigating judge assuage his conscience even if he has need of my help. I could not in my own conscience buy a little personal advantage with your suffering—you who were always the soul of courage and straightforward honesty. I could not do that to my memory of you.

I tried to explain to them that love is the first law; that we must not bow to the other laws when they deny us to love; that an act of humanitarianism is performed for oneself and does not require a thank you that is not honestly felt; that if the customs and the laws are to be changed, we must begin by not bowing to them no matter what the cost. Only then can they be changed; only then can the props of hypocrisy which support them be destroyed. A new system built on the same rotten foundations is bound to collapse.

It was probably neither wise nor fruitful, but I cannot help that. You taught me to be straightforward and honest and I must make your new home in my heart livable and comfortable and beautiful for you. Nothing else is of importance.

Just now the consul arrived. He started to shake my hand but I withdrew mine and said to him quite privately 'I have no hard feelings Mr. Lautz, but I don't think Carol would like me to shake hands with you today.' He was livid but managed to control it in good hypocritical consular fashion. I am doing all the wrong, unwise, stupid and eminently right things today. I know of course that he could not allow himself to understand, that far from making a convert I made an even more entrenched enemy. Someday I may have to change tactics to convert people to our cause but today I can't and I hope I won't because tactics have an insidious way of changing causes.

He had to ask me where I wanted you buried and if he should make the arrangements on my behalf—that is, would I pay for it, I suppose. I had it in mind to say that it was not my concern since as I understood it, it is the murderer's responsibility to hide the body, but then I thought of your mother and my own bourgeois sentiments in the future, etc. and simply said 'I don't think it matters since the people Carol would like to have at her funeral are all in jail.' There followed a question and answer period as to who your friends were, with the information that some of them had been released but most of them had to leave the country.

I asked him 'Why? If they were guilty why were they released and if not guilty and the crime committed against them, why would they be expelled?'[1]

Perfect consular reply; 'It seems those are the laws and regulations in this country. The Italian government has every right to expel whoever they wish from their country. We have no prerogative in that matter.'

This created a little confusion because it occurred to me if I would not be allowed in Italy it would be awkward for you to

1. See Diary Notes pp. 275–276.

be buried here; but since it's your funeral I said 'I think Carol would have no great preference but wouldn't mind Praiano. It was the last place where she was happy.'

All these profound personal sentiments of mine naturally bounced off his bureaucratic shield and were accepted as the usual mortuary clichés that must be listened to with feigned respect. I think he must have 'American consular official' tattooed on his cock! No possible convert there.

I said, 'But don't you as a representative of the U.S. government have any thoughts in such a matter—even if you can take no action? I saw President Nixon here on T.V. and he said the American Fleet was in the Mediterranean to protect freedom and liberty in this historic area.'

Lautz: 'I did not come here to have a discussion.'

I: 'Mr. Lautz, I think the time will come some day when you will have to think and have a discussion with yourself about many matters that are not the immediate prerogative of your office. I think some day you will have to think of your duties as a human being.'

Lautz: 'I am well aware of my duties and obligations as a United States consular official.'

I kid you not. I cannot swear to the verbatim totality of the whole conversation but the responses of Mr. Lautz are word for word. Caricature out of the rule book! They still ring in my unbelieving ears.

I: 'I am not talking to you as a consular official. I am talking to you as a man. I am telling you that one day you will have to think like a man about your actions.'

Lautz: 'Now I realise that your wife's death was very tragic, but she was in the hands of competent medical authorities. I am not a doctor, that is not my responsibility.'

I: 'I told you, Mr. Lautz, on 6 August that my wife was ill, that she needed to be removed from the insane asylum. Carol sent you a telegram five days before her operation pleading utmost urgency that you come immediately. I have your letter answer to that plea which is the most outrageous official bullshit I have ever seen. Twenty days later she was dead. I think some day somewhere you will have to admit to yourself some responsibility in this matter, as a human being.'

Lautz: 'I am not a doctor. I am not competent to judge in these matters.'

Next came the question of my attending the funeral. I said 'I don't think Carol would like to see me there with handcuffs.'

'Well, what if we could arrange that you not be handcuffed?'

I said 'I don't think she would like to see a *carabinieri* guard.'

'Well, what if they were in plain clothes?'

Isn't it amazing how much the American consular officials can accomplish when the mission is death and not simply life.

I said 'I don't think where she is at that Carol would be that easily fooled.'

'Then I take it you do not wish to attend the funeral.'

'If the choice is between my absence and the presence of cops Carol would prefer my absence. I speak of course of Carol's sentiments symbolically transferred into my own images.'

A clearing of throat. 'Yes well I think that would be stretching it too far. I don't believe it would be possible.'

I knew I would reach the limit of his omnipotent powers even in this field of speciality. 'I will then be willing to forgo my . . . er. . . .'

Mr. Lautz: 'Rights. . . .'

I: '. . . privileges in the matter.'

Some discussion about his ability to find your mother's address in files here or in Washington. My God, how efficiently the old machinery works for what it's built for. We parted with stilted nods.

I have become so used to communicating with you over impassable barriers that death does not even seem such a profound change.

It seems the released are David, the two 'English girls' (Widget and Desna), but not yet released Miss Woolhead and Allain, who he was certain had to leave the country. Still held are the German girl, the French girl. . . .

I interjected 'Petra and Florence?'

He replied: 'I'm not familiar with their names, and the coloured boy, Ted something.'

Can you imagine an American still referring to a spade as a 'coloured boy'? I'm sure he is no older than I am, in spite of the little silver in his curly blond hair to match the silver in his twinkleless blue eyes.

I hope I don't have to listen to the doctor's self-justifications, although they may have an autopsy performed. 'My God,' I said, 'they really have to find somebody guilty for everything to excuse the rest of us—when in reality we are all guilty.'

I'm not sure how far that spontaneous truism went really over his head or through it.

A few more phrases perhaps, I'm not sure. I am trembling as I write this but I wasn't then. That amazes me. I never even raised my voice. I realised all that could possibly be said, had been said. I saluted him *addio* with: 'You are nothing but a goddamned I.B.M. machine, I cannot talk with you.' With that I terminated the interview, shaking hands with his interpreter friend who had suffered through all this in embarrassed silence and from whom I sensed some shame and sympathy, and left the room. If that is what is running the Sixth Fleet, that is protecting freedom and liberty in the Mediterranean . . . God help freedom, God help liberty, God help all of us!

One more incident that was quite accidental but very actors studioish. Just after I had withheld my handshake the little priest appeared out of nowhere, and since his sympathy has always seemed truly genuine, I unhesitatingly and spontaneously accepted his condolence. Only as I finished I realised the zing that this counterpoint had produced in Mr. Lautz's otherwise implacably controlled eyes—unpardonable snub of a representative of the United States government by a lousy hippy! No doubt if he gets the chance he will make me pay dearly. But I don't care my love, if you're pleased.

I tried so hard for a tiny glimpse of recognition in your staring coma-filled eyes last night during our common battle against death. If only I could have had that glimpse my present battle for love over resentment, blame and hate would be less difficult. I did use you in my discussion with the director to pull rank, but I didn't think you'd mind. I told him I considered myself Italian—I live here—I pay the taxes here and I suffered the injustice, I think I've earned the right. A most difficult right for a *straniero* to get conceded by an Italian. I went on to say that I thought I had earned the right also to speak for love against laws that restricted it, to the extent that I am desperately trying to win love over hate and judgment in my own heart at this moment. It's hard to put down a man who by his own standards has made a sincere and herculean effort, for not having done enough. People like the director are an entirely different can of peas than the consul. People who sincerely try in their own hearts are convertible, no matter how impossible it may seem. People who are terrified of their own hypocrisy are a maginot line. They must be outflanked.

God, how right it all seems and how beautiful, if only I didn't have to do without you approving and guiding and comprehending it somewhere. I feel so terribly utterly alone. They have cut the guts out of my soul. It must be something the way you felt after the hysterectomy. I weep for you for that, as I haven't before. My poor glorious darling. It would be easy to take if you were still here. I can't spend the rest of my life writing dead letters to keep feeling alive.

I want to die too. I suppose what I mean is that I want to be dead too. Here in this insanity I can't even say it. They would think I'm crazy and tie me to a bed. Here they think everyone normal is crazy. But the craziest notion of all—that your way of dying was not evitable—they think is normal. Perhaps I am dead. They say it will pass, that no grief lasts forever. That's crazy too. It's because I know that no grief lasts forever, because I know it will pass that I want to be dead too, so it won't 'pass'—but simply won't exist. How sweet a thought, not to exist. How sweet a wish, to be like you: not be.

I can't stand their condolences, even when they're sincere. They all think I've only lost a wife. At least that part is good— being here in this cold cheerless place. Death is more acceptable here. Death is the absolute pure beautiful perfection of the horribly deformed ugly counterfeit that is this place. I think in the initial grief it is easier to be reminded of our mutually shared horrors than of our joys. That will be the really difficult part of the amputation. I hope they let me stay here for a while longer; here it is at least bearable. I hope they don't torture me by offering me a quick release, to ease their consciences. I don't think so—they do not have the sensitivity. But if they do, how can I not turn it down? How can I pay the ransom with your suffering, with my fathomless loss?

I don't care now what they do to me but I'll care later and that knowledge may make me a coward today. I don't have your single-minded straight courage that way. I'm always aware of tomorrow. Now I don't even have the courage of the coward's fear that you might put me down. If I go on trial I might prosecute them, but they'll get even and really prosecute me for it if I insist on a trial. That is the real guerilla theatre though, ain't it? Not just running off to the *estero* and writing pamphlets.

Today I still feel the warmth of your breathless body and I think I could do it. In a few days I will have had time to rationalise, to be sensible, to bank my fires.

What rankles me about Lautz is that I probably helped him off the hook of his conscience by being 'nasty' . . . in *his* mind. What the hell, I couldn't be devious just to make him 'feel bad'. It wouldn't have done any good anyway, only fed my revenge instinct, if it had even been possible. On the other hand, if he's able to slip off that lightly he can't be helped—at least not by me. He'll probably organise your lonely funeral, send me the bill and convince himself he's done *more* than his duty.

I would have imagined it to be horrible to have to endure such enduring grief without privacy, without a dark hole to crawl into to nurse the aching wound of the soul, the bloody amputated stump; to let the hatred of the surgeon out into the open and kill it or kill him or kill oneself; to have the freedom to allow this terrible thought to play itself out in fantasy. This is not possible here—the spy holes are always open; the light never entirely extinguished; the 'compassionate helpful human' never more than a few paces away . . . all of which makes it difficult at times to find one's God. Here God is classified—he is Catholic, Protestant or Jewish; he is clearly depicted, clearly defined, clearly visible and tangible and therefore non-existent, in the sense of his utter infinity.

Yet somehow it is not so horrible to endure the enduring grief without privacy. Here in the no-privacy world, there is the privacy of no pretence. In the sense that there is no freedom, there is freedom. Strange that where privacy is limited by prohibition, where freedom is limited by bars there is infinite privacy, infinite freedom. Where God is limited by his idol image there is infinite

God; there is infinity turned inwards, the infinity of the micro universal.

I just read a long detailed account of your death and the precise events and causes leading up to it. It is a total defamation not only of you (of course they found the guilty party—you, *the victim*), not only of the facts pertinent to such an interpretation but even as if for pure exercise. Suffice it to say that hardly a line passes without an easily contravertible untruth. It is even quite difficult to find a blacker person than our dear Edward Joseph Theodore to describe as a mulatto! I am glad you don't have to read it unless of course it might have made you laugh. If however such incredible laxness (I cannot even assume it is totally base in intention) is possible with such easily verifiable local truths, how can we possibly give credence to reports on the Middle East or Vietnam or such totally partisan issues as politics? If the news media have not the slightest sense of responsibility, never mind propriety, what is the possible significance of democracy which is totally dependent on an informed public? These things never interested you too much and I am sure do not now as they do not interest me now.

My reaction is much more personal. They defame you even in death. I might accept for the sake of convenience, due to a feeling of futility, an earlier termination of my incarceration in exchange for accepting a false guilt. I cannot accept that choice for you who can no longer defend yourself. Even if you no longer care, the part of you that is now united in me, the part of you that continues in my body, its existence on this side of eternity, that part of you for which I am now responsible, I cannot allow to be defamed without a struggle. If I did I would corrupt a part of my memory of you which is my dearest possession. I would corrupt my self-respect, all those things we blatantly call honour—not the 'honour' of pride, not the 'honour' which hides fear, but the 'honour' without which a soul cannot grow, cannot live just as a body cannot live without breath. I must stand trial at least to attempt to prove your innocence if not mine.

16 October   It doesn't seem possible that one day has passed. It seems like an eternity without you. My sense of time has stood still. Each moment is an eternity in itself. Yesterday I fasted. I do not want to follow a formal ritual of mourning that may formalise my natural grief. My tears are sporadic. They are more tears of joy for the beauty to have known you, to have loved you, to have been loved by you than tears of sadness that bemoan the abyss your leaving has left in my heart.

I know that you want me to laugh and to sing and to dance for you and I promise you it will come in due time. As yet it seems absurd for me to brush my teeth in a world that is without you! Just now I tried to play checkers. I could only finish one game. I have played too many here before and after writing my daily letter to you. They are beginning to come back to me one by one —the ones you never got to read. The last one that arrived at the hospital I read to you in your coma. Did you hear any of it in those shadows of death where you were wandering? If only you could have given me an infinitesimal sign of recognition. Oh God, why ask such small 'if onlys'. They are as impossible as the big ones. It seems so futile, so outrageous to arrive so late, to be able to do nothing but hold your lifeless hand. Yet when I try to imagine what it would be like not to have had the last touch of your warmth, the last kiss of life from your dead lips, then I consider it one of the greatest good fortunes of my life.

Today the vice-consul (I didn't know he was vice, I would have guessed him to be more versa) came back. This time I made a point to shake his hand. He relaxed ever so slightly but there was a difference. Perhaps there is hope of reaching him. Anyway the arrangements for the Praiano funeral are being made—the under-taker wants three hundred dollars and is willing to wait for it. There is not much hope I shall receive a *liberta provisorio* (the only condition under which I declared I would be able to attend) because the 'analysis' has not yet been made! That only seems dramatically fitting and proper for the final act, which is now beginning. Your 'remains' will be properly certified and put to their 'final resting place'. They still have not understood that your remains have long since been certified and put in their final resting place, in the most private corner of my heart where they belong.

I have resumed playing checkers with Blasi. It was not as difficult as I assumed after the first attempt. I am already begin-ning to resume our life together. I had some pangs when I started eating again today. It was chicken, wine and *dolce* which the wife of the director distributed to everyone for her son's birthday. I misjudged her at first. Her heart is in the right place. It was delicious.

I am glad I am in this place with the 'bad' people— the murderers, the robbers, the thieves and the guards. They have an intimate knowledge of what human suffering is and their compassion is real and acceptable, even if they cannot understand the extent of my pain. It is something I prefer to keep private anyway, just between the two of us. You are the only one who could have understood. Strange but now that you are gone your spirit is closer, more tangible to me than when you were breathing a few kilometres distant. I feel your presence, almost physical, in whatever I do or dream. My pee had blood in it today. My cock is grieving for you.

I am still torturing myself with the 'what ifs'. What if I had pleaded more eloquently, what if I had grovelled and begged more humbly. They are bitter thoughts but it is a necessary trip that will allow me to overcome the bitterness in my heart for all the 'what ifs' the others did not do. What if I had offered to assume total responsibility, admitted to whatever crime they wanted to accuse us of in exchange for your transfer to a private clinic. It does not matter. It has all passed. It is all part of our destiny, yours and mine.

I look forward now to finishing the brief time that is left me. How many births, lives and deaths will we have to go through before we meet again? Death would be easy to accept if it came now. That's why I do not seek it now. I want to share the fullness of that experience with you. The beautiful thing is that I no longer have any fear. I no longer fear death nor pain nor boredom. They will all bring me closer to you. I feel terribly free. There is no longer any anxiety about anything. I no longer mind not making love. I no longer object to getting old. I can accept everything now that I have accepted losing you. I can go with the flow. My dearest darling, I never realised how very much I loved you.

17 October   I have written a short synopsis of the important events. I am trying to get it out with a letter to Perrone, asking him to try to find someone with the courage to print the truth.

The lying hypocrisy of the newspapers even in the sacred face of death is insufferable. How horrible it must be to be incapable of looking into the mirror of truth. What terror they must feel when their hour comes. You were so very fortunate, at least in that regard. You never feared to look into the mirror, even when what you saw terrified you.

But I will make them look by all that is holy to me. I swear to you I will make them look into that mirror, because they must. I will shout all our most beautiful private thoughts of these horrible months. I will shout them out. I will turn on all the lights I can find till they no longer have the strength not to hear, not to see, not to think. They will find their little rationalisations. They may protect themselves behind their barbed-wire hearts from the wrong enemy. The truth may not penetrate their defences where it might do them some good, but they will have seen it, they will have heard it, they will have had to contemplate it. The more they continue to cling to their lies, the more eloquent, the more blindingly bright will the truth blare forth. This is the most vital purpose of my now *senza-te* existence.

The weather has turned cold. I shiver in my 5 August clothes. I never asked for warm clothes to be sent me. After all, it was always to be just a few more days till they finished the analysis—they haven't finished it yet—but they're supposed to in just a few more days! It seems the judge turned down a request for *more* time! I shiver, I am cold—cold like the grave, cold like you, my love. I welcome it, I embrace the shivering cold that makes me . . . like you, since I can no longer embrace your soft radiant warmth.

Oh my darling, how I wish you could have been on stage for the final act of this oh so tragic farce. It is all too predictable to be truly good theatre—a second-rate road company with a cliché-ridden play. I was just visited by the magistrate. Dang! Can you guess what it was about? They have now begun an inquest into who is responsible for your death. The same old sleight of hand corny stage trick: find the guilty victim so we can all be pure and innocent. The *procuratore* (of Naples this time) was much more *simpatico*. Naturally we are now witnesses or are we accusers? But the game is the same. I tried to say what I really feel—that we are all guilty, that justice is not 'finding a victim' or finding the absence of 'crime'. They will, I'm sure, decide on the latter, only this time no one will rot in a *manicomio* jail until they decide on *mancanza di indizi*. How I wish they could pull it off really, that the analysis will prove there was no crime, that presto! you will step sparkling out of the wings and the poor destroyed body I held in our last embrace was really only soapsuds.

In short I tried to explain that justice in human terms can only be valid to the extent that it reduces suffering; that their concept of simply adding suffering on suffering, pain on pain, murder on murder is as mistaken as trying to avoid nuclear war by building nuclear bombs. But the secretary who writes down the deposition is a machine that can only write down the 'facts'. Everything else is irrelevant and is dismissed with a yes yes yes and an impatient wave of the hand. They asked me, after the 'facts', if I had any specific accusations against anyone. I was sorely tempted to play for the cheap laughs instead of the dramatic truth—to put all those Pozzuoli doctors, guards and nuns on the other side of the bars and let the *detenuti* run the place for a few months. I think you would somehow return to the boards for a script like that.

You see how very much I miss you. Who else can I tell this to, who would understand? You see how utterly lost and lonely I am without you. As usual, my darling, you are not listening. As always, my darling, you are too lost in your own scene.

But no, I simply said that the only person I wanted to accuse is myself because I did not plead eloquently enough to be heard, did not beg and grovel enough to be paid attention to. Oh dear, how easily they translated that into their own judicial language. . . . 'You mean, it's because due to restrictions to your legal position that you were unable to secure proper medical and hospital care for your wife as you wished to do.'

I gave up, just nodded my head in 'Yeah, that's it' style. Before I knew what was happening they were nominating Pirrongelli to represent me if there is a trial.

Sure, why not? Why not, why not, why not? Why? Why are you not here? Why are you . . . not? Why . . . not? Not is like *todt*, *todt* is like *tot*, like the *tot* of your own you wanted so much, so very much. Instead we have given birth to a *processo* (trial), which is like cesso, which is like chess—where the cold ruthless player always wins over the emotional one, who plays with his heart.

What I do have to prepare myself for is the opportunity when I will be allowed to speak through the television that projects its laser beams into the privacy of homes, into the privacies of millions of hearts, who over their private *spaghetti* plates feel at least somewhat secure, are at least somewhat offguard of their fears and so can be reached. I now feel sure I shall have that opportunity. It is a God-given opportunity, paid for with your death. I must not waste it. It is the guerilla theatre you yearned for.

Jimi Hendrix, John Dos Passos, Carol Lobravico—all in one turn of the moon. Why are all the beautiful people flying away to glory? Is it a sign of impending spring or a warning of imminent disaster? I cannot read the omens, but I have learned to accept all of destiny. I no longer fear. I am free to tread the lonely road that remains. I am free with your remains.

18 October   It is Sunday. Of course they have done nothing further about me and I am certain they will continue to take their time. Now more than before. The judge will not grant me a *liberta provisorio* I no longer seek before the analysis is in. The analysis will not finish sooner than the allowed thirty days. The consul will not raise his squeaky voice to allow me to attend your funeral copless as I requested. Dr Testa will not now recant his 'error'. Not one of the fifty policemen will step forward and give the lie to the story that was abroad concerning the circumstances in which they found us that fateful night, to which they were all witnesses. The lie which gave suspicion to the 'proofs'. The legislators will not admit the absurdity of their rules and the experts who know better will not find the courage to shed light on the ignorance about *droga* on which the witch hunt is based. The *squadra mobile* will not admit their anti-drug campaign is a silly theatrical farce used for political purposes, used for the power game.

I shall make it very difficult for them to ignore it. One by one. How silly they are. After all, their sin is not so great, not so tragic. It is the result that is tragic. A result none of them ever intended. They are guilty not of your death, they are guilty only of being too afraid to love and so they continue being afraid. If they could lift the fig leaves, they would discover that original sin is as simple, is as human as a cock, and they could begin their road to salvation from guilt, salvation from shame, salvation to glory, they could begin to make love. But they will now blame the doctors, blame the system, blame destiny. They will even gladly blame each other. Blame the *droga*. They will minimise the importance, plea for the inevitability of death, hide behind destiny. They will not blame themselves. They will not correct the wrong they have done to their own souls.

If I truly wanted vengeance I would not interfere. But I do not cry for vengeance, I cry for what I have lost—for you who is love. I cry out for the free melodious life-giving flow of love, against the restricting constipated strangling clutch of fear, which is death for all mankind. Not your kind of death which is natural, which is a road to regenerated life on the next plane of our evolution. But the death caused by fear—that death is not divine, it is man-made, man-failed. It is total and absolute because it destroys the soul, destroys its promise of love, its glorious promise of God.

I wonder what it will be like the next time I fuck? It was never a problem for me when you were alive, when you were in the same room, the same bed. Not even the times you objected. But now the prospect frightens me, and yet I look forward to it—not because I am suffering the supposed sex starvation of the prisoner, which I find non-existent. Here I am asexual. I find the result of the castration effect of prison is not at all the greedy thirst for perversion which so excites the non-prison fantasies. I find it a rather pseudo-romantic distortion of 'liberty'. No, I both fear and look forward to the experience of the first fuck, because it will be a painful reunion with you. I know you will be there, I know you will not object, I know you will welcome it, as you will welcome me to laugh again, to sing again, to dance and to fly. I know you will help me in all of it. You will be there.

I remember a T.V. programme in Paris. A man who had lived in India for something like thirty years was trying to explain what yoga is—that the guru is the guide but that the mountain must be climbed by oneself; that the search for the basic truth is so difficult, not because the truth is complicated, but because it is so eminently simple. It is invariably something we have known all our lives but never really saw, because it seemed unimportant—

not unlike the man who searches for his car and keeps walking past it, seeing it but not seeing.

On the mountain I've been climbing I have seen such clear visions as never before. It all seems so simple, so pure, and I *have* known it all my life. It is the simple message of Jesus. We all know he said love, love, love is the answer, and we said 'Oh yes, yes, yes, how beautiful, why doesn't everybody love me? Oh wicked, wicked world, you have denied my saviour!' And we forgot about love except when it was biologically motivated or . . . convenient. But he said 'Love one another, love is salvation, love is the way to God.' Jesus is incompatible with envy, greed and jealousy. He is capable of anger but not of hate; he is understanding but not compromising; he preaches but he does not judge; he is not afraid; he is dedicated but not competitive; he is rigid but he is no hypocrite. He is rigid on only one thing, one basic truth: love, do not fear, and you shall have eternal life. He is not proud or arrogant or dogmatic. If he said he was the son of God, he also told us we are all brothers. He is humble but not self-effacing. He does not destroy the temples of others, he simply protects them from corruption, by driving out the merchants; but he does not preach in them. He does not need to overthrow Caesar. He does not need to defrock the high priests, but he does not seek them out to convert them either. He simply accepts and ignores them. He knows salvation cannot come by overthrowing them, since they will always be replaced by others. He knows they cannot bring us salvation from their lofty plane of power, so he does not convert them to enlist their aid. He does not ask for new legislation, for reform, for flood controls. He knows these things will shrivel away, will be unimportant once the human heart has conquered its fears and accepted its love. So he speaks to the human heart. To each one of us. He is the prophet of Moses, he is the brother of Buddha, but he is only a guru, a guide. Each one of us must climb the mountain. God is omnipresent in every living organism, in every cell of creation. He is so omnipresent that he has no definition. We cannot distinguish him with our eyes. He can be 'seen' only with our hearts.

How silly of us to try to define God, to describe him. How Lilliputian to try to tie him down to sight, to reason, to metaphor. That is the meaning of 'Blessed is he who believes but has not seen'. In the blindness of their pride they interpret it as meaning that belief can be dogmatically transferred from the superior intellect, from the superior faith to the inferior. Did not Jesus say: We are all equal in the sight of God?

You who have passed through the great door, who are perhaps now in a state of such total simplicity, may smile. Oh God, I do hope you can still be amused; that amusement and beauty like love are part of the eternal, part of the divine. You may smile at my fumbling joy at finding a simplicity in the fact that it takes me all these lines to say: God is love. A phrase that in microscopic terms is in itself an eternity of mere words that try to define, that try to explain a something . . . that can only be felt.

Have you already begun your new embryonic growth in some new womb? Or is it no longer necessary? How I wish I could know. I remember how we used to talk of reincarnation. You believed and you made me believe. I said it was unimportant because without conscious remembrance it would no longer be you. I know now I was wrong. I knew it when I embraced your still warm lifeless body. What conceited importance we place in so absurd a thing as a body. Your body was nothing without you. I was merely trying to hold you back for one more precious instant of eternity; but I only held a pressed primrose that may be an aid to memory but is an insult to the blooming flower that was you, that is you in whatever form you have chosen to inhabit. I, the Orpheus, shall be looking for you in whatever form, in whatever infinity of forms you now exist. I shall find you with the divining rod that is you encased in my heart.

I believe they think my protestations of not hating the poor instruments of your suffering are less than genuine. They do not yet know how utterly unimportant that all is compared to finding you. They do not yet know how utterly unimportant it is to me what they think. They do not yet know how free you have made me with your love.

Sunday here is still the best. There is no anxiety that the outside world will burst in. We can be alone. I am now quite calm. My eyes still fill with tears sporadically, but the tears are more soothing, more beautiful than painful. It is only terrible still when the outside world bursts in; when I have to deal with your murderers in whose power my stupid body still is. I do not speak to them because they control my body; I speak to them because I do not want to let them off the hook, because I must reach them to make them see, to give significance to what might otherwise have been pointless futility. I couldn't stand that. Yet when I weep before them it hurts—not because I'm ashamed, but because my tears are too precious for them to understand. It is pearls cast before swine. My tears are the part of you that is me, because I had to part from you because of them. What is beautiful here is that we are alone, where my tears bring me closer to you who understand. Down there—downstairs—makes me more aware of my utter loneliness.

19 October   Today they gave me a note from Pirrongelli—left yesterday with mail from Jaquotte and Yaguel. I think it means he's on his way to Salerno. The others are all free. I am glad. A week ago the news would have filled me with joy. My heart would have started beating with the hope of seeing you again, of holding you in my arms and helping you recover from the operation. It would have made me dance and sing then stop for fear of being disappointed but beating all the while full blast. Today it leaves me indifferent. It has no meaning anymore except that I may be expelled—expelled from the safe private cell of my sorrow, forced to face that insane reality outside . . . to begin to cope . . . to have to consider the opportunity of punching Mr. Lautz on the nose.

Yaguel thinks it likely I will be in Paris, in America. Quite likely. After all, it doesn't much matter where I am. I should like to see Petra and the others. I should like to share our grief, our memories. Aside from that I have no desires. I am so free I shall just go with the flow or stay with the stagnation that is here. I shall talk for those who are able to hear. I do all that, here, now. It will be a small difference outside. The others are free, only you and I remain in prison. We who are so free that prison is meaningless. It is the first 'just' thing that has happened in so many months.

Now they won't let me have your things, your personal things. In *nome della repubblica* they must establish your 'heirs'. They must be correct, they must not make mistakes . . . with things! It seems you had with you a *ghitarra* of a *certo valore*. How can they know? How can they know who cannot sing, who cannot dance, who cannot hear with their hearts how much *valore* had your precious *ghitarra*—when they were torturing you, when they were keeping me from you, you from me? How can they know who cannot love, who cannot feel, how much *valore* your personal 'you' had for me? The secretary was much surprised you had a *ghitarra*. Wouldn't it have been better, he asked, if you had left it at home? Had you no place to leave it? He didn't ask if it wouldn't have been better to have left you at home. It seems *ghitarras* are of a *certo valore*. They must be kept in safe places, they must not be used in prisons. It seems it is against the rules. Rules are necessary to protect *ghitarras* from harm. *Ghitarras* are of a *certo valore*. He does not know that *ghitarras* have no *valore* when they are not played, that life has no *valore* when it is not sung.

20 October   In all your letters your main concern was that I be released. In all my letters my main concern was that you take care of yourself. It's almost like the O. Henry story of the hairbrush and the watch chain. I know if you were here, you wouldn't have wanted me to write that letter to Pirrongelli.[2] You would tear it up because more important than anything to you is that I be free, that I be happy. You were always so utterly, singlemindedly concerned with that, but you were not always right. You left me for that very reason once and made me more unhappy than I have ever been—till now. And yet deep down we both understand and ultimately you were right as ultimately you were always right because you were always pure. That is why you are not tearing up my letter now. If you really wanted to, you would even now find a way.

You began this book with 'The Final Judgment on Us of Ourselves'. I read those words this morning and I knew I had to write the letter. Not because I give that much of a crap about some rigid idea of 'honesty' that usually satisfies only pride with a *grande geste* while violating the profound honesty of soul. The *geste* is of no vital importance to me at this moment, even in terms of 'The Final Judgment on Us of Ourselves'. But it is vital because without having made it, your words would create difficulty for me later on when I shall say what I want about compromise, about 'reasonableness' and about hypocrisy. If at that moment I think of your words, I shall not be a good enough actor to 'wing

2. See Diary Notes pp. 277-278.

it' without betraying ever so slightly to a severe critic a slight falter of insincerity; and it is always to the discriminating audience that we must direct the scene—not go for the cheap laugh, the melodramatic ploy to satisfy the groundlings.

Just read your letter again—the one of 16 August—the one they wouldn't send till so much later, the one that ends with Baudelaire's

Permit my heart intoxicate with spring
To plunge into your eyes as in a dream
And sleep beneath the shadow of your lashes.

And then: 'I love you. Caroline.' How prophetic. I can now go back to sleep and hope to see you there. I love you Caroline.

The world is up in arms for a man killed in *nome della Quebec 'libre'*. Since I came here the world has been up in arms so many times. They were up in arms when the passengers were kidnapped, when the passengers were threatened in *nome della Palestina*; up in arms when the tupamaros slew the Yankee cop in *nome della liberta*. It is not difficult to get them up in arms when, in the name of something, there is a death that is extraordinary. Your death was ordinary. How much more reason to be up in arms when murder is ordinary. Ordinary means not unusual, usual, means often repeated. Your case was different. You were the spirit of love. Perhaps they think it is less dangerous to lose a spirit of love than a spirit of war, a spirit of fear, a diplomat or a cop. They are up in arms not for the person but for what the person represents. They were not concerned for the passengers as persons; they were concerned for 'The Passengers'. Passengers represent travel, commerce, profit—that is important. You it seems were not important to them for what you represent. That is why your death was 'destiny'. That is why the slaying of the Yankee cop was an outrage. I do not want them to be up in arms about you. I want them to fold their arms about you in love as I do.

I keep wondering about the investigating judge. I have no wish to see his face, I am curious to see his face. What can he be like, this man who persists even now in playing a shabby god? This man who can have no possible grudge against us whom he never knew. And yet—he touched us so intimately with his cold hand of death and hate. How horrible it must be to have so much hatred, so much fear, to dispense it so generously, so impersonally, without grudge. How many similar sufferings must he have caused to have gained that surgeon-like attitude towards pain? A surgeon can pretend the right to save a life; what does the hard impersonal judge pretend to himself in the mirror when he does not see what is there? That he is saving the law? For which he can have no respect? How can the pimp believe in the whore's virginity? That he is curing the malady of crime? How can the doctor believe in the cure when all his patients die? When all his hospitals are fuller every day?

It is hard for me to imagine the hard judge. It is hard for me to conceive the word 'judge'. Yet he is a man; he must suffer pain from the cancer of his soul. I don't understand his suffering, because it is suffering I have not had to suffer. I have judged, I have hurt, but my judgment was thought-less. I have hurt with a grudge; when thought came I stopped judging; when grudge went I stopped hurting. I don't understand his suffering that has made him a robot. I can feel no compassion; I can feel only pity which makes me ashamed. I cannot write a thank-you note to a machine in which I cannot sense the man who I know is there only because reason tells me that what looks like a man is a man. But one cannot feel reason, one cannot think without feeling, one cannot note thanks without impulse.

In *nome della republica* you are now . . . not, you are deceased. The American embassy having ascertained this fact, will not now or ever again issue you a passport, will not allow you to travel. *Tu n'as pas le droit de voyager sans passport.* You who now have all *droit*, you who no longer need . . . *droit*. As usual they are only most superficially right and most intrinsically wrong. In *nome dell'amore* you are not *now*. You are forever un-ceasing. You will travel unrestricted in my heart, with my thoughts, in the vast universe of my dreams. The American embassy shall realise your presence when I make them realise their absence of humanity, of love.

I do hope that Donald Lautz has made his final exit today. I told him all I can tell him, but I could get nothing but a 'consular official' response. Though he was trembling, though his steely blue eyes blazed in their dead sockets, he could not get a human

word across his lips. He came to give me your brother's and
mother's address. Your brother called after hearing the news.
It seems there's been much publicity. He wants me to write to
him and not your mother! Oh dear, what can I say to a brother-
in-law whom I know only from his little-boy-photo and the fact
that you threw a glass of red wine at him at your father's funeral?
Your mother would be easier. At least I read some of her letters—
that you could not answer.

A beautiful letter from Debbie in which before the news she
writes how you were in her dream the 16th, I think. You must
have taken a slow flight or did you tarry with me—as I thought,
wished, hoped, felt—or did you have other stops to make on the
way? She writes how much she loves you. How beautiful she
had a chance to say it before she 'knew'.

Things are now happening fast. There was a man with a sad
frigid face, a messenger of doom, downstairs. He brusquely
handed me, with an 'I don't want to get involved' process-server
manner, a piece of paper. It seems the investigating judge did take
notice of the 'event' and sent the request for *liberta provisorio* to the
publico ministero who . . . turned it down. The curtain is not yet
down on the first scene of the final act. The entrance cue has
sounded for the shadow that has hovered in the wings since
before the beginning. On 16 October—the day I started eating
again, the day it seemed absurd to brush my teeth, the day I
found out officially that the consul was vice, the day he thought
we decided the final resting place of your remains, the day my
dearest darling I realised that I had never realised how very much
I love you—that day this man, this mere man, this bit player had
the effrontery, the presumption to think he could upstage with 'I
reject'. What poor, what incredibly poor . . . bad . . . taste.

The radio has absolved me this morning. It says I will be out
in a short time. Why did they not act in time when there was still
time? I could not care less. I have no 'time'. It is an incredibly
heady feeling you have given me when you took away with you
my fear. It's cool man, it is so cool. I speak, I act, I feel so straight,
so very straight from my heart, from your heart. I do not tremble,
I do not shout, I do not keep silent. I am above it all. I am not
anxious, I do not worry. I am with you.

I know I shall lose again this heady air of freedom—when I

am happy again, when I care again, when I have something to lose again. I know it will all happen; I cannot yet imagine it. But when it does start again, I shall remember this feeling of free, this feeling of you. I shall not go back to the prison of fear again. As yet I am still with death where there is no again, where 'again' is a sound with no meaning, an echo. But I'm beginning to think it, beginning to say it, beginning again, as I know you want me to, my love my love my love. My love is with you, comes from you, is you that is me.

21 October   It is the dawn of the seventh day. I have passed, with your help, my six days of mourning. I commit you, dear love, to the grave of my heart where I sense the first stirrings of a new spring, where the seeds we have sown with our love are beginning to stir, where we are consummated forever, where the flowers of your spirit will bloom in their glory in the next *primavera*. Till we meet again in the ultimate orgasm of beauty and knowledge and happiness that is God, I bid you *à dieu*. I love you My love My love My love. Billie.

8. 22–31 October

22 October The doctor came by to 'cheer me up': 'Are you glad you'll be getting out soon?'

I tell him it does not much matter now. 'This is as good a place as any to ferment my grief.' (*The prisoner does not want his freedom*).

'What do you think you'll do when you get out?'

'I'm not sure. Perhaps I'll try to save humanity from itself.' (*Megalomania*).

'Ah! Interesting. How do you propose to do that?'

'By trying to show men how to love one another.' (*Homosexual tendencies*).

'But you do have family and friends, don't you?'

'No one can fill the void Carol has left in my heart.' (*Afraid to face reality. No close contact of family and friends*).

'Come on now, cheer up. *Coraggio!* Wouldn't you like to go to a good restaurant and eat anything you want? Eh!'

'My hunger cannot be assuaged with food.' (*Lack of appetite*).

'You must learn to accept the misfortunes of life.'

'What is difficult is to accept brutality, cynicism, hypocrisy and indifference in the hearts of men who are afraid to love.' (*Rehabilitation doubtful*).

'Ah, I see you're making a drawing. Interesting. I don't judge drawings as art, to me they are a mirror of the mind. D'you want me to tell you what the drawing means? It means "I'm all alone in the world".'

(*Conclusions*: prisoner in confused mental state, unable to respond clearly to simple questions; lack of appetite; homosexual obsession; morbose fantasy; depressed; unable to grasp reality. *Recommendation*: imperative to keep under observation.)

He who does not know what art is, how can he hope to know mind which is the greatest art when free? His concepts of life, death, art, love, loss, law, beauty and do, do (in the sense of what will you *do* when you get out?) are all so foreign to me—not because they are different from mine, but because they are not his. They are definitions studied in the dictionary of common usage. If he refuses to allow himself to use the words of his heart, his truth, how can I explain to him my truth with false words? How can I explain to him my love if he will not permit me to kiss him? He watches my lips for my words; he is not used to searching truth in the heart with the heart.

They do not listen, they hear. They do not look, they see. They do not think, they repeat. They feel, but they only express feeling that is not private. What is feeling that is *not* private?

It will be harder outside, if they let me outside now that they think I am truly mad, because I speak private truth and not the clichés they want to hear which is the only speech they speak. The prisoners and the guards understand much more easily because they are wise—they know there are things they do not understand, they listen, they try to understand; they are not so used to sort out, analyse and classify everything while they are hearing, before they have listened, as those others who think they know everything because they think they know much when they only know more and therefore know nothing. The intellectual can explain the bomb, the illiterate cannot understand it. Which one is wise? One song, one kiss, one joint, one touch are all worth a thousand pictures. You know all this, my love. It must make you impatient that I use so many words to say you cannot talk about love. But if I kiss them all when I get out, they'll put me right back in again.

They say we must accept . . . the will of God. What do they mean 'accept'? When there is no more choice, there is no more 'accept'. One simply is. I think they want accept to mean: adapt, resignation. *Coraggio!* What does the coward know of courage, keeping the taste of fear in his mouth because he is afraid to swallow? Their 'accept' is a spitting out, a rejecting. My 'accept' is a swallowing, a digesting. It takes courage to swallow, it takes time to digest the bitter medicine that can cure the soul. In their superficial way they who might be profound if they allowed themselves to suck their fear into their lungs and dive towards the ocean floor of knowledge, they tell me to have courage to accept, to enjoy.

R. told me his story last night. Like most here he is illiterate. I asked him why he didn't learn to read and write.

'Because I always played around instead of going to school.'

'But it's easy.'

'Oh it's easy for you because you know how.'

No one here has tried to inspire him to try. I haven't yet. Anyway, he went to work in Germany—three years near Ulm. What little money he brought back he spent. He likes to drink wine, he likes to have fun, he likes girls—he's 'bad'. Why does he flinch instinctively each time I want to express the tenderness I feel for him by touching his head, his shoulder with my hand?

R. thinks he's stupid because he can't read. The doctor thinks he's smart because he's a doctor. I can talk easily with R. R. thinks wars are stupid, that policemen should not be violent and arrogant and provocative, that the rich and powerful are hypocrites. He accepts what is only because it is, not because he thinks it's right. He's no more capable of violence than anyone else who is confronted with violence.

He came back from Germany and he spent his money. He married a girl because she had 'money' in his village. What a concept! But his wife would tell her mother not to give him any because he buys a bottle of wine, runs after other women and doesn't work. He told the mother: 'I married your daughter because she had money and now you won't give me any.' The mother said 'If you don't want my daughter, give her back to me in the condition I gave her to you.' R. got mad and locked his wife in the apartment and went away for five days. When he came back his wife and mother-in-law called the police and charged him with kidnapping. The cops took him in. There was a cop with a typewriter, 'but he wasn't writing what I was saying'. The cop said 'Don't tell me what to write. I write what I want to write, I run this place.' R. got mad. He picked up the typewriter and threw it at the cop. The other cops beat the shit out of him. He was lucky. They judged him mad and they've locked him up here for two years. He may get out in a few months.

Todo is sweet. His greatest joy is to share little goodies he gets from home. Sometimes he gets excited. There was not once when he was mad that a 'come on, it's too absurd' look didn't get a smile from him. Todo had a toothache. For three days and three nights he groaned in pain. The second day they gave him a *nisidina* pill. Sudden fainting spells about ten times a day. Here there is nothing but iron and concrete when he falls. He's supposed to wear his leather helmet everytime he stands up, but he hates to wear it. Todo is about thirty-two I think. For fifteen years he has suffered from meningitis. His right arm is useless and his whole right side is semi-paralysed. He heard there was a clinic in Russia where they might help him. He got the money, he got the visa from the Russian embassy, but the Italian official refused to give him a passport. Todo got excited. It took five men to restrain him, he who can use only one arm and hobbles about. They sentenced him to two years.

Tonino was in a fight. The other man died. The judge gave him fifteen years. Tonino said 'I was in a fight—I had a knife, he had a knife. We were mad. He was unlucky, it could just as well have been me. I wish it hadn't happened. But you destroy my life—fifteen years! And you do it in cold blood—you're not even angry.' Five more years for contempt of court!

C. the shepherd from Sicily who washes the sheets and cleans the shit for the white-haired old man who can hardly move. He who with his simple cheerfulness and compassion does so much more than the doctor who passes through every few days to complain. The shirts hanging to dry on the bars are unsightly and must be removed! C. has been here for two years for a murder he says he did not commit. The *maresciallo* accused him because he was a stranger in the *paese* from another *paese* over the mountains. As yet there hasn't been an indictment for trial.

These stories are not told for sympathy; they are hardly told at all in this place with so many stories. They are told when spirits are good, they are told as a 'joke at life'. These are the people who had sympathy for me from the very beginning, who gave me their precious cigarettes, who forced me to accept their 'goodies', who were concerned when I didn't eat, who understood all the things I could not make the others understand, who had sincere compassion in my grief without knowing my loss but sensing my pain. They are all 'poor' people who lived their lives in poverty but who are rich in spirit, ignorant of writing but wise.

How can you judge a man without knowing him? In the courtroom that encourages lies and provokes fear, how can you hope to find truth? Without emotion, without ideas, only the 'facts', how can you hope to understand? When the only admissible evidence of love is 'mercy', how can you hope to please God . . . in the name of Jesus? To believe there's been an injustice, one must believe there is justice. To believe there is justice, one must believe we have arrived at a state in our development where truth and reason and love are integral needs of our consciousness, not merely conveniences wherever useful, wherever practical. As long as our lives are dominated by fear, we will have supersonic jets, we will have nuclear power; but justice, freedom, civilisation will only exist as beautiful words in our dictionaries.

There has been no 'injustice', only an absurd tragic accident.

Today I felt hatred. Or was it anger? I don't know, but I could not speak to Dr. Testa. He came to play out the farce today seventy-seven days after our arrest, twenty days after Carol's operation, seven days after her death . . . to give me a medical examination. Again of reflexes and poking around, of squeezing my hand and look here look there, to determine if I was or had been—'drugged'. Something he has known to have been a lie. He had the nerve to be sanctimoniously 'nice', to ask me how I felt.

I said 'I don't feel anything anymore.'

He had the audacity, the lack of taste (or was it guilt?) to say 'You feel weak?' to pretend to understand I was speaking of my physical condition.

I finally forced the issue by saying 'You know my wife has died?'

At that he nodded his head and we spoke no more while he continued going through the motions of his 'examination'.

For comforting me he had come up with 'We're almost finished with our investigation, it will be over soon.'

I could only imagine his having said the same to Carol a month ago when he visited her and she wrote 'This time he was very nice and polite.'

I must have sent out some pretty strong vibrations at his conscience. I recall now, though I wasn't aware of it then, at the end—though throughout he had worn the unctuous gentleness of a missionary—at the end he somehow slithered out of the room and was gone in the instant, with no attempt at words of parting or even ending. When I walked out after him, the guard at the door very kindly waved me back into the room and bid me wait. I think he sensed my vibes right out in the corridor and wanted to prevent me from doing something rash.

23 October   Good news. Last night I was happy. C. has returned from his clemency trial in Campo Basso—absolved. After fifteen years this man who was so kind to me with his heart, may soon be free. In fourteen months!

Last night I began making copies of all your letters. I'm strong enough for that now. I am ready for it—it was good. I stayed up half the night. I was close to you, I was you. I realised how you were covering up your pain, your suffering; how you were trying to spare me. I know that now from your diary. But why did you keep from me what you had the infinite courage to taste? That wasn't fair. I know also that you were writing truth when you said you were happy. But you didn't give me the whole truth, only the beautiful truth. As I copy your letters now I feel how you out-censored the censor. But I also understand your not wanting to share the pain with me, though I would have wanted you to. There are some things even love wants to keep private from the beloved. But my dearest secret heart, I think you knew while you were censoring that I knew, that I felt—as I did. That the hiding of the pain was only a game, a game lovers play to expose the most profound truth of their love.

In the *manicomio giudiziario* once you realise the doctors are mad, you do not get sick if you can help it, you do not flip if you can help it.

Time has begun ticking again. It is slowly beginning to take on meaning; only meaning has not yet taken on meaning. I would like to be out, but it is not important. Still, it is painful to realise that time exists when you do not, that I am time-full when you are time-less. It is trying to seep in between us. I shall not let it. It will seep in regardless, I cannot stop it, but I shall not allow it. It will do so without my permission, against my desire.

25 October   The eleventh day. When all this is over I hope they'll grant me the right to call myself nigger! Soul ought to be something you can earn if you're not lucky enough to be born with it in your pigment. I'll just say: I'm an albino spade. But who gonna teach me to swing my ass?

My undying love was dying, they took me to her in chains. Yes master. I begged for your mercy—to let me sit by her and watch her, who no longer could see my tears, and clasp with trembling fingers her lovely feeling-less hand. I grovelled—you grant me that favour—but thank you I could not say. I'll look for the power to love you, for you are more fear-full than I; my song if you want I will give you and I'll try and teach you to fly.

Like Debbie, I too go over in my mind not just the beautiful moments, not just the joys, the laughter and the song; but also the ugly moments, the terror, the anger, the tears, the nightmares that make a total voyage of love, a total voyage of life. And I see—not the romanticised version destined for the local houses—but in the stark realism, your beauty of soul. There is not one moment when you were false. You were incapable of a false smile, an unfelt kindness, a compliment. A false laughter did not exist in your musical scale. You could make harsh sounds but could not sound a false note, you could hurt, reject, ignore, but could not give a false embrace. Your love was true. Not all were fortunate enough to feel it, but no one ever received its counterfeit. That is why all the memory of you is true. There is no need to select, to romanticise, to beautify. You suffice, as you have always sufficed for me for everything, even when I was too blind to see it. The ultimate romance of you is that there is now no need to romanticise. The ultimate truth of you is that you may be dead, but you will never die. This is the truth above the facts that they who search for facts, who try to censor beauty, will never know. The ultimate love of you is that its *geste*, at times withheld, was universal love for all. You loved too much to give what you did not have to give, to destroy the depth of love by being 'kind'.

There is word about that I will get out today. It's not that I don't want it, I am ready for it now; it's not that I don't believe it because I fear disappointment. Yet I do not look forward to it. It will be . . . whenever it is . . . a painful moment. Whatever joy, whatever release there will be in that moment, will be perverted by the deep sorrow of what that moment would have meant, what joy there might have been had there been you. It can now be only . . . a fact.

I've always loved cunt, but I was always too cocky to understand cunty till I found you—in me.

26 October   The game continues. *Faites vos jeux messieurs dames. Les jeux sont faites rien ne va plus.* They all know it's a game, certainly those who play it day in day out—the men of the law. Our case may have become more absurd more tragic than was planned. It is not the most tragic, it is not even unusual. If you haven't yet understood, look in the faces of the players! No one is truly shocked, no one loses, not even for a moment, the beat of the music. Death, unreason, tragedy and tears are a daily part of their game. None of these faceless men wanted that Carol should die, none wanted that she should die in total solitude. They cannot understand how much she hoped and prayed, how much she desired to have me at her side in her final hours. They cannot understand who have not loved as we have loved, or else they could not play the game. But they *are* men who heard her pleas and my 'request'. (How hard it is to recall that I only did request and did not grovel on my knees). They are all men who'll die one day, who know from their secret nightmares what it means to die in total solitude.

For ten interminable days, Carol lay dying, suffering and alone. . . . They knew it one and all, and no one broke a rule. Because of one half gram of hashish Carol had to die. Because of one half gram of hashish Carol had to die . . . alone. Because of one half gram of hashish they would not let me comfort her in her hour of death. And no one is ashamed . . . because they all acted according to the rules. It is *because* they acted according to the rules, not according to their madness, according to their emotions, according to their instincts of jealousy, of hate, revenge, but according to their rules that they should be *ashamed.* I cringe in shame that I 'requested' according to the rules. I accuse myself, condemn, torment myself, admit my infinite guilt. No longer do I fear humiliation, I am free now of that ultimate chain of fear which Carol took from me and buried in her grave.

They who continue the game still think to hide behind the rules, still play with the lies and words of their hypocrisy. They will continue without asking why, as they'll continue their witch hunt of hashish while never asking . . . why? Never asking: What is hashish? It does not matter if it's good or bad, it matters only that it's part of the game. I shall ask you: Why? I'll ask against the rules. I do not care if it isn't cautious or practical or wise; I do not care if my effort is imprudent or impudent or pointless.

I will not play the game to the end. I have seen the hand that will press the nuclear button. It is well manicured and clean, polite and utterly 'respectable'.

What is the purpose of your 'justice game'? What do you think will happen if you no longer play according to the rules? If you begin to act according to the dictates of your heart? Six million died in the extermination camps without a single infraction of a single rule, a single law. Hiroshima, Nagasaki and all the wars have passed into your history books according to the rules. What are you waiting for? What's waiting for us at the end of the road, according to the rules? What do you fear will happen if we begin to act according to our reason, according to our humanity, according to our love? Could it be worse than where we're heading with 'things as they have always been'?

Carol's death I can accept as she accepted it—as part of her destiny. I have no wish to be revenged, to share my grief with you, to seek your sympathy. But on the cancer of fear and indifference, of slavery to rules, on that I can keep silent no more. I see too clearly its results if we continue to ignore the little fears that hide it in indifference.

Debbie's letter—so simple, so beautiful. I cried with joy each time I read it. Though it's in her hand, her words, her way—you could have written it. No bullshit, straight love. She wants, needs to be with me. God, how I wish she were. She is. No need for words. I dig.

27 October   Still here. Still no word from Pirrongelli. Still don't mind. Still. Still. Mom wants to come. Still don't see how I can bridge the gap, the chasm between love and understanding. She represents everything I must change. She thinks she's too old to change. That very resignation to all 'as is' is the basic fear that leads us to the abyss. Yet if I can't reach her, how can I reach anyone? I understand now your problem with your mother—you have left me it with mine. A half truth is still false. If truth offends, hurts, despairs—then how love *and* truth? How love without truth? How truth without love? What is half truth, half love? How can I put her down for accepting what we must not accept, while I accept that enigma? I think Debbie knows—I must let her teach me. She is not yet corrupted by words. I don't think there is danger of my corrupting her, but can she give me my innocence? Now that I have found the simple pure truth, it is beginning to sprout its own complexities! That is the life of all truth. I shall go on with the new stream, the new flow to where it leads . . . in time.

Allain, Nona, Henry and Ben came to visit. My first contact with any reality outside. It's a little frightening. I see how easy it will be to 'adjust'; how hard not to dilute the truth I have found here; to get involved in the 'deals' behind the scenes, the practical considerations; to assume one's rôle in the farce and let the farce continue. But the farce must not continue! We must not be reasonable to gain a small improvement, a few more votes for communist-socialist factions, a revision of the stupid drug laws. Is that all we can ask for? All we can hope to get? Whatever we get will be precious little anyway—not a revision of the laws but a little bit of discussion, not a change in the political power structure, a reduction of the American influence, but a small political football to kick around. The little things add up. But goddamn it, there isn't time to make the addition.

What deal? A few less days, months, years in hell not to speak out? Knowing that speaking out can effect so little? I know, I know, I know I cannot bring you back to life to help me. What do I care if they fire some head cop in Salerno, if Dr. Testa is in trouble? Another head will take his place. Dr. Testa will be more frightened, more incapable of love, just as stupid. Is there no way out of this cycle? I know a way—but what if it's futile? If the most they will do is listen but not change? How can they otherwise but listen, applaud or reject, but not change—if I don't change, if I compromise? If I don't compromise they'll really think I'm mad and lock me up forever.

I couldn't ask Henry and Nona—why? I don't know, I can't yet care enough to know, to do, to face 'reality'. It doesn't seem real without you. Real real real real real real really—real. Henry sent some earth from your grave to Rufus in India. A lovely thought, but it shocked me because I have not as yet accepted the earthy reality of such a thing as your grave. How many shocks will I have to feel on re-entry to earthy reality when I leave this incubator of sorrow, of love? After death comes birth, pain—promise—life reincarnate.

This waiting every day for the *scarcerazione* they say is imminent. This waiting every day for news from Pirrongelli which does not arrive. This daily delusion, this gradual resignation that this absurdity, this cruelty will never end, while knowing that one day it must end—is painful only because it is a repetition of what we shared when time was urgent for both of us. A re-run of anxieties and frustrations felt what seems like an eternity ago. The recalled impact when the drama still had suspense, when the finale was not set.

Yaguel's letter confirms what I knew from your words, what I felt in my heart, that in all the suffering, in all the terror of your compassion, you did find glory, you did find happiness before you left us your memory. It was only the confirmation of what was there, of what we knew was there that we so desperately sought from that final conscious togetherness that was denied us, my dearest love. Let us go on to destiny without tears of regret but the music of joy you still sound in my heart.

29 October   Dear Debbie. Today is Thursday and I'm beginning to suspect I may have been wrong in assuming that they would let me out. It seems that what began as an absurd comedy and passed through tragic farce to tragedy may yet turn to something more significant.

There are some beautiful things. I have had much time to reflect on many things and I have found some very important truths. The gist of it is in the letter I wrote to you about love and fear. Carol and I had the chance through our letters to find beautiful communion of togetherness and love that might not have been otherwise possible. I'm not exaggerating 'to make the best of things'. I have found that one can speak truth from the heart when one is no longer afraid—and be *understood*. The rationalised clichés we usually use, no matter how 'brilliant', may produce nods of agreement but not understanding. Without the truth of love, the truth of the heart, words are meaningless sounds. They may impress like the telegraph, the radio and the telephone; but of themselves, without the life of love, they communicate nothing.

I have told my lawyer that since Carol died under accusal of a 'crime' and can no longer decide for herself, I must do all I can to exonerate her in the letter of the law. I have no other choice in my conscience, even if I consider guilt or innocence of the 'crime' immaterial, even if I would gladly exchange my own liberty for complete exoneration. That if this means I must remain here and stand trial with a chance of further imprisonment, I must take that chance. It's beginning to look like that is the one request that will be granted to me.

I do not like it here, though everyone treats me very well, though I find understanding and compassion in this unlikely place—not only from my fellow prisoners but also from the guards and the authorities. I would much prefer to seek your company, your compassion, your understanding and that of my friends. I also do not want to play the martyr—I prefer the rôles of the lover, the buffoon, the villain. But it is much deeper than that, much deeper than our tragedy—Carol's and mine—which makes up only a small part of the whole drama. Our tragedy like that of an infinite number of avoidable tragedies caused by man's inhumanity to man, is the product of our fears. There is not one person in this whole unfortunate chain of events who is evil, who should be 'punished'. The 'evil' occurs and continues to occur because each one in his own right gave in to his own particular little fear and denied the urging of his heart. I see this much too clearly now to deny the demands of my own heart because I am afraid. I am afraid. Fear cannot be avoided or suppressed, but once it is faced it loses its power and we can see how much more powerful, how much more preferable is love.

One of the most precious things I have found here has been your letters. You may still get a telegram from me that I am 'out'. I write you this letter in case you don't. As for your coming here, what can I tell you except that I desire it more than anything. But for me the mutual desire suffices. It would be most difficult. They do allow visits by the family. Tom I think would send you the ticket. Oma is at Hotel Atlantico, Estoril, Portugal. But I

think until I get 'out', the effort is too great for the recompense.
I love you dearly. Billie.

30 October   How well I understand why you did not want to
stay. The death you faced must have been sweet compared to the
putrefying death of soul of those who, even now, persist in
keeping me here. They can no longer feign to themselves a
sbaglio; their putrid 'evidence' has been excreted and with the
stench in their nostrils they still persist. How much decay must
those nostrils have scented, those eyes have seen, those hands
permitted—to be this numb. The shit pile of their evidence is here
around me every day, as it was there with you. I too would rather
be dead with you than here breathing in their foul vapours. It will
take more than a *scarcerazione* to purify the air. The love that Debbie sprays into my cell does help; it also intensifies by contrast
the pungent odour that remains. It needs a giant flush. *Quelle
tristesse!* How difficult it is not to hate, not to despise but to understand, to love the judges—who lack the courage to judge themselves, who seek to punish without suffering, who seek to justify
their fear with their pride, who seek to be proud without self-
respect, who think they can avoid the smell of their souls'
excrement by hiding it in prisons which they command others
to build and to keep, who think they can wipe themselves clean
with legal briefs in *nome della repubblica*.

31 October   Yesterday was a bit of a down day. I had to accept
the probability that my release is not imminent, that neither the
tragedy nor the innocence of my circumstances nor their initial
absurdity have had any effect on those who judge and execute the
law in Salerno. I'm quite sure I know why.
    I still miss you so terribly, my love. I realise now how all the
time I was trying to help you stay cool, to laugh, to understand,
to love, not to be afraid, I was doing it for myself. I could do it
for you—for myself. I can't do it for myself alone without you.
    Now I have fermented my grief, have passed from the bitter
sweet grapes of the immediate sorrow, I find myself confronted
with the ugliness of the reality that keeps me here. The hypocrisy,
the indifference, the cold hand of death that is these gentlemen of
the 'law' pounds in my brain incessantly. The newspapers, the

television, the interminable bullshit is insufferable here where I cannot cry out, cannot scream, cannot mellow it with song, with touch. This psychological torture not even *voluto* by the insensitive torturers who think of time, who think of freedom only in terms their stunted imprisoned spirits can conceive, who think of beauty not at all for they are blind. How much preferable a sadistic torturing fiend who at least knows the subtlety of what he does and glories in his evil. I could accept that in my masochism and feel at least a human contact. To see the sweating fiend in Salerno clutching his psychic whip with glee! I might be able to come to that vision. But no, I see just so many spirits crippled into machines like Mr. Lautz. That is what's so insufferable. To have no one for whom to summon my strength except myself just seems like so much jerking off. There is no strength required to wait and wait and wait and think and think and think. Only oblivious patience, only the vegetable state is of use to me now. That you are not sharing my suffering, needing my help, absorbing my love, that you are not. . . . Oh God, why have you forsaken me?

> *I am afraid*
> *my soul may die*
> *that I might live*
> *to hate*
> *just as*
> *your body died*
> *to free your soul*
> *for love*
> *and we shall never meet again.*

The spirit of your murderers is the force that keeps me here in chains in the immediate shock. My soul was numbed in the immediate grief, my eyes were filled with tears and could not see, and in the immediate re-birth of our hearts I was too consumate with you to notice. But now soul, heart, eyes, brain make me confront in every instant the very symbol of my slavery, in every image of my fantasy the horrid putrid nightmare spirit of your murderers. The battle against fear and hate is not yet won. My ebbing strength is weakening my resolve. I cry for help, I cry for help . . . for love and beauty, soul music and free spirits for my company. The fiend is suffocating me in loneliness. I need to dance, to sing, to laugh.

The battle cries of love do not desert me in my dreams. I need your sustenance as I never did before.

One thing to learn here is how little we really need of what we think are necessities. To find out what is important. It ain't how to get more that's important; it's how to get more out of less. Reduced to nothing it's easy to judge one's needs by what is missed most. I miss the free company, the touch of the beautiful people, the sounds, the beautiful sights, the warmth of laughter and of course the obvious—sex. Though not as much as I might have thought. The two-bathroom privacy, the Rolls Royce respect, the *bella figura* are less than mere frills. They're traps that hide the very thing they seem to signify. Privacy is much too private to be symbolised. True privacy has no need to hide.

It's easy to see why prisons have always been such good training grounds for revolutionaries. One is brought face to face with the injustice of society, its hypocrisy, its brutality—at a time when one is free of 'responsibilities' which lead to compromise, at a time when contemplation is unavoidable, at a time when one has nothing to lose, at a time when one realises how small and relatively insignificant are the needs of one's existence. It is very beneficial to revolution that they who put revolutionaries in prison are too obstructed by their own immediate petty needs and fears to be able to realise this.

Lovely telegram from Peter just arrived. Patience patience patience. Fuck fuck fuck. I wrote to your mother today. I sent her a copy of yours you sent me on your birthday. It is so beautiful I cried all the time I was copying it. I hope it means as much to her as it says to me. If only you could still be—it would all be so exciting, so important, so filled with hope—guerilla theatre sublime—but what is theatre without the audience that can discern? It's all as cold as a dress rehearsal, a run through that never ends. If you were, it would be exciting. The boredom, the exasperation, the hope for a good finale would be dramatic, but this drama is life-less, love-less, you-less and thus seems use-less. The star has gone home, the projectionist is asleep, but the projector keeps running on and on and on. . . .

9. *1–21 November*

1 November[3]   Last night I lay awake for a long time passing through the moments of our eight years. It was hard to keep them in time sequence. Time didn't seem to exist.

I saw the telephone booth backstage at the Billy Rose. Arthur Peppini had just handed me a white piece of paper with your phone number. You had called. I'd left tickets for you at the box office as per request per Roscoe Lee Browne. I called you. 'Why don't you come over?' you said. I came over.

That nineteenth century whorehouse wallpaper in the beauty parlour on the first floor. I remembered how the night of the opening of *The Cool World* I had climbed that dark stairway . . . to your throne room with Calvin Lockhart and various others, no one was sure it was the right building. Each time I'd seen you the years before I'd felt the attraction and had made stupid efforts at 'contact' conversation. You always rebuffed such polite stupidities, always made me slink away determined *not to give that bitch the satisfaction of recognising her next time!*

This time was different. Can't remember what we said—wasn't much—there was a popper in your sewing basket—you gave me a slight encouragement and I exploded the lovely thing into such a magnificent ball . . . in such a magnificent bed . . . in such an enchanted place. We balled for hours. I was sprawled inside your web of enchantment—but wary, oh so wary. I escaped to my village pad—the pad I had just taken, the pad I kept as a symbol of my 'independence' for a whole year. The pad I never lived in!

You phoned me. With mischief I told you I was on my way to an orgy. You said 'OK, pick me up.' I didn't know then you didn't really dig scenes that much. That night you fairly leaped in and were the life of the party. It was your total cool that turned me on. No bravado exhibition, no shy footsy poo, just 'Well, if you all

3. See Diary Notes, pp. 278–279.

want to fuck, let's fuck.' I remember how you slipped out of your clothes—total natural virginal public privacy . . . total beauty.

You had to go to Paris for the collections for three weeks. 'Would I mind your apartment?' Fausta, the black cat that was so like you. . . . Fausta and I and your paintings, and I wrote you a poem and you wrote me. And you were back in a flash, less than a week I think. Roscoe said 'Take Douglas with you to the airport, she'll dig figuring out a way to get rid of him.' There you were, with the brown leather bag you'd brought for me, imperiously tolerating the customs man, with your eyes on me and a piece of shit in your purse.

I saw the Christmas Eve party at Rosemarie's, all *en famille*, when you called from Johanna's and made me leave the inner *sanctum familiaris*. What magic to make me 'dare' such a thing in those days! But I just left then and drove through the snow to Long Island.

That room, Donald's paintings, Johanna and Geist and you— all magic. . . .

The day Monti came back from Paris . . . his little dog. Monti was the hard rock symbol of your friends I had to seduce. All shocked at your being with a square like me! But you made them accept it. Louis Faure and Ivy and Albee Baker, Debborah and Donald and oh God yes . . . Melinda Rogers! and . . . Denis Deegan. Only Johanna intriguing for you, casting spells for you. Next thing I knew I was building the terrace, always one foot out the door.

Then that day I made it out—bags and all—around the corner to that hotel. Gone for ever, gone for good—T.V. set, typewriter and all. Had to call to tell you where I was . . . *in case there were any messages.* The scene with the manager of the hotel who thought you were a hooker, an outside one. Our common battle against that uptight hypocrite, till we both got thrown out of the hotel and wound up gloriously back 'home'.

My first trip at Monti's and the next day to get you at the airport, still flying. . . . Billie Dee calling at 3 a.m. on his first trip and down to that loft on Houston Street and your first trip. The girl with the shaved head and what's her name, that lovely sprite— 'the peacemonger'.

And Bellevue . . . God Bellevue! I came with the ambulance to take you to the private clinic and they weren't going to let you out and they almost put me in I got so flipped out, and then finally OK. Before I'd been balling somebody I think, can't remember who, and when I came back you'd taken all those pills. I saw me carrying you like a sack wrapped in your fur coat, hailing a cab to Columbus Hospital where they gave you caffein and I talked our way out of there so they wouldn't keep you for 'observation'. Then home. You so wide awake—you wouldn't sleep and flipped all day and all night . . . threatening to jump off the roof. And then arsehole that I was, I listened to Dr. Briggs and sent you to Bellevue. 'It's the only thing you can do at this time of night' he said, 'just for the night!' And you forgave me. You even blamed yourself and wrote in your diary 'When I saw the look in Billie's eyes when he came for me, I realised what I'd done.'

That woman who asked you to ask me to go down for her. I tried to ignore it politely and you said 'She wants to know if you'll go down and get her cigarettes.' Grace Clinic, that was it.

That other time. The doctor with the electroshocks. God! how long it took me to find out that they're the mad ones.

The scene at Ruth's with the dildo whip—Roxanne who came back for the glasses—the Porto Rican chick who wanted to be whipped at that party and you obliged with aplomb.

When you finally insisted on coming to the workshop and I was sure you'd destroy the whole thing and instead you swung with it totally as you always swung with everything in your own way.

I went back to Teterboro airport and our flying lessons, our cross-country flights . . . neither one of us sure what the fuck we were supposed to be doing up there in that machine, but alone up there together, always alone together.

Sarah Churchill and Leontyne and Elaine Stritch and the Dutchman and the Last Minstrel and Dennis again and the Café Cino and *The Edge of Night* and the brief comet that was Sergio and Nico's début at the Blue Angel and Monti's début in that club on Second Avenue and balling balling balling. . . . Those first few years we must have averaged four five times a day . . . it seemed so limitless, our drive to make love . . . so easy, so fluid, so . . .
x x x x x.

The Edward Albee—Dick Barr—Clinto Wilder scene you managed to zing zang out with your vibrations. You cut a lock of Edward's hair and made a wax doll to make him grow his hair long—and by God he did!

The time Edward fell out on Champagne—I'd got you a case of Dom P for your birthday and Dick kept pouring it out to finish it off—and Edward crawling in bed with us. When the C.I.A. man knocked on the door wanting to know if Douglas was of 'sound moral character' and could be trusted. I asked him what he meant by 'normal' and he stammered 'Well, you know, like you and me . . .' and I was able to give Douglas a 'clean bill of morals'! Expecting all the time that you and Edward would come crawling out stumbling over the empty Champagne bottles on the floor.

The evenings on the terrace and all the people who passed through that pad—that pad that floated above 57th Street, that was like arriving in another world for everyone—the world you permeated.

The hamburgers from the Chambers Delicatessen, the poppers from the Buckingham Pharmacy, the answering service who knew everybody's business.

The lovely peace that is Norma and Charley at Steepletop.

The time the three of us get stuck in the fog on the Jersey turnpike with Douglas and we left the car and never went back for it, and Arthur Peppini bought it for fifty dollars I think.

The first trip to Europe, the lost weekend with Sarah and Lobo . . . no, that was the second time we went. The first time when I left you in Paris and got just out the door and you slammed it after me trapping my thumb in the door so I had to knock and ask you to open it—that blue thumb that those who 'know' can see in *Von Ryan's Express*, immortalised!

Lobo and Leontyne again and Douglas in Bad Tolz and the little hotel *auf der Hungerburg* and the Innsbruck family—Tante Dora in the sun-filled room spieling off her Italian she'd learned in Sud Tirol during the war.

The time I showed you the lovely fairy-tale castle in the rain—piling into the car in front of us and the police station then the garage in Schwatz where we had to stay overnight.

And back in Rome with Roscoe at Coleen's and George's—while George was chasing Ava Gardner in his shorts in the

Sicilian streets and neither he nor you were there but both of you were oh so present . . . Coleen conjuring up George and I you.

When I called you from California to say we had to get married or I'd lose the custody suit and you came in the twinkling. The wedding in the sunset wedding parlour and the wedding night. You so despaired that our love was now over that you tore up the wedding certificate into tiny shreds.

With Cynthia and Hugh in Gardner's House and there at dear Nate Rosenberg's where we were hiding out playing detective so badly.

And Fausta left us in St. Tropez where we were stuck with Douglas and no bread, where Vidal Sassoon split after I balled his chick—but that was all later. You see how I get mixed up in time sequence . . . purple mountain lightning, chrysanthemums in Bombay.

In 1965 the Bill Willis scene and again Leontyne's scene. Ugh!

The time I was shooting in Spain and you sent all your friends like postcards. One day Barbara Steele, the next Douglas and then you called from Saragossa—'I don't have enough bread for gas to get there'—and Douglas and I hired a car to meet you half way and waited at a deserted Spanish crossroads in the middle of the night and you showed up with the Jaguar you'd bought from Bill Willis with the money you'd conned out of William Morris. You dug that car so much you never let me get rid of it till one day I laid it on the *autista* for 150,000 lire when you were 'out of town'.

The night you and Barbara made the *sangria* and we had a horrible fight and finally flaked out . . . to wake up in the flooded apartment with the maids screaming. The water had been turned off at midnight; when it was turned on the sink was blocked and everyone so stoned they never realised it.

The time in Rome I was going to leave you and you threw the passports out of the window but only mine fell out and we had to run around from *questura* to the consulate to get a new one. And I was so proud of having a crazy kooky chick like you crazy about me I told all the details the way they happened—amused the *questura* but shocked the Americans who couldn't see anything funny in such a sacrilegious act as throwing a U.S. passport out of a 'foreign' window.

Arrecia and Orestes and the Linda Christian epic.

And Michele who was always more jealous for you than you yourself. I had just seen her in Madrid and she pulled a scene on me because I was with another chick and I finally wound up tying her to the bed and ignored her. And you dug the whole story, as I knew you would.

The apartment in Rome and Attilia and the workshop at the Goldoni at the church and *The Owl and the Pussycat* and *Two for a Seesaw* and Spain again for *Faccia à Faccia*.

The night you put Thomas Millian on a trip and left him raving all over the lobby. Who was the cuntiest? You, Thomas or Gianmaria?

Tangiers, Marakesh, Egypt. Tony Hunter and Serge and . . . Paul and Talida. The Twentieth Century party for *The Bible* we crashed and you crashed the private party of Darryl Zanuck because you were so outraged he should have a private party within a party.

The time the party at Linda's where we started to fuck oblivious of all the people who came in to watch and giggle. That awful party where you balled the cat with the moustache in the bathroom and the hostess got so uptight.

My god, all the beautiful balling, the sweet togetherness, the screaming fights, the ridiculous sweet aftermaths, the penetrating reunion. All the departures and coming together and never out of contact for one instant.

Israel, Dubrovnik, Marco Ferrei and Tony Futz and Renato and Annie.

And then it seemed like it had happened . . . gradually, inexplicably. It never happened. But it seemed like it was happening, like it was getting less and less and your depression grew and I split to the Hotel de la Ville and met Fred Segal and two or three days passed and this time I left no message to be reached for a couple of days. You found me. We had dinner and I fell in love again or realised I'd never fallen out and couldn't. And I think you did too, that's what made it more serious. I took you home, I wanted so much to make love to you but you for the first and only time refused—quite soberly—you made me go back to the hotel. We were apart, but somehow we had dinner together every night. And I came back. But you had decided.

You went away with Talida and Paul and Onassis on his yacht and you were gone but I didn't know for how long. You left them in Jamaica, flew to New York, and next thing you were calling me to send you a ticket. And it seemed all right but. . . .

Then one day I came home and Peter said you'd gone to Taormina with the Living Theatre. He bit his tongue as he realised you hadn't told me, but it wasn't true—you came in a short while later and told me. But it was true, and for the first time I had a premonition it was final. When you came back you still went through the motions of asking me if I minded if you went to Avignon. And that was it.

Two trips from Avignon to Basel. I came there with Igor and I 'knew' I had lost you.

That horrible trip, that nightmare Avignon–Rome when you had a toothache and were digging digging at me. And I hit you and you got out on the autostrada and I didn't coax you to come back. I made Rufus do it or not have it done at all.

Togetherness again in Geneva, but that was togetherness before parting and you sailed away to America, a member of The Living Theatre Company.

Six weeks later I went to Orly, bought a ticket and went after you.

New York . . .

STONY BROOK!

You decided to come back but then . . . *you get on the bus*! I'm in despair.

I cry with joy all the way up the autostrada to Paris. Up on the Mont Blanc tunnel.

Two weeks of ecstasy . . . despair—as you come, as you don't come. All the time—Yaguel.

I trance you into sending a telegram. You arrive.

Ten days you don't let me through to you. You are with me but never there—running running. You leave with Di. A tender goodbye—but you leave and no trace, no word when you go on to New York.

I get the message from Dr. Fribourg. *Cancer*. I phone all over America and find you in Ithaca, New York. Awful phone call. Boston–Stamford–Woodstock. You call, you want me to come *and I don't*!

Back from the operation. Fumicino airport, you with your guitar. It's all right. You accept my coldness, I'm afraid of being hurt. The Living Theatre returns. You light up, you and Steve-Son. I walk out of the house. I don't want to say goodbye this time. I come back. You're still there, flipping because you think I'd left without saying goodbye. Another moment together. This whole nightmare period. A coming so close, a pulling apart.

The French tour—London. You call me in Spain, you come to Almeria. I think I could have asked you not to go to Esauria. I don't know but I didn't.

Debbie—Venice—your letter from Esauria. Maya says it says 'Help!' I reach you by phone but you won't leave a sinking ship, was that it? I don't beg you.

Napoli—*Cristoforo Colombo*—Taormina. Bad. But when we leave *you are with us*. Positano—Praiano. You flip before we went to Cairo, flip in Cairo, but the healing process, the magic of Praiano takes effect.

You go to London—to leave me and Debbie and Carin together. Paris—brief and beautiful. Together, the four of us.

Praiano. The beautiful people, the realisation that whatever changes . . . changes, but we are together. A blending together culminates in the final ride handcuffed to Naples.

The vibrations from prison. The greatest, most intimate coming together is in the letters.

What eight years! Not a dull moment—the full spectrum of emotion, of physical and spiritual experience of togetherness.

When Yaguel told me she saw me in Africa, in Moscow—you never for an instant questioned that you might not be there.

And you were right. You will always be there.

I went into a trance to be with you and it worked . . . for the first time. At least I remembered clearly for the first time. They had just let me 'out'. At first you wouldn't let me tell you much; as always you were so full of your own thing, your own theories. Still sick but O so alive, so alive. It didn't occur to me for a long time to ask how you could be so alive when you had died in my arms. I told you about the consul, I told you about the scene in the hospital, the scene I thought had been our final togetherness, how I tried to breathe air into your lungs, massage your heart, do all the things one hears about but doesn't know how to do, how the doctor pronounced you dead, how I sat with you for another half-hour before they took you away.

'Those doctors,' you said, 'what do they know!'

When I awoke it was no shock. I knew throughout that you were both dead and alive—dead in their sense, eternal in life . . . in me.

I said 'But the funeral—who did they bury in Praiano?'

'Oh,' you shrugged, 'they probably found some skin and bones and put them in a box.'

If only I could wake up from this nightmare and find it was not true. You were more real just now than this 'reality' has ever been.

3 November   Rudi seems to be doing something about the publicity.[4] It's the only thing that's important now—that the truth be known. The judicial process only serves to cover it up. I don't want to implicate or indict any victim. The fact that the judicial process is based on fear makes any remedy futile. Waiting wouldn't be so bad if I knew they were doing something. That's why Rudi's note and Allain's visit meant so much. Oh well, it's not so bad. After what happened, nothing can be bad, I keep telling myself.

5 November   I would have preferred it if bandits had come the night of 5 August. They might have stolen, they might have destroyed—but that's not so bad when one is ready to part with 'things'. They might have raped—but rape is not so serious a violation of body, of dignity of soul as what was done to you. You had suffered rape.[5] That at least you could understand, could even forgive. It is bad, but at least it is human. You didn't even bring charges because you were so loving you could understand. You knew the punishers of the crime were more warped than the perpetrators. You did not want to inflict suffering. You did not keep silent because of shame—that was not a word in the vocabulary of your fears. Bandits might have hurt. they might have killed—but at least they would have been quick, would have been human in their inhumanity. What did happen was far worse.

4. See Diary Notes, pp. 279–280.
5. See Diary Notes, p. 280.

Today begins the fourth week without you. I'm still here. Still no word, still still. Oh God, *quelle tristesse, quel ennui.* The letter and the money I sent to Petra came back. She's disappeared: no trace, no word—poof! Also all the others. No mail. Only Allain came once. Pirrongelli—one letter and yet I can't even complain. After what they did to you, how can I complain because of the *tristesse,* because of the *ennui,* because of indifference.

Today begins the fourth month of this everlasting never-ending psychic horror, this exposure to the foulness of the human heart which is part of me as I am part of it. They will not even let me resign myself to it. Each day they say may be the last, which makes each day last for ever. Yes each day is also one day less. Is infinity less one day still infinity? It could be worse, I suppose . . . I cannot imagine it. The depth of despair seems always to be bottom till we sink deeper; and yet how happy I would be if I could go back in time and do it all again, if I could have you in my arms just one more time . . . again. That's why I don't mind awaking to this nightmare, when I've been with you in my dreams. They cannot understand my grief who have not suffered it, who have not loved my love, and I am glad. I do not want to share it.

I don't know why I get so upset because the lawyers don't come or don't write or because maybe they're doing nothing. So far whatever they do, served absolutely nothing. It may well have gone better had there been no lawyers—at least there would have been no hope, no disillusionment. No, there would have been the despair of thinking that had there been lawyers, it would have gone better. So they do serve a purpose. But I will not give in again to the seductive thought that a better lawyer, another lawyer could do better. That is a vicious cycle that never stops until the nightmare stops. Pirrongelli is at least the lawyer you chose. Good, bad or indifferent, he is yours. I will not discard him. He connects me with you; and whatever does that, even if bad, is much better than good. There cannot yet be good that disconnects me from you.

6 November   Let me take a little guess what's happening in the little minds that are hesitating to decide what's to be done with the 'case'. It seems quite certain that it had been decided to drop the whole thing 19 October when the investigation was finished. Even Donald Lautz, who is not prone to giving encouragement, told me then the judge now had all the facts and would give his decision the following week. The others were released but I am held. The only difference is that they were guests and I was host. So what's to decide? There either is enough evidence to indict the host and have a trial because he is host or there is not. There are no new facts to be investigated. But even Lautz's prediction is now three weeks overdue. Why? My guess is this.

They are waiting now for the investigation into Carol's death to be legally concluded. That is the proverbial whosigootches in the woodpile! For *if* it is officially decided, which is not likely, that Carol's death was caused by the arrest—then the legality, the 'responsibility' for that arrest, for that imprisonment might then become a culpable issue. If previously the judge has ruled that the whole thing was a mistake then the 'mistake' will be the cause of death and thus might be a legally culpable matter. If that farce of 5 August is legally declared to have been a farce—a farce that led not merely to the detention of some foreigners but to the death of an American citizen, who knows who might jump into the act . . . perhaps even the American embassy who is supposed to protect the lives and property of United States citizens abroad. In that case it will be important to prove that all was done within the letter of the law and thus unfortunate but no one's fault.

God help me if that inquest has the courage to find the truth. There'll have to be a victim and it will be me, it will be Carol and it will be 'the law', if they who are guilty can help it. If my guess is true, that would explain why even Pirrongelli cannot let me know. I might not play according to the rules and muddle up the game. Of course, if the inquest decides that Carol died of unavoidable natural causes, then they can safely do what they had in mind doing all along—on 19 October. They'll let me out and send me *via*, and go back to their *spaghetti* plates. Quite likely I haven't heard from Lautz for the same reason. Poor darling. I'm sure you thought your dying would end this thing for all of us. The judge did rule the others were arrested by mistake and detained by mistake. They were got rid of to the *estero* with minimum publicity and who's the worse for wear.

But you and therefore I—for we are the *coniugi* Berger—are a different matter. It's the difference between reckless driving and manslaughter.

I have no illusions it will be an easy battle. Good sense says leave it alone and go with whatever deal Pirrongelli is cooking up. There'll be a lot of sound arguments, especially from my friends. After all, what's done is done and cannot be undone. But the question is: How often will it be redone? Our fight is to turn people on, to change the system—you said it yourself. But the system is a myth. It is the men who run the system that are the system. We might enlist a higher *instanza* or a parallel *instanza* that may make some heads roll to improve their own power position, but nothing will change. They'll use it as an example that in the long run the system is good, that in the long run justice does triumph, and they'll make it tough for me to live in peace. . . . The long run to where?

Secret agent X to Mr. Bond: 'Listen, I'm your friend, I too work for the organisation. I'll now take off your gag so you'll be more comfortable. Please don't scream—you'll get us both in trouble. Dr. Kazoom can be very rough Mr. Bond.' How can one resist arguments like that? You could! I might just possibly scream to find out if Secret Agent X is telling the truth. Let's hold on tight a little longer and see what Mr. Fleming will come up with next.

The air is full of the sounds of the Woodstock Festival, full of your sounds. They're building to a giant crescendo. Debbie's avalanche is rolling and nothing will stop it. We don't have to help it along, just clear some obstructions to make the path a little smoother that it may reach the valley in all its giant splendour.

I'm not a martyr by nature but if somebody puts you on top of a tiger you have no choice but to ride it.

Today I feel truly well for the first time since I came here. In the beginning was the shock, the absurdity, the helplessness and yes—humiliation. Then the separation, the need to be with you, the loneliness without you. Then I found you in the letters in a new closeness, a new dimension sublime. But there was always the impatient anxiety, the interminable waiting for what always seemed imminent, for what we thought was inevitable, the re-union that was not to be as we had thought, as we had dreamed—yet was to be and is forever. The endless days when every minute I was sure they'd let me come to you, when you were 'critical', when you were 'as well as could be expected'—as they said—all the time dying, as we now know. And yet they never let me, until it was too late, until I had to bid you farewell when you had already left, when you had passed the *controllo* of consciousness preparing to board the final flight and left me here alone. When I came out of the shock, the despair, the grief and found you within me, I realised we were still here. Each day they said the *scarcerazione* was imminent and I was impatient to hear your music, to drink the beauty of the sunsets we had shared, embrace the people we had loved. I was impatient to be *out*. But I am still here, and today for the first time I feel truly well. There's no more waiting, only being; there's no more expectation of what may happen, only acceptance of what is, what is to be. No disappointments, at most—surprises. There's no uncertainty of what is 'best' to do, just going with the flow—not carried by the current, but going with the flow.

9 November   Of course I'm still here, but it's quite cool now. Letter from Pirrongelli has no details but says hold on a few more days. I'm in no hurry. The *maresciallo* paid me a visit, says the secretary was in Salerno today for 'other matters' and looked up the investigating judge for me. He mentioned their phone conversation the day he got me permission to stay with you. Oh yes . . . the investigating judge seemed to 'remember' vaguely. (I hope I'll make him remember very well one day.) The secretary asked if he couldn't do something for me—after all, I'm the only one still 'in'. The investigating judge promised a decision this week.

'Oh by the way,' said the *maresciallo*, 'that letter you wrote this morning[6]—do you think there's any point going over that again? After all, it's all over and done with now—practically. It's the way things run, it's nobody's fault.'

'Yes' I said, 'I feel I have to say and do what I have to, even if no one will listen, even if it accomplishes nothing. If there's something wrong with the machine, we must operate it to expose the defects.'

They may not send the letter, but I ain't going to retract it. That too is part of the machinery. It's true that what's done is

6. See Diary Notes, pp. 281–282.

done, but why are there cats here for what was done thirty years ago? The fact that I can accept, the fact that I can understand, can be rendered innocuous does not mean that I can endorse it with my silence, because it's *piu comodo*. It is precisely that thought which makes the horror persist. Pontius Pilate may wash his hands, I will not dry them.

I began today to make copies of my letters to you. I'm glad I started it; it is not a sad task—it makes you so alive. It's as if I were writing to you again; knowing that you have read them gives it even more closeness, more intimacy than when I wrote them, when I could only be sure that the censor would read them.

I really can't regard it as a kindness on the part of the investigating judge that . . . 96 days after our arrest, 22 days after the close of the investigation, 26 days after your death . . . he says that 'sometime this week' he will decide if there is cause to hold me further or let me go. With all the comprehension, all the universal love, with all my understanding, my dear dear judge . . . FUCK OFF!

11 November   Each day more and more people seem to tell me more and more definitely that I will soon be gone. I can feel a mounting anxiety. Just now the *brigadiere* came in.

'Today or tomorrow, I'm sure. . . .'

I just say 'Yeah, yeah, I'm in no rush.'

They really want to get rid of me. It's beginning to get to them what got through to me a long time ago.

Wrote Rudi that they say I'll be out in a day or so but that I'm not so sure. Seems now I'm the only one who does not think it was all an absurd mistake. There were mistakes but not the ones pretended. I'm not so ingenuous to believe in so much ignorance. I must fight the case as Carol would not have wanted me to do but as she herself would have done—without hesitation. I know now life is too brief to make it pointless by being afraid.

I finished making copies of all my letters I found with you in the hospital. It was extraordinary writing to you again . . . reliving the writing of them! It was not morbid, not sad. You were so much alive, as you were then, knowing that you had absorbed them. I lived my writing them, I lived your reading them, I lived your holding them close to you, to the end. It was beautiful. It was only difficult writing the ones you never got to read.

Three photos just arrived of you from Raffaela. They are nothing in themselves—you are much more real, much more vibrant in me—but with what I have of you within me, they are everything.

12 November   If it were a question of mistake, there would be only the need for understanding. If it were a question of ignorance, there would only be need for explanation, for 'education'. If it were a question of injustice, it would not matter enough to fight—there are too many injustices to warrant making a big deal of a small one, since by making too much of a small injustice we only obscure the existence of the large ones. No, the only purpose of harping on the injustice is the hope that it may be ignored. The ignoring of the injustice once the injustice is brought to light, is a matter of sufficient weight to warrant a fight. It is, therefore, counter-productive to have me 'sprung'.

If it were only a provincial matter of a provincial fault in the machinery at Salerno, of a local medical incompetence at Pozzuoli, at Cardarelli, at Incurabile—it would not be of sufficient interest to me to commit myself. If it were only a battle to liberalise the use of 'drugs', to legalise pot and other harmless stimulants, to agitate for medical aid to drug addiction—it would enlist my sympathies as would a campaign against cancer, a campaign to improve the legal machinery, a campaign to increase traffic safety; it would not induce me to surrender my personal liberty. I'm not that much of a campaigner. Ignorance about drugs, imperfections of laws, incompetence of provincialism, the suffering of individual injustices and unfortunate mistakes are all part of the fibre of human fallibility that will perforce continue, even if a small system here and there gradually is removed.

The issue I would like to make clear, though it is too abstract to be resolved, is this: that judgment is not possible when rules obstruct reason; that justice is not possible without truth, and truth is not arrived at through fear; that the torture of punishment is a primeval instinct; that revenge is neither a cure nor a preventive for anti-social activity; that love is not possible if we continue to fear. These are all matters that can be spoken, that can be lived by example but cannot be 'taught' in a courtroom. No, the issue for which this 'case' may be useful as a tragic absurd example is the use of arbitrary legal-police power in a democratic society.

The tactics, as maladroitly applied by the Salerno provincial police, are in use and ready for more important use in every police-judicial power in the democratic world. They are inspired and guided by the American apparatus, where they were first developed. They are the sophisticated model the F.B.I. first experimented with during prohibition. Once the narcotics persecution is accepted and as long as it is accepted, a police department controlled by a legal-judicial power structure (the three are interdependent and inseparable) can arrest and confine any possible opponents or rivals with impunity, circumventing all the supposed guarantees of a democratic constitution. This is quite evident in America, where such subterfuge has long been an accepted fact of life. Examples of persecuting mobsters for income tax evasion or abuse of union funds are numerous, well-known and publicly 'approved'. Income tax evasion and abuse of union funds must be proved by evidence that is often difficult to come by and then involves cumbersome legal battles. Possession of narcotics is a much more simple matter that can be proved and, when necessary, fabricated at will. It is a method particularly well adapted against the poor, the blacks and the young by whom the power structure feels itself most threatened at this time.

After thirty-five years the difference between marijuana and heroin is still being obscured. In America it looks as if it might finally be clarified because, in spite of official suppression, the truth has leaked out to a significant part of the population, and not because the police who have for thirty-five years been in complete charge of fighting the 'malady' have finally discovered a fact that is so easily discovered and verified! In fact the police are *still* trying to prove the contrary by absurd experiments of intoxicating mice with overdoses of marijuana smoke! In Italy there is not even the beginning of a discovery of an enlightenment of the 'dangerous malady' that is being 'combatted'. Why? Why are those arrested for the 'crime' of smoking a joint almost exclusively foreigners and youths? Why are these arrests made with so much fanfare and resolved a few months later with so much secrecy? Why are all people who might shed light on the 'malady' intimidated with imprisonment and expatriation? Why are the quantities seized of the 'dangerous' substance always in matters of grams when the commerce is obviously conducted in tons? Is it really credible that the *squadra mobile* disposes of no better counsel than a doctor who is incapable of diagnosing opium intoxication? That they are so naïve to believe the seizure of half a gram of hashish is a successful operation, while at that very moment six hundred kilos are being prepared in Athens for shipment to Naples? If the drug is truly a grave threat, is it possible that the authorities in charge of combatting the threat know nothing about its nature? That they are ignorant of the varying effects of hashish, cocaine and heroin?

The 'case' is not against police methods but against the whole legal, journalistic, political machinery that supports it in Salerno, as in all of Italy, as in all of Europe, as in America. It is important that the rest of the machinery is implicated in the absurdity. It is not important that Mr. Lautz, the vice-consul of the Naples consulate, be implicated for his 'negligence' and perhaps reprimanded. It is much more important that he be exonerated and protected by the U.S. embassy, by the State Department, because only then does the invisible hand of Interpol or the F.B.I. become visible. If the judicial investigators correct the 'error' of the local police, it remains a local 'error'. If the judicial investigators delay a permissible amount of time for the 'evidence' to be examined, even if that delay leads to the avoidable death of one of the victims, it is only an unfortunate delay necessitated by the exigencies of the legal process. If after the death, after the examination of the evidence, there is a normal delay, it is only a bureaucratic delay. Only when the delay becomes exorbitant does it begin to be significant; only when all of this is attacked and successfully defended, in spite of the absurdities, does the collusion of the legal process to cover the police process become more evident.

I don't think that the actual participants in the drama, at least so far, are aware of the implications of what they are doing. That would make them too wise, too evil, too corrupt to content themselves to the provincial level. No, they are all more or less reacting to their limited impulses, conforming to, evading and stretching the rules, the customs and the attitudes they accept as being the 'facts of life'. No more than the personages involved in the Dreyfus case, for example, were following any masterplan. After all, the Nixons, the J. Edgar Hoovers, the Kaiser, the imperial high command and the marshals of France are imprisoned by the limitations of the 'facts of life'. They manoeuvre within their spheres, they do not create them. They are all players in a game they've inherited, whose rules they dare only to innovate. Being the stars they naturally are prone to innovate them to their personal advantage, certainly not to destroy the game that has made them stars. The same thing is true of the starlets all the way down the line to Salerno.

All we can do, aside from becoming the stars ourselves, which is dangerous, aside from protesting to the referee, which is pointless, is play according to the rules (insisting that the referee enforce the rules which is all he can do) where the flaws are most apparent, where the flaws are most absurd. Only then will the public boo, only then will the public either avoid the match or tear down the goal posts.

Rudi came by. How beautiful he cares so much to get me out. He gave me a start, a spin into the might-have-beens! When they tried the same thing with him, he refused to go to the police station without force till they brought a warrant of arrest, and they left—of course. But 'might-have-beens' ain't no good as long as time only runs out in one direction.

The Banque of Switzerland fucked up again. Sent the cheque to Nicola's father here. I'm deeply touched by the fact that he is deeply touched. His father had written him not to be disappointed if his 'friend' didn't come through, that he would find a way—'he' to whom 1,000 lire can only be saved by sacrifice. It takes so little to restore faith in human nature, in love, to make one forget a thousand disappointments. What a shame we find the opportunity so rarely, what a shame we do not seek it out more often. My God, it's such a slight thing. A man has spent fifteen years in prison, he shares my life in this cell, he shares his friendship with me, he needs a hundred thousand lire to pay the lawyer to save him years —how could I possibly not offer it? What's there to thank for something so natural, and yet he's bubbling with joy, with faith, surprise and gratitude that it makes me feel ashamed, yet joyful at this exchange. I got by far the better bargain. He doesn't know what hope, what faith, what joy he has restored in me.

One little lovely dream destroys the fear of nightmares past and lets us hope for sleep again. Now I can go to sleep, my love—to you.

14 November   Today is the ending of the first month without you. It is the ending of the first month that you are no longer without but are within my heart, my love. One and a half million miles of moon travel. One season of the moon ago. . . .

Had a strange dream—we were both 'out', had gone to New York. My mother was with us. You were you but you looked like my sister—but it was you, your love, your vibes. My mother was cool, though she still had that disturbing 'I don't want to disturb' quality she always had when we were together—the suppression of her desire to be possessive spotlighting what it was trying to hide or seem to hide. At one point in the dream I was in a Hotel Atlantic on West 57th Street. I'd gone around the block and remembered to call Fred Segal in Rome to tell Pirrongelli we had left the country but would be back, told him to tell the hotel to clear out the room but I would be back. At one point my mother said 'Don't cry', and I said 'No, I've cried enough already'. There was the strangeness, the old familiarity of the American coins.

I celebrated the first moon by fasting and not smoking. I went into trances trying to reach you, trying to communicate; but I don't know if I succeeded. I have no recall. I would have danced and laughed and sung and cried had I been somewhere else. It is not possible here. I did all the stunted limited things that pass for ordinary here. I read, played checkers and wept a little.

It's hard to keep faith here. It seems futile, like batting your head against the bars. The fixedness of the inherited ideas of those who 'run things' in the only way they can envision their being run—is much harder, much more rigid than even the bars. It's so easy to arrive at the point of 'why bother'. I can manage to make my own niche, to make my own way even without joining their stupidities, but simply ignoring them. Let the cataclysm happen if you can't stop it! Maybe cheer a little the ones who try to avoid it—from the sidelines. Buy your 'freedom' with the coin of accommodation, of hypocrisy. Crawl into the shell. . . .

Then I look at your picture. I think of what I wrote to you

about 'the cell that is *io*'. And I get more strength. I think of Edna's:

> It well may be that in a difficult hour,
> Pinned down by pain and moaning for release
> Or, nagged by want, past resolution's power,
> I might be driven to sell your love for peace
> Or trade the memory of this night for food.
> It well may be I do not think I would.

But it's hard, baby; it's hard with only words and thoughts to sustain you. Don't ever leave me!

16 November[7]   I dreamed we were all together here, you and the others who had been transferred here. It was in the *infermeria* which got to be bigger all the time with more and more rooms. There was a terrace where waiters served coffee, where tourists came by. All that we lacked was music. Strange but we didn't speak, we didn't really contact. I seemed to wait for you to let me know how much you missed me and I suppose you did the same with me. No one spoke much of the past. I who want to know so much about all that happened, asked no questions and learned nothing new. But it was groovy—cool. You were all sure the *scarcerazione* was imminent. Someone was still in Aversa. I think it was Steve Thornton, though there was another name. It seems he was getting ready to flip out which was one of the reasons they were sure he would be out soon. You did not speak, as I recall. Not 'not speak'—you didn't happen to say anything.

They just told me Avv. Tamarro is coming tomorrow. He's the one Rudi recommended to consult because he feels Pirrongelli is doing nothing. It's the fourth *avvocato*. Each one so far told me the whole thing is absurd and I should have been out long ago. Each one has then disappeared behind a rare letter now and then. What can I say to this one?

20 November   I've received incredibly beautiful letters from Tony Kent, from Katherine, from Carol M. and from Corrine. Each day gives me the answer to why I must still be here. When

---

7. See Diary Notes, pp. 282–283.

will I learn to accept the all-rightness of the flow of things and not despair with the seeming futility of the stupid momentary presence! When will I truly have enduring faith that all the answers will present themselves in time!

Today for instance: C. insisted to allow me to share his family. We were all together at *colloquio*—his mother, father, daughter, niece and the guards. They were all concerned I could not understand all that was said, they were concerned because I didn't have much to say . . . I who was so very content to drink in their atmosphere, their vibrations. It's incredible how the human instrument can transmit love's vibrations in spite of all the obstacles imposed by the finite minds which construct prisons, guards and fear. Yet in spite of their faith in rules and bars, the guards are human and subject to vibes. I have no trouble at all in communicating with them through their meaningless armour of rules, laws, bars and guns. Only those who stay at a safe distance, obscured by defensive ramparts of their laws, their pride, their self-righteousness, seem like machines and are non-contactable. *Tant pis* for them.

Allain just came by. He says the judges are cool but the cops have the pressure. Everyone was supposed to be out on 18 October. Lautz is now doing something—big fucking deal. Bob Peitscher has a million bucks for a film—George Harrison will do the music—Moravia is interested—better no publicity to get me out at the moment. I say publicity now! Don't let the cats run it who've already run it to the ground and into the grave and now want to fly away from the blame.

21 November   Black black day. Why do they still keep us apart? Why do they try so hard to make me hate, when hating will keep me from finding you again who are all love? I shall not let them, but why does it have to be so very difficult? Why can I not rest beneath your lashes and find peace with you? Why can I not go to sleep and not wake again to this absurd nightmare of life? Couldn't you speak to your director where you are now *detenuto* and have him get me transferred to your cell of universal rest? The knowledge that those S.O.B.'s are rushing to their own hour of death and recompense is not sufficient recompense for me to stick around for it to happen. I only want to be with you and they won't let me even now. Having done their worst, they will not do their best and let me die.

My strength of soul is ebbing while my strength of body stupidly persists and breathes and thinks and thinks and thinks of nothing that can truly compensate the absence of your presence. Today I feel abandoned even by you. Where are you now that you are not here? Have you found another lover? Another Living Theatre? I feel the impulse of jealousy to take that trip to where you are, to the new Stony Brook, although I know you won't return till you are ready, till things are right with me again. Here there's no Orly, no Diners Club Card ticket to launch me on that futile trip; no razor blades, no potions, no high precipice that is not barred.

There is NO EXIT.

10. 23 November– 18 December

23 November   I went into a trance. I feel better, I feel you have returned. It was all a bad depressive dream.

Mr. Ezelle, another vice-consul, came today and wanted to know what I thought they did wrong. I said nothing, it's what they didn't do that was wrong. We had a charming discussion, but of course he couldn't agree whether the consulate or the vice-consul had been remiss. I didn't insist. I told him I thought if the evidence was sufficiently analysed a month ago to absolve the others, it ought to be sufficiently analysed to either absolve or indict me and that it seems to me the delay is obviously because it was my wife who died under mysterious circumstances. He said unfortunately these things take time . . . another month or two! He asked me if I needed anything, I said no. He asked me if I preferred being visited by someone other than Mr. Lautz, I said yes. He said he'd be back in a couple of weeks, I said thank you. We said goodbye.

What can you do when you can't yet laugh and no longer need to cry? Watch—wait and—wither. At least they're all getting on stage, the consuls, the ambassadors, the lawyers and who knows who else. I hope someone shows up soon who has some decent lines! If there's enough of them standing around with nothing to do, maybe they'll get as bored as I am of the whole endless thing that seems to be to no purpose. Without an end and to no end.

Blasi is driving me out of my friggin' mind. I can't talk to him anymore. He keeps pretending that men, especially the police and the state, act in good faith—they just make mistakes. Nietzsche is much less ingenuous, I let him talk to me. He's only discouraging because he shows me nothing has changed in a hundred years. Of course he says it doesn't matter, the superfluous people don't matter. We must find the missing link to the 'overman'. What would he say if he knew the superfluous people have their superfluous bomb?

All this, my darling, is so superfluous to you, as it always has been. What can I write to you of joy and beauty and of love amidst this boring hateful ugliness? What can I explain to you who have no need to know, to whom this finite nonsense is irrelevant? What hurts me most of all, I can no longer make you laugh, you who must be all laughter or no laughter at all. I see you in my dreams, but it takes endless hours of work to earn a little tiredness and sleep. I hurt much less, but this insane loneliness just makes me feel the more the pain of hurting less. Oh God, when will you let me out of here!!! Out of this prison madness! You've sentenced me to a life of hard labour in search of truth and beauty. Wasn't that enough? Not only did you take away the one spirit who understood, but you leave me here with those who understand me not at all. I'm not as strong as they all think I am.

'Is it not folly to be alive? Alas my friends, it is the evening that asks thus through me. Forgive my madness. Evening has come, forgive me that evening has come. Thus spoke Zarathustra.'

I do not want revenge that you call justice, as Carol would not want it. But why are you afraid to unlock the doors of your souls that I may enter and find that half gram of guilt? I would say to you: Oh dear, that is nothing, here I'll give you some of mine, let's make a joint of it and seal our love as brothers, forget the 'regulations' that want me to destroy our love, let's suck in our common guilt and let it fill our guts a second, then let it join the universal air, and Carol's smile could smile its sweetest smile, sniff in what's left and bless us both with peace.

I watch love scenes in a good film (*Zapata*). First I was sad, it made me think of us; but then I see they have no idea, no idea! What we had was too glorious to paint with words, to act it out. How can I ever be sad again? There are eight years of glory in my heart, how can I ever be impatient with time? How can I let myself be touched by fools and their foolishness? How can I ask of God anything more?

24 November   Blasi is flipping. His wife and child have returned home. She's expecting, I think in her seventh month. They've been staying with his sister in Salerno these past seven months to be closer to him. He's having a bad '*crise*'. We're trying to keep him calm so they won't tie him up. It's obviously the same reaction of madness he had when four months ago he reached into his pocket and with 'no motivation' pulled out the pistol he had carried for two years and fired all the bullets hitting a friend—the accident that brought him here. To calm him down seems more humane than to tie him up—both are completely wrong. If only he could be allowed to expose his madness without fear, both he and we could learn something. I see so much more clearly the thing that runs through all our interminable discussions I find so frustrating that I have to stop 'discussing' with him, though he's the only one I can talk with—this thing that superficially we might call blindness to logic, cowardice of thought, rationalised resignation to what is and seems unchangeable. He is terrified of all he cannot see and hear and touch, what he thinks of as 'unreal'. He is terrified of madness, which he thinks is abnormal. That's why the *allontanamento* of his family is such an unhinging shock to him. He who counselled me to be strong when I was separated from you by the eternity of death, flips out when his wife and child have removed themselves by a few kilometres! His wife who has need to be where she calls home to bear his child; he, the engineer who thinks that reason is all.

I understand your secret, dear friend, but I cannot explain it to you who are afraid to face it. If only we could take an acid trip together, enter that Alice-in-Wonderland world of madness that is in all our minds, in a secure ship that promises a safe return and thus, removing all anxiety, allows us to examine the beauty of the terrors. But I can't speak of acid to someone who is afraid of the trip. You can't explain swimming to a non-swimmer except as a way to prevent drowning; you can't describe letting go to someone who has only experienced being pushed; a bird cannot convey the feeling of flight to the rhinoceros except as similar to sliding in the mud. Lack of fear to someone who has always felt fear can only seem foolhardiness or courage. That is why love is feared and distrusted by those who have only observed its effects. That is why mind-expansion terrifies those who think their brains are held in by their skulls—for them it can only mean a bursting of skull. That is why drugs and fantasy and dreams are feared by those who think of sleep as an interruption of reality, a surrender of will, a losing of self.

Dear Blasi, you are so 'normal' like the rest of them. Your fear of what you do not know makes you clutch your reality in a stranglehold till that lifeless reality can no longer give you a living comfort. If they give you sedatives the fever in your brain will subside, you will return to your senses, they will think they have cured you and will have learned nothing. If they tie you down till the fever subsides, your fear will force you to forget all you may have learned. They who are afraid to face the sanity of their madness, will never understand the madness of their sanity.

When will these 'evolved' land creatures understand their origins in space and sea; when will they realise, who now grope into space, that we crawled on to the apparent rigidity of land to find a launching platform, not a tomb of dried mud; that we have come from ethereal space, have incubated in eternity in fluid and must use the trampoline of apparent rigidity to return once more into eternal orbit; that this static illusion of reality is the only unreal thing in our universe? You, man, who cannot stop the waves, cannot arrest the wind, cannot hold still the tremors of the earth's crust, you try to halt time which is the motion of a universe so vast you cannot yet fathom its extent. What you call earth is but a slight veneer of crust formed around a tiny ball of fire; what you call sea is but a thin drop of perspiration on that crust; what you call wind is but the gentle movement of the vapour that surrounds this tiny ball that spins about its sun whose diameter is three and a half times the distance from earth to moon and is itself but a small star. All this macrocosm whose limits you cannot detect with your aids to sight and thought and all the microcosm that composes all you can see and touch, is all in constant motion and has been for longer than you can conceive. Yet you attempt to set finite limits on your micro-spectrum that you call reality beyond whose borders you are afraid to look. You build castles in the eye of the hurricane and think their seeming instantaneous calm will protect you. The nearest thing to infinity you could conceive, if you were not afraid to look at it, is the pride of your ignorance, the ignorance of your pride.

Today again nothing in the mail. Allain said he'd be back yesterday for sure. Tamarro said he'd let me know something. . . . Oh dear, how quickly our thoughts readjust from heady flight through space to earthy pettiness.

'This, indeed this alone, is what *revenge* is: the will's ill will against time and its "it was". The will cannot will backwards, cannot break time and its covetousness. Punishment is what revenge calls itself; with a hypocritical lie it creates a good conscience for itself.' (Nietzsche, *Zarathustra*.)

I just remembered something. I think I wasn't quite ready to tell you before, though I knew instantly you'd dig it. When Raffaela sent your picture, the one I had taken in Rome, somebody came and I have no idea what idea was in his head, but he said 'This photo was taken before she died, eh?'

The doctor came. Blasi was perfectly calm, he just couldn't talk sense, he just wanted to be left alone. They took him away. They'll put him in an isolated cell and if he flips they'll tie him down. Doctors! I tried talking to this one, but he 'knows so much better'.

25 November　　Blasi has now flipped completely. All night we could hear him raving all the way over here. They have now tied him up and put him in a strait-jacket. They are strangling him with ever more constricting reality, his only escape is into total madness. When he finally calms down he will retreat into ever tighter 'sanity' till that becomes too much for him and he will flip out again. His whole problem is to reconcile the two in his spirit. Their solution is to drive an even wider wedge between the two.

I was with Blasi all night and day. He mumbled morosely to himself, he moaned quietly to himself, he did not relate to reason, he was a peevish little boy. The doctor came, took one look and prescribed the 'cure'—isolation and sedative. When the sedation wore off a few hours later he was smashing windows and screaming. The doctor prescribed the next cure—strait-jacket and tie him down. Now he recognises no one, can relate to nothing.

'You see', says the doctor, 'I diagnosed it just in time.'

How many wrong diagnoses did they make on you? Opium poisoning, typhoid, peritonitis . . . and the coroner—heart failure. The opium and the typhoid they had to admit were wrong (heart failure is always good because once the heart has stopped it has obviously failed)—and still they claim they did 'all they could' and don't consider that phrase an indictment of their capability. They don't even have the wisdom to include in their report that the hearts that failed are still beating. . . . And what of the judges, are they any different? They also do 'all they can', but crime does not decrease. Criminals become more cautious, they do not become more moral except in as much as they were already more moral in their honesty of crime than those who pretend to be moral without being kind.

Went into a trance. Dream. The sailboat was finally finished and we launched it. It was all natural wood, as Carol wanted it. Carol wasn't there but she was present—i.e. I wasn't aware she was dead or not dead. The boat started to move. There was one final barrier—a wall with a rough narrow opening—but the boat slid easily through out to a calm sea. I came to. The sense of it all was very calm. It seems there had been much frustration until the last minute but that was only a sense. I remember only the launch into the water; there were people helping I didn't recognise. I was pinned by the boat on my side for a brief moment and with one slight force it smoothly slid into the water. The boat had no motor yet, no sail, but moved on its own with easy steering. That's all I remember.

26 November   I have a people, I am of a people. We are not linked by geographic proximity as plants are, we are not united by common interest of the hunt as a pack of hounds, nor can zoologists define us by appearance and habit, nor by co-habitation of our ancient ancestors. You cannot tell us by our tongue nor by the colour of our passports—there are no external signs. Yet he who can distinguish laughter, can translate touch, can read behind the iris of the eye, can hear vibrations of the heart insensible to normal ears that only hear the stethoscopic beat, he who can understand what words cannot express—can spot us in the instant, is one of us and all the rest are foreign. We have no country for we are of space, we have no armies for we are at peace within our sometimes tortured hearts. Our marching songs are rhythms of the dance, our dreams are not of conquest but of glory. We will at times adopt your dress, your customs and your tongues; we will at times defy them. But these are superficial things to pick up or discard as one discards the winter coat in spring or preens oneself with feathers for the ball—they are not rooted to our souls. Our time is now, is yet to come. We have no tombs, no monuments. Our past lives on in memory, that of the past which fed our present dream. The rest is buried in oblivion. Our wealth is love that never does decrease but feeds itself with sharing. As we have wealth that can never be robbed we have no need of fences, no need of laws, police and prisons. Our judges are our counsellors, our judgment final and of ourselves.

The medical orderly came by today.

He said 'See, we were right. Blasi is dangerous when he gets like that. He's been screaming, broke the windows.'

I said 'Maybe *I* was right. He wasn't violent till you put him in isolation and tied him up.'

'But he's the way he was when he came here,' he replied. 'Who tied him up when he flipped out and shot all the bullets in his revolver? Tell me that.'

I said, 'Evidently something made him have an attack, but he was all right for forty years before that. We should find out what caused the attack.'

I tried to explain my theory about the fear of fantasy closing the safety valve, but he just said 'No, no, it's a *malatia*. I know, the doctors know. Fifteen years and I've never seen one who could be cured.'

I said 'Maybe it's the "cure" that's at fault?' But I doubt if he really 'heard' me. Fifteen years without a cure and they still use the same methods and still think they're right because they're doctors.

27 November   I still don't know how to answer Pirrongelli.[8] I have the feeling he's playing their game: no publicity and maximum delay without trial. His first interest is the Arab. He doesn't write from the heart; it seems like a big camouflage of fancy words. If he believed his own *memoria*, I don't think he could be that outraged I asked for other counsel. There is no counsel in his letter, only hurt vanity. The results of his actions have been nil—he got no medical intervention for Carol and he did not get me to be

8. See Diary Notes, p. 283.

with her to give her final comfort as the secretary was able to do
with a phone call. He's part of the 'deal' for the release of the
others. He knows much more than what is being said. He must
know the implications much more clearly than I—he is not an
uninformed fool. He doesn't talk straight to me, I don't trust him.
On the other hand, who is Tamarro? There is no good will
towards me. They're all wrapped up in their own bags, playing
their game and I'm the football who doesn't know the rules. The
ambassador hasn't answered my letter, just shoved it back to the
consulate. God, they're all part of the system. Of course, I could
just settle back in my seat and watch . . . and wait and wait and
grow bitter and either cynical or vengeful.

Just now the director called me. We had a rather long talk
about 'law' and 'psychiatry'. You are guilty once accused until
you prove yourself innocent. You cannot prove the half gram of
hashish was not yours unless someone else claims it as his and
tells how he got it. Italians can't eat French cooking because the
natural tastes are no longer discernible. It's like that with our
legal system. Truth is so confused by so many spices of argument
that it can no longer be tasted. And after all, what is truth? Look
at Rashomon. Pirrongelli's argument—that I put the blame on
you—is quite brilliant. It's the only way to get me out. Put the
blame on the dead. That is customary practice in Italian law. In
this case it is not even a moral blame because Carol was sick. . . .

'But it's not the truth,' I said.

That's when we went into the bouillabaisse and Rashomon.

'I don't think I can do it,' I said; 'there's such a thing with us
as respect for the dead, for love.'

'It's the only way. You cannot prove it was not yours otherwise. No one else will take the blame.'

We spoke of Blasi. I tried to tell him of Ron Laing.

'No, the Anglo-Saxon psychoanalytic technique is wrong because it refuses to recognise the illness. Schizophrenia is in-
curable, it is a terrible disease. We follow the methods of the
great German psychiatrist Kranpe.'

'But', I said, 'that's entirely Laing's point—that insanity is
pervasive. We are all sane, we are all insane; there is no borderline
between well and sick in the head, only degrees of symptoms
whose effects may be made more or less harmful.'

'No, that's all wrong. There definitely is a disease called schizophrenia.'

He called in one of the *detenuti* to demonstrate. The cat came in and they started kidding around. I didn't understand all. But afterwards the director said to me: 'You see, one minute he says he likes me and wants a '*licenza*', the next he says he'll kill me and he doesn't even change expression. It's all said jokingly—that's not normal.'

At one point he said 'I'm a psychiatrist, I don't even understand myself; how can we try really to understand others when we can't even understand ourselves.'

'Only through others,' I said.

'The way they react towards us, the way they look at us?'

'Yes in a way,' I replied, 'but more because they are like us, we are all alike.'

'Everyone is also different.'

'Yes but also alike.'

Why do I feel frustrated when I cannot find agreement to my truths?

My mother wrote. She won't wait any longer, she's on her way. I understand, I'm even glad, but I'm concerned. What will the stench of all this mad foolishness do to her? She's really only smelled it once, when she was young and strong and even then she thought it was only the bad guys. Here there's no brown shirt *Heil* to separate them from the good guys—they all have haircuts, ties and clean fingernails that cap their bloody hands.

I have to do it. I understand it all now. They say that unless I put the blame on you I can't get out of here. I know you would gladly take the 'blame', not only because you're beyond their reach. You would do it even if you were still alive because you would rather have me out. You wrote: 'If only I knew you were free in the world I could take anything.' Well baby, it's my turn now. What I do will not likely have any effect on anyone except that they'll be certain I'm mad. That doesn't matter. We can't do 'right' only when there's an audience. Jan Hus, Giordano Bruno, Jesus . . . they did not recant, did not surrender the principle of the truth they held in their hearts in the face of death. Why should we suppose that it was easier for them, that their sacrifice was more important because more people know about it?

If truth and principle are such pitifully finite things that they increase in significance by the number of people who may applaud or be awed, they would not be worth the sacrifice. If there must be a firing line we must stand there, stand or fall. Can't turn and run so that more people will hear us preach courage where it's safe. He who fights and runs away lives another day only to run again.

Words have to have meaning. We cannot keep saying love, peace, honour, courage, freedom, faith, hypocrisy and then give them other meanings as it is convenient. That is why this tragedy happened. Why Dr. Testa signed his false diagnosis, why Fiorentino signed the commitment order. Why all the other players in this farce played so much for real, so without heart. Why no one 'believed' when I said you were sick.

The handcuffs were real. Your death was real. This prison is real.

I know now how the ridiculous legal process works. Those who have money to hire 'good lawyers' can find the right lies that sound like truth; the poor, the illiterate cannot and they suffer, but they have no power to change things. It's not only the legal process in Italy that won't change. As long as we change the meaning of our words to suit convenience, all the disarmament talk, all the peace talk, the freedom talk, the social justice talk in the whole world will remain the half hypocrisies, large and small, to cover our petty fears and our greeds. The idea that as long as we can do nothing effective one has the right to look the other way, entrenches our indifference. I do know what love means, what truth means, even if I can only see a foggy relative part of it. I know what pain and sacrifice and integrity mean. You are too firmly embedded in my heart that I can betray your truth.

28 November   Well, I did it. I sent the letter to Pirrongelli.[9] I told him to withdraw his argument that it was Carol's hash. Tamarro says Verasani is a hard square who doesn't like hippy-kids-foreigners. He's pissed off because the others were let out while he was on his vacation. Only chance seems if the *publico ministero* decides to withdraw, which is unlikely, but even then it goes back to Verasani though it could be more difficult for him to keep me in. He has up to a year to decide! Looks quite hope-

9. See Diary Notes, p. 284.

less. Nobody's willing to publicise it. That's not really my concern. Or is it? Whether it is or isn't, there's not much I can do about it. One day the Verasanis will rest in their graves with the other dinosaurs.

My mother is coming Monday!

Last night I saw Blasi. He just lies there feebly mumbling for his father who was here yesterday, but of course they wouldn't let him see him. He doesn't seem to recognise anyone or anything, though I felt a slight recognition in his hopeless staring eyes. Oh God, what suffering we cause, and shut our eyes and go to sleep.

They're all delighted with the argument that I put the 'blame' on you. They want to help me. They can't understand that I can't see it their way. The trouble is I see it too clearly both near and far, and far is so much more terrible. It makes the near bearable and inconsequential. They think I won't do it because I'm afraid your spirit will curse me if I betray you. They try to tell me spirits don't mind. You wouldn't mind even if you were here. What a laugh! I talk to the wind I know. There's more hope you understanding what I say and feel than they, you who are an eternity beyond understanding. I must really begin to understand that they are mad mad mad. If only I could go with that and treat their madness for what it is. When I speak to the madmen here I don't try to reason with them, though they at times understand very well and they can laugh and scream and cry. Those 'sane madmen' cannot even laugh—how sad, it makes me want to cry.

29 November   Let's orbit a little through and around the mind of Billie Berger. What is this insistence of playing Horatio Alger to Snow White—my letter to Pirrongelli, my stubbornness not to mince words, my insistence on truth and significance of words and at the same time, refusing to 'indict' Carol of a 'crime' that no sane person could judge a crime? You who keep insisting that words cannot communicate, that truth has an infinity of variations, you who can think of a thousand logical arguments to expose the absurdity of what you're saying—what are you doing Billie boy? I don't know. Okay, that's a good starter.

Since truth itself is moving we can't pin it down, can't examine the 'foundations'. We *can* try to find its core, predict its path and thus define it, as we define the atom nucleus without pinning it down to sight or the static state. I wrote two letters to Ezelle. Both have as good a structure of logic, both tell an aspect of my truth. I could have written twenty more and if challenged, defended each with equal vehemence against all challengers—or if admired, exposed each one to ridicule for its absurdity, to condemnation for its dishonesty, to derision for its shallowness. The same is true for what I wrote to Pirrongelli. When I wrote the first letters to Ezelle and to Pirrongelli, my instinct was not satisfied. I didn't feel 'good'. No amount of examining the logic of the path would change that. The second letters satisfied my instinct, they made me feel 'good', made me feel right. It is important to determine if the satisfaction is a satisfaction of love or an ego satisfaction of fear.

That is the core, the nucleus of our system. Instinct tells me that the nucleus of fear leads to collision with the meteor, while the nucleus of love avoids the meteor and leads to ultimate absorption into the energy of God. The core of fear, as the core of love, are too intense to be studied directly, though we can feel the warmth and the cold they emit. We can study fear in ourselves most clearly by their refraction: hate, pride, envy, jealousy, tension, anxiety, etc. *It don't feel good.* The refractions of love are peace, joy, harmony, relaxation, etc. *It feels good.* That's all that's important.

Worrying about the results is obviously a product of fear. I don't think whatever I do or say has much effect. They'll let me out when they decide. Pirrongelli will or will not do something, he'll take me at my word or ignore it, he'll be offended or not as other things move him, not by what I say—much more likely by what I pay. Maybe the tactic my instinct is leading me into is to make them deal with my absurdity rather than my logic. 'Shock-guerilla-philosophy'. If our absurdity seems obvious, their absurdity does not feel itself attacked, does not need to defend itself and becomes more naked.

For some reason I left out the argument that might give my absurdity some weight. Perhaps I saved it for later, who knows? Anyway it goes like this. . . . I would gladly accuse Carol of being a whore, a liar or a cheat to get me out. She would certainly be in favour of any manoeuvre. Her honesty was too profound to be concerned with stupid technicalities and words. But if I join the argument of her accusers, I do in some slight way justify their actions. I cannot come to the defence of her murderers. If I were to admit to the *possibility* of it being Carol's hash, it would be true but not the truth in question. The truth in question, the deeper truth is this. . . . I am not the lover of the facts. I am the lover of the spirit that is Carolyn Lobravico; I am the lover of myself; I am the lover of man, the lover of beauty and of knowledge and of love itself. I am the lover of God; I am not the devil's advocate.

3.30 p.m. In my trance a letter arrived from you dated 28 November and was left at the door. You say the police were out in swarms searching everybody and looking for guess who, that you made only a half-hearted attempt to see me. You think they might have let you if you insisted. The director made a half attempt to embrace you which you rejected. You had a letter from Peter which said we would be witnesses of a great event in the next twenty-four hours, also something about the death of Mao Tsetung. You left me with your letter (which also contained dates 4, 5 November) and a very delicate old pretty iron grill. I was in an apartment-like cell with a refrigerator where I found some cream puffs which I ate. I couldn't read all your letter at first glance and didn't finish it all. When I ate the cream puff I came to.

1 December   My mother. We spoke for twenty minutes and fought for fifteen about the length of my hair and my beard. She loves me, I know that. We both know it—the words get in between. She's so sure she knows that her values are right because they are rigid, because they are rooted in generations of tradition. That's why they are neither right nor wrong, but are useless. To allow herself to accommodate the flow of her love she can only stiffly bend. She has so much love for me, so much strength, it is miraculous how far she can bend that oh so solid brittle structure of conviction. It takes such effort. I went and cut my hair and shaved my beard. It was to show her we can flow. I'm afraid she'll only be able to interpret it that she was right and snap that little box closed again and put it where it 'belongs'. She will not understand that comfort can be found on any mattress, that warmth is generated from within.

I hope, I think that you, my darling, *do* understand. Oh God, I hope you do as much as I know you do, but I don't blame you for being peeved, disgusted with things as they are here still. I miss you still, miss the still you so terribly, so very much. Don't leave me for an instant, even if I do foolishness to please where love is greater than foolishness. Each time I touch my hair or lick my beardless lip, I feel a pang of betrayal—the symbol of the first compromise—then I feel better because I still feel the pang . . . that reminds me.

2 December   Another vision. If they now let me out and I return to visit, the doors to here—to the inner sanctum of upstairs—will be as firmly locked as the doors are now to outside. How many visitors who come here want to visit this inner sanctum and how much! How much desire to ascend those steps I sadly climb each time they send me back to my cell. That is the secret of the lock. It locks both ways.

It is the seventh day of the seventh week. You and my mother, you both have so much love for me, you're both so strong—you are all fluid, she is all rigid; you are inside me; she is outside; you fulfil me, she caresses me; you who are dead make me alive; she who's alive makes me feel death; you joy, she sad; you free, she prisoned. How can I give her—you? To free her for life, for joy—she who finds it so hard to accept me? Her essence too is love for me; but her truth is judgment, your truth is love. She wants to mould me to her image, can feel my real of love yet wants to dress it in her robes, not seeing how beautiful you've made the soul of my nakedness. The fashionable elegance of tradition and convention she thinks is the proper dress of respectability and dignity; she thinks that clothes can hide the imperfection, when all they serve is but to enhance the natural difference of perfection. She has no faith is her sense of beauty, a sense that for you was natural beyond the hesitation of question. Your '*mitleid*' was instinctive; hers is reserved and saved up for the right occasion. And yet I mean her so very well. I want to give her the fit of you that is me. Unfortunately gifts cannot be given but merely offered till they are received.

3 December   My mother wants to leave me an inheritance when she dies. I hope when I die there'll be no inheritance. I hope when I die no one will be in need of what I have, that I will have been able to distribute all I have had to give and leave only memory.

Somebody came to the house to help me distribute my 'possessions'. Raffaela writes that the robbers broke in, took the movie camera and the two tape recorders, and killed the cat. Must have been someone we know—they went in through the *cantina* window, the one that if you don't know the house you don't even know is there. The only thing I'm sad about is the cat. But then maybe you asked for her wherever you are. I hope the director will let you have her. Why haven't you asked for me? Or are the rules there as cruel as they are here? Do they also think it improper for the male and female part of a union to cohabit while in prison? I will write Raffaela to drop the *denuncia*. I am only tempted to make one about the cat, but I doubt the *carabinieri* would be interested in that. I'm sure there's no law against killing cats unless they are registered property. How ironic that the thieves profit from the fact that the judge cannot decide after four months and keeps me here because I might do harm to his law. I'm grateful to them for that irony. Raffaela is very upset, she does not yet know that after they robbed me of you there is nothing of 'value' anyone can take from me.

I really thought today was the day, but it is not over even yet. I spent the day translating my letters to you. It is the only reality —beautiful with infinite sadness, a bottomless void that has more substance in its fragile dream of memory than those ugly fools I can no longer conjure up in hate-filled fantasy.

4 December   My mother has now disappeared. It doesn't matter. How can anything matter when matter no longer houses you. Remember when we rehearsed *The Exercise*? Real real real REAL REALLY REAL really really real REAL real. The more the word is repeated, the falser it sounds. I'm bored to death with waking up each morning. I'm dead tired of no sleeping. Dying to hold you again, to make you laugh again, to make you come again, to dance with you and watch you sing. Oh God, why can't I sink off into mad oblivion?

Dream. I'm supposed to do a film. Have to wear a wig. It's a Western. I play a kind of naïve bumpkin who I think later gets wise to the 'reality' of the West and puts everything straight, probably with his guns and fists. It's with the Burtons. Liz and Dick come to see us. You have hurt your ankle or something and I'm fixing you an ice pack. Liz and Dick act out the 'nice' conventions à la showbiz. You are in your bed-throne with two or three friends around you holding court. You are starting to be sweet truthful cunty, i.e. beginning to call them out shooting 'straight from the cunt'. I know you're right but I also know you're about to fuck up the whole deal. I tell you to cool it. You have the innocent air of—'Who me? What am I doing?' and retreat into the impregnable aura of your 'court'. I'm doing all the sophisticated whore things. When Liz comes in I readjust the blanket I have wrapped around me, 'exposing' myself to her for an ever-so-brief 'cool' instant. Liz and Dick go to 'wash up'. Liz is hungry. There's no food in the house, at least nothing that pleases—Raffaela didn't buy anything because we were in jail.

My mother's come back. Pirrongelli says wait—in a few days we'll know something! She trusts him. What does that mean? I can't talk to her, we don't speak the same language, seems hopeless. If I don't talk 'bapt' (bourgeois artificial paradise talk) she flips. Bad scene. Later she cooled out. Got to treat her like a junkie—she's hooked on 'bapt'. Trouble with giving junkies their stuff is that you eventually get hooked again yourself—if you don't,you make them suffer and drive them to despair. She's delighted I cut my hair. She can't understand how it drives us farther apart that she's so delighted. What is love? What is understanding? What is hope?

Letter from Yvonne. Yeah baby, I need to hear from my people or I'll go mad in isolation. After my mother left I went back to translating my letters and feel better, felt a little security. That Pirrongelli telegram got me hooked again. I really thought it was over. Two months ago he said a few days, maximum a week. What does he mean by '*prestissimo*'? Big bring down. Think I'm over it now. Back to the flow.

5 December   My mother came. I tried so hard not to talk of what was on my mind, but she insisted and I did it badly. How can I explain? I can't explain, and yet I can't pretend and smile. She represents everything that's wrong. She can't even understand why she can't understand. I can't pretend so she'll understand what she wants to understand in the way she wants to understand. Can't stand her fear of hippies, fear of drugs, her admiration of the consulate, of the doctors, of the system. But why am I critical of her? What the fuck do I expect her to do? I know she's not a hypocrite, but she believes in all the bourgeois hypocrisy. Everything she talks about reeks of it. I can't stand it—not here, not with Carol in my mind, in my heart, in my soul. I've got to get out of here. I've got to be with my people. I can't think clear any more. It all comes out bullshit. I can't think pure —the purity is becoming a pose. It all begins to seem so hopeless when you can't recharge with touch, with beauty, with freedom. Yesterday I said 'bullshit'. My mother doesn't even understand the word. How can you talk to someone at a time like this when they don't understand what bullshit is.

OH GOD . . . !

I was just here with Nicola. The guard opened the door and there you were! This time it was no dream, this time it was real. My God, how beautiful you were, delicate but alive. Nicola was surprised, but he left immediately. I took you in my arms. I told you they had told me you were dead.

You said 'I know darling, but I was so weak and the last time you were so hard with me I had to pretend.'

I took you in my arms, so delicate, so warm, so real. I held you in my arms and cried. Oh God, I whispered, if only I could tell you how often I've dreamed this scene.

I was still warm, my arms were still in their tight embrace the tears were still rolling down my cheek. But I was awake! Never in my life have I had a dream so real, a reality so false to wake to. It was a vision. I can't believe it yet.

Before that I remember dreaming I had handcuffs on me and went to the infirmary. I told the guard I was returning them. He believed me, unlocked the handcuffs and put them away. I remember thinking 'What a wonderful ruse. Now all I have to do is just walk out the gate and I'm free.' But first I decided to go and tell you about it. It seems later I did walk out, but I don't remember what happened next, though that dream continued into other things. But that was a dream dream, completely different. Strange thing that after the shock of waking which was like your dying again, I felt so wonderfully free, no more depressed, no more lonely.

6 December   Last night I saw today's paper's big story, also in *Oggi*.[10] Pirrongelli must be flipping, though I really don't see why yet. How much worse 'disposed' can the investigating judge be? I know now the publicity is right. It may not get me out faster, it may bother the investigating judge—but that is exactly what I want. I want some significance to the whole thing. *La lutte continue*. I cannot let Pirrongelli or my mother or any of them dilute the significance of our suffering 'for my own good'. He'll either assist me the way I want to be assisted or not at all. I sure read the cards clear yesterday!

There is a powerful force here. Had a long talk with the *brigadiere*. They all see things quite clearly. They know they are the victims, just as the 'victims' do. Though they feel themselves powerless to change things, they don't lose sight of the wrong. They may at times be tough, as they've had to learn to be, but there is heart.

On T.V. they were talking about the reform bill (five years and now it's at the talking stage, the amending stage—two or three years before it can go into effect). The *brigadiere* takes one look and says 'First remove the causes of crime, then talk about justice.' What else can I say?

Almost finished translating letters. Mom came—much better. I feel her now, I know how difficult it is for her. Lovely *festa* today—San Nicola. Sent out to a restaurant. Had rabbit and *frittata mare* with Nicola, Remo, Fosco—groovy, sad, groovy. Can't explain it.

There is life, hope, strength. Mom asked me to write down what I can't say. No, I have to say it, got to put it straight. Today I felt her really. I owe it to her, to myself, not to hide behind an essay—precensored, well thought out words. It's not clarity that's important as much as spontaneous vibration. Tomorrow I'll try.

10. See Diary Notes, p. 284.

7 December   Yes, we must talk but the din is already so strong. Yes, we must send out vibes but the range is so short. An action is worth a thousand pictures. Talk diffuses into argument, talk diffuses into sympathy, talk diffuses into agreement—agreement, sympathy and argument diffuse into talk. For our actions we cannot manufacture the fitting truth nor can we disentomb the truth of yesterday nor put the tinsels on today's truth. To stage the truth most impressively we simply must not hide it, neither in exaggeration nor in privacy. When the enemy is all evil, all wrong, all perfidy, it's time to doubt the firmness, justice, goodness and honesty of our own position. Our measure is in our friends; our measure is also in our enemies; and in the distance between the two. It is also in the rate of increase or decrease of that distance.

Today I had a fabulous *colloquio* with my mother. I know you were there. Everything is working out. Nicola says that tonight there is word I'm leaving tomorrow. Out or to Salerno? Who knows? I can wait.

9 December   They're always using the phrase 'violence against innocent people' whenever there's a political kidnapping. How many have been kidnapped *and released* by the 'irresponsible' terrorists since I've been here? Since you had to die of your incarceration? Who is outraged? What do they mean by 'innocent'? The phrase seems to imply that 'innocent' describes people against whom violence is not justified! Of course, it's possible to be partisan in one's outrage against violence, but then is it really outrage against violence? Planned systematic violence is a tool; emotional instinctive violence is a reflex. The conscious use of violence is a part of the conscious threat of violence to create fear in order to get what we want. The policeman's gun, the pointed missile, the prison gates or the kidnapper's pistol are threats of violence. As long as we vary our outrage, depending on whether we agree or disagree with the ends the threat of violence is trying to achieve, we are only criticising the goal and not the method.

The kind of torture. . . . A change from corporal to mental torture is a change, but only a change in kind. It's highly doubtful which is more and which is less humane—the pain, mutilation, the killing of the body or pain, mutilation, the killing of the spirit of the mind. The sensitivity that can accept the justice of ten lashes, in its vanity might yet revolt at a hundred strokes, though it concede politely one hundred years of isolation and not admit the loss of its humanity. The heart that turns away in shame at wilfully inflicted pain, walks calmly by the prison gate and does not skip a beat. The scars of mental torture are less evident, more easily concealed but the pain is no less felt, the wound not quicker healed. The symptoms of the cancer of brutality and fear, of lack of love are easily hidden from the unsearching eye—the cancer's not removed. It will burst out with deadly certainty in other portions of the system, while we in innocence and incredulity ask—why?

> *If justice really does exist,*
> *You who play in its name,*
> *You who dress her up in your lies,*
> *You who treat her as a whore—*
> *How do you think justice will treat you*
> *When you arrive at the judgment day?*
> *How do you expect to meet your death*
> *You who are terrified of life?*
> *Do you really believe that erecting your idols,*
> *Burying your heads in the sands of ignorance,*
> *You will be able to change God?*
> *You will be able to make God disappear*
> *If he truly exists?*
> *If you do not believe the existence of God,*
> *What use are your idols of clay?*
> *What use is your justice?*
> *What do you hope to gain*
> *While losing your immortal soul?*

Just saw Avv. Dario Incutti who was sent by Pirrongelli as his representative, evidently to cut out Tamarro without him having to make the trip himself. He says it is definitely not a matter of days; probably many many more weeks, possibly months.

I asked him why Pirrongelli had sent me a telegram saying that we would see each other 'soon, very soon in Rome'.

He said 'Sometimes a lawyer has the duty to keep up his client's spirits.'

He told me I would soon be transferred to the jail in Salerno, as if it was good news. . . .

I said 'You mean to tell me I must stay locked up for a year or two with the best lawyers working for me? How long would I have to be here if I had no lawyer?'

He started to tell me the story of a man who is eighty-five years old, who has served thirty-seven years for a crime that has a maximum penalty of thirty years and that he can't get out of prison because no one will certify him to be sane enough to stand trial. . . .

I said 'That doesn't answer my question. There's also Auschwitz, there's always somewhere worse.'

He started talking about war. I let it drop.

10 December   Last night they spoke two hours on T.V.—the judges. All more or less reasonable and intelligent. But isn't it the greatest bullshit of all, the greatest madness, to appear to be reasonable and sane amidst such madness? How can you deal with bullshit if you don't call it bullshit, but give a scientific explanation of its component parts? What is *buona volonta* that goes along with hypocrisy? What are the various viewpoints of half truth? Forty per cent of cases result in acquittal, sixty per cent in guilty. The vast majority of trials result in freeing the accused because he has already served the time of his sentence. The vast majority of the forty per cent innocent therefore serve the punishment of the crime they did not commit. Once that is admitted, how can there still be two hours of intelligent discussion? Wouldn't it be more reasonable if they all just screamed and raved for five minutes? What meaning have words like 'basis of law,' 'constitution,' 'respect for law,' 'judge,' 'law,' '*amegliorare*'? What meaning has '*soluzione*'?

The *reunione* we had here with two visiting magistrates made more sense. One of them said the situation is hopeless as long as the situation outside is hopeless. Improving the conditions inside the prisons is impossible except for minor 'slow improvements', until the whole concept of crime and punishment and society is changed.

I think the T.V. programme depressed me more than anything else. It all seems more and more hopeless—not just 'getting out', but the world getting out of the morass. The more I see and hear the men of intelligence, of reason and of vision, the more I realise that they who 'know most' are most resigned, most hopeless— and *ipso facto* they know least, are most unreasonable. If the answer is death, the argument cannot have life.

It is very tempting—the thought of violence, of tasting blood and consumating the evil and stupidity in one great flash of fire and pain on the barricade, and have done with it. I cannot bear the hypocrites like Incutti. Their ugly ties and regulation suits and tailored minds—all symbols of their ignoble fear. I want to grab him and shake him at least into naked violence, naked stupidity, naked fear. They all seem impregnable to love, incapable of courage and inaccessible to reason that is not convenient for them. There are so many hands to push the infernal button. They are not even eager to push . . . not eager to refrain.

12 December   A conglomeration of all the ideas that have been firming up in my head. Buckminster Fuller, Che, evolution of myself, family chains, success chains, small scope in particular goals or larger scope getting fucked up in small responsibilities. Very possible they'll take me to Salerno. Supposed to be a rotten prison. What is rotten, what is not rotten about prison? Maybe finding the answer to that question is what will be good fortune in the long run. Okay, I'll go with the flow, but I sure would prefer sometime soon good fortune in short hops, even if less spectacular. I'm getting tired from all that long run. Not sure I can last the distance. Stitch is beginning to bother me. Let's have a little sprint even if we're not yet on the final lap. Flow flow flow. How about a little blow . . . job?

The devil does not have horns and cloven hoof. There are no goodies and baddies, only men reacting to various stimuli. If we want to isolate evil, we must look much more closely and not only with our eyes of the conscious. The search for God may begin with the symbol of a powerful grandfather image. The search for the devil may begin with a serpent or fright images or people who are perpetrator-victims of actions that cause us pain. The search itself, however, is endless. We may pursue it to the finite depth of our perceptions. We must not stop in the forest or the desert and there conclude or refuse the pact. The pact with the devil like the covenant with God was made before the beginning of life. It's possible that when I meet Verasani, he will be quite comprehensible as a human being, he might even be *simpatico*. I mustn't be disappointed, I mustn't be confused. For the devil hath power to take a pleasing shape. We must stop trying to waste our combined energies trying to slay the poor dragons who are simply poor creatures like ourselves, like the unfortunate maidens. We are all dragons . . . we are all maidens.

They came today with influenza shots. I refused mine. I am here because I was falsely accused of injecting something into my system which, even if true, I cannot consider a concern of the state . . . not even of the state that claims to own my body. If they now want to inject something into me, I refuse to accept it voluntarily.

Just had a powerful dream about Carin and Debbie. I woke up and meant to write it down but went back to sleep and now have forgotten. Am dreaming long vivid complicated dreams each time I fall asleep.

At the *colloquio* with my mother—difficult. She asked me what I was reading. I told her *Che*. Weird—once people have an idea association, can't get them out of it. There is no reasoning. Nazi—communists—bad. She tells me how hard she worked and sacrificed for what is right. I talk of the good things in Cuba.

She says 'How do you know? You only know what you read.'

I say 'I read this on the back pages of the *New York Times*.'

She says 'Communists are like Nazis.'

'But the communists are the only ones who fought the Nazis. The Nazis are an extension of capitalism, of the idea that each must fight for his pile . . . etc.'

Seems pointless to explain, pointless to keep quiet.

Why should I be concerned if and when I get out? It's only when it seems imminent I start making plans. Plans that transport me into things that suddenly seem important, that makes me want to give meaning to what happened to you—as if that mattered when you are not here . . . when nothing matters. You always had the instinct, the good sense to leave when the party was dull. I've always stuck around too long. I've never known how to walk out gracefully, when the only thing graceful is just to leave when you've had it. I feel very calm, but it's not a good calm. It's just resignation—let the frantic buffoons play their stupid game. I don't even want revenge. Not because I'm afraid, not because I'm too positive (unfortunately), but simply because it has no significance.

I'm tired and I want to go home. I want to find that river along which you're walking. I want to go with you and keep walking till we're both home.

I surrender, I surrender. I love you, I love you, I love you. It's shameful, ignoble to want to get out of here and start caring about stupid shit, to want to find meaning when all is meaningless —that is, you-less and useless. Forgive me Debbie, I don't exclude you but you have your own thing, you'll have your loves. I know I'm not alone, I know there is much love for me from you, from all the others, but my thing is gone. I feel so empty, so void. I'm ashamed to keep going through all the motions of being alive—it's a bad scene I'm playing. It lacks conviction, it all lacks heart, it has no pace, no life. I don't want to go to sleep because I'm afraid I'll wake up again.

13 December   *Basta* with everything. I'm in the tomb. The dead have a right to the privacy of not responding to the needs of the living till they're ready. I'll not put on an act. To act one must be alive.

I can't stand it when people think I'm upset because there's been an injustice. There's been no injustice, only cruelty, hypocrisy and indifference. I can't stand it when people think I'm sad because I'm in prison; I'm sad because here I cannot forget that prisons exist. I can't stand it when people think I'm lonely because you are dead; I'm lonely because there is no one who can share with me the profundity of our love. I can't stand it when people think I'm frustrated because I don't understand them; I'm frustrated because I do understand them. I can't stand it when people think I want to die because I do not want to live; I want to die because I do want to live but find myself in a world where the most alive sensation is your death. I do so much want to be dead too, though here I can't even say it or they'll make me wait that much longer, though I know that once I no longer have to wait I'll no longer want it. But the truth of this moment is that

I want to be dead, no longer to care, to be able to let go ultimately of everything, as I've done in a small way inside this
small tomb. How well I understand why you stopped breathing,
you who no longer wanted to care, in a careless way in a careless
world, where care-less is to be careful.

Things are bad with me, baby. The only thing that makes it
cool is knowing I have not yet arrived at what you suffered in
your heart. You always felt things so much more quickly than I.
I'm not as sensitive as you—it takes much longer to seep through
the thick covering about my heart. But I do want to be where you
were. The harder it gets to bear, the closer I'll be to you—and
still you also went through to the other side of it and I will too
and we'll be together. But I can't get to that 'up' without going
through the down.

Nicola, Di Lorenzo, Blasi . . . they're so preoccupied for me,
for my mother. Knowing less, being less involved, their caring
is the most powerful thing to get to think-feel positive again,
to restore the hope-faith in humanity that my mother with all
her love, all her concern, completely destroys. I'm beginning to
rise again to fall again—how much lower? Where is the point
zero in the fathomless pit of despair?

15 December   Another bad scene with my mother. I just can't
make it any more. She says she's going away. I said 'Yeah, OK.'
It's sad, it's terrible, but she can't understand me. I need someone
who understands or no one at all. Each time I see her I go into a
depression. If Debbie were here she might bridge the gap, she
could at least compensate it. But my mother doesn't even understand that. I've stopped asking her to help Debbie get here.
Yesterday she spoke with Ezelle. He talked to Incutti who's
talked to the judge for two hours. Result: the judge will now
question the police on 22 December then turn it over to the
publico ministero who'll then give his opinion and send it back to
the judge. . . .

The Sonda launched two weeks after we were arrested has
arrived on Venus.

18 December   Tomorrow morning they're coming to transfer
me to Salerno, the regular prison.

19 December   Nicola broke down and wept last night. He cried like a baby. He wouldn't give a shit about being sent to Salerno himself; I mean, he'd probably be pissed off as hell but he'd be too tough to show it. I could sense the vibrations of all the suffering he's been through 'going to new prisons'—what they must have put him through in those thirteen years. It just all came out of him . . . he was naked as he'd never let anyone see him for himself. I was cool then, comforting him, telling him I'd be all right; but I have tears in my eyes now as I think of it.

The director let me phone my mother. She was a flood of tears, but all the tension was gone in her voice. She sounded so beautiful, she just let it flow. I hardly recognised her voice, it was full of tears and heartbreak and yet so young and true, like a lover. I do hope she's all right. It was the moment I should have held her in my arms and pressed her to me. . . .

You would have let me protect you for once for real and maybe so much of the bullshit between us would have melted away and we could have been free for a moment together and would perhaps even not ever have had to go back behind our bars again. You had that moment of freedom for that moment when you said you loved me. You'd never said it like that before, not to me.

The director tried to convince, to practically plead with me to tell the investigating judge with a form 13 and say the shit was yours. I kept saying I couldn't do that. I could feel his almost physical urge to persuade me. He even embraced me and kissed me goodbye. It was all lovely, but all the emotion started to give me second thoughts about my cool.

This morning up at 5.30. The fuzz about two hours late. One went to Poggioreale, the other to Pozzuoli—that gave me a jerk! On the way down it occurred to me to have an auction of your paintings. You never wanted to sell one, only give them, but I could give the money to the Living Theatre or something else that could be more fitting. I'll have to think about it. I want the one of the two of us on the bed and the one by Bob Thompson and one of you. Time to think it over, I'm sure.

Here I was a little upset when they took my books away and the notebooks with the copies of your letters, also much upset when they wouldn't let me have your photo. They brought that to me later in the day, also the books, but not the poncho Jenny had given me—my God, that was my top coat! The cat at the sign-in went through the religion bit. Catholic?—No, Christian. Protestant?—No. But do you believe in God?—Yes, God. You believe in 'him', pointing to a crucifix? I pointedly dismissed the idol on the wall and said yes I believe in J.C. but not that—with a vague gesture towards the wall behind me. He didn't quite follow that, but considered it 'good' that I at least believed in God and J.C.

Five minutes later they took away the little crucifix I've been wearing about my neck, the one you had on the piece of string about my letters in the hospital. That bit of sacrilegious hypocrisy outraged my spiritual cool somewhat, but I made only a slight protest, having already lost on your photo. Having to do without the physical you, I can surely do without the physical tokens and reminders. But that those idol worshippers of the store-bought-Jesus could be so insensitive to personal sentimentality, even when the outward form of the cross is the same—ah yes, but you see, they who only live by touch and sight think one cross is as good as another. . . . He told me I would be allowed to keep a plastic one.

20 *December*   I already feel much better. Just talking, being with people who aren't Italian (there are four Greeks here) makes me realise how hermetically sealed in I've been.

25 *December*   Today I began my hunger strike, to protest against the law which is all Caesar's and no Jesus. You are so very much in my thoughts today. Strange, we never really celebrated Xmas and all that stuff. I also refused the 2,000 lire the *ministero* gave all of us. They also gave us *salsice* and potato chips

and *panetone motta* and desserts and stuff. Wonder if Jesus gave or received Xmas presents? The Roman letter and number of the law is administered for the expediency of the 'protectors' of the empire. All outward show and pomp, inward corruption, pride and greed—but the first and only law of Jesus—LOVE—is not admitted to the judges' chambers, and here it comes in the form of *panetone motta* and 2,000 lire. Somehow I don't think that's what Jesus had in mind.

26 December   Debbie arrived. Wow! Yeah! with Pat and Henry. Continued fast till midnight, then I had to eat something —my friends kept insisting.

Just called to the 'doctor'! Seems I've seen this cat before, but all these oily no-look-you-in-the-eye cats look alike. How do you feel? *Bene.* Stethoscope two seconds. OK. I think it was Dr. Testa.

They tell me that man is inherently evil, that the most evil must be imprisoned for the good of society. Isn't it strange that after four months in prison I have yet to meet an evil man? Isn't it strange that in all this time I have not yet met a man who refused his compassion. Isn't it strange that I have not yet met a man who refused to share his precious cigarette or food with me? What does this 'evil' consist of that 'they' who build prisons and mete out punishments are so firmly convinced of its existence? Could it be the reflection of their bathroom mirrors?

I've gone beyond the point of being amazed at absurdities, but just for the record: Deb brought me some books yesterday. *Moby Dick*, a book on hypnosis and others. They haven't given them to me because they must go through the censor. Why must they censor a book? How can they censor it without reading it?

2 January   Dream. I am approaching a villa by the sea with someone. It belongs to friends—a little like Johanna and Geist's on the island—but we drive up the path of the villa next door. We get out, start going towards the beach. There are a lot of hedges, dogs with snifflers that seem fierce. We beat a retreat to my friends' house. More dogs—this time friendly dogs. It is Jack and Vivian's house! We go inside. My friend with me is a young man-boy aged sixteen. In a room there is a body on the floor quivering, there is a group of people doing acting exercises. The boy with me is a painter; he reminds me of Aaron. Carol looks at his drawings. Her attitude is complete cool. She is impressed with the boy's talent. She says 'I'd like to see your work in a couple of years, I really would.' The boy starts to explain something about the technique. Carol assures him she's understood completely what he was doing and how and what he's trying to get to. She has lost all the kind of uptightness of 'I don't want to get involved with your work because I must concentrate on mine and your problems might dilute mine'—that kind of isolation she kept herself in as an artist, afraid to divert her own individuality.

I am awakened by the man who collects the post. I want to stay with the dream but have to give him a letter for the bank!

I was called again to the doctor. Same bit on the stethoscope. How do you feel?—OK. How is the food?—OK. Are you getting enough to eat?—Yes. If not we can prescribe you special food— No. Close your eyes.—OK. I don't trust the bastards. I keep asking him why. He says it's routine with a sheepish air. It may be they're trying to give me special food to be nice! Not bloody likely. It's just as possible they want to give me something that'll make the first 'diagnosis' not impossible. In this rotten set-up anything is possible.

14 October was real. Ever since then the only sanity is to nurture paranoia against reason.

4 January   A terrible thing just happened. It's rocked me to my soul. I was pacing up and down and a thought slipped into my mind that I tried to suppress, but then I forced myself to think it, as I'm now forcing myself to write it.

'Oh Carol baby, why did you have to die just then?'

I tried to whitewash it to mean 'You thought your dying would free me' but no, it's 'Why couldn't you have waited a few days till I got out?'

Oh God, what swine we are to have such thoughts. What is a little nobility compared to our abyss of evil? If you put every noble beautiful thought and act on one side of the scale and all the evil in this species on another, where would the balance tip? When even the noble and heroic is tainted with ego satisfaction?

Is it possible that there is really no salvation for this fungus of life? Is not evil the rule and goodness only one of Satan's tools to spread it? There is no argument in history to contradict this. More serious evil has been done by Christians than anyone else, since the evil is done with the professed knowledge of love, which is good.

What if the creation of life, the human concept of God, are all creations of Satan? What if the creation of life was the archangel's 'fall' and the nurturing of the thought of God the original sin? If we are truly the children of Satan, I must stop wishing to delay the apocalypse. I must fulfil my vendetta in its specific sense—not turn them on, but punish and be punished, revenge and be revenged. Is that not as powerful, as pure an instinct of our soul as this search for God? It is certainly more manifest in our actions; and action is the only tangible proof that is universal. Thoughts—we can only know our own. It would certainly be the surer and easier way. A few years compared to half an eternity.

Debbie, the thought of you still holds me back from the thought I am toying with. But Carol too. I felt you so very strong just now. If I felt that plunging myself into the abyss of hate and fear would let me share an eternity of hell with you, I'd do it yet. Still I know-think-feel Carol did not take that plunge and I'd not find her there and then be separated by eternity and not mere life and death. The flow is all we have to go with. All thought is static when it does not help us navigate and float.

I wonder how much Verasani can conceive the infernal tortures of the mind and spirit his prison is afflicted with? I suspect he does. I suspect much fear in him. Even if I suspect him too much a coward to put it into word and thought. *Tant pis, tant pis,* the unsaid fear, the unthought terror makes the worst quake of soul. I cannot yet find the power to pity him, I cannot yet understand him enough to find compassion.

Love, love where are you love?

Went into a trance, then a deep sleep. I've cooled out again. Back to *Moby Dick.* Back to 'waiting it out'—no point in getting impatient. After all there is a reason for it all far above and beyond the silly reasons of the bit players who are merely acting out my destiny. Whatever the stupidities that are causing it—it is a most important point of my life, wherever it leads. Mustn't lose sight of the course for the squalls. Back to Ahab and his big Dick.

5 January   Incutti came. Marchisiello now has the case and says he'll do it 'rapidly' in about ten days. He'll recommend either dismissal or trial, *but* it then goes back again to Verasani who *then* makes his decision on which there's no time limit. I put the question to him if he is aware of President Nixon's involvement, that he could answer yes or no.

He said 'Don't ask me questions I can't answer.'

That's a good answer. He laid the 'injustice' bit and a 'little bad luck' on me, but I stopped him with 'My wife has died because of this treatment. We cannot use words like "a little bad luck".' Even if Marchisiello recommends dismissal he is sure Verasani will say no. The question now is how long he'll delay in saying his no. Incutti wants me to nominate him. I think I'll wait till I see Pat on Thursday. There's no more reason for me to rush. It's my only luxury.

7 January   *Letter to Debbie*: Though we can keep trying and hoping, we must now count on my not getting out in time. When do you have to be back? This is the hardest question for me to ask, but I have learned to accept all. There is a point in all this pointlessness, and perhaps it's just precisely that for you as well as for me. The will can steer, the heart can hope, but we must accept the body's going with the flow of the tide. The only thing I really still desperately wanted was really to be with you, to share the values I've found in this experience, not the nervous paltry anxieties; though perhaps the meaning of it is that these paltry nervous anxieties are the most fleeting—the values will stand the test of time. Love is best felt when things are bad. We're now in the wake of the frustration of the bad which will subside without a trace or scar and maybe that is what you were meant to share. I can't communicate to you here and share the soothing freeing joy of the great pain of love and loss and rebirth I've gone through, though I most desperately need, want, desire to share it with you—for your sake as well as my own. But that can be done only in an atmosphere of peace and serenity. It looks now like that will have to wait. Depending on what time you have, I would like you to try and get Carol's guitar—I know she would want you to have it as I do—and collect those of her things that are in the various places.

7 January   For man to cage another man, to torture the body, the mind, the spirit of another man—what crime is there comparable to that? It's true, we do the same and worse to beasts of other species, but there at least we can plead ignorance of their sensitivity—a hollow plea at best, since the sensitivity violated must always be our own. We have no measure outside the hermetically enclosed universe of self.

Most prisoners are here for theft. What is theft but stealing, taking for one's own use or need some object, outside the rules? It is a doubtful moral sin, as long as the only measure of the morality of the 'rules' is the power to enforce them.

Less than ten per cent of the people living within the arbitrary boundaries of the United States (which boundaries in themselves were fixed through the morality of force and violence) 'own' about ninety per cent of the wealth. The people living in this world area of the United States as a congregate claim about fifty per cent of the world's wealth as their 'property', although they are but seven per cent of the world's population. Seven-tenths per cent claim forty-five per cent of all the usable goods! They mean to defend that claim by pretending to seek peace in the name of laws they have made themselves 'democratically' without consulting the world's society and only tokenly consulting the other ninety per cent of their fellow creatures they call Americans whom they manipulate to fight the wars whose violence and threatened violence maintains this unjust distribution. Worse than that—they torture tens of thousands of their offspring, treating them liked caged beasts for the 'crime' of having refused to kill their fellow man.

How can we speak of injustice, when 'justice' is mere greed and pride and brutality clothed in velvet robes of expediency but devoid of even such morality as we imperfect creatures are capable of conceiving? A 'justice' that in every aspect is an affront to truth, a denial of love, an avoidance of the truth of love, a suppression of the love of truth? To believe there is justice, one must believe we have arrived at a state in our development where truth and reason and love are integral needs of our consciousness, not merely conveniences wherever useful, wherever practical. As long as our lives are dominated by fear, we will have supersonic jets, we will have nuclear power; but justice, freedom, civilisation will only exist as beautiful words in our dictionaries.

Yaguel came to see me in a trance. When I pulled her to me in an embrace, she stiffened slightly and I woke up. It was about two o'clock afternoon. Deb didn't come. I have no bread again. Haven't made yet the nomination of Incutti, waiting for word from Pat or someone.

The Death of Vengeance. . . . I've overcome another hurdle—how not to kill for vengeance without submitting to the fear of earthly punishment. It has seemed ignoble to me till now to forgo the vendetta in name of a love I cannot yet feel truly in my heart but only abstractly realise in my misleading brain. I haven't voiced this thought, though it's been ever lodged inside the purpose of my brain. Vengeance—an eye for an eye, a tooth for a tooth is not served by striking out at the obvious surface level of life and pain which are not within the province of our will when that will merely serves as slave of destiny. That's the point where the parallel lines of Christ's love, Jehovah's vengeance and Moses' barter meet in the infinity of justice.

The reason why I must remain still in this prison of life is because I am so fumbling slow to learn.

8 January   Dream. Four or five people sitting on a sofa. They're all dressed, but there's a sensual orgiastic atmosphere. Insert images of girl's arse, black panties, just small areas of exposed flesh about to be spanked in a kind of orgy ritual. One of the people on the sofa is a little girl of about eight or ten who looks on in a wide-eyed look of first orgasm. Could be Carol. She's all wrapped up in her own experience. The whole feeling is warm, pleasant, sensual.

Agnello, the little forty-year old Neapolitan con man. He measures time by the months-years he spends outside of prison. I keep telling him they don't put him in because he steals, they put him in for doing his job badly. He says this last time he was really smart. He stayed out for four years! 'But not because I wasn't working' he adds quickly to preserve his self respect.

Everyone teases him constantly, but he has the natural comebacks of an Eastern sage.

'Agnello, do you own a big car?'

'What do I need a car for . . . ? When I need a car I steal one.'

'Agnello, how come you never got married?'

'Because I'm always in prison, that's why. If I got married while I'm in prison my wife would cheat on me and so she would bring me dishonour!'

9 January   Letter to Deb: What I read to you today was not meant to teach or explain anything, except perhaps the fact or process of my own floundering search for truth. Like most of my thinking I've been writing down, it doesn't come up with any answers that can be passed from one person to another like an apple. They describe a way of clearing a path that is quite personal to me and thus perhaps has some significance towards understanding how *my* mind works and where it is trying to go. In any case, I know that it's not clear and precise enough to be understood in one hurried reading, even in terms of my meaning. It may hopefully stimulate quite different images and stirrings in your own consciousness. It is basically not my understanding but your own you must deal with.

I have a feeling (beyond proving or disproving) that we each contain within ourselves all knowledge which is finite during our brief conscious physical existence of life. We try to bring as much of that as possible into our consciousness. That is the process of learning, of seeking truth. Books, words, experiences, both sensual and emotional, are all only tools for unlocking that comprehension that is within us. We can have visions of truth without being able to put them into words, even perhaps without being able to organize them into thoughts, which are words we use in talking to ourselves. Carol, I think, had this gift to a high degree. She had enormous faith in it which made her psychic struggle so violent within herself. We only saw the outward manifestations of it like the fire of a volcano or the convulsions of the earth we call earthquakes which are only surface symptoms of the enormous energy raging at our planet's core. That's why, in spite of the hysteria, she extended such vibrations of calm. I think your spirit, in a different way, your own way, has enormous possibilities for understanding, for comprehension of truth, quite possibly more than my own.

I don't say this because of the love I bear for you and wish to flatter your pride—all such concepts are meaningless on the level I speak of. I say it because you must have complete confidence in your instrument even when it may at times seem completely out of tune with everyone else's, even when it seems contradictory and confusing to your own conscious self. I'm talking again as always more to myself than to you, because it is precisely that deep confidence, that cool that you have within the energy that makes me think so. Carol had that confidence, Osiris has it. Words are difficult. The most appropriate I've found is 'to go with the flow'. The importance of all experience is to grab it and delve into it and not either to seek it or avoid it.

10 January   The great significance of Christ, as of Buddha or Mohammed, is not so much in the truth they found or their teachings with which they tried to share that truth; the great significance of these phenomena is in their enormous magnetism of personality which transfuses itself over centuries, even when their teachings are totally misunderstood and misinterpreted. It is this unquestionable magnetism that is felt, sensed by people who have neither the intellectual nor spiritual freedom to accept the teachings on any but the most banal levels and by people who have need to distort them.

What I say now is rather difficult for me to say out loud. I say it because first I find the difficulty itself intriguing, second because I now feel it much more strongly and third because I no longer think it is any subjective ego gratification but simply an interesting phenomenon.

To my surprise I find a certain magnetism to emanate from myself, without any personal effort or consciousness of it, in this environment. People seem to sense something in me that I am not aware of projecting. Various people whom I've made almost no effort to cultivate form strong attachments to me. I have been aware of this before, but in free social intercourse there is always mutual selectivity. People who enter into one's personal circle of contact identify by some common mutual interest, intellectual, spiritual, materialistic advantage, sexual, artistic, etc. Perhaps you can make them laugh or suffer or have an orgasm or stimulate their thinking or spiritual process, who knows?

The people I'm speaking of now are for a large part people who cannot be intellectually stimulated by me, cannot respond to my sense of humour, can't (I don't think) arrive at orgasm from my presence—people who cannot profit from any of the things I'm aware of being able to bestow in some measure. This magnetism is a great mystery to me and I set it down to begin my search for its understanding. I know that it is a very dangerous thing to possess. It easily creates fear in others. I think it is at the base of the few extremely strong and seemingly unaccountable antagonisms I've encountered in my life. It attracts animosity and persecution like a lightning rod. That is something that can be taken into account, but what is more dangerous are the counteractions, the effects of this attraction set up in the self that so often divert, block and diffuse one's own search. It takes constant awareness and more understanding of the phenomenon than I now possess to discern the positive as well as the negative effects of this magnetism on one's own search. Rejection of the people thus attracted can in itself be a most negative effect; on the other hand, acceptance can cause over-involvement in the psychic needs of other animae when my own needs my attention to grow.

I have a feeling that Nietzsche suffered from the rejection effects which left him in a kind of brilliant sterility. I know it will take me a long time to find the answer, so I'll just shelve the problem for now.

Carol—Osiris—Debbie.

11 January   Yesterday I sent a telegram to Peppino: *Sono pronto per uscire dalla mandala.* Today the guard came to tell me from the director that he can't pass it through the censor because of the 'secret' word at the end. I happened to have the Jung book that has a picture of a mandala which I sent to the director in explanation of the strange word. Half an hour later the guard returns with the telegram.

'The director says you must explain it more clearly in the telegram—mandala is not in our dictionary.'

I said 'The telegram is a *poesia*, one cannot "explain" a *poesia*', and started to crumple up the telegram to dismiss the matter.

It seems that is an act of sacrilege or something. The guard immediately said 'No, no,' and took it back from me and disappeared once more.

Diamantis, Constantino, Argiris, Jonis finally got out today. We exchanged memoranda. It was quite an emotional parting.

Diamantis whispered to me 'You know he (I think Constantino) just said to me he feels very sad that he has to leave you.'

Jonis gave me the cross he'd worn around his neck, and later C. gave me his with the black beads. I now have two crosses round my neck to take the place of the one Carol left me when she died, the one that they won't let me keep here. It has the beauty-love-irony significance.

Also the professor is leaving, but for another cell. Agnello is worrying about the next cell-mates. I should have thought he'd learned acceptance of these changes by now. I look forward with curiosity to the next passengers, the next chapter. Next time I hear Greek music, it will be embodied by four Greek visions and their vibrations.

Conscious fools, that is fools who are aware of their foolishness, warrant attention for their honesty, warrant listening to that we may decipher their wisdom, warrant gratitude for the music of laughter they bring to our hearts, warrant respect for their humility and love, for their generosity. I will pay attention to such true fools. I will listen to them. I am grateful to them. I can respect and love them. But you false fools who parade in judge's robes with policemen's badges, who wear the mortician's mask under your general's cap, who spout synthetic knowledge and counterfeit ideas, you I can only dismiss with pity for your own sakes and mine. For you possess neither honesty, nor generosity, neither wisdom nor love and your respect even for yourselves is but a fantasma of your pride. I shall tolerate your presence when I have no other choice, but otherwise give you wide berth for your souls cast a putrified smell about them in their decomposition. Under your fine habits, gentlemen, you stink. Behind your dead serious mask you are ridiculous, your unfeeling brutality in half-masking, accentuates your cowardly fear and your half-knowledge is half-stupidity, your counterfeit wisdom exposes your ignorance, and your titles are the scrotum of your dishonesty. You do not warrant another page.

12 January   *Letter to Deb :* I've been thinking about the pie they wouldn't let you give me. I thought of telling them that the meaning of the gift is not in the eating of it, that it would be far better to let you give the gift and then eat it themselves or throw it away than to interfere with Christ's message of love whose symbolic act is the act of giving. But then there would have to be so many things explained first and no explanation can reach understanding, if the heart is not able to receive it.

As the Pueblo Indian Ochwiny Biano said to Carl Jung, the great white medicine man: 'The whites always want something, they are always uneasy and restless. We do not know what they want, we do not understand them. We think they are mad.' Jung asked him why he thought the whites are all mad. 'They say that they think with their heads.' 'Why, of course. What do you think with?' Jung asked in surprise. 'We think here,' said Biano, indicating his heart. The brain-reason is an instrument to translate the message of the heart. When in our brain's pride we undertake to censure and interpret instead of translating, then words and ideas interfere with heart to heart communication and become but sterile static.

I would have to explain, for instance, that theft is a very venial sin compared to the mortal sin of indifference. All sin is a private matter of the soul and God. The only effect of sin that can be of matter is its effect on one's own conscience, on one's own soul, on one's own relationship to God. You can only steal from the miser, you cannot steal anything from generosity which is love, which is common with God; just as the miser is fear which is censorship of God. Indifference, on the other hand, does not affect the miser, but greatly offends love and is therefore a most serious sin.

I write you this to show you I tasted the fruit of your pie and received nourishment from it, to let you know that your gift was not only received, but consumated.

I had another thought. If I leave my cell and go into the courtyard, I increase my freedom of movement, my freedom of social communication, but I'm all the more aware of the extent of the walls of my prison. Such relative freedom is pointless, as freedom beyond these walls is pointless and relative. Life itself is a prison. We are imprisoned in our bodies, we are forced to breathe, to eat, to feel—we are even imprisoned by divine providence or destiny. The only possible 'escape' is in the spirit of man, not in ignoring the bars that surround us, but in accepting them and comprehending their futility. It is the people who in their pride, their fear create prisons for others who in doing so most imprison their own hearts in indifference—it is they who suffer the evil effects of the prison. All negative voodoo has a way of bouncing back. We can find the way to God in the acceptance of suffering, not in the imposing of it. That is why he appears to us in the form of Jesus and not in the form of Pontius Pilate, the Pharisee or the Caesar.

It seems inconceivable that they will not let you see me except once a week when you have worked and saved for three months to come half way round the earth and can stay only ten more days. But as I said, there must be a reason. Perhaps it's to let you find more clearly how you can communicate with me through Pat, as she through you, through Osiris who by the way I've become convinced is my guru, through all the people who are close to me, through the flowers, the house, the sunset and the sea that are pervaded by Carol's spirit. There are times when we are prevented from the contact of physical sensations to force us to develop our mystical sensitivity. 'Scavati bambina' means 'dig yourself baby'. Love. Billie.

Before I wrote the letter to Deb I had another dream. I was cross-examining the judge. It was real but also followed the lines of a play like the Caine Mutiny court-martial. I knew I had him. I asked him what time it was. He started to put on his glasses. I said 'No, without your glasses.' He started to break. I pursued the point. 'You do not know, you do not admit you are blind, but only pretend to know, pretend to see.' He became extremely embarrassed. I felt sorry for him, because he was becoming ridiculous to the others though he struggled on valiantly trying to find the answer to what time it was with mathematical equations, but even his notes he had great difficulty in reading.

We are in a theatre prison. I go down a flight of stairs. Outside there is a mob. Debbie is there. She is about five years old. We communicate beautifully, giving each other strength and cool. Carol is at the trial though I do not see her; I know she admires, approves my performance, though she too feels for the judge and objects to the ridicule of the crowd.

Previously I had a dream where I was in a tower climbing up furniture, which is not at all secure, to reach a terrace. I get to the top where everything is very shaky. The dream ends before I get on the terrace, though I don't have the feeling that I will fall.

14 January   Tomaso had a dream last night that I was leaving. He was all excited about it. Agnello has turned into Attilia. [The woman who worked in Bill and Carol's apartment in Rome before they moved to Praiano.] He won't let me pick up a broom, have to do it when he's out of the cell. Antonio is cooling out, but depressed. They let him out on provisional liberty and then arrested him again! He's got three kids. What madness with these *persone per bene*. My friends here, these 'hard' characters, are so easy to turn on. A little music, a little cool. . . . Agnello's hit on the right idea. If you need something, steal it. If the uptight people only realised how weighted down they are with their possessions, tied to the cord of pride about their necks. If someone needs something, let him 'steal' it, what's the difference? Stop pushing them around, laying fear and pride on them, and why should they kill each other when there's nothing to prove? If only we could get rid of all the useless bullshit and spread whatever there is around and work when we feel like it, feel responsibility when we feel like it, dig each other, dig life, dig love—I'm quite sure there'd be no need for fear.

An incredible load was lifted off me when I went through the vendetta concept. All is cool, oh so very, very cool. I feel you guiding me baby, I feel you so strong. I dig it. I dig . . . everything.

It's incredible how beautiful things come to you when you're free from trying to 'get yours'. The Greeks left me cigarettes for three days and extra meat and wine and 5,000 lire on the bill! Back to Gibbon and his story of greed and power, fear and bullshit pride.

15 January   Giovanni was drawing last night. I drew a figure that seems to have three arms. He wanted to show the drawings to his teacher but said 'Better not show him this one with three arms because it's not right.' I told him 'If you can't be free in your fantasy, what's left? Art is fantasy, it doesn't have rules of right and wrong.' But in the 'schools', especially here in Italy, they still 'teach' rules about drawing. The fact that they are the most stupid rules is not what upsets me so much, but that instead of absorbing the freedom of art into their lives, they insist on infesting art with the prisons of their rules.

Refusal to apply reason to 'things as they are'—i.e. to accept what is obviously absurd by authority of law, custom, tradition or fear—renders the service of *all* science and recorded knowledge impotent of the advantages that might accrue from them. To this extent a more primitive, i.e. less recorded and rigid inheritance of knowledge and science, is preferable and less dangerous because it at least gives more free and open rein to the currents of mysticism and need. The advantage of cumulative time-wisdom which the recording means give to mankind is no doubt extraordinary and can reduce the otherwise ponderous time element of evolution of knowledge, comprehension and wisdom. It does the same, however, for ignorance, error and stupidity. The evolution of the first is only possible if there is no censorship of 'common sense' and if the elimination of absurdity is given top priority. Nuclear bombs are absurd, regardless of the clear thinking, technical skill and ingenuity that is invested in their manufacture. Disproportionate distribution regardless of need of food and goods is more than injustice. It is absurdity since it makes any organic social order impossible and forces us to adopt the rules of fear and ignorance, thus damaging all mankind—the privileged as well as the deprived. Wilful destruction of ecology is absurd regardless of the immediate minor comforts it may provide. The acceptance of fear and denial of love is absurd. The acceptance of any absurdity is absurd.

17 January   Deb, Pat, Allain. Allain is concerned that it will be blown over. Yesterday's headlines. Of course, that is their game and to that extent they are absolutely right. So many horrors have since passed under and over the bridge with the result that last year's crime interests only dusty judges moiling over dusty acts and that of course is not our way. He asked me if I were interested in a private autopsy, but I said no. Too many wrong hands have already touched your poor body that should only have been touched for pleasure, for beauty and for love.

They are right, yet they are also eminently wrong. I am not at all concerned. The very essence of Carolyn Lobravico is that she was incapable of making an unnoticed entrance or exit. I never quite understood why or how, but that was always an undisputed fact of your existence. You did it in so many unexpected ways, but it was invariably so. I know your last exit will upstage even dear Sharon's and as ever in a different manner; you were always above competition. One of the things I look most forward to now is how you will manage it. It may well be that not all the world will have noticed, but those who were meant to notice in whatever way will mark it well regardless whether or not they search it out or shut their eyes. If the Salerno dwarfs are to be included or not, is not for me to decide. If they are not, I will not give them the honour. You may keep us all waiting for yet another moment, but your curtain call will be memorable. Your timing was always perfect and could not be second guessed.

Today eight or ten guards burst into the cell. Special perquisition! Ordinarily they do it every couple of weeks in the early morning when everyone is still asleep, to search for home-made weapons and escape tools. This time they concentrated on my cigarettes and tobacco for rolling cigarettes when I run out. I get it all from the prison commissary. What do they expect to find? They don't have to 'find' anything, only suspect and keep me another six months while they 'analyse'. The only good thing is that it shows someone is worried of standing one day in the bright sunlight of truth without his jockstrap.

19 January   A new arrival. His vibrations depress me. He just sits and stares. He's got six kids at home. One gets used to everything here in time; it's just the getting used to of the others that I haven't got used to yet. On top of it yesterday's episode. Just shows how hard up they are to pin something on me. First they steal the marmalade, then they have to find some victim somewhere because the cowards are so afraid they might become the 'victims' of their own action. When you cover a manure pile with fine democracy silk it still smells just the same—if one has the courage to step close and does not content oneself to look at it from the safe distance of the bourgeois household with a rose-coloured telescope. Tomorrow is my birthday.

20 January   Geburtstag! Debbie brought me a beautiful necklace she'd made for me, and Pat a groovy leather jacket. They 'may' let me have the jacket but haven't yet. Second day hunger strike. Debbie-Pat supposed to come back tomorrow. Debbie is down —she has to go back Saturday. More fucking *pacienza*.

21 January   The first hundred days without you. I suppose it's only fitting this new life should begin with not being easily able to forget what they did to you—not that I think I ever could. They'll never be able to do anything more to me again. These hundred days plus however many more of 'prison', only confirm my freedom and their *scavitu* of fear and ignorance. Like you I have accepted my tomb. I too have passed a birthday here whose little joy is magnified a thousand fold by the horrible depression that surrounds it. I only lacked the joy of being able to communicate my joy to you, but at least I don't have to censor out the shit for fear of making you depressed. They won't even let me have your letters here so that I have to read them from memory. That too is fitting after all, after all, after all . . . before the conscious significance of 'before' has begun.

Before all . . . the next all is still in embryonic unconsciousness, a vague promise of hope of life as yet untouchable by conscious reality—more exclusive, less defined, more infinite as you are elusive; less defined, more infinite in my heart where you is I and I is you, and we can dispense with the separating gulf of we and you inside the intimacy of I, of one. You had to die, I had to live. You live in the place where I died—we now are complementary in ultimate consummation. I now know what made me go on a hunger strike. It is the living symbol of death, a joy of deprivation, a deprivation of joy. How else can one commemorate a sad-happy birth-deathday! My love, you are where I am not. One hundred is the one at the unity of multitude of universal love.

Letter to Debbie. How could I tell you with words how much it means to me that you were here? How the fact that the fools gave us only five final minutes is immaterial to us, how their not letting you give me back Carol's wristband has its own significance between you and me and Carol and keeps them separate from disturbing the peace of our love with their frantic unenlightenment? How words and presence are only symbols of our union and communication and their very miserly permission or retraction of these symbols only enriches our love, our freedom, our experience, while they impoverish their own understanding to enrich the ignorance of their pride which fastens the strangling chains of their ignorance and confirms their slavery to their fear. We can only gain where they cannot even lose because they ain't yet got.

I love you, baby. Your joy is my joy, as my tears are your tears, your beauty my beauty. I fly with you over the ocean as you stay here with me in this so-called prison. Fly, fly the road, to glory. Follow the sun that never sets though the earth must refresh and absorb while it shuts its eyes and shades itself from the source of energy in the cooling moon which is the mirror of the sun, the memory of light, as ignorance and fear keep alive by contrast the presence of wisdom and love. By the absence of wisdom and love they prove their existence and hold out the promise of the eternal sunrise, when we shall be strong enough to accept the glory of eternity without contrasting contradiction, without need to 'repose' and absorb. Billie.

How do you pray? How do you see? How do you hurt? How do you feel? When you have no ear for others' prayers, when you have no eye for others' beauty, when you have no sense for others' pain, when you are numb to others' feeling? Are you so devoid of faith that you believe God is inside the cage of your catechism and nowhere else? Are you so accustomed to barren darkness that beauty's light must smart your eyes? Are you so filled with your own pain of soul that you cannot bear empathy? What horrid noises fill your inner ear that our screams to you are silence? Who are you, insensitive man, who seem not to hear, who seem not to see, who seem not to know of pain, seem not to feel and pray and yet in seeming not to have these functions common to all show but your fright, show the nakedness you cover with vain feathers of your pride and numb brutality? I can but pity you, poor man, who waste the beauty of your sensitivity, the essence of your soul to purchase but cold comfort of frivolous complacency. I can only pity but not understand or perhaps will not yet admit what I do clearly seem to understand since I still sense too much the poverty of my compassion, to soothe the utmost horror of your pain of soul, and thus dismiss you simply for an impoverished ignorant fool. And yet I know that underneath your hard core of stern self-righteousness, under the tangling netting of your foolish ignorance stirs a volcano of fear whose trickling lava has but scorched my outer skin.

I dread you man who cannot sing, who cannot laugh, who cannot love, who cannot truly pray, who cannot dance, who must needs choke on tears. I dread you for you must needs destroy all that to me is dear, all that you might enjoy, all that is most important. I dread you man, but you can never touch what is essential in my soul. Your blindness lets me the more clearly see, your numbness lets me the more truly feel, your misery's avarice of spirit makes me feel wealth beyond belief amidst my spirit's poverty. That which you steal from me and in your envy trample under foot enriches me. In utter desolation of my sadness I think I've found more happiness than you in drunken laughter of your caged-in ecstasy.

23 January   Today Debbie flies home, or is it tomorrow? Fly baby, fly and keep flying, God bless you my joy.

Incutti came. I just listen to the explanations. I no longer react. How can I react? There is no rhyme or reason, and the mystical and emotional vibrations of these people are not on my wave length. He, I feel, is quite conscientious and sincere. He will do what he can do, but the game is still played by the other players with their funny rules and tricks for which they have their own reason or motivations, none of which are on my wave length. I wait and flow, and what is worthwhile will come to me in its mysterious way. Incutti says Verasani will give his 'sentence' in two or three days when he gets his shit back, that the *tribunale* will set a date 'as soon as possible'—translated he estimates now March or end of February . . . maybe, maybe! How can I even feel any anxious expectations or anxiety at this point? It's their problem. I have more worthwhile things to contemplate.

Finished five days hunger strike. Don't really feel even hungry. Strange, doesn't have much effect, except that it makes everyone else flip out because they all think they'd starve to death after one or two days. Maybe it's to cause at least some doubts about pet convictions.

Giovanni and Felice got up in the middle of the night and made me anchovy sandwich and cheese and everything they could scrape together. I really couldn't eat much, wasn't very hungry, but it was a great great feast of good vibrations. Life could be so simple and beautiful if we could only let ourselves go with the flow. It takes so little water to make the deserts bloom.

Oh yes, Marchisiello came by to say hello and let me know he's doing what he can. Weird feeling. He's the man who signed the original order!

25 January   Felice . . . what a beautiful name, and it fits him. Such a happy disposition, a real life Billy Budd. Yesterday he learned to play chess. I've never seen anyone pick it up that fast. Last night he was laboriously drawing letters into his lettering book till 4 a.m. At the moment he wants to learn writing because he gets a kick out of it. He has a lust for life, a lust to learn. The judges could learn much from him if they were not so blindly learned. The 'holy' system which they prefer to defend rather than comprehend, prefer to exploit for benefit of their little egos, produces out of such a fantastic human being a twenty-three-year-old illiterate convict. I can no longer get upset that they fear hashish without the slightest inkling of what it is. They have as little comprehension of humanity itself and are also afraid of it.

Enough about the fools, more about the wise. Felice knows a ghost who comes to visit him. He is all white and the others can't see him, but Felice gets along very well with him. A couple of times when he had problems and was depressed the ghost even helped him out. They went out stealing together. They had to be careful to keep to curved crooked streets and avoid cross-streets. Then his ghost friend would show him where to break in. There was a small opening in a grilled entrance and when Felice got stuck the ghost gave him a hefty push. Felice is delighted he has this 'gift' of seeing ghosts. It's due to the fact that the priest left out a few words at his baptism.

27 January   Begins the 26th week. On the 176th day. One hundred and five days of limbo. Fifteen weeks without you. 115 days since you last spoke to me, since you last warmed my heart from the outside. Fifteen weeks that you are I and I am you. Your love warms me, your love sustains me, your love gives me strength as never before when I need it as never before. That is the justice of destiny. . . . You give warmth to my warmth, light to my meaning. When I try to imagine what warmth, light and meaning would be had I never known the joy of you, I realise what can exist beyond the conceivable limits. You are my gate to the conception of infinity—the sun itself is but a valley of shadows, there is no ultimate. What joy to think there is no ultimate, no bars, no prison of limit. What joy to know that there is you in my heart that of itself could never have conceived you had you not been sensible to touch and sight and love.

28 January   The question is what do you have to show for it? It's really pathetic if you have only bitterness or sympathy thirst, if it can't take you to a higher level. Everyone's suffering is private anyway. How can you compare it if you can't get inside another's soul? Neither the sound of the scream nor the blade of the knife nor the size of the scar can define the pain. That's why it is easier to become immune to the pain of others than to stop screaming. It's an immunity you were unfortunately immune to, my darling. How can they who have anaesthetised themselves to empathy begin to understand the pain they made you feel? And yet even that pain exists in a moment of time that is now past; in the now and future of my heart is only the bitter-sweet joy of knowing you had the courage of your sensitivity to feel it. They are tears of beauty that keep swelling up in my eyes and leave a choked feeling in my throat when I think of it. I have no need to show my scar to the blind who neither know the pain nor see the beauty of it.

12. 4 February–29 March

4 February   You may listen to my words—I should be pleased, I should be flattered, I might even in my egotistical loneliness be grateful to you for your attention. I should know no more, no less. You might as well listen to the song of a bird or watch the sunset or hear my laughter or touch my tears or hold a rock. In any case, as you absorb, as you feel, as you think—you shall understand what you may understand today; for all these things are part of God's creation and will bring you closer to him in the consciousness of your feeling, in the consciousness of your understanding that this moment of time has brought you to. The seed of your consciousness may be watered by my words—I should be pleased, I should be flattered, I should be grateful if it were so. I should know no more, no less. The seed of your consciousness may be nurtured by my words, by the sunset, by the song, by the rock, the laughter or the tear in this moment of time; but do not, I pray, mistake the water for the seed. Absorb, absorb, reject what you will. Assimilate. Do not try to retain the fleeting water in your grasp and think you hold a treasure in your empty hand; do not repeat from memory. The dried up prune is not a plum, the dried up water droplet is but air. All that remains as long as you remain within this temporal state is the seed of your consciousness which may transfer itself into your longer lasting soul in some unforeseen, unheard, untouched, unscented and as yet uncomprehended way. This seed of consciousness must feed to grow, must feed to live, must feed or die; it gets no nourishment within the sterile grasp of rigid memory. Do listen please, do touch and see, do taste and scent and feel, then try to comprehend what you are capable of comprehending and tell me of your thoughts that I may in turn absorb them into me. Then I shall be richer in my knowledge and pass it back to you . . . with love.

Well . . . at least another month here. We have to point for

12 March 'if all goes well'. The law-people say I'll go free after the trial but as we well know for dramatic impact and potency those predictions have substance of wind. The Salerno Mephistophelians will not so easily concede on their pact of blood. I'll watch the play to the end. I never could walk out, even on a bad performance. No point crying about spilled tickets. The ante is too high to drop out even if I could. As for my own part—another month, another year, whatever it is, is just punishment, just contrition for my guilt for all the times I withheld a pleasure from you—be it a smile or a caress, a comfort or a fuck that I might have placed in your oh so limited grabbag, that grabbag that you consumed with such loving appetite. It's a light sentence when men who never had the measureless joy of being loved by you, are punished with *ergastolo* [life sentence], having committed such venial sins as murder. What minor trivia compared to me who struck you with my hand. I shall expiate my sin knowing the clemency is in payment for such pleasure, such warmth and such love as I was able to give. In the profundity of my suffering I will also accept the growth it gives me as the reward of the punishment. In true justice there can be no punishment without reward, no reward without punishment—or else where would be the justice? I am my judge, my scourge, my cornucopia, I am my universe. I am I . . . and also you.

7 February   I'm OK now but this afternoon I slept and must have dreamt. I can't remember what, but when I awoke it was bad-bad-bad good. I must have been with you. I missed you so terribly I ached to wake to the you-less world. But it keeps my soul from shrivelling and preserves appetite. It is a joy to wake to consciousness of painful lack, it signals unremembered joy and makes me wish return of sleep. My love, my love continues growing in my heart more that you're gone, more you are here with me.

A most unlikely case . . . I did the cards for Pasquale before he left. The cards have a strange power. They allow you to say things, not only say, but communicate in a way that transcends or circumvents. They have a similar effect of intimacy as the sublime act of fucking. I never would have dreamed of piercing through his armour of pretended self-satisfaction and square opinionatedness; but suddenly, involuntarily I found myself speaking to him of love and sentiment and warmth, his warmth, and search for truth and I felt communication, felt an intimate touching of soul. The next day he had me write two letters, one swearing vendetta to the death against the man who now is mate of the woman he loves and father to his son. The sentiments expressed were from the vicious cycle of vendetta-honour rules, impotent in effect as misguided in intent, something he had to get out and it would have been worse than useless to do anything but write them as he said them. But what was real and touched me was the truth of his emotion, the truth of the tears that welled up in his eyes, the truth of the fact that this hard boiled egg allowed me the intimacy of witnessing them. Love communicates in mysterious ways. Pasquale spontaneously embraced me and kissed me as he left. I never would have expected that in a million years, as they say. The break-through lay in the cards.

This morning I did the clean-up detail. Even though I cautiously wait till all have left for school or *passeggio* there is always a Felice who straggles behind. It is a custom in Italy that work is a social affair. One man is incapable of doing anything. It needs at least one other who carries on a running commentary of advice which is at once supervision, entertainment and command.

They've all come back from their free play period. No point in trying to think. Anyway, it may be impossible to attack the problems of the Latin soul with the mind of Teutonic rationalism that has fed on the Yankee brine of expediency, affected by Hebrew mysticism, spiced with Bakunin, with a mind resting in a body whose soul is drawn into the magic magnet of Lao Tse, with a heart ruled by a gypsy poltergeist and a wish to transcend the infinity of space to God. Amen.

Last night Giovanni made his protest. He asked to be sent to the isolation cell, the one they use as punishment. He explained to me that way they have to bring in a magistrate to question him. The guards and the *brigadiere* refused to send him. He started to flip out, methodically. First he yelled, then he threw all his things into the cell corridor. Next he banged his cot against the door and barricaded the door. They still ignored him. He picked up the broom and broke out all the little windows one by one. At last about ten of them came and broke down the barricade. Giovanni clutched the bars with his arms, broken glass gripped in his hand and wild determination in his eyes. They backed down. Finally the *maresciallo* came to 'negotiate'. He gave his word nothing would 'happen' to him and that he would call the judge in the morning. I offered to go down with him as a 'guarantee'. The *maresciallo* agreed, Giovanni agreed . . . he went to the isolation cell. The same night we were all moved to a different cell. This morning Pietro left for his trial in Gubbio. We are now three.

12 February   Today the *brigadiere* showed me the letter I wrote my mother express *raccomandata* thirty days ago. It has come back from the U. S. consulate with translation! I told him what I thought of their formalised mother-love, their formalised humanity, their formalised freedom.

He said 'But it's written in English, I don't speak English.'

I told him that's why the atom bombs will come, because everyone is so nice and conscientiously does only his bit, without thinking.

'But I don't speak English' he kept repeating.

'I told him bombs won't speak English either or Italian but he'll understand them all the same; that it's not enough to speak with the mouth in any language. One must learn to speak with the heart. The thing that really offends me is that the American consulate who offers a car and an interpreter to my mother and brings me the Christmas package and explains to the Italians the necessity for the American invasion of Laos, the horridness of the Russian invasion of Czechoslovakia and the great benefit of the nuclear base in Naples for the preservation of liberty and human rights—holds up a letter to my mother for thirty days to make a translation for the censor.

13 February   Last night I did arithmetic with Felice. His mind blocks at abstract numbers. Fascinating! I suddenly realised how multiplication-division is a purely theoretical concept. The decimal system is a magical invention—nothing at all natural about it. If you try to explain it with Roman numerals it's impossible. What is this magic quality about 10?

Anyway, the *brigadiere* came in and saw I was helping Felice to learn reading and right away—'Aren't you ashamed of yourself? He has to teach you to read and he's not even Italian! Why don't you go to the school?'

The whole performance is a dramatic example why this boy who can learn chess in twenty minutes, can't read, write or multiply. Instead of helping, instead of inspiring learning, the one who knows the slightest bit more lords it over the one who knows the slightest bit less. The *brigadiere* has to get into the act and play 'school teacher', which is another version of cops and robbers, of cowboys and indians.

He said 'I have 1,200 lire and have to divide it among seventy-five people. How much does each one get? D'you know how to figure it out? Good, when I come back the next time you can give me the answer.'

Then turning to me he said 'But you mustn't help him. You know it, don't you?'

I said, 'I would give the nicest one the whole 1,200 lire.'

'No, no. . . .' He gave an elaborate explanation, assuming I did not understand the Italian.

I said 'No, I understand. You want to divide 1,200 lire amongst seventy-five people. The point, however, is that it is a useless calculation because not one of them will get even the price of a cup of coffee.'

The *brigadiere* retreated and Felice plunged into a frantic search for the answer. It took me two hours to get him to think about the method and fuck the answer.

15 February[11]   Tried to explain to Rolf, i.e. to myself, the difference between wanting suicide and not caring about life or death. I know the answer, but I cannot yet explain it.

> *I do not wish to live*
> *I do not wish to die*
> *I do not wish to do anything*
> *I do not wish to do nothing*
> *I am not undecided*
> *I am not frustrated*
> *It's all the same to me*
> *I am not at all disinterested*

11. See Diary Notes, pp. 285–286.

That is the riddle. I know the answer, I cannot explain it. It's cool.

21 February   Outside our window, below on the roof of the guard shack, there are always pigeons, pecking away at the left-over pieces of bread the prisoners throw out to them. Bread is then thrown to them with a weight on a long string. The string is made by unravelling the yarn from a pair of socks. Tied to the string near the bread there is a small weight. With this home-made trap hours and days and weeks are then occupied trying to entangle the pigeon's legs in the cord and pulling the bird through the bars. I find it most depressing to dwell on this prisoners' passion for entrapping these animals who are in total liberty of flight, to pull them inside their own cage.

Today Felice caught a pigeon. I asked him to let it go. He didn't understand—he says he won't kill it. He tore out its feathers—he wants a pet. I do not understand why I wept for the first time in so long. Did I weep for the pigeon? Did I weep for Felice? Did I weep for me? Did I weep for you? I felt bad, bad, bad, good—good because my feeling bad made me sense your presence in me. My sensitivity is joy in having found your sensitivity inside my futile silent tear to share my loneliness, in having sensed my loneliness that is defined by you.

26 February   Telegram Incutti—Verasani's indictment for trial has been deposited! Incutti arrives with it. He left me a copy but the censor is still studying it. They haven't yet let me have it. While Incutti was here Tamarro also arrived. I hope I'll have more contact with Sottgiu. I cannot talk with the other two. They are incapable of thinking beyond 'getting me out'. That would have been important six months ago. How can I discuss absurdity with people who treat it seriously? To talk of justice where I cannot find the slightest spark of interest or conception of morality, of truth, of love, of sense even? There is no outrage, no sensitivity, no commitment—not even commitment to the political reality. Sottgiu is a communist, perhaps he'll at least have that. These lawyers are the same ilk as the judges, the cops and the jailers. Eeeeek! When will I be able to speak with human beings again? If Sottgiu is no better, what can I do? I cannot lend myself to this nonsense and deign it with attention and yet I'll have to do either something or nothing. What would they do if I do nothing, say nothing? Refuse to give a persecution the appearance of legality. Or should I simply wait and speak later? To refute the charge is to veil it with reasonableness.

27 February   You have all been civil with me. Each of you has done his part, his duty. Not one of you accepts his responsibility! You policemen, you doctors, you nuns, you lawyers, you consuls, you reporters . . . not one of you accepts responsibility and today you ask me to defend myself against your accusation: *the responsibility for the presence of a half gram of hashish in my house.* Today you ask me to do my part, to give my consent to the inevitability of this horror by defending myself. You say that it's always been like this. I tell you it will always be like this until one of you, until each of you shall follow your dream instead of doing your duty. It's true, it is the way things are—from My Lai to Hiroshima, from Auschwitz to Golgotha, from the Cardarelli hospital to the *tribunale* of Salerno.

I could not avert the suffering nor the death of my dearest love. I cannot stop the wars nor the construction of the bombs. I cannot avert this trial and I cannot avoid either your condemnation or your acquittal. Yet I protest! I protest not because our suffering is exceptional, but rather because our suffering is *not* exceptional. I protest against what is useful for my dream of humanity; against the rules—for reason; against duty—for love, against the law of Caesar—for the law of Jesus. I cannot avert what will happen but I, one three-billionth of humanity, will not do my part. I shall not defend myself against your accusal. Like Carol I am prepared to suffer for our dream but not to dream for the suffering to continue. I am prepared to die for life, but not to live for death.

28 February   I dreamed again of Carol. She was alive. I asked her how it could happen that they all said she was dead—even Verasani's sentence which makes it official—and what should I say at the trial? Should we tell them or keep it secret? As always she just shrugged her shoulders and gave me her enigmatic smile. We were standing by the window. I turned for a moment. When

I turned back she was gone from the room, though she could not have passed by me unnoticed. I was terrified, I raced around looking for her. I found her in the bathroom doing her make-up. She just smiled. I understood everything, but now I cannot remember what I understood.

1 March The *procuratore della repubblica* came to check out the scene in the cages. No devil, kindly old gentleman. I didn't say anything. He knew all about my case and gently told me it would only be another fortnight. I could only say *'finalmente'* and all the entourage smiled so very politely and understandingly. If your last terror-stricken, half conscious look just before the end, when they lifted you to change the piss-soaked sheets, had not pierced through my memory at that point, I would almost have felt grateful. They've waited five months and now it's 'only a fortnight' and justice will triumph or get shafted as usual and then what?

Oh baby, give me your strength. I need you, need you, need you now. Oh God, why couldn't they let me go the road to glory with you? Why must I still be here and watch and speak and care?

3 March Extraordinary letter from my mother. She's never spoken to me so directly from the heart, from out of herself, the being behind the mother. A metamorphosis is taking place. Have faith in the language of the heart. The first surprise was when I spoke to the secretary and the director of the *manicomio* after Carol died. I spoke not what I thought they expected to hear, not even what I thought they would understand, not what I thought they would agree with. I simply said what I felt in my heart. I spoke to them of love and life and truth and I found a response, an intimacy—and now my mother. When communication is pure, without the compulsion of ego, it can burst through the barriers of title and station and relationship that separate us— even of my mother! It doesn't change the relationship, it robs it of repressiveness. It's similar to the metamorphosis that takes place in people after they have made love.

I am an explanation junkie, I am a logic addict, I dig the high of reason; but what I understand is more than what I know, what I know is more than what I say. The secret of my heart is in the touch of my caress.

4 March   I went into a trance to find Carol, to find out how I should act. I was teaching. Carol, Anne Bancroft, Rolf and others. Annie and Carol did a scene. The curtain was closed. Orange peels and other garbage started raining out on the audience. We all moved back a few rows keeping a wary eye on the source of our distress. As the curtain opened Carol said to Annie (part of the scene) 'We must get their attention' or, 'I think we got their attention.' Rolf did a scene and also a few others. Rolf in particular all words, indicating reactions. The scene with Annie and Carol was the only good one. I took some good notes but when I wanted to give them I couldn't get the attention of the class. They were only interested in showing off their 'work' and being praised. The more I tried to explain with words, the more there were interruptions—coffee, lunch, etc. I kept getting more and more frustrated. Finally blew up at Rolf who was actually only telling the others to pay attention. Rolf was very hurt and left with the others. I was left with Carol and Annie who were the only ones who wanted to learn but who had shown they knew how to do it.

When I woke up I realised what I have to do. I must not try to explain. Carol is the star. Guerilla theatre: don't get in the way with words even when you think you know. To act is to do— not to talk about it.

Last night I concluded . . . the important thing is to let the others talk as much as possible. Let them condemn themselves. Don't attack so they can defend. That is our strength. They have the onus to explain. The more they try to justify, the more they attack, the more they incriminate themselves. I will tell Incutti not to attack Dr. Testa, not to ask for his disbarment. Ask questions. The important fight comes afterwards—it must be fought with questions, not answers and accusals. I know the answers. Those who are ready to know will only really know when they find the answers themselves. Carol is the silent witness, five months since her death are the silent witnesses. We must not take away their majestic strength with words that can be refuted, can be questioned, can be derided. It is not up to us to mention Carol.

They must bring her into the courtroom or leave her out. She will fend for herself. I do hope they'll leave me the handcuffs.

Verasani's twenty-seven pages;[12] the State Department's letter to Buckley,[13] Lautz's letter to Carol [quoted on p. 131]—those are the things that will make the collage. They have all the physical strength—the guns, the bars, the bombs. Jujitsu works only when the opponent is goaded into applying his power. A letter is sent from the U.S. Senate 7 January—it contains a carbon copy of a 19 December letter from the State Department—it arrives Naples 13 February—stamped again Naples 15 February —arrives to me in Salerno 4 March. That is more important than the exaggerations, rationalisations and lies it contains.

7 March   The life-boat-drill voice of Padre Riccardo burst in on our consciousness over the loudspeakers. 'Holy mass. Come to mass, come to holy mass. Today is Sunday. Everyone is under obligation to come to mass. Whoever's not Catholic mustn't come. The sooner you come the sooner it's over and the *colloquio* will take place. Come to holy mass, all must come to hear mass. . . .'Followed by the scratchy record of Sant'Antonio. Franco went. It turns out that there were so few in the audience that the good padre refused to say mass until the guards descended to the cells and rounded up more of the faithful. Ten days to go, though there is now talk that when the lawyers end their strike the magistrates will begin theirs. It only hurts when I laugh.

What must change to change the tyranny of the power pyramid is the individual. A mass of individuals whose hearts are split by fear into command and obedience, whose only concept of liberty is a loosening of chains, a distancing of frontiers—such a mass must inevitably divide into masters and slaves. The heart that is truly free, that is filled by love and does not acknowledge fear— that heart can neither be tyrant nor slave. The revolution must happen inside me, inside every one of the three billion people who populate this earth. I have only little reason to believe that such a change is possible even in my heart, yet I believe that it can happen for every one of us because it *must* happen if our

12. See Diary Notes, pp. 286–288.
13. See Diary Notes, pp. 289–293.

species is to evolve, if our species is to survive. In terms of the eventual revolution we must concentrate on the microcosm, on the individual. We must concentrate on individual responsibility. We must concentrate on the insignificant. In our analysis we must go from the complex to the simple, to the underlying cause, the origin. We must reduce to the common human denominator. Fear and love are common denominators. They govern the emotions and actions of the master as of the slave, the powerful as the weak, the sage as the fool.

Franco Diotti just arrived—he's a truckdriver from Piacenza. On his way through Salerno he bumped into a bus on which there was riding a *maresciallo* in *borghese* whom he told not to break his balls or something. *Offeso publico ufficiale!* Anyway, we're having coffee and *panetone* brought by Felice's family or maybe Franco's. We are now a jolly six and I really feel your presence in me. You always attracted a crowd. I languish on my cot and play Carol Lobravico paying occasional scant attention to my court, allowing them to amuse themselves and dropping an occasional bombshell.

8 March   Dream. A long table. There are about ten or twelve men seated. Each one gives his political views. They are all Americans—various expressions of left. I am the last one to speak. There is a slight hesitation and I say: communist. At first there is a shock but then all their faces register agreement at the pure simplicity of it. We were all of one mind to begin with, but each one had tried to couch it in words that were 'acceptable' to the others and also to himself. In my moment of hesitation I was tempted to do likewise but something made me choose the pure and simple truth over considerations of the practical, the effective.

I am on top of a long flight of steps. People are coming up the stairs to get some kind of blessing. I walk over to where the ceremony is and want very much to have it although I don't know what it is. It turns out it's to declare yourself black. It's all very religious.

I say 'Yes, I want to declare myself black' and the very gentle black holy-lady is about to take me in when she asks me what part of Italy I'm from.

I say, 'I'm American.'

She shakes her head sadly and says, 'I'm sorry, in that case it's impossible.'

I tell her I'm not a native American, I only have an American passport, that I don't consider myself any particular nationality.

'Sorry,' she says, 'I'm afraid it's quite impossible.'

I'm very disappointed. I go down the long steps envying the people I pass coming up. At the bottom I meet my father who tries to cheer me up. Then my father, my mother, Carin and Debbie—we're all in a kind of Howard Johnson's. My father is getting me a teddy bear to cheer me up, pretending it's just as good as being black, if not better.

I'm in a car, a kind of V.W. bus. There's a blonde girl. I'm taking off her panties but I'm not supposed to see her cunt. I do see it but it's very vague and doesn't interest me. I don't feel at all horny, I just don't want her to be embarrassed.

Incutti came. He has a book with all the 'case'. It's enormous, about two inches thick! He'll leave me a copy in a few days. I only leafed through it. A strange feeling seeing Carol's name in the medical reports and interrogations and gossip talk. Her prison photo! In a way I want to relive those moments with her, even through their dirty hands and keyhole eyes and warped minds. On the other hand, I dread it. The horrible outrage, how dare they? How dared they? And it all looks so legal and correct and 'explanatory'. Oh God, why did you take away my power to hate? It would make it easier. If only at least in my fantasy I could relieve the aching aching void by smashing my fist, by drawing my sword, my lance. I'm left with impotence, even of fantasy—limp. And yet I'll have to go through it and yet I want to go through it. Dying, being dead, not being would be easy still. Why do I have to wait till it will matter again? I know I know I know.

Peppino was downstairs at the *colloquio*. I felt his warmth. Why do we have to talk when talk is so much less? When talk is not possible without letting those clowns have centre stage of the conversation. It's good to feel Peppino's warmth, to hear that everybody is with me, and yet I dread getting outside this isolation. It will be a more difficult adjustment than coming in. Then I couldn't imagine what could be worse than finding that everyone is mad, that all sense is shattered into the absurd. Today I know even that. It will be finding out that all the world is sane again, that there are rational explanations for everything, but that you are not here, and life must go on. 'They who are near to me do not know how much nearer to me you are than they are.' Why did I have to learn the meaning of those lines so clearly?

9 March   Carol appeared in a glorious way. I think I was with some people coming up a path from a beach. Carol was strolling down in her cool dignity wearing or carrying a contraption that was at once a huge straw hat, a sun umbrella and a tent. It defies explanation and yet it was totally simple. The kind of thing where you wonder why no one's ever thought of it before. A total gas. I can't really tell now, and I think we couldn't tell then, whether it was attached to her head and shoulders or carried. It seems it was more carried but her hands and arms were free and yet it wasn't floating. Still, it was no mystery, it was completely obvious. From the edge of the *sombrero* she had hung coloured bands which gave it the impression of a tent. Just one of those outrageously lovely creations she was always coming up with, one of those bombshells she would introduce without fanfare, that centre of attention she so involuntarily managed to attract. It was a symbol of Carol that I can no more explain with words than I can explain her, that all those who knew her will understand instantly.

Felice knows quite readily all the letters and sounds of the alphabet. Confront him with a word like *risposte* he can immediately give you the sound of each letter but comes up with guesses like *romani, revisione,* etc. He instinctively likes too much the attention of having me explain it to him to learn it and lose that attention. I think that at least is the technical block. I'm sure there are other emotional psychological blocks that go back to infant experiences. Still here we have a mind that easily grasps the graphic complexity of chess and yet refuses to make the slight step between the spelling and laborious reading. At the same time he expresses infinite delight and application in the mastering of the most absurd and useless problems and tasks. I've decided not to help him for a while and disinterest myself in his progress or lack of progress and see what happens when the 'reward' of 'not learning' is removed. I told him I was convinced he was just pulling my leg. Subconsciously that is exactly what he is doing.

The idea of the divinity of Jesus is meaningless until we can define the idea of God. In the vaguest possible definition of God, the 'sacrifice' of his becoming man is infinitely greater than the pain and death of the crucifixion. Sacrifice signifies depriving oneself of something of value. The humiliation of becoming man far outweighs the humiliation of being spat upon and exposed to public view in the trappings of punishment. The terms sacrifice and humiliation have no significance to God, nor can the words 'pain, death, significance' have any meaning when applied to God. If God has chosen to personify himself in the apparition of this one man, then if we believe in God it is blasphemous to reverse the process, to oppose the will of God by deifying this man, thus destroying the very purpose of God. It is only through concentrating on the human form of Jesus that we can hope to find in some measure the word and meaning of God. If we do not believe in God, then all talk of divinity of Jesus is by definition impossible. For Jesus the God it is not his death that represents sacrifice but his birth, the pain of becoming man, not the pain of returning to God.

The example and preaching of Jesus the man can be understood and emulated by man. The example and preaching of Jesus the God can only evoke awe devoid of meaning. If we wish to personify the specific will of God in Jesus, it is even more rather than less imperative to consider him a man, to consider the myth of Jesus as a prophet of human influence and propagation rather than divine creation and command. The argument of whether God created man or man created God can be resolved only in favour of man, since 'argument' is a human concept. Since 'created', although a human impossibility, is still a human fantasy, a human concept, since the concept of God itself is a human concept, a technique of the human mind to reduce something beyond its comprehension within its own limitations—the concept of God is not yet God. On the subject of God all is possible. What is least possible is certainty. What is least permissible is intolerance and dogma.

10 March   Incutti is trying to round up all the 'good' witnesses, the *persone per bene* to prove that I am hospitable. I think that's a mistake. The persecution must be exposed. If only the good *persone per bene* amongst my friends were hospitably received in my house, I would not be here. The fact that I should have to prove my 'generosity', my 'hospitality', that I should have to explain that my friends with long hair are 'worthwhile' and 'important' people—that fact is the indictment, let's make that very clear—the need to defend one's actions that are the interpretation of the gospel of Jesus, that the practice not the violation of the commandments of Jesus Christ are suspect to the Caifas of the *Democrazia Cristiana* of Salerno, that hospitality towards the poor and uninfluential is suspect to the Pontius Pilates of the *Democrazia Cristiana* of Salerno.

12 March   I can't concentrate on the *tribunale* scene, I can't really concentrate on anything. Instead of time flying, it's standing still again all of a sudden—probably because it doesn't even look like it will happen on 17 March. Those fucking lawyers are still on strike. Depressing again. Also the cold is still with me and doesn't help energise. I only know I can't now allow them to force me to take them seriously. Their game is stupid, their traditions are atrophied, their game pompous, their players ridiculous. We must not make it less stupid by allowing them into our argument. We can submit to the terror, to the force, to the guns of their traditions. We must never endow them with dignity, we must not bow when there is no whip. Take them at their word, it is enough to let them display their stupidity. The truth is revolutionary. Make them pull out their whips—they are eloquent displays of the strength of their fear. Their self-conscious pomp betrays their lack of freedom. Though they may seriously hurt we must not take any of these things seriously. In taking them seriously we endow them with substance. Don't argue with the tiger who devoured your child; don't kick the car that deprived you of your arm; don't curse or adore the hurricane that destroyed your house. The importance of their effect does not change their substance. Tigers are tigers, cars are machines, hurricanes are natural calamities . . . and windbags are full of hot air. Just let them open their mouths and fart.

13 March   Today there's a military coup in Turkey. Greece—
Turkey——? Is Italy next? In their smugness they all think 'it
can't happen here', which is precisely why it can easily happen.
As always, as always, as always . . .! It's this habit of accepting
everything. The chain reaction of acceptance, the ability to
swallow without outrage, to digest without revulsion, to regur-
gitate with complacency—that can make it happen so easily here.
I only wonder why I should still care?

Incutti—he's certainly conscientious but I can't get with him
—no fantasy. He takes it all so normal and serious and so endows
the horrible absurd senselessness with a veil of sense. He leaves
me very depressed—makes me sense how entrenched is all this
madness. He is but another face of the police—judge—prosecutor
apparatus. Part of the testimony is that they had information
that I was the main supplier of drugs for Positano. How about
that? Did they ever ask themselves what possible motive I
could have to conduct such dangerous commerce on so small a
scale that all their search uncovered no supplies anywhere? In
the interrogation I said I had asked my friends not to bring drugs
into the house if they used them. That is as far as I will go—
I will not search my guests and their belongings.

Salvatore is the new arrival. The comedy continues. He had an
argument with a post official. In the post office there happened to
be a judge (thirty-seven years old) who insisted that the postman
make a *denuncia* for '*offesa a un publico ufficiale*'. When the postman
refused, the judge threatened to denounce *him*. Oh dear, these
guardians of the public morals! These Catos! Not even a crus-
tacean judge of eighty-five but a young cat of thirty-seven. No
wonder the merchants of the fascist drug are uptight for the love-
drug competitors. Do not confuse, dear hearts, honour with
pride, love with desire, order with slavery.

14 March   Incutti—today we had some contact. I'm not depressed like yesterday, although the news is that the 17th is off
—still a strike and they have to fix another date. We went through
the 'book'. I told him I did not want to explain that my house is
furnished '*normale*'. It is not according to the taste of the Salerno
policemen; but it is my taste, it is Carol's taste and it is to the
taste of our friends. If that is a crime, then let me condemn me

for it. It would be closer to the truth. I will not say that 'although only my name appears on the lease that I shared the right with Carol to invite people, because Carol was present at the signing of the lease'. Whether or not she was present, she certainly had that 'right', as has any friend the right to invite whomsoever he wants. I will not 'explain' this and thereby infer that it is something unusual. It is unnatural to lock your door, to lock your heart. There should be explanations for the action of locking, not for the act of not locking. These are absurdities I refuse to dignify by discussing them. I read him excerpts from the Gospels that explicitly refer to the arguments of this case and the whole law and punishment game they are playing.

Matthew 5:6, 10 . . . 'How blest are those who hunger and thirst to see right prevail; they shall be satisfied. . . . How blest are those who have suffered persecution for the cause of right; the kingdom of Heaven is theirs.'

Luke 6:27–38 . . . 'Love your enemies; do good to those who hate you; bless those who curse you; pray for those who treat you spitefully. When a man hits you on the cheek, offer him the other cheek too; when a man takes your coat, let him have your shirt as well. Give to everyone who asks you; when a man takes what is yours, do not demand it back. Treat others as you would like them to treat you. If you love only those who love you, what credit is that to you? Even sinners love those who love them. Again, if you do good only to those who do good to you, what credit is that to you? Even sinners do as much. And if you lend only where you expect to be repaid, what credit is that to you? Even sinners lend to each other if they are to be repaid in full. But you must love your enemies and do good; and lend without expecting any return; and you will have a rich reward: you will be sons of the Most High, because he himself is kind to the ungrateful and wicked. Be compassionate as your Father is compassionate. Pass no judgement, and you will not be judged; do not condemn, and you will not be condemned; acquit, and you will be acquitted; give, and gifts will be given you. Good measure, pressed down, shaken together, and running over, will be poured into your lap; for whatever measure you deal out to others will be dealt to you in return.

Matthew 15:6–9 . . . 'You have made God's law null and void out of respect for your tradition. What hypocrisy! Isaiah was right when he prophesied about you: "This people pays me lip-service, but their heart is far from me; their worship of me is in vain, for they teach as doctrines the commandments of men." '

Incutti's answer was, 'Yes, but that's theology. Not everyone can understand it.'

I said, 'No, *that* is most simple and most clear; it is the *codice penale* that is difficult to understand.'

What is religion and theology if it cannot be put into practice?

16 March   They can't put us all in jail, they can't kill us all; they can only threaten us all, they can only reach us with fear. If we refuse to fear, their weapons are only bullets, their weapons are only jails. Their purpose is to control us all, their purpose is not to imprison or kill some of us—that is only their method which tries to control all of us through fear. If we all refuse to fear, they will disappear. They will no longer have need of their purposes, they may become 'we'.

17 March   To the *tribunale*. Benedetta, Raffaela, Gaetano, then friendly faces and curious faces and some people in black robes who all seem like extras. It's only appropriate in this farce that although all concerned knew there was a lawyers' strike, they still had to put on their costumes and say the lines that set the new date. Next show 14 April! At least I got a look at the stage. I can't imagine the play but looks like a good advance. I don't forsee a long run.

Wrote C and D and M and bank. Goodnight sweet hearts.

18 March   The inquest. . . . Once you accept the nonsense that there *are* 'other valid considerations' beyond reason, beyond compassion, beyond love, then all makes sense. Once you accept the nonsense that there are 'considerations' that outweigh human compassion, then all is reasonable. We, poor players, of the guerilla stage, must play our parts that some few more of you may seeing, understand. What hearing, feeling you've till now ignored.

Today was just one more small scene. They all know now quite well the facts of 5 August, they all have now a pretty good idea of all the why and how of then and all the why and how since then. And yet because of 'other valid considerations', by a mere stroke of the clerk's pen I am imprisoned for twenty-eight days more. On 5 August 'they' knew what there was to know, but there were 'other considerations' that to them made their actions imperative, that superseded justice, kindness, love, that overruled their human reason, their human feelings. And so the same for seventy days when you grew slowly weaker, for seventy days when you wept and pleaded for the slight humanity to let me come to you and hold your dying hand, to let me travel the slight distance that separated our touch. Also for that they have their explanations.

And so the same: the consul from America who can explain so nicely his duties, limitations and responsibilities which make all that he does and did not do, all that 'possibly could be done'. And so the same: the day the hard judge no longer could delay, no longer could misunderstand the crystal clear findings of his examining delegates and yet delayed his 'judgment' for three more months for 'other valid considerations'. And so the same: the day the same stern judge explained to us with comma, paragraph and clause why in his 'judgment' the trial must now take place, which judgment in itself in its effect is sentence of x many months more of my confinement in this cage. And so the same: today the clerk's stroke of the pen, today the turn of the policemen's key and so today and so today and so today. . . .

When they explain to you why napalm bombs must sear the flesh of a Vietnam child, do you then understand the 'vital other considerations' that make this act of madness but a regrettable inevitability? If you say yes, you are a blessed man, for in your final flash of consciousness enveloped in the nuclear flash you'll have no doubt of why and how; it will make sense beyond reason, beyond compassion, beyond love for 'other valid considerations'.

19 March   Today is San Giuseppe. Everybody gets a *dolce* and a *salsice* and Padre Riccardo sends us his come to 'messa' message. Met the padre in the hall. He smiled. 'Just a little more' I said. Now it's starting again like so many times before. But I have news for you, my friends. You can't do me a favour. I will not smile and be happy and say thank you. What you never took from me, you cannot now give me back. I did not protest while I was here, while you had me gagged and bound. I will *not stop* protesting when I'm out. I will not let you forget.

Carol is buried in my heart, she is resting well, she has no need of you. I have no need of you. It is you, dear sick sick sick brothers, that have need of me, of Carol—to see yourselves. I shall be your mirror. It is a mirror that did not cloud up with my tears—it will not cloud up in the sun. I shall not blind you with my glass, but I will make you see.

What has not changed with time is you, my feathered ones. But I have time, had time, have time till there will be no more time for me as there is now no time for you, my darling. What happens in the time that's left for me is cool. I know the way, I care not how far I must yet go or where it ends, but you will never lead me down the path with the false promise of your false smiles.

The wrong, the hurt they've done me is much. Compared to what they did to you the much they did to me is nothing. I cannot even complain. Yet I will not belittle my suffering because it is a measure of the grievous pain, the most grievous wrong they did to you, they did themselves—they who now wish to forget. That all my suffering is not worth mentioning compared to what they did to you I readily admit. I more than they because I truly know —I know the pain at which they can but guess, I also know the benefits of which they cannot possibly conceive. I readily admit my suffering can be annulled—I do not even care to speak of it. But of the fact that it can *easily* be annulled, that I do *not* care to speak of it—because that much is nothing compared to what they did to you—of that I'll speak, of that I'll cry and scream so that they will not easily lull back to sleep their conscience and responsibility. But who will stop the bleeding in the will to live? You people who are so good at turning off, how can you give me such a tourniquet and keep safe distance that I cannot turn you on?

Incutti asked me what I intended to do when I got out. I told him I would visit your grave. And then? Then? How can I think past 'then'? Then I think perhaps I'll search, I'll look and think and search for reasons, signs and dreams that somehow will make life less meaningless.

20 March   I am not outraged, I am not surprised because I do not believe in the justice, the freedom, the love of humanity of the men who control the system. I am outraged, I am surprised that those who profess to believe these things are not outraged, are not surprised.

Trial set for 30 March—telegram from Incutti.

21 March   Beautiful bit. Franco's students made a demonstration for him. They protested because with him they could learn, with the new teacher they don't. There's probably the clue why they 'picked' him. The authority people don't like the popular teacher who thinks discipline is a by-product of teaching knowledge. They want knowledge to be an excuse to teach fear. Schools are training grounds for obedience. Where will it all end if schools become breeding grounds for freedom, for knowledge and for thought? Good heavens, that would disintegrate our society! Babies, it's happening. I've got news for you, it's already happened. The old diploma and *maserati*, the prison and poverty and all your versions of the carrot and the stick are losing their magic.

22 March   Before it happened you told me: 'You can't complain, you can't scream—nothing's happened.' Today you say: 'What's the point of screaming, it's over and done with.' But while it was happening, you had me bound and gagged! I scream not because it happened, I scream because it happened and you think there's nothing more to be done. I scream because while it was happening you bound my hands and gagged my mouth and refused to listen. I scream because it will happen again and it will be worse. I scream because what will happen will one day be in the past and you will say to me then: 'What's the point of screaming, it's all in the past.' It's not that your words are not reasonable. It's not that your words do not calm me, it's that I do hear you and yet I scream. I scream because your words do calm me, because you *are* reasonable, because I begin to listen to you.

24 March   You speak of *equality* and I see the poor, you speak of *freedom* and I see your prisons, you speak of *brotherhood* and surround your hearts with walls of indifference. Explain to me the meaning of these words you use so freely, then explain to me one word more . . . *hypocrisy*. I understand very well what you say, I do not understand what I see. Or perhaps I understand it all too well and it is you who must learn the language of the heart.

The courts have started working again. Felice came in to give the count with a smile on his face—roughly twenty years! I screamed at him and threw whatever I had handy. You can scream, you can weep, you can shoot the sons of bitches for all I care—but don't make light of their rotten inhumanity . . . with a smile! We may not be able to prevent their brutality, we may not be able to show them the light; but we don't have to accept, we don't have to join their inhumanity. If they came each day in the public square and shot one hundred people, then should we be angry when they massacre 101? Should we praise their humanity when they only shoot ninety-nine? Not one death, will I consent to, not one day. There are no mathematics for man's inhumanity to man.

25 March   You've imprisoned me all this time but you don't know why, you silly arseholes. I've been imprisoned all this time —I too am a silly arsehole but at least I know why. I find it just, I deserved it, I needed it, I accept it. All my life I've been too 'well behaved' to tell you what stupid shits you are because you've left me alone, because I was afraid of offending you. I saw your ugliness, your petty narrow stupidity, your blind brutality, your slavish idolatry of tradition, your absurd egotism, your despicable fear. I saw the bullshit that you slobbered out of your fat mouths, and I was too polite to mention it. I was afraid to incur your displeasure, to hurt your feelings, to lose your petty favours and praise. Yeah man, I'm guilty Mr. Judge, I promise *not* to be good. I shall try to do good, to speak truth, to unzip the fly of politeness and expose the hypocrisy.

'Paradise is for those who command their anger and for those who pardon offence and for those who return good for evil.' (*The Koran*)

26 March   It's not that I can't believe you're dead. I believed it from the first, and yet I know you're here. Each time I go to sleep I want to dream of you. I command my subconscious. You do not often appear, not in the part of the dream I remember.

Yet each time I awake I'm not too disappointed because I can't remember where you were in my dream. I know you were there, you are always there, you are in everything. I do not have to think of you. You are in everything I do, I feel, I think, I dream. When we lived in the house I sometimes did not see you for days, but your presence was always with me. We did not have to talk and touch to communicate even then. Now it is so much more. Now you are in everything. You are my key to God, to universe, to mystery, to omnipresence, to the divine cool of knowledge without words, of wisdom without thought, of love without possession—without touch. You've taken me one step further into eternity.

Now I know what it was I noticed in the courtroom. Here in the prison there are no uptight faces. Why is it that the 'criminal face' is so much softer? Why is it the imprisoned face is so much more relaxed, so much freer? Why are the judges' features hard, so impenetrable? There's something not quite right with the righteous.

There is as yet no motive for me to defend myself, and by doing so grace a persecution, a cover-up with another name. That's where the nitty gritty is at. That's why I get depressed each time I find myself being sucked into their game. The high priest has a motive for conducting the human sacrifice . . . but what motivation is there for the victim?

Mr. Ezelle, the consul. . . . He wanted to know what Incutti told me, what he anticipates of the trial, how he intends to defend me, etc. I told him I wasn't much interested—one day or another they would have to let me go. He tried to persuade me how important it is for me to get out. I explained to him that is of small consequence. What is important is that the American consul, the Italian policeman, the Italian doctor and judge find out for their own sake why the evil, the suffering continues; that they will never find the answer in the presence or absence of a tiny piece of hash, that all this concern over such an absurdity can only confuse what is important.

'Still,' he said, 'you are the one who is suffering.'

I told him I wasn't suffering, that my suffering was ended on 14 October 1970, that he and they were suffering by suffering the evil to continue; that I didn't honestly know what crime I should defend myself of; that a woman wept and pleaded for seventy days while she was dying, pleading that her husband who was ten minutes away be allowed to comfort her and that all that time the fine gentlemen stood by and refused. I asked him why I still only had the funeral director's bill in explanation of Carol's death.

He told me they had inquired and had the whole medical history 'so thick', but had thought I wanted to wait till I get out!

I asked him why he thought that I was so uninterested when I had asked six months before for an investigation.

He asked me if there was anything they could do for me.

I asked him to get out of Vietnam.

'But I'm not in Vietnam,' was his reply.

Oh yes, he wanted to know who the unidentified woman with the child was. I told him I wouldn't tell, I'm not a policeman. Just as they did with me, they could then put her eight months in a *manicomio*. You can play your silly games. I know full well that you can hurt me, but I won't play. He asked me what I planned to do when I got out. I said I didn't know yet. He said he was sure I'd see things differently when I got out, that I'd snap out of it. I told him I'd snapped out some time ago, that it was time he snapped out of it. I was quite sure I wouldn't snap back in. I'm sure he thinks I'm mad. I'd love to know how he'll put it in his report.

Photocopy of Western Union telegram to Italian consulate, sent I think 2 March 1971, arrived somehow—don't know from or through whom, but it's a lovely assurance that somewhere in this blind world of no sense some lovely words of sense and beauty filter through the apparatus of absurdity: *The imprint of the heart floats in space untarnished by the flames of changing form. The eternal committee for William Berger.*[14]

How did those words get to me? How precisely at the moment I was struggling with the man behind the consular face inside the bars of a Salerno prison? What sublime timing in spite of Western Union's instantaneous over-technical perfection which tries to anticipate the time of destiny yet sometimes fails so beautifully. We'll win, my love, because we cannot lose.

Incutti came. He seems to feel he's got it all under control.

14. See Diary Notes, pp. 293–295.

I'll wait and see and see and wait. I learned to wait, to wait and see, to wait and see. The consulate had asked him to find out about the 'mystery lady with child'. Why is the American consul so interested in the mystery lady? He spoke to the *publico ministero*. The *publico ministero* is interested. It's the point in the whole case that most proves the police persecution. Is the consul just a patsy for the *publico ministero*? Perhaps the *publico ministero* told him *that* was the way to 'get me off' and he wants to show Washington he 'got me off', and so the *publico ministero* has the bit he wants. But then, why didn't in all this time the *publico ministero* have me interrogated? Did the consul really just read it in the papers as he put it to me? First he asked me if it was true 'like it said in the papers' that we were all naked in one room, though he didn't really believe that himself, as he said. That was the hooker for the next question. They knew in Washington right away about all the injections and treatment and everything. There's been a lot of busy little lieutenants and secretaries. Nothing is casual anymore, not even the consul's good will visit three days before he thinks I'll get out to ask me if I need anything—after all this time. He also asked me again about the mail censors. Kind of strange that after that 'unfortunate' misunderstanding there's been no more 'delay' at all for censorship! Eight months they didn't know anything, couldn't do anything and now he tells me I must do all I can to help end my suffering.

Whatever happens, I'll keep playing it by ear. . . . Just whisper me the cues baby—blow 'em in my ear, I sense you strong. Your sensual sense is the only sense.

29 March   I can tell you my story. I can try to be objective. I can tell you the 'facts'. I can give you my interpretation. I can show you my tears, I can show you my grave. You will understand what you are free to understand with your heart. You are bombarded each day with thousands of stories. If you care to look . . . there are oceans of tears. There is an avalanche of words and images and interpretations of facts that can confound you in their deluge. Your brain has to sort out, analyse, execute, absorb what it is safe for you to absorb. But you can understand only with your heart what is in your heart. I have no wish to share with you my anguish and my loss, I have no need to seek from you agreeing nods. You need not be afraid of me. The battle you must fight or flee is only in yourself, as mine is within me.

God must be above argument. If God can be reduced to argument, to concept, even to concept of truth and love, if God can clearly be understood, he is not God but something less than mystery, less than infinity, less than eternity or at the very least of similar dimension. The way towards God may well be love, as I believe—without proof, beyond discussion or analysis. It does not follow even that God is love. The path that leads to the top of the mountain is not the mountain though it is part of the mountain, though it is my means of scaling the mountain. I cannot say there are no other paths. Until I reach or see the top I cannot even be sure the mountain has a top. I can only follow the urgings of that force within me which I sense to be stronger, purer, weightier than my intellect, my reason. The rest I leave to time and destiny.

I have no shame—not understanding what I cannot yet understand, not seeing what I have not eyes to see. Shameful is only not to see what one has eyes to see, not understanding what one can understand, to shut one's eyes and mind because of fear. I do understand that it is absurd, for fear of loss of pride, to claim that God whom we can never fully know is truer God if Roman God or Persian God or Chinese God if I am Roman, Persian or Chinese; that God of man is more or less than God of ant or whale or fly is also naught but vanity. I have my instrument to search what is unfindable and you have yours. If only one of us finds but a speck, then all the foibles of humanity make sense, have value and are justified. If God is any less than that, He is not even—All.

Strange beautiful chance! As I couldn't sleep thinking about the trial tomorrow, I picked up the last volume of Gibbon's *Decline and Fall of the Roman Empire*. I hadn't touched it for months. Out fell the beautiful postcard of 1 December—*We are thinking of you getting out from the trials and sorrows—a great resurrection sun will arise. Pierre.*

It is enough. I have nothing more to say. Good night my loves, my love my love my love.

13. Diary Notes

Chapter Seven
1. By 17 October all those involved in the two cases had been released. As they came out of the separate *manicomios* where they had been for two and a half months, they were handed a telegram which Bill had sent to the two *manicomios*. It simply said: *Carol in total liberty. Love Billie and Carol.* That was the first news they heard of her death. Later they heard from the authorities that Carol was due to be buried that day. In fact, the funeral took place in Praiano cemetery. The only people present were several police, the American vice-consul, Donald Lautz, and a Catholic priest who performed the service. It was a windy but clear autumn day as they lowered her body into the ground. David Naylor and Petra Vogt who had heard about the funeral in Positano where they had gone immediately after their release, arrived as the service was drawing to a close. They stood below on the steps and watched, refusing to participate. But Petra could contain herself no longer—she ran forward before earth had been heaped on to the coffin, and threw herself into the grave, weeping and shouting 'Murderers! Murderers!' After the officials had left in their large black cars, David and Petra stood silently by the grave. Later the others arrived. They all joined hands round the grave and stood there a long time. No one spoke. That evening they all left Italy.

Some explanation of how they came to be released is necessary if we are to understand what they must have felt as they stood around Carol's grave that day.

In Marilyn Woolhead's case what had been found in her house on the night of 9 August had been itemised in a police report—amongst other things, 100 seeds of marijuana, hashish, a small bottle of 'unknown substance', morphine. This and the testimony of Dr. Testa (the same doctor who examined the Berger group in Amalfi jail) who found the four people arrested to be suffering from 'syndromes of drug intoxication', were the accusatory factors which caused their detention in *manicomios*. But in the *sentenza istruttoria* deposited at the court on 6 March 1971 (an official document stating the facts of the case and the causes for release) it was stated, in spite of Dr. Testa's initial diagnosis, that 'it could not be ascertained that the people were under the influence of drugs. The "syndromes" could have been for other reasons—morbid states, nervousness, etc.' As for the evidence found in the house, it was stated that 'of all the evidence taken by the police only the piece of hashish was proved to be a substance with a low percentage of illegal drug content. The other evidence has been proved not to contain illegal drug content'. The conclusion of the *sentenza* was that 'the evidence presented is not enough to justify a trial for the accused and therefore the decision is that there is insufficient evidence'.

The Woolhead and the Berger case were almost identical, except that far more evidence of narcotic substances were found in Marilyn Woolhead's house. For example, the 'unknown substance' found in a small bottle there—which everyone admitted afterwards was L.S.D.— remained an 'unknown substance' in the *sentenza*. Yet Marilyn Woolhead and the others arrested with her, were all released on 17 October.

In both cases large sums of money were paid to key officials by parents, relations and friends of those arrested to ensure their release. It is important to realise that until Carol's death and everyone's release, no analysis of the evidence found in either case had been made. In both cases it was made afterwards and must have been influenced by the authorities' embarrassment at Carol's death. On 19 October it was officially stated to the press that only half a gram of marijuana was found in the Bergers' house on the night of 5 August—in spite of the police reports to the newspapers at the time of the bust that 'a large quantity of narcotic substances had been found' and mention made in the interrogation at Positano police station of 'butt-ends containing evidence of marijuana' found on the night of 5 August.

Because of the money that changed hands and the authorities' desire to get all the witnesses out of the country as quickly as possible, all the evidence that would have implicated the others in the Berger case was removed from the official analysis produced on 18 October. In other words, all the blame was put on to Bill so that he could be kept in prison for a longer period, although as signer of the lease for his house he was legally in exactly the same position as Marilyn Woolhead who had been released.

From Italy everyone who had been released after Carol's death went to England where they rented a large house near Basingstoke which they got cheaply because it was supposed to be haunted. They intended working together to produce a film script of their somewhat bizarre experiences in the various *manicomios*. But after three nights in the house they all left in terror, having discovered that it really was haunted. Reuniting in London, they stayed at the house of Victor Spinetti, who had directed *Hair* in Rome and who knew some of the group, where they employed the film actress Diane Cilento to write the film script. Soon after, in early March 1971, the group broke up.

2. A number of curious incidents surrounded Carol's death and everyone's release, indicating that the authorities panicked. Why Robert Peitscher was released before everyone else remains a mystery, though evidence exists to connect it to President Nixon's visit to Naples in early October, implying that presidential pressure was exerted to speed up his release. Also, Carol died while the investigating judge, Verasani, was on holiday and it was the investigating judge in Marilyn Woolhead's case, Verdarosa, who signed everyone out of the *manicomios*. On his return Judge Verasani was furious that it had all been done behind his back and later Judge Verdarosa was demoted.

From the confusion and corruption of the case, three facts emerge. The first is that at the time of her operation Carol was about to be released and if Robert Peitscher could be freed, why couldn't she? It is significant that although repeated attempts had been made to get Carol transferred to a private medical clinic and refused, on 9 October—the same day as Peitscher's release—a paper was signed granting permission for her transfer. The second is the legal implications of everyone's release—something of which Bill was well aware, as is shown in his questions to vice-consul Lautz. If everyone else could have been released and he detained because he was signer of the lease for the house where drugs had been used, then officially Carol was innocent of any crime because she had not signed the lease. Her detention in an insane asylum and her death had therefore to be justified by the authorities—especially since the testimony of Dr. Testa had been discredited. Thirdly, either Carol was fatally ill before being committed to Pozzuoli *manicomio* and died as a result of inadequate medical treatment or she contracted a fatal illness in the *manicomio* or hospital. Either way the Italian authorities and the American consulate were directly responsible for her death.

Knowing the corruption of the Italian judicial system and guessing how the others had got out, Bill was suspicious that Pirrongelli might make a 'deal' to get him out of prison which would involve some compromise on his part. On 20 October he wrote to Pirrongelli:

> I don't know what you are doing on my behalf but I wish to be sure you are not doing anything against my interests. What is most important for me to know is what is happening in reference to the accusal levelled against Carol Lobravico Berger on that fatal day— 5 August 1970—for which she had to suffer *ergastolo* [life sentence] in the name of the republic. Carol is no longer able to act on her behalf to defend herself and she has delegated me that responsibility. I only know that according to the newspapers she is still under accusal. Even in the obituaries they refer to her as 'the drugged

one'. I should very much prefer that she were still—drugged or not drugged, innocent or guilty . . . it is not important to me. I believe it is all a medical problem and not a judicial one. However, for those who accused her it seems to be a legal problem and a crime against the state of great seriousness, and I must therefore treat the accusal with seriousness. As we know, Carol was not drugged. I have no desire, no intention to leave here voluntarily if that form of liberty should signify that her absolute innocence will not be officially established. Such a liberty would sentence me to *ergastolo* of my spirit.

Written at the point when he was beginning to emerge from a period of mourning and take up the cause of Carol's death, the letter is a manifesto, a declaration of commitment to fight without compromise or thought of his own position. But the letter, written as a direct instruction to his lawyer, contains an indication of the inner struggle that Bill was undergoing at this time, a struggle that is clearly stated in the diary where Bill rationalises every alternative. It is revealed in the sentence. 'I should very much prefer that she were still—drugged or not drugged, innocent or guilty . . . it is not important for me.' The question was whether or not he would try to force the truth and culpability of Carol's death into the open, exposing the corruption of the Italian judicial system, the false testimony of the doctor who had everyone originally committed to insane asylums, the stupidity of the police, the ineffectiveness of the American consul. Certain limited facts dealing with these issues were available to him which were at least enough to open the whole case up and win public opinion to his side—if he could get the facts out. The rest would have to come from his willingness to play the martyr, to act as his own hostage, refusing any offer of compromise to get out, thereby hoping to embarrass or pressure the authorities into revealing details of Carol's death.

Chapter Nine

3. In a letter to Senator Javits, written on 1 November, Bill restated all the facts relating to the lack of co-operation by the American consulate that he had written in a letter to Javits a month before Carol died. Both letters contained essentially the information in the following memo, which Bill handed to Lautz on 15 September:

I have been accused of use and possession of narcotics. The Italian police seized from my home an unspecified number of items in my presence and I understand further items without my presence on at least three separate occasions after my arrest. My wife and I and seven guests have at this date been incarcerated for forty-two days. The authorities continue to refuse to: 1) consult the physician under whose prescription the medicines and syringes seized were purchased and used; 2) perform an analysis of the many varied items seized; 3) present me with a descriptive list of the property taken from my home. I have not been interrogated since my arrest and the examination conducted at this institution has been found negative as to the state of my intoxication and addiction. Communications from my wife and my attorney regarding the state of her health have failed to reach me. Communications from my banks, one in Rome and one in Switzerland, have not reached me. The fact that access to my finances is impeded renders any effort for my defence extremely difficult. I have to date not been shown or been presented with a document of arrest and no such document has been delivered to this institution. My legal counsel, Eduardo di Giovanni, informs me that several aspects of this investigation or lack of investigation are of doubtful constitutional legality. Since you have informed me that you are empowered to ensure that I get just and equal treatment under Italian law, I request that you investigate this matter. Also, since I am allowed no personal contact, aside from my counsel who resides in Rome and my 'immediate family' who is being detained under the same circumstances or residing in the United States, and since communication with my wife in both personal and legal matters is extremely hampered (her letters, when they are delivered, arrive after seven to ten days), I request that you make arrangements for periodic visits by a representative of the consulate.

Because he had received no reply from this first letter, he mailed the second to the American consulate in Rome so that they could forward it. On 16 November he received a letter from the consulate in Naples referring to this letter to Senator Javits: 'Please be informed that the consulate general is forbidden by regulations to use diplomatic facilities for forwarding private mail. Since there is no restriction of your mail privileges by the hospital, the letter is returned herewith for mailing through normal postal channels.'

4. By now Bill's faith in his lawyer, Pirrongelli, was wearing thin. The last he had seen of Pirrongelli was on 3 October and he had received only one letter from him in that time. He and the American consul were the only people who could make regular visits, although Allain Frankel—the only person of all those arrested who was not expelled from Italy—made one visit. Despairing of using official channels to make any effective protest, Bill decided to use a close friend, Rudi, who lived on a farm near Praiano and who came to Naples to try to see him

on 3 November. Permission having been refused for a visit, Rudi left a note about the publicity issue. On the same day Bill wrote to Rudi explaining his position:

How sweet of you to have stopped by, how sad I could not see you. I have much need of the 'beautiful people'. I thank you for your efforts, especially with the press. The most important thing for me now is that the truth be known not only about our personal tragedy but perhaps some light may be shed on the whole terrible inquisition of the drugs witch hunt which was the cause of it, so that we might finally shed some light on the incredible ignorance that enshrouds this 'danger' and so that the danger can be isolated for what it is.

As for my getting out soon, everyone seems to think so, but I have my doubts. My lawyer is already the third and each one thought that at least *liberta provisorio* could be 'easily arranged'. I think the tragic absurdity has been greatly complicated by Carol's death and I don't think a solution is too simple as long as the very people who caused the tragedy are in charge of investigating it. They are all much too frightened now, much too uptight. If they had the slightest sense of honour or humanity (any one of the three would suffice) it would never have happened. They can't continue to repress it forever and the more they persist the more clearly will the basic evil be exposed, the more Carol's suffering and death will not have been totally futile. That is all I am interested in now because it is what Carol would have wanted. She was always ready to give her all—her love her beauty her energy her life—to spread her love her freedom her soul in the battle against ugliness, fear and ignorance. I am willing to go with the flow as long as I'm in the river. If her death can in some way become a symbol of her life, I think that is all we can ask—that is all she would have asked. That's why I think your efforts to let it be known are most important and I love you for it. My and Carol's innermost love to you and Valli for being so beautiful.

5. Carol had been raped while hitch-hiking from Praiano to Positano in autumn 1969. She was picked up by three drunken Italians who stopped the car and forced her to get out at the point of a knife. They tore off her clothes and one of them raped her. But they became frightened and fled. Carol did not tell Bill until many months later because she didn't want any action taken by way of revenge or punishment.

6. On 7 November it was officially established—in a declaration signed by the investigating judge and the *publico ministero* at Salerno—that Carol Berger's death was 'due to natural causes and did not necessitate an autopsy or further investigation'. This conclusion came as the result of a routine inquiry into the causes of Carol's death—a separate inquiry by the Naples district attorney was dropped at this point. Bill sent a telegram to his lawyer, Pirrongelli: *Wish to protest against conclusions of inquest into the death of my wife Carol Lobravico Berger prior to such time as a decision is reached concerning the validity of the accusal under which she had been detained.*

Although Bill had at his disposal facts that related to the initial police raid with which he could fight a rearguard action he knew nothing definite about the most important issue—the causes of Carol's death. There had been various versions: an official version printed in the newspapers saying that her intestines were perforated by intensive drug taking; and later cardio-respiratory insufficiency. The only other official statement about her death came from various statements put out by the American consulate in Naples. The first version, which they held to throughout, was a letter from Donald Lautz to Carol's brother Frank Lobravico on 29 October—after hearing of Carol's death he had telephoned the consulate from New Jersey, asking for information. The letter from Lautz ended: *I should like you to know that she received the best medical care available and was in the hands of competent physicians.*

The only action that Bill could have taken at this time was to have insisted on an autopsy, but this would have been another violation of Carol's body and would only have confirmed the Cardarelli doctor's diagnosis. So on 7 November he wrote two letters, one to Pirrongelli and the other to the U.S. ambassador in Rome:

To Pirrongelli:
The real causes of Carol's death will never be brought to light through an autopsy which can only define the condition of her illness. The victim of an automobile accident may die from loss of blood from a wound. The cause of the wound was the accident, was the piece of glass which cut through the vein—however it is also important to ascertain why the ambulance did not arrive in time, who stopped it (the ambulance) or delayed it and for what motive. I maintain that the entire phase of the investigation, the way in which it has been conducted and the motive for which it was conducted in such a manner, are important factors in determining the cause of Carol's death, in particular the avoidable cause in a similar tragedy in the future. The present hesitation and delay, for however long it may last, in arriving at a decision about the validity

of the original accusation, is an eloquent indication of the forces and motives which delayed the arrival of the 'ambulance'. The fact that these forces, these motives are still at work today, four weeks after Carol's death, indicate that so far nothing has changed. The probability of a repetition of a similar tragedy exists today as it existed yesterday. I have already suffered too greatly to be afraid of eventual consequences. In my interest, in Carol's interest and in the interest of our society I request your aid as my legal counsel to clarify the truth regarding the avoidable causes of this painful event.

To U.S. Ambassador, Rome.
Dear Mr. Ambassador. On 1 November 1970 I communicated some of the events leading up to this tragedy in a letter to Senator Jacob Javits of New York. I maintain that the lack of assistance on part of the U.S. consulate in Naples in spite of repeated requests for aid, to be a serious contributing factor to the resultant tragedy which might have been otherwise avoided. I stated my opinions in this matter in a letter to Senator Javits and sent it through the U.S. consulate Naples to make them aware of the implications. I asked for confirmation of receipt and dispatch of said letter but have as yet received no reply. The investigation into the causes of my wife's death is presently being conducted by the *publico ministero*, Naples, and I herewith request advice and assistance in this matter from your embassy. Since I feel that the U.S. consulate Naples is implicated in the matter I do not feel myself able to direct myself further to that office.

7. On 16 November Bill was informed that his letter to Senator Javits, which he sent via the U.S. consulate in Naples, could not be forwarded and that he should use normal postal facilities to mail it. Also a new consular official from Naples, Mr. Ezelle, was put on his case. Bill never saw Donald Lautz again. In fact, Lautz, who had recently arrived in Naples from South America, was hastily transferred to a new post in Mexico. On 16 November Bill wrote to Mr. Ezelle about the delay of his letter to Senator Javits:

It was not kind of you to delay my letter to Senator Javits, though I am sure it was correct. I shall try to answer you not in kind because I do not think you meant to be either kind or unkind, because I think you misunderstood my intent. It is precisely this usage of 'correct' language that codifies human emotion and makes us appear to be machines. I would have much preferred your telling me to go to hell, though I know that is difficult to do on consular stationery. It is precisely this mechanisation that ignores human contact and human truth, that made Carol's and my avoidable tragedy inevitable. Perhaps with more timely and more expert medical attention her death would not have occurred when it did, but that is only speculation of what might have been, which is useless. I do know what could have been avoided with a little love, a little compassion was the fact that she had to die for twelve days in total loneliness and solitude. It is something I believe you and also Mr. Lautz would have tried to avoid had the channels of communication been open. However, they were clogged by official correctness which locks the truth of our emotions, the truth of our humanity, the truth of our love and leaves us only with the truth of 'facts' that can be classified by I.B.M. machines but are not truth. It is not pleasant to be confined in an asylum for the criminally insane, which by the way is not synonymous with 'hospital' although it might come under a very generalised classification of the term. It is not a pleasant experience but an important one. Here amongst the murderers, the thieves, the madmen and even the guards, I have found human compassion and love in an hour of personal, private tragedy, the profoundness of which I can only indicate but cannot describe to you. It has been a matter of painful regret to me that I have not been able to feel a similar humanity of compassion and love from my own countrymen, but only correct indifference. I know that such humanity is there, that it is only the signs that are obscured by the usage of diplomacy which tries to avoid them. However, even diplomacy is only a means to human ends and should not become an end in itself. I should like to recommend to you some contemplation why the human touch was so totally lacking when it was so sorely needed.

Chapter Ten
8. By now Bill had found a new lawyer, Tamarro, to work on the case—because he had had no contact at all with Pirrongelli. When Pirrongelli heard about this he wrote Bill an angry letter saying that his rapport with the investigating judge could be ruined by the intervention of another lawyer. In a *memoria* sent to the investigating judge, Pirrongelli had tried to make a case for Bill's release whereby the ownership of the half gram of marijuana would be attributed to Carol. In fact, according to Italian law, where a person is considered guilty until proved innocent, the only way of 'proving' Bill's innocence was to put the blame on Carol—in the same way as the release of the others had entailed putting the blame on Bill.

9. *To Pirrongelli* (28 November):

I have seriously reflected on all this for the past two days. The director has clearly explained to me that since according to Italian law I must prove my innocence and that since such proof is impossible without finding another party guilty, it is the common custom to put the guilt on the deceased. He further pointed out that it would not even be considered a moral guilt, considering Carol's state of ill health. Unfortunately it is not the truth. The truth is that I have known a love so glorious, so joyous that I cannot find the words to describe it. The truth is that I must respect this love, that I must respect her death, beyond all personal considerations. I must therefore reject any argument that will betray that love. After much reflection I must ask you to withdraw this line of defence, though I am aware that such action will mean that I will have to stay in prison much longer. I know that Carol would not have wanted me to do what I am doing, but I also know that she would have acted likewise in a similar situation. She wrote in one of her letters to me: 'I could support everything if I could know you were free in the world'. I have loved too much to do less. I cannot aspire to my freedom, to my 'official' innocence by putting the blame on Carol. I would not have done it were she still alive— I cannot do it now that she is dead. This is the significance I give to the words—love, respect, honour and integrity.

10. The article by Salvatore Maffei in *Oggi* attacked the Italian authorities for their incompetent handling of the case and pointed accusingly to its inconsistencies. Bill was described as 'incarcerated with rapists, demented murderers, catatonics in a mute and motionless trance and restless schizophrenics uttering two words a minute until they collapse' —and was directly quoted as saying 'I'm innocent, they have to let me out of here. I'm not an addict, it's all a frame up . . . I'm innocent and I'm not insane, but if I'm held in an insane asylum much longer, I'll really go crazy. . . .' There was also a quotation about Carol from Gianfranco Montegna: 'Carol was with the Living Theatre, she was a sister, a lover and a witch.' Other attacking newspaper articles had appeared earlier—in *L'Ore* (with a cover photograph of Carol and a headline 'Who murdered Carol?') and a Neapolitan magazine—but none had contained a direct quote from Bill about the implications of Carol's death as appeared in the *Oggi* article. As a result of the article, it was decided that Bill should be transferred to the tighter security of Salerno prison.

Chapter Twelve
11. Although Bill had found a new lawyer, he had not yet officially dismissed Pirrongelli. On 14 February he wrote about Pirrongelli in his diary:

I've waited this long because you chose him. But his absence, his peevishness at being importuned by requests for information and offers of help by my friends, his silence to my principal questions of 1) what he did to obtain medical and judicial relief for Carol, and 2) what was the significance of his *prestissimo* telegram of 4 December, and now his letter saying he will come to see me if I pay him a million lire, to discuss preparing my defence—are all too eloquent to be ignored any longer, especially concerning the nature and extent of his 'interest'.

Then on 17 February he wrote a letter dismissing Pirrongelli from the case:

Until today I gave you my full faith because Carol had nominated you with so much faith, so much hope. I did not want to go against one of her ultimate decisions. I have waited to reply to your letter until today because I had expected to see, at least, your representative Avv. Incutti who had promised me two weeks ago to return in three or five days. Since I have seen neither you nor him I must assume that you are holding back until I send you a million lire. If I still had a million lire to dispose of, I would probably have sent you the money already because I do not attach such importance to money.

Some time back I gave a cellmate 250,000 lire for his lawyer without asking any explanations simply because I could not idly watch the continued suffering after thirteen years of imprisonment of a man whose friendship I had accepted without doing what it was possible for me to do. It was not an act of generosity but simply an obligation between me and my conscience. Unfortunately at this point I have no more money of my own until such time as I can again earn some, and I am forced to rely on the help of my friends who are the very people who are responsible for the continuing pressure which causes you so much bother. To ask them for money I must first consider their interests which are I believe to clear up what has happened and to see me in liberty.

The police and the other gentlemen of the law have deprived me of all that was most dear to me in my life. Ironically after the police the robbers arrived and took everything from my house that might still have been converted to cash. On the other hand the men of the law and the outlaws have left me in total freedom to think and react freely without fear. I can do nothing now except wait until such friends as wish to help me will help me. I removed today your nomination as my attorney and have tried to explain to you my state of mind and my thoughts.

12. Extracts from the *Sentenza di Rinvio a Giudizio*—the indictment for the trial of William Berger, deposited 25 February 1971 by Investigating Judge Verasani for the *Tribunale* of Salerno.

Concerning the nature of the substance (found in Berger's house), the investigation has ascertained without possibility of doubt that the substance examined was a small quantity of marijuana of low content originally potent.

The proof of Berger's guilt which requires that he be held for trial, can be summarized as follows: 1) beyond doubt the *tabachiere* containing the narcotic substance was found in the Villa Zingone; 2) that the Villa Zingone was under lease to Berger is another point of certainty; 3) it cannot be said that the drug seized could have been brought by other persons, since the metallic *tabachiere* was discovered in a room other than where the meeting was taking place which the police interrupted—making it appear that the *tabachiere* had been concealed from the persons at the meeting and that the concealment could not have been accomplished without the knowledge of the proprietor of the house. Furthermore, one cannot but observe that, judging from the furnishings of the Villa Zingone, it appears certain that in this villa meetings took place of people dedicated to the use of drugs—especially when one considers the mattresses arranged on the ground in such a way as to permit persons to stretch themselves out on the floor. (See photographs in the Acts.) Also the facts that the quantity of the drug found in a *tabachiere* was smaller than the size of the *tabachiere* itself leads us to assume that only a residue of the drug was seized and that the greater portion of the substance here deposited had been previously consumed. Neither must we over-look the verbal statements which testify to a continuous coming and going of people in the Villa Zingone which attracted the suspicion of the bodies officially nominated for the per-quisition.

Such a large amount of evidence clearly denotes that in this villa people met together who were dedicated to the use of drugs, and that such meetings could certainly not take place without the knowledge of Berger, the proprietor of the villa—to conclude otherwise would be preposterous. On the other hand, if one were to consider, merely as an hypothesis, that it was the guests who brought the drug with them, the situation is not altered in respect to Berger from the moment that he became the custodian of the substance in the house and thus became its possessor. It is not sufficient to cite the fact that the other co-defendants have been acquitted of the charges levelled against them, as outlined below. Even if it is ascertained that the guests of that evening cannot be proven to have consumed drugs, it does not preclude the fact that on other occasions drugs were consumed in the Villa Zingone by other people—taking into account the furnishings of the Villa Zingone, as outlined above, and the continuing coming and going of guests, also noted above.

Berger must therefore stand trial in this *tribunale* . . . and must be held in custody. . . . Penal action, however, will not be taken against Carolina Lobravico Berger since the crime attributed to her has been annulled by the death of the said person.

As to the use of narcotics, the examiner—Dr. Testa—states that at the time when he made the clinical examination there were symptoms which gave evidence with criteria of probability only in regard to the use of substances derived from opium. In places where a more detailed medical–legal examination took place, it was found that the symptoms noted could have been expression of other states of morbidity (for example nervousness which is so prevalent nowadays). It appears evident that no proof can be said to have been established as to the guilt of these defendants in relation to the crime of which they have been accused. Therefore the defendants—Edwards Theodor Joseph, Dunkley Michael, Naylor David Frank, Peitscher Robert Henry, Gelhar Volfgang Florian, Nicaise Florence Margherita and Vogt Petra must be acquitted of the crime ascribed to them, in full.

The investigating judge declares the formal investigation closed; orders the indictment of Berger William Thomas so that he should answer before this *tribunale* in his present state of detention, concerning the crime of which he has been accused; declares n.d.p. against Lobravico Carolina Berger in respect to the crime of which she was accused, due to annulment of crime and to the death of the defendant; declares n.d.p. concerning (the names of seven co-defendants) in respect to the crime of which they were accused for not having committed the act.

On 7 March 1971 Bill, who was given a copy of Judge Verasani's

Sentenza in Salerno prison by his lawyer Incutti, made the following comments in his diary:

Verasani's twenty-seven pages, although they contain only a minute quantity of sense of small potency, must not be dismissed as total nonsense. We must assume, judging by the fact of the events, that the minimum of thought is but the residue of a larger amount of thought highly dangerous to the public welfare, which larger amount was consumed if not on the occasion of filtering through the judge's mind then on some other occasion by other minds but not without the judge's knowledge. It can be clearly proved that the thinking contained in those twenty-seven pages are the property of the judge and therefore, till such other heads are known we have no choice but to hold the judge responsible—not only for the thoughts contained in the twenty-seven pages but for the other thoughts they represent. Such thoughts being: that people who are distinguishable by non-conformist length of hair and non-conformist dress, that people who mingle freely in dance and laughter, who freely share their worldly goods and love one another, without apparent motive of personal gain, that such people who, in short, practise the message of Jesus in acts and not words are dangerous to an uptight society. The thought that people who in their lack of conformity display an absence of fear must be taught to fear and removed from the scene. The thought that fear, conformity, distrust and isolation are essential to our society of law and order; that generosity is suspect and love dangerous; that actions not traceable to financial gain are unthinkable and must have hidden motives. The thought finally that the poor, the non-conformists, the 'niggers' of the world can be persecuted at will; that right, justice and compassion are the exclusive property of the rich and the powerful. The thought that what is different is dangerous, that what is weak must be suppressed by what is strong, that fear not love is essential for harmony.

After careful analysis of the judge's opinion and its small thought content, it is our opinion that the whole operation 'Praiano', its resultant legal and penal actions and their tragic consequences were prompted by this kind of thinking which is attaining highly dangerous and world-wide proportions. It is the essence of the *stupefacente* of fascist thinking so prevalent in today's older generation by whatever name or political affiliation it may be disguised. It must, therefore, be treated with appropriate seriousness, in spite and perhaps also because of its apparent absurdity.

13. Senators Jacob Javits and James Buckley, Congressman Edward Koch, and Congresswoman Bella Abzug all requested an answer from the State Department on the case. Similar letters were sent to all four, giving the official State Department version. All were signed by David M. Abshire, Assistant secretary for congressional relations. The one quoted below was sent to James Buckley, dated 9 March 1971. The italics (my italics) indicate the careless way in which the facts were handled in the 'official' version.

I have received your communication of 25 February concerning the arrest of Mr. and Mrs. William Berger in Italy. Mr. and Mrs. Berger, together with *five* other persons, including two other American citizens, were arrested at their home on 4 August 1970 when a police raid discovered the *presence of narcotics* in their house.

According to procedure required by Italian law in narcotics arrest cases, all seven persons were confined for a *short time* in judicial mental institutions for psychiatric examination and observation, blood analysis and other pertinent tests. According to the director of the Pozzuoli Mental Hospital, where Mrs. Berger was confined, *she did not ask for the services of her private doctor, nor for the medicines he had prescribed*, following her incarceration. However, *after a thorough medical examination by physicians on the hospital staff*, Mrs. Berger was given medication *which she said was the same type she had been receiving from her private physician*. The consulate general also reports that Mrs. Berger *never complained about inadequate medical* care during the consular officer's visits to Pozzuoli.

At Pozzuoli *Hospital*, Mrs. Berger developed a fever *on 3 October*, was transferred to Cardarelli Hospital, a large modern hospital in Naples, where she underwent exploratory surgery for treatment of diffused peritonitis. At that time, the doctors believed that the peritonitis may have been caused by abdominal typhus. *Since there were no complications after the operation* and the attending physicians prognosed a *normal convalescence*, she was transferred to the Incurabile Hospital and placed in an isolation ward as a precautionary measure because of the possibility of typhus, a contagious disease. *Her attorney, Mr. Bruzio Pirrongelli, had permission from the Italian authorities to transfer her to a private clinic or hospital, but since there were no apparent complications, he agreed to Mrs. Berger's transfer to the Incurabile, a public hospital.*

On 13 October Mrs. Berger suffered a relapse and, in spite of all efforts on the part of the hospital staff, she passed away on 14

October. The cause of death was acute cardio-respiratory insufficiency due to bilateral broncho-pneumonia. The consulate general concludes that the medical charts confirm that the hospitals and attending physicians provided competent medical care and treatment.

Mr. Berger who has legal counsel has been indicted and his trial will be held 17 March in Salerno. If found guilty, he could receive a sentence of three years imprisonment, minus the eight months he has already spent in confinement. In that case, however, the death of Mrs. Berger could be considered a mitigating circumstance upon which Mr. Berger might base a request for presidential pardon.

The consulate general, which has followed Mr. Berger's case closely, reports that it is satisfied that Mr. Berger has received all the rights and privileges accorded to an Italian citizen accused of the same crime, and that he has not been treated unfairly according to Italian law. *Under these circumstances, the consulate general has no basis upon which to protest to the Italian authorities concerning Mr. Berger's treatment.*

The consulate general reports that the consular officer who visited Mr. Berger in prison recently found him well, but uncommunicative. The consulate general will continue to follow Mr. Berger's case closely, and to offer all appropriate assistance.

On 23 September 1971 Bella Abzug, who was dissatisfied with the State Department's replies on the case, sent the following letter to Secretary of State William Rogers:

After listening to William Berger relate the details of his arrest and imprisonment for eight months in an Italian mental hospital and prison, and examining State Department reports concerning the death of his wife Carol while similarly incarcerated, I have serious doubts about the conduct and co-operation of the American consular officials in this and similar cases.

On March 8, 1971, I requested answers to a series of policy questions relating to the scope of activity of State Department officials in cases of this sort. The answers I received on April 27, 1971, have not dispelled the questions and doubts which the Berger case occasioned, but rather have increased them. I am specifically concerned with the circumstances of Carol Berger's death, and the cooperation or lack of same that Mrs. Berger received from the American consulate.

Mrs. Berger was arrested on 4 August 1970, and confined to the Judicial Women's Mental Hospital in Pozzuoli, Italy, where she remained until 2 October 1970. As the result of a persistent high fever, Mrs. Berger was transferred to the Poggioreale Jail Medical Clinic, and from there to Cardarelli Hospital in Naples, where exploratory surgery was performed the next day. Several days later she was transferred to the Incurabile Hospital, where she lapsed into a coma on October 13, and passed away the next day.

These are the details of Mrs. Berger's last months as gleaned from State Department reports; however, discussions with William Berger, a reading of the entries in the diaries kept by both him and his wife, a discussion with Petra Vogt who was imprisoned with Mrs. Berger, and a perusal of much of the correspondence between the Bergers themselves and with the American consul, provide many more details, and many unanswered and discomforting questions.

Mr. and Mrs. Berger were arrested on drug charges related to the finding of less than one gram of hashish in one of the rooms of their home. Though Mrs. Berger was convalescing from hepatitis at the time of her arrest, her medicines were taken from her, apparently as suspected narcotics.

The State Department reports claim that Carol Berger was provided with medicines while in the mental hospital, and that she never complained about her health or inadequate medical care (Abshire letter of March 24, 1971). This is disputed by Petra Vogt, who claims that Mrs. Berger lost weight rapidly, and became steadily weaker before developing the mysterious fever that led to her transfer.

Although William Berger made repeated requests to have his wife transferred to a clinic, or even a regular prison with better medical facilities, she remained in the mental institution until October 2. Carol Berger also requested a transfer in two letters to the American consul, when she also asked that he visit her. These visits were not made, apparently because the consul decided that they would be of no value since Mrs. Berger's desire to be transferred, or to change attorneys, could not be complied with by him. Reportedly, even the director of the mental hospital in which Mrs. Berger was detained requested that she be transferred to a hospital clinic on September 16 because of her health, but the American consul himself never attempted to have this done.

On another occasion, less than ten days before her transfer and operation, Mrs. Berger urgently requested the American consul to come immediately. He replied that the impending visit of President

Nixon was occupying all consular officials, but that they would be glad to answer her requests in writing.

Although consular officials are apparently authorized to do only very limited things to aid Americans detained abroad, in this instance the bare minimum was not even responsibly performed. Consular officials may assist arrested citizens in matters of the health (Abshire letter, page 3), but no assistance was provided by the American consul to Mrs. Berger.

Although also authorized to assist in forwarding mail 'if regular mail channels are not satisfactory', the consul also was of no assistance in this regard. From the excerpts we have examined from the diaries of both Mr. and Mrs. Berger, it is readily apparent that their mail was both censored and delayed, if not altogether lost, and that requests for aid from the consul went unheeded.

Another function which the consul is to perform involves aiding in the selection of an attorney. In this instance, no guidance other than a vague list was provided, and when competent attorneys proved difficult to obtain and to communicate with, the consul was of no help whatsoever. At one point, due to the confusion caused by their inability to communicate with each other, William Berger was represented by a different lawyer than his wife, and, at another point, both attempted to appoint a local lawyer for the express purpose of serving as a conduit for increased communication. As mentioned previously, the American consul apparently refused to aid Mrs. Berger in changing her attorney after her request.

Even at the time of Mrs. Berger's transfer to the hospital, the American consul still failed to provide even minimal cooperation and assistance. No advance notice was given William Berger of his wife's operation, and he never was requested to consent. Permission for him to stay at his wife's bedside during her last day was obtained by the extraordinary efforts of the director of the mental hospital where he had been confined, since the American consul 'could not be reached'.

Also troubling are the inaccuracies, missing facts, and self-serving statements contained in the State Department and consular reports in response to requests for information on this case. William Berger received no special treatment from the legal or prison authorities beyond the director's intervention to allow him to be at his wife's death bed—despite the statement to the contrary in the December 2, 1970, memo. Although the consulate was made aware on August 8 of the serious condition of Carol Berger, and made no attempt to have her transferred to a clinic, its report states that it is convinced that she received the best possible care.

A February 1971 memo to my office states only that 'During her confinement, Mrs. Berger communicated with husband by mail and telegram', without noting that both Bergers complained often of the extreme difficulty of communicating with each other. Regular visits were specifically requested because of this, and refused by the American consul.

There are other troubling facets and inconsistencies concerning this case, not the least of which involves the Bergers' continued confinement in mental 'hospitals' over excessive periods of time for insufficient grounds even by Italian standards, and the lack of protest by the American consul to this treatment. However, at this point we must attempt to see what all this leads to.

In the words of William Berger, from a letter to Senator Javits: 'No amount of words and recrimination can undo Carol's and my personal tragedy or assuage the profundity of my grief. I am, however, deeply concerned with the apparent discrepancy between the duties and obligations according to which our consular officials are operating and the basic human needs and ideals our government professes to protect. It is to effect a change in these duties and obligations and their application that I call your attention to the details of this sad affair.'

For the same reasons, I would like to first request a complete review of the facts and circumstances involving Carol Berger's death. Second, I would like a complete review of the conduct of the American consul in this case. And third, I would request a re-examination of our policy toward the consular duties owed an American detained abroad on drug charges. Although I have been told that there is no 'hands off' policy towards Americans detained on drug charges, I fear that in practice this may not be so. The tragic events of the Berger case speak for themselves; in hopes of avoiding a similar recurrence, I urge you to investigate.

14. By early February a committee—'The Eternal Committee'—for the release of Bill had been organised in New York by Ira Cohen and hundreds of telegrams and letters from friends sent to the Italian consulate in America, various senators in Washington, the authorities in Italy and Bill's lawyers—demanding information about the case. On 18 February demonstrations were organised outside Italian diplomatic offices in New York and various European capitals, demanding Bill's release. The effect of the demonstrations was to gain international press comment on the case. A press communique was released:

The Eternal Committee was formed to gain justice for William

Berger, to protest the institutionalisation of some fourteen people as part of a witch hunt by the police of Salerno, Italy, to demand an investigation of the tragic death of Carol Berger, and to protest the failure of the American consulate to protect its citizens abroad. The Eternal Committee does not share the point of view expressed by American consular officials that the standard of treatment accorded to American citizens abroad by foreign police and judiciary should be based on the worst examples of treatment given to the citizens of the country in question. Telegrams stating: *We protest the unjust incarceration of the American actor William Berger in Naples since last August and the tragic death of his wife Carol who died through neglect of the Italian authorities* were sent to the Italian consulate in Washington, the American embassy in Rome and the *questura* in Naples. These telegrams were signed by some fifty persons, most of whom are respected members of the artistic community here and abroad. The list included Allen Ginsburg, Shirley Clark, Ellen Steward, William Hitchcock, Nelson Aldrich, William Randolph Hearst III, Julian Beck and Judith Malina. A delegation visited the Italian consulate and had an interview with Mr. Vieri Traxler, consul general of Italy, who agreed that the trial of William Berger was long overdue, that conditions such as these were usual in Italy and that the whole affair certainly seemed 'Kafkaesque'. Mr. Traxler agreed to forward all mail and a petition requesting the freedom of William Berger to his superiors in Washington and Rome.

Carol Marini, a cousin of Carol Berger, contacted me through *The Village Voice* and informed me that Carol's mother knew nothing of Carol's death until she read about it in *The New York Post*. Joanna Vischer, an old family friend of William Berger, has been in touch with his lawyers in Rome who say Berger will be tried some time in March. Valli, well-known artist who lives in Positano, reports that Berger is not allowed visitors. Mr. Traxler says that the executive branch of the Italian government has no control over the judiciary branch and that only pressure from the American state department will effect Berger's release. Berger says he wrote Senator Javits many months ago through the American consul in Naples but received no reply. I personally had difficulty getting any reply from the senator's office about the Berger case. There is a movie script being prepared now in London on the case by Diane Cilento, well-known English actress. The story has been released through other news agencies, notably ANSA (Italian News Service) and should be getting wider and wider circulation. Public indignation is mounting each day. How much longer must William Berger suffer while the bureaucratic and impersonal agencies of justice, both American and Italian, compound error on error, refusing to declare the truth officially while pretending sympathy and understanding? Is there no voice stronger than that of the fear and ignorance which brought about this tragedy in Positano?

Part Three: *Epilogue*

Whatever is here, that is there; what is there, the same is here. He who seeth here as different, meeteth death after death. By mind alone this is to be realised, and then there is no difference here. From death to death he goeth, who seeth as if there is a difference here.

Katha Upanishad

14. *Author's Letter to Carol*
7 March 1972

I have just taken an acid trip in your womb cave nearly a year after Billie got out of prison and almost the same amount of time since I began working on the book with him. I was inside your body for some of the trip. It was so beautiful and sensuous, and I had the sensation of being born through you. Billie was with me most of the trip. I held his hand and I was you trying to take him with me, though he seemed to be far away and almost dead. Somewhere there was a flash of illumination that seemed to signify the coming of a new religion or era. I tried to find various keys but none of them fitted, and I realised it was like birth—the door had to be opened from the inside and we who are outside could only wait for it to happen and it would happen. It also had something to do with the book, as though the book contained mantras or hidden meanings. The cave, the house, your death were all part of the beginning of something incredible. It is something I never expected to find nor understand fully. I can only walk on blindly, knowing that no one has ever been on this road before and that we have all made a journey in the dark through some valley of death, guided by you.

During some part of the trip there was an eerie sensation that the bust and the police pouring into the house was an eternal moment and had to be repeated over and over again, but then I realised that was not the essence—it was merely a part of some other moment that had a much greater significance. Either you or Billie made some breakthrough that pushed everything further on and left that horror behind. I don't know what that moment is, though it must be contained somewhere in the story. Perhaps it was your death or perhaps it was Billie's return to the house, and the struggle he went through not to seek revenge for injustice, but to let things happen and to make the house a place where you could be and and where we could share you.

Later on in the trip I went upstairs with Joe and sat by the fire with everyone else. David* was there playing the guitar, with Charley singing. The indescribable beauty in David's face when he gets into these guitar sessions. I know he is with you forever and will never return. It seemed you liked being back in the house, but you were surprised at all the people, wondering who they were.

I don't understand what is supposed to be happening, but if I stay in the experience, then it seems real, a liberation that is totally personal, without any rules or regulations or set precepts. Just a discovery of oneself. But more than that in that it had something definitely to do with the house and with Billie—as though everyone here had something to do. I don't know. I suppose it will just happen without our particularly trying. So let it happen.

It seemed I had been wandering around in a maze for so long. I knew there was something extraordinary about being here— glimpses of another reality—though I was never confident about it, trying to rationalise it away and explain it to myself.

So I gave up trying to explain it and make it make sense. I wanted to go back and see what had happened to me during this time—what I had seen on the edges of myself and what the house had meant to me.

I met Billie in London—Teddie† took me along to the flat in Gloucester Road where he was staying—to interview him for the *Guardian*. Julie Christie had given me five free tickets for a charity performance of *Oh! Calcutta!* and we all wound up going to that at midnight. I remember thinking how strange it must be for Billie to have just come out of prison, suddenly seeing a supposedly 'liberated' show. Billie's reaction was to say that if anyone in the audience took off their clothes, the police would be on them like a ton of bricks. So much for the illusion of freedom.

Next day he came to my house where we worked on the article. He showed me photographs of you and I had a sudden flash that

---

* David Naylor who had been Carol's lover just before the police raid on the house and who returned there with his girlfriend Charley, a French singer, shortly after Bill's release from prison.

† Ted Edwards, also one of those arrested in the house on 5 August 1970 and imprisoned in an insane asylum for two and a half months.

you were the person in The Living Theatre who had come up to me in a London performance doing that whole number with 'holy hands, holy hair, holy cock' etc. and touching me all over. It was the only moment in *Paradise Now* that really got to me because of an extraordinary tactile communication between us. God knows why I didn't go up and talk to you afterwards, but I didn't. Anyway when I realised it was you, the coincidence gave me a feeling that you had chosen me. Having come out to the house I thought more and more about that—especially in down moments and it kept me going through the chaos of that summer —though at one point I realised it probably wasn't you but Jenny.* It seemed funny to realise that, but by then it was too late—I was hooked by some magic spell—and it didn't matter.

My attraction to you at first was purely visual—through photographs which Billie showed me and copies of your letters which had funny drawings on most pages and were written in your high backward-sloping handwriting that seemed to paint rather than write the words on to the page. The photographs revealed many different sides of you—the cat-like pouting face of someone who could curl up in one's arms and purr softly or the harsh bitchy face that says 'Fuck off' or 'Who the hell d'you think you are?' The commanding face and the commanded face . . . Always opposites, always alive.

Then Billie went to the States to see Bella Abzug, leaving me with the diary to see if I could find a publisher. For eight days I did nothing—it just sat around on my floor where he'd left it while I did other things. I'd lost momentum when Billie left and I felt I didn't really want to get involved in the whole thing—it was too complicated and I had an uneasy feeling about Billie. One couldn't resist thinking there was something Christ-like or demonic about him, at any rate something beyond a normal state of consciousness. He had that translucent sort of calm and eyes that cut right through all the bullshit to the centre, but you couldn't be sure he wasn't acting out the whole tragedy, enjoying the centre stage and fantasising you into what he wanted you to be. Also I knew the whole drugs thing wasn't so simple as he made out since Teddie had told me that he and several others

* Jenny Hecht, Living Theatre actress who died in mysterious circumstances in Los Angeles just after Carol died.

were on L.S.D. the night of the bust. Billie denied knowing that, so I went with his story in so far as the article was concerned. Then one day I picked up the diary and started reading it through from beginning to end and saw that it was 'abnormal': the story of a unique relationship. Something Billie had said which I had written down, seemed to sum it all up: 'Suddenly our unimportance becomes important. We find ourselves saying "Why should this happen to me?" We start to feel the pain ourselves because it's happening to us and yet most of the time we are indifferent to the pain of others, not treating it as important.' So I got off my arse and found a publisher, called Billie in New York and got him to come back to London.

He walked in the door with Carin who I thought was a girlfriend, not realising he had two daughters, and immediately we set off to go and see the publisher who had just returned from seeing Harold Wilson. In a bombastic mood he asked Billie to talk about the whole thing. Billie was tired and rambled on—the publisher sinking deeper and deeper into his chair, throwing out the odd bored question to which Billie went on rambling. The whole thing was getting stuck in a quagmire when the publisher asked what it was like being imprisoned in a mental asylum.

Billie was silent for a moment then said to the publisher in a sharp interrogating voice 'D'you always stare at people like that?'

The publisher looked alarmed, spluttered 'Yes . . . no . . . no', averting his eyes which were in fact staring intensely at Billie.

Immediately Billie said 'And do you always slump back like that when you talk to people?'

The publisher sat bolt upright and looked nervously embarrassed. It was an awkward moment because it seemed to be destructively personal and rude.

Then Billie said 'It's like that.'

The publisher laughed, everyone relaxed and the point was made. Ten minutes later he accepted the book and we had the go-ahead. It was a fabulous scene.

Two weeks later I went out to the house. There was a black flag flying from the roof and a blonde half-naked girl leaning out of the window to tell me Billie was in London. That was Ilona. Billie came back from Milan that night and the first I saw of him was getting out of the other side of the big bed I had crashed into the night before.

Those first two long frustrating conversations with Billie when I tried to get him to talk about the whole story and he would say 'I was in love with Carol—she was the most beautiful being I have ever known and loved. That's all there is to say. . . .' The first on the upstairs terrace in the bright morning sun the day after I arrived, Billie saying 'I want to be destructive to be creative. The problem with the revolution is that it's more important to turn one person on than to make demonstrations or governments fall— now I feel completely alone. . . .'

He wanted to be left alone to nurse his grief. He talked often of suicide and it seemed I was pushing him nearer it by pressing him to reconstruct the past. Then that second conversation on the terrace by the little house some days later.

After going over the events of your last days very quickly he reached the last seven hours and said: 'On 14 October the police came and took me to the hospital. I walked in and Carol had oxygen tubes in her and was being fed intravenously. I talked to her but there was no sign she. . . .' He stopped talking and sat absolutely still, looking at me as though I was intruding—a long hard look—then he got up and walked away. The tension was so strong I just sat there for about an hour, rooted to the chair.

And all the time the tide of people coming in and out of the house, disrupting the calmness of the place. I couldn't understand why Billie let it happen, why he left the door open to anyone to walk in who wanted to.

But there was your elusive brooding presence in the house, a sense that I had to or wanted to discover more about you—the paintings all over the walls, the doors; the photographs of you; the mystery of the house that seemed a spider's web of dreamland; the changing colours of the sea and mountains; the odd moments of peace I felt were here, in spite of the chaos of people. At that time it seemed dangerous, something that one could get lost in, drawn deeper into the pain of Billie's sense of loss. I could feel it like a magnet and it denied the sureness and clarity of the diary.

Suddenly Billie appeared to have lost his footing and the house to have become nothing more than a cobweb in which to catch pretty girls. He was balling them left, right and centre, sometimes two at a time but not involving himself with anyone—keeping his distance, withdrawing to the secret cave for hours on his own and reappearing with a calmness in his face. I think he was using trances to get back to a sense of you, though it seemed to be difficult for him.

Then Bernard said he had some acid and Billie that he wanted to take it—the day that Fiori, the contessa, turned up drunk at lunch, her tits hanging out of her dress, swaying about the kitchen kissing everyone.

'Last year we had drug addicts, and this year drunks', Billie said. 'Drunks are worse—they are more obstreperous.'

It was the day that Billie gave the impression of having come through some struggle—you could see it in his face because it had lost the usual distant and mocking look. After lunch he told the story of how you had once said to someone teasingly that he was a C.I.A. agent, then two years later a friend in Paris took you aside and said earnestly that he had confidentially heard that Billie was a C.I.A. agent and you had a confrontation with Billie, wanting to know the truth about the rumour you had started. You're crazy.

Billie took the acid and disappeared into a cave. It got dark and I was sitting on the terrace by the little house where you had your easel and used to listen to Anna singing. Suddenly Billie appeared and sat down in the wicker chair.

I said to him 'I thought you were going to take a trip?'

'I have taken a trip' he said. Long pause, then he came out with 'I have to see Valli'.*

'You want to see Valli?'

'I have to see her,' Billie said.

'D'you want me to drive you?'

'You don't have to.'

We both sat looking at the stars, then I said 'I had a whole vision of what I'd paint as a mural on the wall.'

Billie said, 'I have a whole vision of you right now.'

I got up. 'Come on, I'll drive you to see Valli.'

Billie was laughing all the time but got up and we went to the

---

* Valli Myers, the painter who lives with Rudi (the person who visited Bill in prison) on a small mountain farm between Praiano and Positano, with a large menage of animals.

Carol

Manacled at the tria[l]

Bill at the house after his release

Bill, 1972

house to get the car keys. Billie starting arsing around with a torch he had bought at a petrol station—with a pinpoint light in the centre of a pair of glassless spectacles. A martian eye whispering morse messages.

We drove along the road to Positano, though Billie couldn't remember in which valley Valli lived. We found one that he thought could be the right one and I left him there by the roadside to go on up to Valli's farm. I went with Osiris [Billie's dog] to the Quicksilver discothéque, but didn't have enough money to get in so came back. I found Billie standing in exactly the same place where I had left him an hour before. He said the torch had given out and the path up to Valli's was too dark to go on without it. So I stole a paraffin roadside light and used that as a torch. We stumbled up, with Osiris going first. Osiris suddenly stopped and I saw in front of us a deep well that we would have fallen into if it hadn't been for Osiris. We gave up and came back.

Back at the house, people were playing guitars and everything seemed normal. We went back to the chairs we had been sitting in before. Billie started talking about the stars, pointing to one which he said was trying to catch his attention.

I said, 'Maybe it's Carol. . . . .'

'I went down to the meditation room and thought of Carol and cried. . . . I don't know why I cried. Then standing there by the road waiting for you to come back I looked over the cliff and wondered how far down it was. I could hear Carol saying "Jump and see", but I didn't because it might not be far enough.'

Then he said, 'That's a load of bullshit.'

There was a general blah blah about the beauty of the place and the night.

Billie said. 'I don't care a fuck about all that, I want Carol. That's how much I want her. I don't know what I'm doing here. I don't know.'

I told him I thought he gave out a lot to those around him. Billie's reply was to shrug his shoulders and say: 'I know I give out a lot but I don't care—maybe that's why I give out a lot.'

Silence, then he went on talking, 'First I wanted Carol, then Valli, then Karin. . . .'

306 HOUSE OF THE ANGELS

I thought he meant his daughter Carin who'd gone to England for a few days.

He said 'No, not that Karin . . . Karin Christensen.'*

He went on 'One is dead, the other is in jail and another lives high on a dark mountain.'

I asked Billie if he wanted to be here in the house.

He said 'I don't really want to be here—but it's the only place I want to be. I think I have to start from here.'

'To start what?' I asked.

He said 'To go on living, the journey, the way . . . towards . . . the way on up the mountain.' His voice broke down and I wanted to hold him, to embrace him.

He said 'We've run out of cigarettes' and went off to get some more.

Then I fell asleep—it was just beginning to get light.

After that we went to Rome because Billie was making a Western to pay the lawyers. On the drive to Rome Billie said 'Carol never gave any reasons for doing anything. She just did it. If you asked "Why?" she would say "What the fuck do I care why!" She was a painter—she just knew what she was doing, very definitely. That is the whole story of Carol—she lived like she painted'.

Billie also talked about love and being in love, saying that he felt a complete moment of love with Carol but then got frightened of losing it and that was when things started to go wrong. But he said he realised later that he couldn't lose it. I asked about those moments of love because he was also talking about fear, which was what really hit him inside the *manicomio*.

He said 'This kind of love is the total absence of fear . . .' He was silent for a long time—driving fast down the autostrada to Rome, the sun unbearably hot—then he said 'You should take an acid trip because there are certain things you know but can't talk about, and acid makes you realise this'.

I said 'I want to find my Carol, whoever she is . . .'

---

* Karin Christensen, a young Danish girl who had been at the house just before the police raid in August 1970. She was arrested in Rome the very same day that Bill was released from prison—30 March 1971 on a minor drugs charge and was kept in prison a year. Besides looking remarkably like Carol, she also had suspected cancer and was given a serious abdominal operation in prison without the aid of any anaesthetic.

That strange day at Ellio's studios outside Rome when Joe, John and Roxanne* turned up out of the blue and we all sat around on the set—Billie carrying guns and a rifle, hanging around waiting to shoot in the heat. And we all started asking him what on earth he was doing making a Western and all he could say was 'That's where it's at'. It was some sort of fundamental conversation about what we wanted to do with our lives—on the set of a Western movie.

Three weeks in Rome in July. Joe, John and Roxanne taking acid every day, the incredible highs at Parioli, dancing and eating at night. The evening with Fabienne at that restaurant when Billie started playing the tape of Charley singing as though she was having an orgasm and everyone suddenly stopping their conversation and looking round and the argument between Billie and that police-type man who thought the tape was disgusting and that we should all be thrown out.

Coming back to the house—all the people here—the chaos and fighting. It was the beginning of August. Ilona started to flip out. No Charley was the first one—it was while we were in Rome she tried to commit suicide, slashing her wrists and Anna ran all the way to Positano to try to get a doctor.

I shut myself up in the little house and tried to work, reading all your letters and diaries and getting lost in it all and becoming more and more disillusioned with Billie. The diary seemed a complete lie, an illusion—his ego bigger than the Eiffel Tower and all his interests in fucking whoever came to the house. Then in the middle of all that—at the worst point when I was ready to quit—that dream one afternoon when I was sleeping on your big bed, the dream that was the beginning of an extraordinary ten days.

There is a whole area about dreams or acid that is very hard to communicate. What has one thing to do with another? In the land of green and blue nothing else matters. Seen from there the world is a

* Joe Wheeler, 41 year-old American actor who was a friend of Bill and Carol from the days of their Rome apartment. John Thompson, also an American actor, who some years before had deserted from the U.S. Army in Germany, worked in films in Spain, then went back to Germany, handed himself in and served an eight-month sentence in solitary confinement for desertion. Together with Roxanne Palash, a young American girl, they lived in an apartment in a condemned building in Parioli district, Rome.

hell because it's all about control, who's right—it's a world full of tiny crabs, everyone trying to grab everything for themselves; it's a world where justice, love, everything is used for this end. Totally amoral. It's a matter of 'seeing' this, not arguing it, because once you've seen it, then you 'know'. Others will reject it because they don't see, and their logic is another part of the grab-machine-ego system— the human disease.

I was with you—with your dark hair and a wide-brimmed hat and eyes that gazed long distances and smiled sphinxily at the world around. You didn't have the disease people have—there was so much distance in you, it was unbelievable—or space or love—but mystery—you didn't talk. Billie was looking for two men who'd had lunch in a hotel but hadn't stayed the night. This seemed of vital importance to him but no one knew why. . . . Billie playing his detective game. Maybe he still had a bit of the disease and we all had to help him? But he could stand in two worlds at the same time which was clever of him. No one could quite understand how he did it—either he pretended he had the disease or he pretended he was without it. Either way he was pretending.

I wasn't 'with' you because you were with us—there was a group of us—about twelve. But I had a special feeling about you and looked at you all the time or when I wasn't looking at you I was feeling you— which meant that when I found something funny and laughed I could turn round and laugh with you because I knew immediately where you were.

*The way we knew Billie was pretending was because he was playing his detective game and because when we were in the park and sat down in the chairs and all of a sudden, all at the same time, we took off, got high, soared and laughed—after a moment of silence when we all looked at each other and it seemed the universe would explode, which it did when we took off—while we were doing this Billie who had been playing chess with me in an even and only-just-begun game moved all his pieces so he had me check-mate. But when we studied the board for a long time we discovered that he hadn't really got me check-mate as he thought—which was the funniest thing and made us get even higher. You were the only one who didn't look at the board but kept gazing far away into the distance as though looking for someone—*maybe it was for your other Billie to come. *We all knew it was something like that which made you silent and always looking into the* *distance—but it was strange because this horizon-gazing and sphinxiness didn't make you melancholic or in any way unhappy nor did it take you from us or make you seem distant.*

Then I woke up and heard Billie in another room talking into the tape-recorder—it was the time when he was reading the diary on to tape. And I thought: Christ, he's playing his detective game again. . . . What is he doing? What's he doing here, how can he be here? Things like that. It seemed as though he was doing things for or else to do other things which is part of the disease. And I felt such terrible pain to find Billie here when I thought he was there. I didn't feel as though I was here and I wondered about this—if I was here too in the same way that Billie seemed to be here.

For the moment it didn't seem that I was here but that you with your dark hair and deep deep quietness had sent me to bring back your other Billie, who you looked for without looking and yearned for without yearning.

There's something I've forgotten that happened before the dream —a few weeks earlier when Billie started to flip out and lose his cool. It was a day in July when Pierre Clementi was busted and we read about it in the papers. The thing that bugged Billie was they mentioned his name in connection with Pierre, implying guilt by association. Billie was still playing the part of the innocent victim of the system, the police, laws, etc. Suddenly he blew up, throwing the paper across the room and snapping at anyone who spoke. All Billie's frenzied paranoia started to come out. He got so uptight that he rushed off to Naples in the car for a meeting with a journalist which I'm sure he invented since no one turned up, just to show everyone that he was doing something, proving something to himself—God knows what because there wasn't anything he could do. It was the same with Karin Christensen whom he kept talking about, letting out his frustration against the system but doing nothing much about her. It was Joe who really got things organised.

It was only later that he told us what he was planning to do that day when Pierre was busted. He said that he was going into Naples to see the journalist to explain what he was going to do— which was to walk into a police station smoking a joint and admitting that he smoked marijuana. Billie said that if everyone who smoked marijuana came out into the streets smoking a joint, they would have to change the laws because there wouldn't be enough room in the prisons for everyone. Billie went on saying that it was the uselessness of protest that was important and it didn't matter what the end result was, only the strength of the protest. He said it was important to protest against the Vietnam war 'not because the Vietnam war was important but because the protest was against the system which will go on producing other Vietnams'.

Then Billie started arguing that Hitler was the greatest prophet of the twentieth century—using Hitler's careful introduction of extermination camps as an example: Hitler got the idea accepted by just letting it happen for a year during which the generals protested with Hitler denying knowledge of them, then when he officially introduced them no one protested because they had already protested but done nothing, thereby actually condoning extermination camps.

Then Billie admitted that going up to the police with a joint in his hand wouldn't achieve anything, but it didn't worry him because he would be doing it for himself and not for the end result. He said 'It doesn't matter if nobody knows about it.' The trouble is that he didn't do it. He said that on the way to Naples he got into a three hour traffic jam and that by the time he arrived at the rendezvous with the journalist, she had given up waiting and the whole thing petered out. 'It wasn't meant to happen,' he said feebly, showing that his need to publicise his actions undermines his arguments. As a result the whole incident appears nothing more than a temperamental fit of mock heroics.

But all that came out later—at the time we didn't know what was going on except that he was flipping out.

The dream happened on 8 August. It was a great liberation for me as regards Billie because before that I'd been unable to accept the contradictions within him. They were pulling me as far apart as they must have been him.

There had been great hostility in me towards Billie—because of his bullshit half-baked explanations of everything, a kind of lazy cynicism. If he could make the movement into action it would make some sense, but instead he did nothing, which made all his arguments seem like a gaseous substance, completely empty. I didn't think you had this kind of buffooning pretence in you—acting wise and laying on to everyone the past. 'When I was in the *manicomio*,' so the sentence would begin and everyone falls into a hushed silence as the head of the table begins to speak. Billie worship, Billie and his Messiah complex.

The same thing underlies the house. Although it's very open and free to all, Billie is a benevolent dictator, allowing his 'children' to be free. Also immediately after the bust there seemed to be an incredible naïvety on Billie's part—I don't think you had this. All Billie's awakening to the world as it really is seems stupidly naïve—why didn't he realise this before? Before it was too late to do anything about it? He was living in the enclosed world of actors, drugs, getting high and not being aware of the edges of his life. Also he goes on protesting about the half gram of dope found in the house—but a lot of the others here that night were tripping on acid when the police broke in. Billie goes on denying this—because he is frightened of what *they* will do if *they* know the truth. So he manipulates the truth so *they* won't have the opportunity to get him or abuse it. In other words, the truth of what happened in August 1970 is not relevant to him, only the invasion of his liberty. You took drugs—everyone admits that—but didn't care what the consequences would be. Billie seems to have expected everyone to see it his way without making the effort to convince anybody. Therefore your death gives him centre stage and he appears as the great guru, emerging from a traumatic experience—and everyone falls into an awed silence. But in reality your death was expected, a sort of joke on your part. Billie sees it as a murder rather than as resignation, suicide.

Going from this kind of hostility to Billie to appreciation and sympathy for him when it seemed he was the most 'waiting' person I've ever met—waiting for others to make a move, to reveal themselves—which creates a tension and strain at times. He wants to let things happen, not interfering. It is extraordinary when you think what he is doing now—just continuing his life where he left off, working in films, living at Praiano, doing the ordinary things and not creating a splash of new things, as though the prison experience and your death confirmed and focused what he believes in. The changes are inner—discovering his strength. You can see this in Praiano—like the evening when he showed us films of you. He watched them for a while then went down to the meditation room to try to get back to you. The films certainly evoked you very strongly amongst us. Billie must have gone into a trance to get to you because afterwards his eyes had that clear lucid look. Perhaps he had been weeping also.

The sun hot, people going around naked, and yet a distance between us that was hard to define. Everybody hiding from intimacy, especially Billie.

There is incredible violence in him below the surface of coolness and calm. The struggle going on inside him to fight non-violently, using the same outwardly passive methods as before—yet the problem of being inwardly active and fighting for inner truth while feeling the sense of inner emptiness he must have, a sense that nothing is worth doing because you are dead and gone. Yet he goes on searching inwardly for some way. The courage required to go on doing that and not falling down into sentiment-ality—the same struggle as in prison.

The day Kevin left. Billie, Bernard and I at lunch talking about love and acid trips and Billie saying 'The most positive thing that happened to me in the *manicomio* was that I finally got rid of my mother—she became a person I could talk to, someone I dug instead of just a "mother".' Kevin looked happy to be going and said how happy he'd been here. Then he mentioned something about money and Billie said 'Oh, d'you want some?' and went out to get some for Kevin, who then got his guitar and suitcase and left. Ilona woke up and discovered Kevin had left without her. In a mad panic she got her things together and left to find him, though no one knew where he had gone. Five hours later Kevin returned, having forgotten his passport and next day Ilona came back. Finally, after tumultuous rows they set off together.

Good days—bad days.

Back to Billie's whole philosophy of drifting, what he calls 'going with the flow'. It was that kind of ridiculous drifting which was more responsible for your death than anything. Everyone in the house just drifting—it's really pathetic—and a feeling of loneliness and of no one being a part of anything.

So Billie takes drugs. Why all the hypocrisy about it? Every-thing he says about the government and the system are really about him—and what he writes doesn't tell us anything about them, only about him. He is not really interested in anyone else, only his own fucking. When you were here the house was completely different, so people say. Billie puts everyone down and no one can say anything any more. You never let him get away with it. His seductive aura. It takes a long time to penetrate through that to what is really going on. There's a lot of ugly things in him below the surface if you care to dig down.

The time when Charley split to Rome after a row with David. She is jealous of your presence everywhere. She wants to be the star, to be you for Billie and David. A few days later some of us drove up, including David and Fabrizio. One day Fabrizio was walking through Trastevere and saw a crowd of people standing round a fountain. He went over to look and saw Charley swimming in the fountain in the nude. He brought her back to Parioli— that's how we got Charley back—then driving down to Praiano after smoking that incredible hash in Parioli—a nightmare trip with Charley, who had also taken acid, driving some of the way, swaying all over the autostrada.

Billie at the house, waiting for some enemy worthy of him to appear, someone he could murder.

One day at lunch he suddenly said to me, 'You are too much in the conscious—there are certain things which can't be said.' I was arguing with him about Vietnam and individual freedom within the system and he got so angry he stood up shouting at the top of his voice 'Nobody shares, nobody shares a fucking thing, the system destroys sharing between people. . . .'

I said 'Why are you shouting?'

He shouted 'I'm not shouting', then sat down and in a calmer voice said 'I'm not shouting.'

In the space between these sentences I felt he could almost, perhaps nearly did, kill me.

It's still 8 August—the day I felt you, the day I went to the other side and saw who Billie was. Nan arrived some days before with her talk of spiritualism and seances. The day before—on 7 August—I wrote in my diary 'Carol is writing this book'. On 10 August we played chess all day, just going on and on playing, then swimming in the pool. During this time Billie was reading the diary into his tape-recorder and I was working in the tomato room. That afternoon Billie came into the tomato room where Nan and I were talking and we talked about you.

'My whole life now is Carol. She is here. I don't care a fucking thing about anything else in the world.'

I kept asking questions about you, but I had the feeling that Billie didn't want to talk about the past.

'Maybe we should go to a medium,' Billie said then added, 'but that isn't the only way of getting in touch with Carol.'

Billie was sitting in the deck chair, wearing one of your shirts, Nan was lying on the bed and I was at the desk. We sat there for a long time, no one saying anything.

That evening I met Billie in the hallway. 'Listen, you have to stop me whenever I get logical. I was sitting by the window just now watching the sunset, thinking about Carol and the house—that's it, it's magical, it's no use trying to explain it.'

The next morning Henry* came up to me and described a dream he had had about you in which you spoke three words 'Body . . . die . . . lie'. I didn't think anything much of it, except I realised that Henry had seen you or felt you in some way. Later on in the morning I drove into Positano to do something and met Chuck † and Marmory there. We had coffee at the Bar on the terrace and Suzanne who lives in Positano appeared and started telling about a seance she had at her house the night before—the night of Henry's dream.

She said, 'Carol came through and said three words "Body . . . die . . . lie".'

My heart missed a beat at that point. I explained Henry's dream to them and Suzanne said she was going to have another seance in a few days—would we like to go along? I said I'd talk to Billie. I came back to the house and told him of the words you had said in Henry's dream and the seance in Positano. He took it very coolly and nothing happened. On 17 August Suzanne rang up and said she was going to have the seance that night. Chuck was

* Henry Howard, Living Theatre actor and husband of Nona who was at the house the night the police raided it, together with her young son, but who had not been arrested with the others. Henry who after the break-up of the Living Theatre had formed a cell in Paris, stayed in the house with Nona while Bill was in prison, then came back the following summer.

† Charles 'Chuck' Griffith—42-year-old Hollywood film script writer of most of Roger Corman's early horror movies—his best known film being *Wild Angels*, the precursor of *Easy Rider*.

camping at the camping site in Praiano and wanted to come too. Billie said he would give it a try and we all went to Chuck's tent for supper. I remember as we walked away from the house to go to the camping site how much more relaxed Billie appeared when he was out of the house.

Some heavy things had been happening in the previous week. Ilona had tried to commit suicide in the bathroom by slashing her wrists. She had come back to the house from Morocco where she had gone without Kevin in order to find out where he was. But Kevin, who was in Norway, didn't want to see her again. She had tried to commit suicide three times in the past week, leaving trails of blood all over the house. We couldn't take her to a doctor because he would have to commit her to an insane asylum—so we patched her up as best we could and tried to help her. But the strain on Billie was very hard because if she did do it, the police would have arrested him as well—for not sending her to a doctor.

Also just before Ilona started trying to kill herself she had been going into Positano every day, dancing at the Quicksilver, getting stoned drunk, then bringing her lovers back to the house. One day Joe found her in a cave smoking a joint with a Mexican boy she had brought back and Joe freaked out because we all knew it was dangerous to have any drugs in the house—the police were out to get Billie and prove they had been right all along about the house. Joe had screamed at Ilona and threw the Mexican out of the house, protecting Billie from the same kind of scene that had happened a year before.

So the night we went out to Chuck's tent in Praiano, the house had become a burden and it seemed Billie could no longer control it or look after himself. We were all aware that things were getting dangerous but no one could quite get hold of it.

For example on 3 August Billie, Henry and myself had a discussion about discipline and rules after a night of non-stop happenings. We were sitting on the porch drinking coffee, talking in tired philosophical voices. During the night Ilona and Debbie had come back from Positano with two Italians and Billie got angry and threw them out because he was worried about informers and someone planting something here. Charley had been singing all night and making love to David, screaming out at the top of her voice every time she had an orgasm so that all of Praiano could hear. And in between orgasms she and David splashing around in the pool, laughing and screaming. So there we were on the porch —Billie talking about awareness of the outside community—of all the people in Praiano sleeping and getting up early to work, of the cops watching the house and how the whole situation was very uncool. The absence of restraints or imperatives had reached such a pitch that the police were bound to walk in. Billie was saying that the more the restraints fell away, the more people lost awareness of an outside reality—and this is a major problem. The problem was—how to live without restraints and yet keep an awareness of others, a sensitivity to other people here in the village?

Billie said, 'The problem is to have a desire to do something that isn't a rule or discipline but grows out of your awareness of others, so that it is not imposed by anyone but desired. There's a whole difference in point of view and it's something that a community can aim at—the removal of restraints and the opening up of people—which can be very frightening. Then comes the positive process of integration and creativity which maybe has to be lost again when others join the community. Adjusting to a new person is very difficult instead of locking yourself away from them.'

Another thing that happened in this period immediately before 17 August was that after a suicide attempt by Ilona, she and Billie were sitting on the chairs in the porch, and Billie was getting more and more angry with her because she was putting everyone in danger with her histrionics.

We were all sitting round and at one point Billie said to her, 'Why don't you stick a knife in me, why don't you kill me because that's what you're doing baby'—his voice trembling with rage.

Ilona was still covered in blood and bandaged up—she was also drunk and seemed hardly able to hear or keep her eyes open. Suddenly she stood up and shouted at Billie 'That's your trip Billie, that's what you want me to do. . . .'

Billie was shouting 'Go on, do it, why don't you put the knife in me?'

By now he had picked up a knife from the table and was trying to put it into Ilona's hand.

Ilona kept saying 'That's your trip, Billie. It's not what I want to do. . . .'

Then he heard her and stopped talking. It was an incredible moment because she was right and Billie knew it. Suddenly the violence in him was naked—it was very frightening. It was the only moment I've ever seen him utterly dumbfounded.

So there we were—Billie, David, Nan, Debbie* and I—in Chuck's tent, eating supper and smoking joints. The time came to leave and we piled into a car for Positano and went to Suzanne's house.

We all lay around on her terrace for a long time while she and another woman got the room ready, then the seance started. There was a strange atmosphere—it was a bourgeois house and these were people who had seances out of curiosity or for gossip rather than really getting into it. We all wondered what the hell we were doing there. The whole thing seemed so incongruous.

We used a ouija board. Talida Getty † came through first and we asked her if you were there. She said yes and then went to get you, reluctantly. A message came through for Billie from you. It was the word 'shit' which you kept repeating, god knows why. By now the atmosphere was extraordinary—we all knew something real was happening.

The word 'shit' and the initials 'G.S.' were very strong. The glass moved rapidly from 'shit' to 'G.S.' all the time. Nobody knew what this meant.

Then the glass moved to a number—10. We asked if that was a date? You said 'yes' then we asked if you meant October? Again yes, then the glass moved to 14. We asked if you meant 14 October? The glass said 'yes'—the date of your death.

Then someone asked if you had a message for Billie? 'Yes.' Question: 'What do you want to say?' Another question: 'Where do you want him to go?'

Up until now the glass had been moving slowly and indistinctly. Suddenly with alarming speed and clarity it moved to six letters: B-R-A-Z-I-L . . . Brazil.

* Bill's fourteen-year-old daughter who had come to Italy from California to see him in prison. She and Carin, Bill's elder daughter, came to Italy in June and stayed at the house all summer.

† Wife of Paul Getty Jr. She committed suicide in 1970. Carol had gone on a cruise with them just before joining the Living Theatre in 1968.

Question: 'Is there something else you want to tell Billie?'

'Yes.' It turned out that you wanted Billie to go to Rome to see his agent, Perrone, for financial reasons, then he should go to Brazil to see Julian Beck and the Living Theatre—it was only then that we connect 'G.S.' with 'L.T.' because they were close to each other on the board and it was hard to see what letters the glass was pointing to sometimes. You mentioned Julian Beck—that it was important for Billie to see him. At this time the Living Theatre were in prison in Brazil on drugs charges. Someone asked if you wanted Billie to be arrested with them. Immediately you answered 'No', and everyone laughed because the response was so quick and concerned. Debbie asked if she should go with Billie and you again said 'No' very firmly. Debbie looked completely crushed.

Then you said that the Living Theatre would be out of prison when Billie got there and that he should go there before going to Colombia where he was supposed to make a film in September. You also said that shortly after Billie arrived the Living Theatre would leave Brazil—all of which subsequently happened.

Billie asked if he would be with you and you said 'Yes', then if the house was in danger. Another 'Yes'. The word 'shit' appeared again and the fact that Henry was disturbing you. You said Henry should leave the house at once, though the danger was not tonight. Then you said that Ilona was in danger but should stay in the house.

Someone asked if Ilona was in danger tonight? 'Yes.' Was she at the Quicksilver? 'Yes.' Should we go now? 'Yes.' Immediately Billie and Debbie left and shortly after the seance ended.

Afterwards, in the car driving back from Positano, no one spoke. The same all evening. Next morning Billie was different—more cheerful, outward-going, as though something had been resolved in his mind. But still nobody mentioned the events of the night before.

That night we had another seance—this time in the house—Billie and Nan making a ouija board. We put the table in the telephone room. Billie sat by the table for a long time, going into a trance, waiting for David to come. David came and we started. This time the atmosphere was different—less freakish, more simple. First of all Billie's father came through and gave him a date—7 July 1972—when something extremely important would happen. Then you came again and kept repeating the word 'war' over and over again. It was late at night and the vibrations in the room were confused—people kept asking distracting questions of their own and the whole thing broke up, except for a few people who tried to go on. Most of us were sitting out on the terrace by the telephone room, talking, when suddenly there was a scream from the bathroom. It was Ilona committing suicide again by slashing her wrists with an old razor blade. Again blood everywhere and panic—this time she had almost done it but not quite. We patched her up.

Looking back on the events of those days, two things seemed very important, though at the time it wasn't possible to understand it all because so much was happening. The first was the date—7 July 1972. The second thing was the fact that during this time—from 7 August to 18 August—you were trying to reach Billie, using whoever or whatever you could—through dreams, events, coincidences of one kind or another. And it seemed that what you were trying to say to him was—Leave the house. The house seemed to have become a disease for him, living a gypsy life with all the people around—at one time there were thirty-five people sleeping in the house—cluttering up his life. It seemed self-destructive and dangerous for him, as though he was re-creating the conditions of the *manicomio*, though he always seemed able to cut out from it and keep his distance.

A few days later Henry and Daphne left. The house started to cool out. I asked Billie why he was staying in Italy and what he thought about going to Brazil and the whole seance, because I could tell that he knew he was talking to you directly. He said that if you had been there that's what you would have said—you would have been concerned about the Living Theatre and would have wanted to get to them. But that wasn't necessarily what he wanted to do.

At this time there were rumours that there was going to be another bust in the area, and Billie thought the police would be out to get him this time. Billie talked about not running away. I said that was very passive—why doesn't he become more active instead of just waiting for them to come and get him? He replied that it was the only way of bringing the revolution—instead of jumping on the barricades and forcing something to happen. You had to let them come to you and be ready for it.

Conversation on the roof one evening as the sun was setting or was it in the kitchen? Billie: 'Part of the experience is to decide whether or not to go on living, whether to care about poor people in Naples, caring about why Nixon and people are mechanical toys, about changing society. The only way to be free is to be free. You cannot impose it on others with a gun. It's the same with love. You can't arrive at love by intellectual argument, only at the necessity of loving. You just love. . . . Madness is a circle, mad people don't make any sense—they can have one emotion one minute, another the next, but spinning round in circles creates an energy maybe. I'm not interested in converting the whole world to communism or anarchism so that I can have a reason to go on living. If we need some kind of housekeeping to keep ourselves from destroying each other, then that's OK. But love is OK. If police keep running into my house with guns, I can't go on loving. We must find what compels us to love. The choice is between fear and love. What we have been in and are now in is a system of fear and 'talk' about love, except in individual moments and with individual people. Fear works very well as an energy producing force. But we've come to a point where fear cannot serve any more because it leads to total destruction. We have to avoid it, therefore love—which creates energy. If we have to love, we have to find out why it's inevitable. . . .'

Conversations about the significance of the house and the growth of a community went on for several days as well as the issue of whether Billie should stay here or not. This was partly the result of everybody except for Billie being uncertain as to what to do with Ilona. Billie wanted her to stay here and for everyone to try to help her, instead of sending her away to someone else which is what everybody was inclined to do. Billie wanted the community to be able to handle it and absorb her instead of pushing her out. It was a difficult thing to do, but everyone realised what he was trying to say and the significance of it—because we all knew in some way that Ilona's suicide attempts were a judgment on the community as much as on herself. So we tried to reach her and hold her and comfort her.

The other thing that provoked these conversations about

community was the fact that Billie had started working at this time as the garbage collector of Praiano—taking over the job from Gaetano who was ill. And this brought out discussions of the significance of work—of not working for money but everyone doing what had to be done, without thought of the reward. Every evening Billie would go round the village knocking on doors and collecting the garbage. It was far out—this person everyone thought of as a movie star collecting the garbage.

Then there was the time when Nan and I were trying to persuade Billie that it was more important that he should take care of himself, instead of letting himself and the house disintegrate around him. Using the image of climbing the mountain, we were saying it was more important that he should reach the top so that people could see in him an example of what they could reach. Billie replied very firmly that his rôle was to stay at the bottom of the mountain and show people the way to the mountain. We realised that was what he was trying to do in the house.

On 22 August Ilona tried to commit suicide again—after which, as always, playing Carole King's Tapestry record over and over again. There is a sense of evil in the house that is very overpowering.

The same night some people brought some marijuana into the house and smoked it in the little house. Billie found out and was furious that they could be so stupid. I said the only logical thing for him to do was to split for the mountains or impose his will on the house and make sure no one brought anything here. He talked about having patience, waiting for others to understand— even if he has to go back to prison.

'Why not get together a group of friends and do something positive together?' I said.

Billie replied, 'What are friends? I don't see people as friends and others as not friends—that's playing the old game, making oneself isolated.'

I said, 'Any decision isolates you from the alternatives—that's the nature of decisions. Why be frightened of that?'

He didn't answer but stayed silent.

Next day Billie took Carin and Debbie to Rome to get an aeroplane for the States. The night before—the girls' last night in the house—they slept with Billie in his bed. I went in and saw them lying there, hugging each other in their sleep. It was a very moving scene. Debbie's desperate need to cling on to Billie, to merge with him which becomes frightening sometimes; and Carin's ability to let go, to see him for what he is and to live her own life; and Billie watching it happen, letting them be free to do that. Seeing them sleeping in the bed together brought all that out, all that had been happening between them this summer.

That same evening before Billie, Carin and Debbie left for Rome, Ilona tried to commit suicide again. By now it has become a sort of joke, no one taking it seriously, thinking she won't do it. Someone came into the bedroom and said they had seen Ilona waiting outside the bathroom—everyone laughed. Ten minutes later there was the sound of glass breaking and a groan. More blood, bandages and shouting. Billie stayed in the bed, philosophising about it.

While Billie is away in Rome Ilona made a final attempt at suicide—the worst. Everyone has been drumming into her that she musn't do it in the house—she can jump off a cliff or whatever —but here she is putting everyone in danger. It's early in the morning—I am making tea in the kitchen when there is a horrible groan from the garden. I go down and see Ilona lying in a flower-bed covered in blood and a woman from the village standing by her. Ilona had tried to kill herself on the steps outside the house, then staggered in. This time she slashed herself with a broken bottle—wrists and ankles. It is very bad. We bathe her and this time it seems she won't recover. We go to see doctors all over the place but no one will do anything. We phone the German embassy in Rome and Naples to try to get her admitted to a clinic. It seems the only way of keeping her out of an insane asylum. We find somewhere and get ready to drive her to Rome. Then Billie returned and he said he would pay for her to get out of the country. So we drive to Naples airport, arrive with five minutes to spare. They won't take a cheque so I have to give her all my travellers' cheques. She hobbles away, covered in bandages, but happy.

She has tried to commit suicide eight times and suddenly it seems as though she was doing it to make us take her away from the house—the only way she can say it. She is pregnant—she wants to get to Kevin who has 'gone to the North Pole'—and she has no money.

We return to the house—there is still a smell of blood every-where. Perhaps Ilona sensed something about the house—an evilness here—that you also felt sometimes.

A few days later Billie comes to me and says he is glad Ilona left because it seemed as though he was keeping her here to prove something to himself.

He said, 'I realised I was frightened of her—she was sticking a knife into me. But I got over the fear of what she could do, then realised it was no use keeping her here to go on proving to myself that I had got over that fear.'

Ever since the seance and the sense of your reality, your being here, I wanted to know more and more about you and to fight through my idealised illusions of you to the real you. I had a sense that you were evil, the evil spirit presiding over the house, and suddenly objects started to fight me—spilling boiling water all over my legs, breaking my toe on the steps. I tried to keep cool, fighting the devil. I found some of your diaries and saw how you had fought against an evil presence, how you had an over-powering sense of death in the house. It was frightening. Or at least the beginning of a dangerous journey for me.

And all the time David was here—connecting me to you in a much stronger way than Billie was able to do.

Nan and a whole lot of people left. Suddenly the house was very calm, a sort of calm despair—only a few people here and autumn in the air. There was that beautiful morning when Raffaela woke us up at five o'clock—Billie, David, Charley and myself—and we walked up into the mountains to get wine, dawn coming from behind the mountains and the coolness of the morning, then coming back laden with wine barrels via the monastery all the time the sun getting hotter and the leaves on the trees in the valley a golden red.

Quiet days—Billie and I working together on editing the diary —it was beginning to get windy and cold—the quietness inter-rupted only once when Charley got drunk and tried to leave but Billie went after her and brought her back. It seemed for a moment that we were returning to the madness of the summer, but it passed. And a new feeling of trust and openness emerging between Billie and me.

Then there was that peculiar funny day—4 September—the day

it was rumoured there was going to be another bust. Everyone was nervous in the evening. Billie kept saying he wasn't sure what we should do. We sat around fantasising about armed resistance and starting the revolution in the house and how hard it would be for the police to break in if we defended the house with guns. Billie opened up the slit above the front door and made a notice saying 'Bang, you're dead' which he lowered on a piece of string everytime anyone came in.

That night there was a full moon—everyone stayed up on the terrace, waiting for the police to come. It was very beautiful— a thin autumn mist over the sea. And we locked the doors and waited and waited. Nothing happened.

Diana arrived from London. We sat on the porch talking, Billie eating a fig. After a bite he looked startled and showed everyone half a worm wriggling inside the half-eaten fig in his hand.

I said, 'The other half is still alive.'

'So am I,' Billie replied.

Billie showed his Living Theatre film—incessant conversations about acting, learning (how it's impossible to communicate the truth one has discovered except obliquely) and finding the universality of love. Billie gets turned on by reading about Gurdjieff in Ouspensky's *In Search of the Miraculous*, and keeps reading passages aloud.

I was leaving in a week to go to Venice for a holiday with Alison [my wife] whom I haven't seen for three months. One evening—while making tea in the kitchen, with the sun an inch above the mountains before disappearing—I feel an extraordinary peace and have a vision of you and Billie completely at peace, away from all the storms—you playing your organ in one part of the house and Billie mending something in another—both so closely connected in feelings and thoughts.

Another day when I was typing out some thoughts about the night of the bust, trying to imagine what you were feeling, I suddenly got a very strong sense of you and I let my mind go and type what comes into my head.

The police have arrived and you hardly say a word . . .

Touch me. I see you now looking with your dazzling eyes that blur the world for me with something strange. I know you are strong,

strong beyond me. I just want you to touch me, here in this aloneness which may be our last aloneness. Touch me so we are together. Don't look, stare . . . touch me. I can't ask, I can't . . . not when I'm dead. But now when we are not alone but alone . . . it doesn't matter. I will touch you and you will never know my need . . . one last kiss.

Then in the car and the last moment of conscious togetherness.

Now there's wrenching the door open. I can hear the sound of someone coming through the opening of the door, through their voices that are parting us now—that cuts between us like a hate . . . too late. I touch your head and put my hand over your eyes. I am going now. You turn away calmly—you are always calm—but I know how hard won that calmness is because I can stir it into strife. And you look once then leave the car. I sit here knowing what you will feel when I am gone—the togetherness, the inter-knowing, the inner-knowing. . . .

A sense of certainty about you, of my knowing you better and a fear of losing myself and getting caught up in illusions.

Then Bernard arrived back again with some acid and I say I want to take some. We have talked a lot about it over the summer and I have been uncertain about it, especially with all the chaos in the house.

11 SEPTEMBER 9.30 PM—*I take a trip of acid with Billie, David, Bernard and Charley. Eyes begin to water. Just now sitting by the fire in the big room—Billie chopping up wood.*

10.45 by the village clock. Billie just read a passage from In Search of the Miraculous *and we talked about 'remembering yourself'. I tried to describe how I thought we develop a voice for our thoughts to someone—in this case you—and how we go on directing our thoughts towards that person, wanting to share them.*

Back to the theme of 'the poetry of separation' which I felt Billie indulged in sometimes with you.

Charley keeps coming in and dancing in front of the mirror—get bad vibrations from her—she wants everybody to look at her. I send out strong negative rays. Billie and Bernard now lying flat out on mattresses. David is downstairs, I think painting the door into the kitchen with silver paint.

Billie said 'I just woke up and had the sensation of not being any-where, of not existing, of not knowing time . . . I just picked up where I left off'—then he started talking about a painting in the far corner of the room which you did while on an acid trip. At one point Billie said 'My dream is to have three girls in a constant readiness for love—never bothering you with "What are you doing? Where have you been. . . ."'

A beautiful night—with the scent of things after rain and flashes of an electrical storm in the sky.

Talking about George Jackson's murder in San Quentin prison, Billie said, 'It's obvious—just look at the handcuffs, the guns, it's not nice. . . .'

The whole thing of 'being' came up while I was thinking about being here in the house and about you—the whole thing also of why everyone could so easily have accepted the cops coming in without fighting or resisting. Everyone in the house at the time was working from a different level of reality completely, but then Billie had to play the game out move by move—like an elaborate chess game—move by fucking move. His whole vision of things as they are is based on the acid experience—the insights, the stillness, seeing things as they are without the bullshit. People are not able to see things as they are— what are they? Now we're challenging a sense of vision—at least let's get down to asking that question.

Still night in the sky.

There is a beautiful house on the mountain-side where the sun shines all summer and there are people in this house who keep 'losing' themselves and 'finding' themselves again. In one state or the other everything is beautiful, then ugly—moving from heights to the depths. Billie is the only one who can translate this vision into reality.

To the vision-bearer to whom we've given the secret, don't fuck it up. . . .

Anyway you won't, I know. It's slow and hard for you, baby, I know—horribly hard—but it's all here too—the other side, the ha ha side, the ho ho side—both sides of the fence. You're not a baby sitter, you're a fence sitter. . . .

Practising my Carol voice. Why the hell have I got that, where have I got it from? Maybe from Billie's need for her? It's not Carol's voice. It's me imitating Carol, which is crazy. So all our arguments are really about jealousy! The ugly worm worming to the circus surface. The rub—if I can respond to Billie's need for Carol's voice, where is me? Half Alison voice, half wanting someone voice, sitting on the seesaw. Maybe it will always be like that. Who is this someone else?

Just now I looked at a photograph of Carol in the kitchen and saw her weariness with the world.

The candles are still burning, the fire still glowing warm and the Indian music making its mad zigzags as though trying to persuade the flies to go away. That's really what Indian ragas are—the restless impatient movement of the perpetually flicking hand or dog's tail in the drenching sun.

Billie talking about acting and how to recapture concentration— by concentrating on something specific like a cigarette, then letting the concentration radiate out and not being distracted by critics or the audience. When he talks about acting I see the teaching wise side of him—guiding, coaxing.

At one point Billie dressed up in your clothes—a leopard coat and a hat which made him look like Alexander Nevsky or Ivan the Terrible. Now he is in the telephone room, talking to you with the ouija board.

Downstairs I say to David 'Billie's in there with himself talking to Carol.'

David said 'Oh, I thought he was in there by himself.'

We laughed.

I can hear Billie now breaking into tears, his whole body convulsing in terrible sobs, using all his strength to reach you—the real you, not just the Carol of our imaginations, his *Carol, the Carol he knows and loves and holds or has held.*

I would like to give . . . but I can only be here in another room, hoping to catch from the person who's been given the vision and the long horrible slog of living it, what he's really saying or intending. Beyond intention though—just being.

The Carol no one could reach even when she was alive and here. Billie being jealous of that Carol, keeping everyone else away.

Stars emitting great booms of light—pulsating energy in space. I just went to the tomato room and looked a long time at the collage photographs of Carol—saw that her mouth was so alive, the most alive part of her face, and her eyes seductive, alluring, drawing in like the moon. I saw also how she needed the security that Billie gave her, it's in her face—to tease the nipple. She must have been a real nipple-teaser. Carol—the naughty nipple-teaser.

Stars glittering, travelling through space—a vast emptiness like the November wind. The sensation of that distance of space was marvellous, friendly, not at all frightening or lonely frightening. What's wrong with loneliness? How can we ever be alone? Only dead . . . like what we feel when we are jealous—we feel dead. But if we are both fully alive, fully being, how can we be jealous? We can help each other towards doing that, getting there—the difficulty is in not leaving one or the other behind. I see this as the issue between Billie and Carol. It's easy for one to reject the other and say 'I've grown out of it all—you're dead for me.' Because she didn't, Billie isn't dead now nor is Carol. 'They who one another keep alive, ne'er parted be. . . .' Donne. Can't damn Donne well remember.

No hallucinations—just things as they are.

A cock just crowed. I turned round. Through the window dawn is coming. I relit the almost burnt out candle and am writing here by the fire, watching words appear from somewhere.

The book with Billie is not about the book at all—it's about a summer without Carol and how to get through that, how to keep going with her, without her, with her. . . .

Osiris barking. Cigarette finished.

I walked outside and had a piss—could hear the sea roaring below, cracking ceaselessly at the rocks below. The terrible angels who cry— they are below on their black yachts. Let them cry.

Oh Carol, I need you so I can be free of Billie and Billie needs you to be free from us all. Carol, listen, I'm talking to you. Come down and be with Billie now. I'm fed up with playing your part just because you're still throwing a big star number. The audience is getting impatient with my little tricks. They want the real Carol Garbo Lobravico. Come out of hiding now, we know you're there.

Grey sky. I keep looking out of the window as though I'd never seen a day before. It waits on the window-sill like a purring cat—the day I mean.

Billie's desire to reach Carol and lack of sureness that he has, makes total war—everything has to serve that. It means he can never really get into anything because of that mighty ego that demands service at any price, cost . . . what Carol felt sometimes.

The terrible thing for Billie is that all he went through in those eight months in prison he could have gone through in one night—the night of the bust—if he had fought with the same awareness that he

*has now. That is a terrible might-have-been. If he had been differ-
ent. . . . Changing always means arriving at the same point. The
whole thing could have been different—not just the night of the bust,
but before. The seeds of it were all there ripening. That's what death
is I suppose—that gap between what* could be *and what* might
have been, *death intervening. The fight to preserve what* can be *in
oneself is the battle with death to glory. That is the battle Billie
is fighting now. O god, on his own in the loneliness of the cell that is
him. God help him, God bless him in it.*

*Dawn has come now—the sound of human voices, human bangings.
I leave you world to your world. I may come back but I still feel the
options are open. I want to be in your cunt, not just tickling your
nipple.*

Carol—the naughty nipple-teaser.

12 SEPTEMBER 9.45 AM. Woke up with an erection—all systems
functioning, feeling good. At lunch Raffaela made a cake and we
had a quiet celebration of your first birthday in another
world.

It was my last day in the house—I felt Billie wanted to say
something to me. When it was getting dark he and Diana had a
shower together then he came down with her to the fireside, both
of them wrapped in towels. I was typing away by the window. He
and Diana began making love in front of me—by the fire. I went
upstairs to his bedroom where there was a light and went on
working. Later Billie came up and sat on the edge of the bed.
There was a long silence, very long, while we looked at each other.
I felt even more strongly that he was trying to say something—
I didn't know how to get to it.

I said 'How are you feeling?'

Another long silence during which I could feel him trying to
get some words out. I waited for as long as I could.

'Okay?' I said, filling the silence with another question.

He just nodded and said, 'Yes' quietly, then got up, walked to
the window, looked out for a moment, then left the room.

Next morning I left early in the car with Fabrizio and Charley.
From Rome I went to Venice to meet Alison and the beginning of
a long horrible nightmare that I never anticipated.

Ten days of hell in Venice when she told me she was living with someone else and didn't want me. Rows, scenes, grabbing at one another and pushing away. There were some quiet moments when we managed to make love and it almost seemed the same as before. One morning in the hotel when she was lying in bed I read her bits of the book. After I finished she said sleepily 'Was there anyone in the room?'

I said, 'Did you feel someone here?'

She said 'Yes, I felt someone else was in the room while you were reading', then she turned aside to sleep.

I left her in Venice and took a slow train back to London to try to finish the book. I thought I was almost there. Then three months living in the house in London alone, having lost Alison, trying with all my strength to finish and not understanding why I couldn't, but I couldn't—as though I had missed something essential. I felt you sometimes in the midst of all the frustration and anger with myself—calm, patient and sensuous, waiting and watching, but I was losing you. Then Billie's phone calls—from Istanbul and Praiano, wondering what was happening to the book, yet his voice calm and gentle.

Then a few days before Christmas I decided to return to Praiano—I thought to have a rest and a holiday. I thought I would only stay a week. Arriving in Rome and Billie meeting the train with Margaret.* He'd been in Turkey making a film in November. People had come in and out of the house. There had been a fight between Tanja and Anna, Anna stabbing Tanja with a knife because she lost to her in a game of chess. I heard for the first time that Roxanne had become pregnant by either Joe or Billie—she didn't know. She had got pregnant in October—did you arrange it for the 14th? At the time I didn't think anything of it. Rachel was also pregnant by Karl who was flipping out.

Back to the house a few days before Christmas—not many people here. Christmas came and went and we almost managed to avoid it—just a few presents and a cake cooked by Raffaela.

Billie had changed—he was quieter, more resigned. You could see that the pain of the loss of you had gone out of his face but also the life. He was sort of half with us, half alive. I felt he had given up and resigned himself to waiting and watching.

Apparently Joe wasn't coming to the house again. He was in

* South Vietnamese wife of Pierre Clementi.

Rome, looking after Roxanne who was nervous about the baby. I saw them in Rome before we came to Praiano—just briefly. Joe had decided to cut all ties and go to Morocco with Roxanne— he felt the next step was to live totally in the present, without money or possessions. I think we smoked a joint in Parioli and laughed a bit, but there was something missing.

The house has changed too—it feels like somewhere to live, somewhere to breathe and grow and expand. All through Christmas and the New Year warm mellow days with oranges and lemons ripening on the mountain-side and some days we swam in the pool, then in the evenings the candles, the music, the slow burning fire—people talking, playing chess, making things.

Then two days when something extraordinary happens to me. I get an overwhelming sense of death, of complete depression and speak to no one for two days, just lying in a room, unable to do anything. No energy, no power—just a sense of not being here, of dying. I couldn't explain it to anyone or talk. It was the beginning of a battle that nearly killed me, though at the time I didn't know what was happening. I felt I understood what you experienced in the house—the sense of death, the depression, and it was frightening.

Billie was preoccupied with Pierre Clementi because Margaret was trying to do something about him. We were waiting for his trial to come up. Also Karin Christensen was still in jail. But again he wasn't able to do anything except go through anger and rage at the system and the laws.

That day when Chuck and his entourage moved in from Positano, seeking refuge in the house because he had no money and no work—Marmory, little Jessica, Sharon and Sheeliah, Lucretia all carrying his belongings up the three hundred steps. Suddenly there were a lot of children in the house—Jessica, Sheeliah, Balthazar and David who came at weekends.

There was also an incredible energy in the house and strange things began happening.

David and Charley arrived from London—Charley had been making nude photographs in Rome at Alberto's and David was flipping out. Chuck brought one trip of acid with him and gave it to Billie at lunch. Billie wanted to give it to me but walked around with it all afternoon. Then in the evening he came and sat by the fire and said 'I have just taken the trip I was going to give you and I feel kind of bad about it.'

'I thought that trip was not going to come my way when you were talking about it,' I said.

Billie—'Well, it hasn't.'

Long silence as he stares into the fire, then he said, 'I can see everything. It's an incredible trip.'

'What can you see?' I asked.

Billie—'The whole . . . the whole world—everything that's wrong. Seeing it doesn't change it, that's the trouble.'

'It makes me feel sad that you can see yet feel you can do nothing.'

Billie talked on about judges and lawyers, saying that everyone should go to prison.

'There are other places besides prisons,' I said. 'Anyway we are all in some sort of prison.'

I sense the old battle in Billie coming out—the battle between the guru and the führer, the Billie who lives in the house and lets everyone share in what he is and has and the Billie who wants to lead an army to destroy the system. Sometimes sitting by the fireside the house felt like a bandit stronghold, waiting for enough recruits to turn up—at other times it was a spiritual oasis in the world. All through these days Billie seemed to be oscillating between violence as a solution and non-violence, passivity. It was a dangerous and difficult battle, and no one could really reach him.

Later that night while Billie was still tripping I said, 'Why don't you lead an army? . . . Why don't you pick up a machine gun and fire it? It would be a glorious moment, if nothing else.'

Billie—'Maybe that's what it's all about—glorious moments', but didn't say any more.

Then David produced some acid he had brought from London and gave some to me. I dropped it on the floor and we lost it, so he gave me some more. I didn't want to take it then but to keep it until the book was finished, so I stored it away. Everyone else was tripping—music, laughter. A good atmosphere.

Renato arrived from Salerno jail. He got drunk and tried to rape all the women, chasing them around the house. Billie stayed with him, holding him, stroking him by the fire.

The energy in the house was moving up and down very rapidly now. On 3 January I wrote:

The worst night ever. No love, complete lack of love in the world. Where is love? Deep deep within somewhere—reaching hands can't reach it. Who can reveal it? Now there is no one to talk to here, no vibration of love whatsoever—nor anything on the outside as perhaps before. So I have to walk alone, with only echoes to guide me. Maybe it would be better to cut out of here, to split, since there is nothing here for me except silence and death.

Today I can begin to work without illusions—to get out of this tomb, this monument to death. Why did I ever take this trip?

Renato got drunk again, racing all over the garden in the night followed by Billie, Tanja and myself. He kept falling down stairs and climbing trees. He was going through another level. He didn't try to rape all the women now but spent hours spouting poetry to them, playing the gallant poet, gently wooing. But everyone could sense the violence underneath and it didn't work. Still nobody would make love with him.

And all the time Sharon was here—with her quietness, her understanding. She is a beautiful person. I felt very attracted to her but made no move because I felt she needed space for herself but we communicated on some deep level—about loving and letting go of demands and pressures.

Margaret started flipping out, drawing Billie more and more into her web so he was hardly ever with us. She seemed terrified of everything and never left her room. She could feel the energy here more deeply than anyone and was totally paranoid. But we had got over the 'who's sleeping with who' syndrome that had been a tension in the house for a while.

I was getting more and more lost in a spirit-world I knew nothing about, I kept trying to anchor myself down by long conversations with Chuck and Marmory—but they were going through their own changes and we ended up talking about them. But it helped somehow.

Billie and Margaret kept driving off to Rome to see Pierre. One day at about 10.30 in the morning, two shepherds came to the house while we were drinking coffee and sitting by the fire. They were strange rustic-looking characters and started playing music as soon as they came in the door. No one knew who they were, but we just sat there listening. One of them was wearing a shabby suit, except the trousers and jacket didn't match, and an umbrella over his arm. He was playing an instrument that looked and sounded like an oboe, except it had a splayed horn-type end. The other one was playing bagpipes. The music was shrill, piercing and very precise. Marmory gave them some money and they said *Buon giorno* then left. Later I went on to the terrace and listened to them as they went around the other houses of the village.

After lunch Gaetano [Raffaela's husband] asked me if I wanted to go up into the mountains with him. It was a warm cloudless day and there was a beautiful clear view over the sea. All the way up I was thinking—What a marvellous life he leads. We got to Gaetano's father's house high on the mountain. Gaetano unlocked the door and gave me a glass of wine from one of the many barrels there—it had a delicious cool 'ping' to it, very tasty indeed. I only drank a little but Gaetano downed the rest of the glass in one gulp, smacking his lips appreciatively. Then we climbed higher—to the broccoli terraces above his father's house. We got to the broccoli fields and Gaetano showed me how to pick them— it was a narrow terrace on a steep part of the mountain near the top, with an incredible view. While I was picking broccoli and thinking 'back-to-nature' thoughts and about the happy peasant life, Gaetano started talking about him and Raffaela wanting to leave Praiano since the whole mentality was directed towards work, work—and if you didn't work you were considered to be a robber or worse. Apparently Raffaela wants to go with Billie when he leaves Italy and Gaetano would go with them and find work. It looks as though they are inseparable from Billie now—strange village pressures that I couldn't quite understand but could imagine. Then I came down with two bags full of broccoli for the house while Gaetano went on picking to sell to the shops in the village.

Then Karin Christensen was freed from prison and wrote a long letter to Billie which he read out one night round the fire. She had gone back to Copenhagen. The letter ended:

You know, I think you are very beautiful and somehow I'm sad that I didn't have the chance to see you again. But maybe one day. I know that you have done a lot of things for me, but the word 'thank you' just doesn't hold it. You know what I mean, it is much more than that. It is the way you are, the way you think and finally the reflection, to the way you look. It is in your eyes when you look at me, your hands when you touch me and a million other things which made you what you are—something so very beautiful. But I'm sure that sometimes, somewhere we will meet again—though I don't know when, I do know why. Life is just made this way—you get drawn to certain places at certain times and you meet people. You leave them, meet again and leave them—and for always you are on your own, no matter where you are. . . .

Billie's voice cracked, everyone was silent, the fire and candle light glowing, the dogs and cats sleeping. There was an extraordinary communication in the silence. There is an army though it doesn't carry guns and isn't easily identifiable—somewhere out there, in the world, a voice has answered Billie, has called to him. I travelled inside my head and found him there.

I wait for life, for love and grow bored, tired, tense. I wait, destroying what I am waiting for by waiting or is there nothing there to wait for except myself waiting? And waiting turns to wanting someone who is not. I wait for what is, watching it become me. I wait, absorbing the unknown, letting it become created. But waiting or wanting, I feel I am not known.

But suddenly a crack appears and he was known and we knew him—for a brief moment. The great weight of sorrow that surrounded him so that no one could get to him because of his fear of revealing that emptiness, lifted for a moment. It had happened before, but never so clearly as in that moment—times when he becomes an ambiguity, something more than himself.

I feel you again in the house very strongly, strangely—a communication with the dead, your need of something from Billie.

At lunch Billie tells me that he had a dream the night before about the house—that it had more rooms to it than he thought. He went through a door into another series of rooms that seemed to go on forever. The same night Chuck and I had an identical sensation that the house was moving. It wasn't a dream but a definite sensation, and Chuck is one of the most sceptical rationalists I've ever met.

There's been a series of strange dreams—three people dreaming on the same night of a man with a machine gun and a sadistic, maniacal laugh; my dream of you having a baby; Chuck's vision of the mysterious woman you made love to then died.

I become more and more aware of Billie's commitment to the house. This is a rare human love in this world that can absorb changes—what you and Billie had. It isn't just Billie—it's you and Billie—now as much as when you were alive. The house is a crack between worlds. There is a communication here with the dead and between the dead. The house has a strange power or magic that has puzzled and confused me for a long time. It has seemed that I have been pursuing an elusive search into the relationship between you and Billie and getting more and more to the point where complete opposites met—ideas, passions, personalities—so that it seemed two forces, beyond even the human embodiment of them in persons, had been in conflict, and one or other had to die—lovers who kill one another to resolve the underlying duality that exists in the world and which destroys love and yet is the condition of this mortal life. And all the time the house was here, absorbing the changes while people came and went—as though the house itself contained a presence that was beyond change, duality, *maya* or whatever one calls it.

Though I keep peering endlessly into the past and getting conflicting views of the relationship between you and Billie, the important thing is what exists now—you and Billie living in one body in the house. The music, the vibrations, the many rooms, people coming in and out and losing track of days when they arrived here—smiles, flowers, food—sunshine and laughing, the kind of togetherness you feel here.

At lunch one day Billie said 'I want to change the world.'

He is doing it here—in the house—with the sharing and the freedom, the energy and patience. People change, find themselves, grow and gain strength to unite themselves with their opposites.

9 JANUARY. Amazing Pentecostal day of open communication between everyone. Chuck started talking on the porch about the house and how when he arrived here there was a sense of everything lifting from his shoulders, all the difficulties of the last few weeks—something many people feel about the house. The hostility between Margaret and me came out in a heated row in the kitchen

as it was getting dark, and then talking, really talking to Sharon in the little house. I had just read through my notes of August last year and realised how you were trying to reach Billie then. I had a sense of not being in control of my life as I had always thought before, a sense that we are all delicate instruments. Sharon talked of a time in Los Angeles when she had a sense of everything being dead and that she had been receiving too much spiritual energy—so she went and lived on her own, taking off her clothes and lying in the sun, eating carefully, resting her body— otherwise she would have been burnt out by so much energy. I mentioned that I felt I was being bewitched by you—not being able to make love to anyone so that I went on living as though dead. We talked about the struggle now between Billie and Carol —either for Billie's soul or Carol's—Billie resisting Carol to save her or Carol sending out rays which move everyone around.

Next day I went to visit your grave for the first time. There was peace there but also a feeling that I wanted you to come alive. At one point I closed my eyes and felt a buzz of peace, then on opening them again the light all around seemed much softer, paler, unreal. But mainly these were self-induced sensations and I felt the absence of what I wanted or hoped for—as Billie must have felt the night he returned to the grave after coming out of prison. I try to let go completely and let whatever thoughts there are come. I feel certain you are saying something very hard to understand unless we can let go properly . . . going with the image of being in another world, an ethereal city or house, in the light of a presence, bringing the foetus subconscious to birth out of the womb of consciousness.

14 JANUARY. Long journey to my writing room after waking up —via long cup of coffee and talking to Sharon in the kitchen— feelings of waking up and calmness coming back. Second cup of luxurious coffee, then a long crap in the bathroom, then walking around to see who is up and about, then watching the sea from the terrace below the little house, smoking a cigarette and waiting for the sun to come out. Thinking about the hash experience of last night and all the strange things that happened. Smoking hash by the fire with Fenja while playing chess; thoughts about Billie—'a character with some deep psychological flaw in him' came into my head as a sentence and stuck, though I couldn't easily justify it,

but it seemed to be true to my dream of him—living in two worlds at the same time, always trying to fill the hole, the gap inside himself and barricading himself off from anyone discovering it. Maybe it's the same flaw that I have—something to do with relationships to women and the mother taking over too much of oneself.

Then I went to bed and tried to fall asleep but felt the vibrations of the house very strongly—a sense of orgasm in the house perhaps because I could hear Billie and Margaret making love in the other bedroom, Billie playing out his *karma*. It seemed as though everything that had ever happened in the house was present in one moment. At several points I seemed to have to get up and wander about for no apparent reason—just because I felt strong vibrations somewhere.

A sense at one point of being a total eye—being content to watch and observe instead of getting involved in power games.

I felt your vibration too—how fucked up you were and maybe controlling, manipulating—and how perhaps I wouldn't have liked you at all, which seemed strange since I've been living with you for nine months and always had such a strong romantic attachment to you. But I didn't see you as generous or gentle, but more greedy and grasping. I think that romantic bag is a good one to be rid of. . . . Maybe you and I would have had big fights and are doing now. Perhaps you are trying to imprison me?

There is something I don't like about the hash experience—it leaves you suspended, in-between doing and seeing, so that it takes time to integrate yourself again. Sharon talked this morning about 'vibrations'—how you had to quicken up your vibrations to received vibrations from around and how she could really feel people which is what I am beginning to understand. She is an incredible person. We also talked about the difference between letting something happen and trying to make it happen—one living without illusions, the other constantly enacting illusions and blinding yourself from what is really going on.

Linda, Fabrizio and the other Tania arrive. Everyone who is here is invited. Why? Is it because of Billie's need for people around or is something going to happen to which we are all witnesses?

Beverley Axelrod* comes and there are long discussions about dropping out.

She says 'To be "radical" you have to believe in the system—that it can be changed. But the system needs "radicals" to foster the illusion of change. One day I stopped believing in the system and realised the only action I could take was to drop out completely.' Then she went on to talk about 'Waiting for the revolution to happen . . . if it ever will', with a note of provocative amusement in her voice.

Her beauty, her presence, her 'soul' stays with us and takes us all through to a new level. Later in Rome I met her again and she tells me of her year in Grenada, living completely on her own with the only decisions of the day being whether to lie in the hammock or sit in the deck chair. She asked me why there weren't any female bitches in the house, any mother souls.

Billie goes to Copenhagen to see Karin Christensen. He is away for two weeks. While Billie is away David and I go one night to your grave with two of the girls, climb with difficulty over the high railings and put candles on the grave. I have an uncanny tingling sensation in my hands as I sit by the grave silently, something very definite which I can't explain.

Then there was the day when the different dimensions of reality on which the story of you and Billie took place suddenly unfolded. It was frightening because of all the contradictions, though somewhere there seemed to be a point beyond the contradictions. There is another world but it is this one. . . . I saw you as the black queen of evil powers and Billie as the bright god with flaming sword of radiating vibrating love light. I saw Billie as having a silver of infinity in him, a tiny drop. I saw the struggle that went on between you and Billie as the struggle between two forces that were interchangeable—the source of light (different from light itself) and the source of darkness—but the struggle took place in infinity so there are an infinite number of levels, not limited to our clumsy language. We live in infinity veiled by time—a convenient necessity for our physical bodies—but all time is eternally present. In world-language—i.e. conceptual and

* Ex-lawyer of Eldridge Cleaver and the person to whom *Soul On Ice* was dedicated. She lives in Rome, running an underground Italian magazine *Il Fallo* with Italian anarchist Angelo Quattrocchi.

visual and very limited—we have to make do with such concepts as light and dark, good and evil, a force, a divine light, the presence, the dark glob, the flame of darkness. But even these words 'struggle' and 'conflict' cannot convey the true meaning— it can also be seen as a dance, a vibration, an impulse, movement. All this is going on behind the masks these forces wear in the physical world and the silly actions we invent to achieve their purpose.

Then reaching through to a point of stillness beyond the contradictions to another version of your whole story. It went like this . . .

Billie the Guru and his tribe are living in an old and beautiful house on the mountain side, seeing visions and dreaming dreams, sending out energy into the universe of cosmic love. But there is a level they have to reach if they are to go on. Then the police come to the house and put everyone of this tribe into prison because they are different. The police idea is to convert them back to straight society so they can work in the system and obey the great dark force which is the subconscious purpose of this planet—for life to become so regimented that it becomes extinct, squeezed out slowly by machines, regimentation and conformity. The police are the jailers—as are the lawyers, the judges, the ministers, etc. The tribe are the prisoners, fighting off the pressure of conversion back to the system. Carol realises everything is going wrong and that the forces of regimentation and conformity are winning, so she dies in a dramatic action to relieve the situation and enable Billie the Guru to win through. The chief policeman is Billie the Cop and he is interrogating Billie the Guru about his way of life, asking him why he lives as he does, why he doesn't have normal furniture, why his guests don't pay him and why he always keeps an open door and allows people to use drugs. Billie the Guru is caught up in self-doubt, wondering if that wasn't the right way to live after all. But then Carol dies and Billie the Guru starts to win through and begins to interrogate Billie the Chief Cop about his way of life—why he wears uniforms and has so many rules and regulations and prisons and laws and organisation. At this point the rest of the tribe are let out of prison and become jailers and all the people from the system are put in the jails. They have to turn on in order to be released. In other words, the situation is reversed, though in effect it is the same—

there are still prisoners and jailers, though the requirements are different. Finally Billie the Guru realises, as does Billie the Cop, that they are really the same person and they begin to absorb one another. At this point there are no longer any prisoners and jailers— everyone is released and they all begin to merge, each absorbing his opposite in various ways—through some force of attraction or repulsion that has existed throughout. Each one is the other's redemption, though at first the attraction is dim and perhaps expressed as total opposition—as with Billie the Cop and Billie the Guru. Once they have fully absorbed one another, then the house is again restored to what it was, but now it is larger and more full of love divine, light incandescent, spirit energy which renews the universe—because now there is an extra dimension via Carol who is in the spirit world.

A few days later David started making a red Indian tepee, imagining all of us living in tepees in the mountains—a tribe.

Then Billie came back from seeing Karin—he had been staying in a snow hut in Austria, going from Copenhagen to Paris to there. For a few days he seemed far away, talking about politics in an obsessive way which didn't chime in with what had been happening here. It seemed as though the revolutionary, machine-gun Billie was winning; then he started relaxing and being 'with' us more. But there was tension there, largely because of his appeal* in Salerno which was due on 16 February. He wanted to make some gesture, to do something positive towards the revolution, but apart from admitting that he smoked marijuana there wasn't much he could do—it was in the hands of his lawyer.

The day of the appeal came. Billie dressed up in his suit and tie. It started at 11 in the morning and didn't finish until 7 at night. It was a long horrible day in another world. His lawyer was trying to get him acquitted and bring the facts of your death out into the

* The appeal was made by Bill's lawyer, Incutti, after the trial on 30 March 1971. In Italian law if one side appeals, the other side automatically appeals as well—in this case, the public prosecutor on behalf of the state. Also, since no official transcript of the trial's proceedings was made, the appeal court had to refer back to the original evidence. In other words, it was a retrial, but without any witnesses. The purpose of Incutti's appeal was to try to bring to the court's attention the circumstances of Carol's death and to demand an investigation into the whole case. The public prosecutor's appeal aimed at proving Bill guilty of the charges for which he had previously been acquitted. The public prosecutor's appeal, if successful, would mean a further term of imprisonment for Bill.

open. Billie sat in the dock in a corner watching it all with grim determination.

At one point the presiding judge called him forward and asked about a statement he had made in an original interrogation— that he knew about marijuana and hashish. The judge asked him how he knew? It was a tense moment. Billie replied that he had smoked them in Morocco, and his lawyer had to jump up and say that he hadn't gone to Morocco just to smoke marijuana but to make a film.

There's no concern for truth in a court of law, only words and definition of words.

Then the judge said 'It's all right, I'm only asking because I've never seen it myself'—in a benevolent, friendly voice.

They were trying Billie for letting his house be used as an opium den on the evidence of half a gram of marijuana and none of them knew what marijuana looked like, let alone what it was.

Next the public prosecutor started repeating all the ridiculous phrases of the police who had come here the night of the bust. The public prosecutor was strong, determined and insistent. He prefaced his remarks by saying that Italian justice owed nothing to William Berger and that the furore that the case had caused in Italy and in other countries was threatening the stability of Italian justice and the whole basis of law and order in the country. . . . His exaggerated arguments, delivered in an impressive stentorian voice, revolved around the fact that the doctor who put everyone in *manicomios* couldn't be wrong because he was a doctor, the police couldn't be wrong because they were the police etc. At one point he started twisting the facts— saying that Billie was friendly with a lot of known drug pushers and that he was responsible for Carol's death.

Billie jumped to his feet and shouted out 'You are talking about my wife, accusing me of killing her. I can't sit here and listen to that. . . .' Police and lawyers rushed over to quieten him down.

Then his lawyer tried to show that you had died from negligence and lack of proper medical attention. The judges went out to deliberate and returned an hour and a half later with their judgment—confirming the decision of the previous trial—acquittal for lack of sufficient evidence.* Nothing had changed except to reveal the total lack of concern for truth. Later Billie said that he had had the impulse to get up and walk away.

The night before the appeal Billie had been smoking a joint—the next day he was in court facing a charge about half a gram of marijuana. That same night he was smoking another joint. What's it all about?

The next day we drive back to Salerno to see the lawyer about whether Billie wants to make another appeal to keep the case open. His lawyer thinks the authorities will expel him from Italy. Part of the sentence of the previous day was that Billie had to bear the costs of the whole legal process. Billie says—no, there's no point in making another appeal just to prevent them expelling him from Italy. He says he's tired of it all. R.A.I. television are at the lawyer's office. They came to make a film of the house, expecting it to be closed down and Bill ordered to leave Italy. R.A.I. television crew arrive at the house and make an interview with Billie who sits cross-legged on the porch. It seems like the end of the house. Billie says he is not sad about the court's sentence since he didn't expect anything else—the more the system reveals itself, the more people will realise its corruption and redundancy. He says he doesn't care about what happens to him, only about what is happening in the minds of the judges, lawyers, police, etc.

A few days later Pierre Clementi gets two years for use and possession of drugs—a heavy sentence. It seems as though the clamp-down has come and it is time to fight or flee.

That night I lie awake in my cave thinking of many things. There are times when I reach the point of needing to be rescued, and this is one of them, though there is no one to do it, no one I feel I can talk to because of people being bound up in themselves. Reading Graham Greene's autobiography made me think back over my own childhood with something of his detachment and

* The result of the appeal was a victory for neither side, though the fact that Incutti was unable to persuade the court to open an investigation into the circumstances of Carol's death was the *coup de grace* to Bill's determination to raise the issue as to why she had died and who was responsible. After the verdict Bill could appeal again; but since the evidence he needed was unavailable, it was pointless. The only advantage of another appeal, as Incutti pointed out next day, was that it would prevent the police serving him with a *foglio di via*, i.e. expelling him from Italy as an 'undesirable alien'.

compassion—that more than the words, incidents or characters is what I value about the book—and I saw myself in my teens living in Somerset and having a sense that something vital was missing, though I couldn't say what—those long walks on the moors, the loneliness. I saw myself as a boy looking for someone, something. I realised that it was my father I missed because he was hardly ever there. He was always away in Nigeria or Malaya. I began to think that my attachment to Billie and a sense of confusion or betrayal over him comes from him being a father-figure to me, someone I can live near and learn from. But I want to be free to be myself without these attachments.

Billie sees the whole world committing suicide in some form or other, everyone mesmerised by the mass accumulation of individual self-destructiveness—leaders of nations being nothing other than the embodiment of that self-destructive energy. He sees the house as a place where people can live without the conditioning and pressures of conventional society, discover that destructiveness in themselves and work to detach themselves from the so-called 'civilised' world that is inevitably heading for collapse.

The people who come and stay here for a while certainly discover it but, like Ilona, they can't always make the trip out.

I think his vision of the world stems partly from your suicidal tendencies, from a feeling that someone like you couldn't survive in this world unless he loved you with a totality that he found difficult to find in himself and unless he was able to create the right conditions. Having tried to do that for eight years, he feels he can extend the same energy outwards to include many more people. But unless he is totally aware and attentive of what he is doing, he can so easily induce or provoke the very thing he is most frightened of. I think this is what happened with you, and the terrifying thing was that he only arrived at the point where he could have saved your life when it was too late. That was why he fought to exorcise fear from inside himself in the letters and in his diary.

I can't stop myself from thinking that Billie murdered you in some subtle way—psychologically or psychically. It's a terrifying thought that has been drumming inside my head for a long time and I keep trying to erase it, but I can't. The murderer who takes on the soul of his victim. But there is no judgment. It happened in some area where there was space for various possible destinies, long before the actual events happened which caused it—what we call 'accidents' or 'events' being manifestations of a state of consciousness. In his diary Billie has tried to recreate that space in order to go on living. It was the edges of conversations with him and all that has happened in the house that gave me the clue to what he was shutting out of his mind. The only way he can get to it is to bring you back to life. I think that is what he has been trying to say to me, but without words.

It is almost finished now.

There's a cock crowing and the smell of Vicks ointment I just rubbed on my chest to fight this awful cold. That's about as far as I got in my sleepless state. I go and make myself some tea.

Then suddenly I break through to your world, to the other side. In these months I have wandered about thinking of you and searching, but I have been lost, struggling in a cobweb of ideas and uncertainties. Mainly I have been thinking about those last seven hours when Billie sat by your bedside holding you and watching you dying. Something extraordinary must have happened to him—as though he went with you beyond death.

That day Rachel and John had come down from Rome. In the late afternoon Billie lies on the mattress in the long upstairs room and starts reading from *The Tibetan Book of the Dead*. He reads for about five hours and everyone listens, except Rachel who starts walking round the house, looking more and more distracted. Suddenly she decides she is going to leave for Rome—after only a few hours in the house. She invents some story about an angry landlord and everyone tries to persuade her to stay. The situation is exactly one that is described in *The Tibetan Book of the Dead*—of wanting to preserve something in oneself, an illusion, and not letting go. But she is determined and leaves. Only later do I realise that she is frightened of something in the house and picked it up very quickly.

Then John produces some hash he brought from Rome that he says is the best he's ever smoked. I take three puffs from his pipe and start to feel dizzy. I go to the bathroom, then to Billie's bedroom—the nearest bed I can find—and lie down. The room is dark but the light comes in from the next room where the others are sitting around talking. Suddenly something terrifying starts to happen to me. I start going away—the voices become more distant, blurred, the light gets dimmer. Objects and sensations no longer have any solidity—everything is in perpetual motion but I am leaving.

I think—I am dying, this is it.

I want to call out to the others in the next room, but it seems useless because they won't know what is happening and can't do anything. For a long time I do nothing—I no longer have an 'I' that can call out even, I am disintegrating. I don't feel I can ever get back into the rhythm of life. I am going and nothing can hold me.

Summoning all my strength I call out the name 'Chuck' because I hear his voice and because I feel I just get into the rhythm of his voice.

The shout is like an electric shock in the room. Everybody stops talking and jumps up, not knowing where the shout came from. I know what is happening yet I can't speak any more. I breathe louder and louder so they know where I am. Billie comes in first then everyone and they sit around me, holding me.

I know I am dying and that this is how it happens and nothing can stop it. I want someone to reach me.

I say, 'Billie, be here, be more here,' because I feel he is helping me—I don't know why, I just feel it.

He doesn't say anything nor does anyone—I think this is because they don't know what is happening to me. I desperately want to return to that level of reality I think is normal or ordinary but I can't get back. I feel an extraordinary energy in my body and this energy is burning me out. There are no visions—just a complete dissociation with reality, a loss of something.

A phrase Billie had read from *The Tibetan Book of the Dead* kept echoing in my head—that the dead don't know they are dead. I thought I was dead, that I had left my body altogether and was already in the after-dead world. I remember I kept saying as though to reassure myself 'It's the trip, the trip. . . .', then 'Is this what it's all about?'

Only the sounds of Charley singing and Jessica crying seemed real though far away.

I remember Tania asking if I wanted any tea and I put my hand out and grasped the cup. At first I couldn't feel the cup at all and then I knew I was dead, that it was all just an idea. Then I did and that reassured me—the hardness of the cup, though my hand felt as if it was melting—I couldn't understand how it could hold the cup.

Then I began to think that if I ever came back I would be mad forever, that if I woke up next morning in the house I would only think I had woken up, whereas in fact I would just be watching my body in the bed imagining it to be alive.

One of the extraordinary things about the experience was the intense communication I felt with Billie—beyond words altogether. I knew that during the experience I had been you, that you had come into my body in some way, that I had experienced something of where you were and what you were wanting. Next day Billie said he had felt an extraordinary energy in the room and that I had spoken with your voice. I felt that although it was the most terrifying experience of my life, I had experienced something of those last seven hours of your life—the journey away from the body. I wasn't to know that it was only a prelude to something else.

Next day Alison came from London and stayed for a week. Perhaps it was the beginning of our journey back to each other. We went for walks and out for meals, and at night lay in the cave talking, keeping a little distance between us, never making love. But it was a good week, a chance to share each other again. The night before Alison left she and Billie got into a heated discussion about dropping out because Billie was advocating that everyone should drop out of the system and just stop whatever they were doing for two years, while Alison was arguing that it was more effective to work within the system. During the discussion Billie started to talk about the last seven hours with you—saying that suddenly in that time he had felt the reality of Biafra, Vietnam . . . as he looked at your helpless body, the victim of the inhumanity of the system. But Alison cut him short, not realising that this was the first time he had ever talked about that—though obviously much more had happened than just a political awareness awakening, but that is the kind of indirect way in which Billie reveals himself.

That night in bed I tell Alison that I have felt all along that there is some darkness in Billie, some area that he can't get to—that I have had this sense from the beginning though I haven't been able to comprehend it fully but that I am beginning vaguely to now, still not knowing however exactly what it is I have to do or reach. I said I thought that the more I became aware of Carol, the more I felt this was true. Only when this happens can I finish the book. I never thought I would be involved in this but I am now and it's something I have to see through, whatever it is. I told her I thought that this was what had come between us, though it need not—if we can learn to be free enough to accept each other's destinies and not try to destroy that which is the most essential part of us.

Billie organises group work in the house that goes under the name of acting classes. We begin to reveal ourselves to each other more.

Billie goes to Rome for a few days and Chuck leaves the house in complete despair and chaos—Marmory has left with little Jessica a few weeks earlier. We all have to sit round the kitchen table and go through a totally negative despair trip with him. He feels that the house, although apparently free and a place of love, is actually dangerously anarchic. In a more intense way, it is a trip we all go through—some leave and some stay to see it through. Chuck left. The potential here and the energy can so easily become an instrument of one's own illusions, feeding and fanning them so that it becomes frightening—to be faced so starkly with oneself. It is very clear that this is what happened to Chuck and Tania who left with him—feeling the security and peace that Billie provides here and the freedom, they let their illusions of what could be here take over instead of working towards what they see—their visions, their expectations—and naturally the whole thing collapses. But it is hard and Chuck's despair shook us all because we all feel it sometimes.

Everyone is changing so much and at different speeds that it becomes hard to see it. Renato has gone through so many levels. After his poetic trip he thought the answer was to go off and find a job. He drove off to Naples and we all imagined him looking for a job in a restaurant or something like that.

When he came back he said to Billie 'They wanted me to use a machine gun. I refused—I did right didn't I?'

Then he started to reveal a whole mechanical, practical side of himself—he mended the broken machines in the house and set up a photographic laboratory. Then Giovanni got out of jail in

Salerno and came here—he was in for armed robbery. A rough-looking tall man, more violent than Renato, even he started to change. And Billie was coming out of himself more—you could feel it in the acting classes, as though it connected him to something positive in the past. He was easier to reach and talk to. He no longer seemed to keep the distance in himself, the need to be detached, watching and waiting.

Joe and Roxanne came here for a few days. Roxanne's baby is due in four months—she seems much calmer now and more friendly towards everybody.

For two days nothing much happens, then one night Joe and Roxanne are in the little house. Joe is talking about going to Morocco in about two weeks. I go to the main house and find Billie and Fenja in the big bed.

We talk for a while. Billie says at one point 'The profoundest thing I have discovered is that I am still in jail.'

I say, 'Joe is in Morocco—Morocco is the little house.'

Billie leaps up, grabs a paintbrush and some paint and paints 'Morocco' on the little house, then we all talk to Joe about his going.

The next night Joe talks with Raffaela and Gaetano who persuade him that he should stay around here. They say they know of a house in the mountains where he can grow his own food and be in the kind of place he wants to find. Joe breaks down into tears—he doesn't know what to do.

The next morning I tell Joe I want to take my acid trip with him there—he is leaving the next day. I have kept it for three months, waiting till I finished the book, but I feel I want to take it with Joe there and this could be the last time he will be here in the house. I never thought of taking it with him and I can't explain why I chose that moment, except that I felt that the moment had a special meaning . . . a concourse of energies.

That morning Joe goes with Gaetano to Aegerola to look at the house Gaetano mentioned the night before. I wait for him to come back, writing in the little house—Roxanne coming in every now and then and watching me though talking little. It rains all morning and Joe comes back soaking wet. He changes his clothes and we talk for a while in the little house. I go through a moment of resistance to taking the trip, then it passes. I feel somehow it will be a great release, then tell Joe I want to take it in the cave.

I go and tell Billie I am going to take a trip and say that I want him to be there. He is shaving in the bathroom. He just nods and I go down to the cave with Joe. I take the acid and we sit talking about the house Joe has seen in the mountains. Roxanne comes in, then suddenly I am in it.

I feel I am in your body. I sense you, see images of you, feel you very strongly. I am in your body and I am being born. It is hard and slow and I want it to be over. I know that when it comes something extraordinary will happen in the world, the beginning of some new era.

Billie comes in and sits with me. I reach out and hold his hand. I see something extraordinary in his eyes—a light and depth that has something divine about it. I see the same in Roxanne's eyes. I feel an affinity to her, a strong pull towards her. Joe is lying beside me, talking sometimes.

The cave is a womb, a heart and it pulsates with this energy of birth. I-you are being born.

I still hold Billie's hand—everyone is quiet now . . . Joe and Roxanne. It is the beginning of a new religion, a new age and the child that is to be born is the start of it all. It is Joseph and Mary. I feel a tremendous energy, flash of light, awakening coming . . . coming but not yet. We must wait for the birth. Roxanne is Mary and Joe is Joseph and I see that Jesus was not the son of Joseph. Billie is the father of the child in Roxanne but you have chosen Joe to look after her.

The child is you being born, your rebirth, your re-incarnation. Billie is the father but you have chosen Joe to care for Roxanne.

The date of your birth is 7 July, the day that Billie's father told him was important. You are re-entering the world, you are coming back—a Christ-child, it is a second coming.

It had grown dark outside. Billie has left the cave and Roxanne too. I ask Joe to give me a pencil and write:

Message for Billie. He will understand. Tell him that amongst other things I am the child he and Carol wanted. I came through Carol. It feels like being born—very slowly—lots of waiting but knowing it's going to happen okay.

There were other visions—I saw that the book was a series of mantras that contained a secret voice, I saw a knife and had the feeling that something terrifying was going to happen but not yet, not now or perhaps it could be averted—a murder, a death. Judas is the only one who did not betray Jesus.

Then Joe walked with me into the garden and we looked out over the sea, feeling the wind. After that I went upstairs and sat by the fire.